T0244307

NOBLE
VOLUNTEERS

NOBLE
VOLUNTEERS

The British Soldiers Who Fought
the American Revolution

DON N. HAGIST

Foreword by RICK ATKINSON

WESTHOLME
Yardley

Facing the title page: *Soldiers Cooking*. Hand colored lithograph printed in London, April 1798. (*Anne S. K. Brown Military Collection, Brown University Library*)

Westholme Publishing, LLC
904 Edgewood Road
Yardley, Pennsylvania 19067
Visit our Web site at www.westholmepublishing.com

ISBN: 978–1–59416–349–4
Also available as an eBook.

Printed in the United States of America.

To all soldiers who have fought bravely in unwinnable wars.

CONTENTS

PART III. *ENDING CAREERS, ENDING THE WAR*

Illustrations

FOREWORD

FOR NEARLY TWO AND A HALF CENTURIES, the British soldier who fought in the American Revolution has been little more than a caricature. Derided as bloody-backs and lobsters, the troops sent across the Atlantic on behalf of king and country remain largely anonymous, their motives suspect, their behavior condemned, their military prowess ridiculed.

Yet they had names and personal histories, families and fates. Individually and collectively, they were a ferocious adversary, occasionally undisciplined but always formidable. Their defeat may be attributed not to a want of fighting prowess or martial spirit but to the strategic incoherence of their national leaders, as well as spotty generalship and the tribulations in fighting an expeditionary war for eight years across three thousand miles of ocean in the age of sail. They deserved a better cause.

No one has studied the British enlisted ranks in the Revolution with greater diligence and insight than Don N. Hagist. Now he has given us a remarkable group portrait of these men, illuminating who they were, why and how they fought, and what their lives were like. He dispels myths and limns the human features of those often seen as anonymous redcoats.

Most of the men who fought for the Crown in the Revolution had enlisted in a peacetime army, unaware that they would be swept up in revolutionary events far from home. Under the British system, they joined the service for life, or until physically disabled—although to stimulate recruitment, that open-ended commitment would be modified during the war to allow enlistments for either three years or the duration of the rebellion. Contrary to popular misconceptions, few were pressured to join in order to avoid jail or to escape poverty. Indeed, Hagist's exhaustive review of recruitment records and personal accounts leads him to conclude that "not a single man who left a record of his rationale gave unemployment or impoverishment as a reason for becoming a soldier between 1765 and 1775." Earning eight pence a day, or about £1 a month—minus various deductions for uniforms and food—no private could expect much more than a subsistence livelihood.

Many were farm laborers, but a majority enlisted from the trades. They had been shoemakers and coopers, bakers and blacksmiths, barbers and bricklayers, and thus derived from the core of British plebian society. They were also surprisingly diverse, as Hagist reveals, not just English, Scottish, and Welsh, but also Irish, Nova Scotian, Swedish, Polish, Austrian, Swiss, Dutch, Danish, and even the odd American. An army that had excluded Roman Catholics relaxed that rule in 1775 under the pressure of meeting enlistment goals.

What drew them to the colors? Thomas Sullivan, who joined the 49th Regiment in early 1775, described being "strongly bent upon rambling." He added, "My chief intention . . . being to travel and traverse a stretch of the seas, occasioned my enlisting." Andrew Scott, a twenty-one-year-old Scottish farm worker who liked reading and writing poetry, reflected that signing on with the 80th Regiment in 1778 "afforded me an opportunity of seeing the world to an extent which, in another situation, I might never have had an opportunity of doing." Less romantically, James Andrews, an Irish linen weaver and the father of two, saw the army as a chance to be "freed from the clamours of a wife." Still others heeded recruiting pitches that offered an opportunity "to win honor and fame for your native land," as the 42nd Regiment urged, or to rise above their station since, "The lands of the rebels will be divided amongst you, and every one of you become lairds," or so the 71st Regiment promised.

They proved adaptable and resilient, both as individual soldiers and as an army. Rather than fighting only in exposed, tight ranks, as stereotypes of the British army have long depicted, "we have learn'd from the Rebels to cover our Bodies if theres a Tree or a Rail near us," one light infantry soldier told his mother in April 1777. That same spring, a brigade in New Jersey practiced firing on broken ground in order to learn the requisite adjustments in firing uphill or down. A year later, the 71st Regiment learned "to spring from tree to tree, Stump, Log, & etc with the utmost Agility." As the Americans quickly recognized, British attacks were notable for agility, speed, and ruthlessness. The army itself adjusted the size of regiments as the rebellion in North America intensified, and again when France entered the war to make it a global conflict.

Certainly the British soldier was forced to endure rugged, even brutal conditions in the long war. Disease killed many more than bullets. Of 1,325 recruits shipped to New York in 1779 aboard a slow-moving convoy from the home islands, 43 died during the voyage and nearly 300 others were sick on arrival. Of nearly 1,200 enlisted men who served in the 38th Regiment from the time the unit arrived in Boston in 1774 and departed New York in 1783, nearly 300 died during that span. Service in America for thousands of British soldiers led to an excruciating death and an unmarked grave in a foreign field.

There is a poignancy to the stories of these men. Don Hagist's demonstration that so many British soldiers, like soldiers through the ages, sought little more than "the comforts of a pension in old age, and the pleasure of recounting my adventures to others," as one put it, reveals their humanity. This book shows that beneath each red coat could be found a beating heart.

RICK ATKINSON

INTRODUCTION

SAMUEL LEE GOT NO SLEEP AT ALL on the night of April 18–19, 1775, and his work kept him up the entire day of the nineteenth. He was a tailor in Massachusetts, the American colony that had become the flashpoint of unrest against British government policies. The London native had come to America eight years before and moved around to places including Philadelphia and New York before arriving with his family in Massachusetts in 1774. At thirty years old, Lee was quite accomplished at his trade, a master tailor supervising a staff of eight to twelve in serving as many as 450 clients a year. He was the same sort of "mechanic" as most tradesmen in Boston's Sons of Liberty and the region's militia companies, and his colleagues had warned him on the evening of the eighteenth that something was afoot: the regulars, those professional soldiers in the British standing army that occupied Boston, were preparing to sally out into the countryside.

Tailoring could wait. Lee dressed for a march, took up his musket and premade cartridges, and a day's worth of food. Leaving his family behind, he joined his comrades in the darkness, headed toward the edge of town, met up with others on the way, and walked off into the night. They probably all hoped nothing would come of whatever lay ahead, that the militia would simply monitor the movements of the British march, and everyone would be home again before the next sunset, as had happened several times in the months before. He had no idea that by the following evening, colonists would be at war with the British government. This would change his business and his life, and the lives of everyone with him.

Samuel Lee was not a Son of Liberty, and he was not a militiaman from a Massachusetts town. He was a private soldier in the grenadier company of the 18th Regiment of Foot. After learning the tailor's trade, he had joined the army at around the age of twenty and fitted the regiment's uniforms in addition to mastering the military arts. His regiment came to America a few years after the French and Indian War, traveling from garrison to garrison, while Lee tailored and soldiered all the while. Like many British soldiers, he had a wife and family in tow. He became the regiment's master tailor and also served in the elite grenadier company, among the regiment's most fit and reliable soldiers. With tensions rising around Boston in 1774, the soldiers of the 18th Regiment in New York departed and joined the Boston garrison, which led to his company being among those that marched out on the night of April 18–19, 1775, to seize warlike stores cached in Concord.[1]

Samuel Lee was in many ways typical of the men who filled the ranks of the British army when war broke out in America. Most had joined the army in the 1760s and early 1770s; they enlisted during times of relative peace, after a force reduction when the Seven Years' War ended. They joined the army as a career, expecting to serve until they were no longer physically able. They were regulars, professional soldiers, distinct from militia and other temporary forces. Occasional flare-ups of violence, from police actions against smugglers on the English and Irish coasts to a slave rebellion in the Caribbean, gave some of the new soldiers experience bearing arms in anger. Long overseas deployments were routine for men in an army of empire. Even when they were posted in Great Britain, army life was itinerant in nature, as regiments regularly shifted from town to town and encampment to encampment, moves that maintained fitness and readiness while also avoiding overburdening any single location with extended military presence. But there was no major war in progress when men enlisted before 1775, nor was there any reason to expect one. The prospect of going to war was certainly abstract, something that could happen but was not expected or imminent. There were veterans of the Seven Years' War in the ranks to teach, train, and tell stories to those who otherwise had no direct experience with combat, but most of the army was composed of men with military experience but only minimal exposure to war fighting. They were, nonetheless, very well trained and accustomed to adapting to changing conditions.

While Lee was very much an average soldier in terms of his age, experience, and background, he was nonetheless different from his comrades. Among the private soldiers in his regiment were some as young as eighteen and some in their fifties; Lee's age was somewhere in the middle, but not representative of the majority. His ten years of service was also in the middle for a regiment that included some new recruits and some thirty-year veterans. Over half had learned a trade before enlisting, and many used those skills for military work, skills that ranged from hatting to shoemaking, from stonecutting to thatching. There were well-educated soldiers, illiterate soldiers, and regimental schools to transform the latter into the former. There were men from every county in England, Scotland, Ireland, and even some from mainland Europe and from North America.

To understand what sort of men were in the British army that fought in the American Revolution, it is essential to look at broad ranges of attributes rather than homogenize them. The soldiery must be characterized in terms of diversity rather than in terms of common factors. It was a population drawn from nearly all echelons of the society that created it. There was such a range of nationalities, ages, skills, and socioeconomic backgrounds among British soldiers that we can only get a feel for the social makeup of the army by looking at many individuals and appreciating how they were different rather than how they were the same. There was no "typical" British soldier.

"The Conduct of the Noble Regiment of British Volunteers, shall prove that Englishmen never wanted Courage," proclaimed a recruiting poster for the 88th Regiment of Foot. Throughout the 1770s and 1780s, the British army relied almost exclusively on volunteerism to raise recruits; with an exception discussed in chapter 10, the army was an all-volunteer force, composed primarily of men who enlisted as a career rather than for a fixed term of service. Reasons for enlistment varied, as will be seen, so the title *Noble Volunteers* may lean toward hyperbole, but it captures the desired spirit if not the actual motivations of the red-coated soldiers in America.

This book is about soldiers—the "other ranks," that is, privates, corporals, drummers, and sergeants. Officers were different and require a different study. Writings of officers are used throughout this book, but the writers themselves are discussed only to the extent necessary for understanding the men they commanded. Officers left more writings than the other ranks, but in this text their names seldom appear except in the citations.

During the 1770s and 1780s, the era covered in this book, the lowest rank in the army was called "private soldier," but the word "private" was not used as a title to denote rank. Period writings refer to, for example, "Serjeant Wright," "Corporal Thompson," but "Thomas Rogers, private soldier"; nowhere do we find "Private Rogers." This book follows the same convention: if the name of a soldier is not preceded by a rank, it can be assumed he was a private solider.

This book is focused on the infantry. The British army of this era was composed of infantry, cavalry, and artillery, but most of the soldiers sent to America served in infantry regiments, called regiments of foot. Much of the information in this book applies to cavalry and artillery soldiers as well, but those branches also had their distinct methods of recruiting, training, living in barracks and on campaign, and so forth. The king of England reigned over England, Scotland, Wales, and Ireland, although Ireland was still a separate kingdom with its own government subordinate to the English government. There were some differences in how the army was managed in the two kingdoms, but those are out of the scope of this book except where noted. Within these pages, "British" refers to anyone from England, Scotland, Ireland, or Wales, and "British Isles" refers collectively to those countries. Military documents of the era seldom distinguish Wales, instead including Welsh counties as part of England and people from Wales as among the English; for that reason, this book generally does the same.

Regiments of foot and cavalry were designated by numbers, but each with their own number sequence beginning at 1; there was a 17th Regiment of Foot and a 17th Regiment of Light Dragoons, both in America at the same time. Throughout this book, full titles such as 10th Regiment of Foot are used when necessary to distinguish between infantry and cavalry regiments. There were many more infantry regiments than cavalry, so regiments numbered higher than 23 are often called by a shorter name, for example, 35th Regiment. In all cases where "of Foot" or otherwise is not explicitly stated, foot can be assumed. Besides British regulars, the British army in America included Loyalist regiments, composed of men enlisted in America for the war in America; German regiments, often referred to as Hessians and as mercenaries, contracted by the British government; and native North American, or Indian, allies. This book is concerned only with the British regulars.

Many quotations in this book are from handwritten manuscripts. Writers of the era frequently abbreviated even though there were no standard abbreviations, made extensive use of superscripts, capitalized whatever words they liked, and punctuated with irregular dots, dashes, and scrawls. For this book, the emphasis is on readability rather than exactly rendering the original text. Abbreviations are spelled out if their meaning is not otherwise blatantly clear, without using square brackets or other indications. Capitalization is not always consistent with the original. Original spelling is preserved except in cases where the words might not be understandable. This may seem like taking inappropriate liberty with primary sources, but the focus here is on understanding rather than replication.

This is not a chronological narrative of the events of the American Revolution. Some knowledge of the events and flow of the war is helpful, but not necessary, to understand this book. Many major battles and campaigns are mentioned, as well as some unfamiliar ones; remember, though, that for the soldiers experiencing them, every event was immediate, and no outcomes were already known. Standing sentry on a storm-swept shoreline in the middle of a winter night, fending off a rising fever while fearful of imminent attack by assailants unseen, may have been one man's most difficult hours of an eight-year war, but histories focused on pivotal campaigns are unkind to such personal experiences, trivializing or entirely overlooking most of the hardships endured by most of the soldiers.

This book is about soldiers, and about men—who they were, and what they experienced.

PART I

A PEACETIME ARMY PREPARES FOR WAR

CHAPTER I

Seduced, Kidnapped, and Cruelly Used

TENSIONS IN AMERICA

On the evening of July 18, 1774, John Young stood sentry on the wall that crossed Boston Neck, the stretch of land connecting peninsular Boston to the mainland. Other soldiers milled about the nearby guardhouse, ready to take up their weapons should any sort of disturbance occur near the fortifications through which travelers going by land to or from Boston must pass. The sun was setting, a few boats plied the adjacent waters, and a gunshot rang out. The soldiers heard the whiz of a musket ball, and from his vantage point on the wall, Young saw it splash into the water just twenty yards short of them. A telltale puff of smoke demarked the boat from which the shot was fired, and the three men on board rowed hard toward the town. In the fading light, the soldiers lost sight of it. An officer reported it, but nothing came of the incident.[1] It was just another insult by Bostonians to the soldiers garrisoning their town, harassment that began when they arrived and would continue, and escalate, in the ensuing months.

Boston was teeming with soldiers. For the past decade, tensions had run high in the American colonies as citizens used various forms of protest against new laws passed by the British Parliament. The fundamental issue was whether these laws were just, given that the colonies had no representatives in Parliament. Opinions ran high on both sides of the issue on both sides of the ocean, with laws and protests and repeals and new laws from 1765 into 1773. That year, things took a new turn with the destruction of a cargo of tea in Boston Harbor. Parliament, overruling objections of many members sympathetic to the colonists' motives, passed a series of measures effectively suspending the Massachusetts colonial government and imposing martial law in the colony. And marital law meant soldiers.

Four regiments of foot, infantry regiments, sailed from Britain to Boston—the 4th (King's Own), 5th, 38th, and 43rd, each with about thirty officers and four hundred men.[2] They were joined by the 23rd (Royal Welch Fusiliers) and the 47th, each of which had been in America for a year already in New York and New Jersey. The 59th Regiment had shuttled back and forth between Boston and Halifax, Nova Scotia, since 1769; now it, too, came to Boston. Supplemented by companies of the Royal Regiment of Artillery, and the 64th Regiment posted at Castle William in Boston Harbor, by mid-summer 1774 there were around four thousand British troops in Boston. In October, still more came—the 10th and 52nd Regiments, which had been in Canada since 1767 working at various posts along the St. Lawrence River from Quebec to Niagara; they had packed their baggage to return to Britain but were diverted to Boston, briefly, it was assumed, until the tensions there died down. Part of the 18th (Royal Irish) Regiment was sent from New York, as was part of the 65th from Halifax. A contingent of marines from English garrisons landed in Boston, equivalent to an infantry regiment, so that by early 1775 the garrison numbered around six thousand, similar to the number of male residents of military age in the city.[3] The soldiers were not welcome, and the populace used various means to let them know it. The last time soldiers had garrisoned the town, from 1768 until 1770, altercations between soldiers and residents proliferated, escalated, and culminated in five deaths at what came to be called the Boston Massacre.[4] The locals were experienced in instigating conflicts with soldiers, and although now martial law instead of civil law applied, from June 1774 through March 1775, British soldiers in Boston were taunted by townspeople who refused to tolerate them.

Soon after the 4th and 43rd Regiments encamped on Boston Common, the large tract of open land set aside for grazing livestock, someone left a letter addressed "To the Soldiers." Signed by "A well Wisher to the soldiers & a Friend to the Poor of all Denominations," it offered an intriguing proposition:

Friends & Brothers this is to Inform you that it is the Hearty Desire of the Inhabitants of all Parts of this Country that you would as many of you as are Posses'd of a Spirit to Push your Fortunes in a New Country where you may have Liberty & by a Little Industry may obtain Property that you would march up either singly or in Companys & you may Depend on a welcome Reception, kind usage, Encouragement of Being Employ'd in any Business occupation Trade or Employment that you have been most used to or shall Incline to follow. that the Country People are Determind to Protect you and Screen you from any that may attempt to betray you to your (at Present) Cruel Masters & Misguiders.

The letter offered assurance that "being in a Country now where all are upon a Level you may by one Push Lay the foundation of your own good Livings in a Land of freedom & Plenty & may make the fortunes of your Posterity."[5] This was a straightforward attempt to persuade soldiers to desert the army and start new lives in the colonies. Within weeks, Robert Gaul of the 43rd was "seduced away by some of the inhabitants of Boston."[6] Perhaps Gaul was influenced by the letter, more likely by face-to-face encounters. And the seduction was not limited to promises of prosperity. John Man of the 64th Regiment, on trial in November 1774 for his second desertion in two years, testified that "Each time of my Desertion I had such offers & Insinuations from these designing Bostonians and Country people that deluded by their first making me drink to excess and then conveying me away in an obscure manner, lending & assisting all help and means to forward me from my Regt."[7] John Winters of the 59th Regiment explained that it was not Bostonians who had tempted him: "he was seduced away by the persuasions of an Inhabitant of Dedham, near Boston, and one William Whyte, a soldier in the 59th Regt. who deserted with him."[8] Robert Hall and Timothy Bremer left the 43rd Regiment in October 1774 because they had "for some time had an unfortunate Connexion, with a Woman living in the Country, from whom they had often received pecuniary Favours. That she prevailed upon them on Tuesday the 11th Instant a little before Evening Roll Calling, when they were heated with Liquor, to accompany her to a house near to Dorchester Neck in a Boat."[9] Even more extreme were the measures used against Thomas Watson of the 23rd Regiment, who "had no intention of deserting, but was kidnapped away . . . upon his coming to the wharf, a man knock'd him down" and four others "tied him, and put him into the boat."[10] He, like many British soldiers who left Boston willingly or not, was quickly hustled westward to prevent any possibility of returning to the ranks.

Soldiers in New York and New Jersey faced similar treatment in 1774. The 18th Regiment's Thomas Sewell "went with two other Soldiers into an Orchard near Elizabeth town, with the intention to gather Apples, when they were seized by five Countrymen, who carried them off."[11] John Jermon (or Germon), a twenty-one-year-old from county Sligo in Ireland who had moved to New York, enlisted in the 23rd Regiment there in July 1773 but twice absconded. He described the challenges soldiers faced, particularly those with local connections, to stay in the ranks in the face of temptation:

> I, John Jermon 22d June last went into a house next door to the Hospital where Liquor was sold, being two or three of my acquaintances there, I drank pretty freely, and they persuaded me to go to the Town to another House where I got drunk & staying late, when I returned to the Hospital the gates were shut, they then persuaded me to go off, which advice I being in Liquor too readily agreed too.[12]

For the soldiers, this was no merry cat-and-mouse game. Desertion was a capital crime, and those not sentenced to death were often punished corporally instead, with sentences of from 500 to 1,500 lashes. From June 1774 through March 1775, eleven soldiers were tried in Boston by general courts-martial for desertion, of whom two were executed, one sentenced to death but given a stay of execution as an act of mercy, seven lashed, and one acquitted.[13] At least thirteen other men returned from desertion during this same period (including some who had deserted months or years earlier) but were not tried by general courts;[14] no records survive to tell whether they were tried by regimental courts, which could sentence only corporal punishment, or were not tried at all.

Search parties that ventured out of Boston into the countryside to track down deserters faced obstruction from inhabitants who resented both their presence and their mission. In early 1775, "two good men" of the 10th Regiment made their way forty miles south to Middleboro, where they learned that the deserters they pursued had sold their weapons. The trail going cold, they met up with four more British soldiers, "disguised and on horseback," who came to support them. The six headed back toward Boston "when the Country rose upon them, to the Number of about One Hundred and forty Men, with Arms," surrounded them, and ordered them to stop. The sergeant commanding the party refused, and although outnumbered, they managed to outintimidate the assailants, taking two of them at pistol point to a justice of the peace in nearby Plymouth. The soldiers returned to Boston unharmed but without the deserters they sought, and with a clear understanding of how much the country populace despised them.[15]

Several regiments in Boston had recently come from Ireland, where they had also experienced harassment by local citizens. While those in Boston were being inveigled to desert, their comrades posted in Irish cities were enduring much more savage treatment. In Limerick on the night of October 16, 1774, "a soldier of the 17th regiment was assaulted at the back of the old slaughter house, Irishtown, by some ruffians, who barbarously cut out a piece of his tongue; as the unfortunate man cannot write, the cause of their committing this inhuman action, or the villain who committed it, is not yet known."[16] More common was a practice called houghing, or hocking: cutting the Achilles tendon, or hock, a wound that could not heal properly, thereby rendering the man lame, no longer able to serve as a soldier and maybe unable to work at all. This was the case for Thomas Thompson of the 24th Regiment and Charles Dowley of the 35th who "were houghed, and otherwise so cruelly used, that they are rendered incapable of earning their bread" in Dublin on January 28, 1775.[17] Five days later, Thomas Shaley of the 57th Regiment "had his skull fractured in three different places, haughed in both legs, two of his fingers cut off, and stabbed in many parts of the body, by a number of butchers who met him on the Inns-quay."[18] The following week, when a corporal of the 35th Regiment was houghed, a newspaper called the perpetrators "some merciless miscreants, who are a scandal to human nature and a pest to society."[19] Newspapers reported one or two such incidents in Dublin during each of the first three months of 1775.[20] In September 1776, the War Office awarded pensions to twenty-three soldiers "who were houghed and thereby rendered unfit for the service," and to the widow of one "who had died of his wounds, and left her with 4 children."[21]

The soldiers, although discouraged from and ordered against mixing with the populace, did sometimes retaliate. On the evening of January 30, 1775, a large number of soldiers went to Dublin's Ormond Market to seek revenge on those who had attacked Thompson and Dowley; they assumed it was butchers who had lain in wait for soldiers and maimed them. Finding no butchers, they broke open butcher shops, stole and trampled sides of beef and mutton, stole choppers and cleavers and other effects, and destroyed shop books. "From a hat that was found the next morning in the market, it appears that some of the 35th regiment . . . were concerned in this illegal adventure."[22]

So, too, did soldiers in Boston fight back against those trying to trick them into desertion. Corporal Phineas Baker, a Yorkshire native, and Henry Drennan of Antrim, Ireland, were both in the 38th Regiment. On December 26, 1774, they went into a public house where "some countrymen" offered them plain clothes and assistance in deserting. Baker took up the offer of being snuck out of town on horseback; the countrymen had only one horse, so Drennan declined. Baker donned the clothing, stuffing his uniform into one of the men's saddlebags, but when the guide told Baker to ride behind him, the corporal explained that he had to be in front because he was unable to ride without stirrups. With control of the horse, Baker set out at a gallop to the nearest barrack, upon which the countryman "leaped from behind him, and made his escape, swearing he would not wait to be shot." Baker was allowed to keep the horse, tack, and clothing since no one in town would admit owning them.[23]

In March 1775, soldiers of the 47th Regiment caused a stir when they detained Thomas Ditson, a resident of the town of Billerica, in the streets of Boston. Ditson was told that they were "going to serve you as you have served our men." They made Ditson strip to the waist, poured tar and feathers on him, sat him on a chair affixed with a set of wheels, and paraded him through the city wearing a sign that read "American Liberty, or Democracy exemplified in a villain who attempted to entice one of the Soldiers of His Majesty's Forty-Seventh Regiment to desert, and take up Arms with Rebels against his King and Country." Ditson claimed to have been inquiring around town for a gun to purchase when a soldier offered one for sale and invited him into the barracks to conduct the transaction, after which the soldiers seized him. John Clancy, the soldier who accused him, gave a quite different account, saying Ditson had approached him to buy used clothing. Clancy invited him into the barracks to look at some garments; Ditson sent out for hot drinks for them, and while they drank, Ditson whispered about purchasing a gun and eventually struck a deal for the purchase of two. Now believing he had a good mark, Ditson told Clancy that "if he would desert his Majesty's Service, and go over with him to Charlestown, he would furnish the Deponent with any Sums of Money he wanted." He could arrange for a boat to take them, after which "to the Devil you may pitch the whole Army in Boston, and all those that command the Soldiers," and any deserter who would help train Massachusetts soldiers "should be made a Gentleman."[24]

This scene from an encampment near London in 1780 was probably echoed frequently in Boston in 1774. A corporal is saluted by two grenadier privates and a battalion private. Two mocking townspeople look on, while a young drummer plays with a dog. *The Relief*, H. W. Bunbury, circa 1780. (*Anne S. K. Brown Collection, Brown University Library*)

Clancy's story was believable to his officers and comrades because it was so familiar. People of Massachusetts knew well how to harass soldiers, having had two years of practice from autumn 1768, when the 14th and 29th Regiments arrived in town, through early 1770, when several redcoats, beleaguered by brickbats and chunks of ice, opened fire on the mob that harangued them. Throughout those years of frequent and violent conflicts between soldiers and civilians, the inhabitants knew that the law was on their side; soldiers could easily be provoked into fighting with townspeople and faced military punishment for doing so.[25] There were many more soldiers in town in 1774 and 1775, more to tempt with alcohol and taunt with insults. Each regiment's commanding officer was directed to "prevent his men going into town, and from having as little intercourse or Conversation with the Inhabitants as possible,"[26] but prevention proved impossible.

Undeniably, the soldiers brought some of the animosity upon themselves, exacerbating sentiments that were already against them. On August 2, 1774, Corporal Charles McKenny of the 5th Regiment assaulted a local woman, Sarah Muncrief, in an outhouse; he was thwarted by her housemate Katy Derby. His actions were punishable by death according to military law, but Muncrief asked the regiment's commanding officer for lenience as a show of mercy. He was tried by a regimental court and sentenced to be reduced to private and receive one hundred lashes. Muncrief was then defamed by town gossips as a lewd woman, forcing her to defend herself in the newspaper.[27] Another incident that made the papers was provoked by James Hamilton of the 4th Regiment in September 1774. Enoch Brown, a store owner, was "alarmed by the noise of six or seven soldiers, who I observed greatly obstructed business with customers from the country." He asked the soldiers to leave, but Hamilton instead "called for rum," indicating he would drink it right there. "I will have no rum drank in the store," admonished Brown, upon which Hamilton called him "a damn'd saucy fellow, and walked out with the rest, and stopping at the door, he not only insulted me with the most abusive language, but attempted to strike me with a large club, which was prevented by one of his companions." The soldiers disputed this at a regimental court-martial, saying instead that Brown had assaulted Hamilton. In his newspaper account of the incident, Brown made one indisputable claim: that Hamilton complained because "the people were using all means in their power to have the soldiery punished, by getting them drunk, enticing them to desert, &c."[28]

There was ample animosity, even though there was no war. The garrison was in Boston to maintain peace, not incite war, and the soldiers were peacetime soldiers. Among them were some veterans of the Seven Years' War, which had ended a dozen years before, and of minor conflicts such as riot control or skirmishing with smugglers in the British Isles. As with most armies at the beginning of most wars, the majority of the soldiers in Boston, elsewhere in North America, and back in Britain, had enlisted during times of peace. Each regiment was at a peacetime strength; daily routine was focused on fitness, discipline, and military work, but not combat per se. Enlistment in the army was strictly voluntary, for British peacetime doctrine dictated a small army of career soldiers that could be augmented in time of emergency. Men enlisted not to defend the realm against an explicit enemy but as a career that might last twenty or thirty years, partly in far-flung reaches of the empire. Now, that far-flung place was Boston, and the emergency they were sent to resolve was instead accelerating.

On March 21, 1775, soldiers manning the lines at Boston Neck stopped two carts headed out of town to inspect the contents for smuggled military stores. A crowd gathered, and some taunted the soldiers; one said "he would whip the Arse of any Regular there, and challenged them to turn out and fight." A man on horseback brandished a stick. Pushing, shoving, grabbing. A servant, pushed away with a musket butt, attempted to strike back but was hit on the head with the musket's muzzle. While this was going on, a man with a bag of tinned-iron camp kettles passed by, and "lifting up the skirt of his Coat, struck his Hand, as an Insult to the Soldiers, on his Backside." A soldier kicked the man, the man struck the soldier on the face with his bag of kettles, and a scuffle ensued.[29] This was the British soldiers' life in America. It would soon get much worse.

CHAPTER 2

Roving Dispositions and Soaring Spirits

ENLISTING A PEACETIME ARMY

THOMAS WATSON'S MOTHER DIED when he was fifteen years old. His father had died when he was an infant, leaving six children entirely in their mother's care in the village of Nessholt, a few miles northwest of Chester in Cheshire, England. It was coal-mining country, and young Thomas had toiled at that dark, dirty work since the age of seven, "amongst a very wicked company, and soon became as bad as any." Eight years of that was enough, and the death of his mother prompted him to go to London to live with one of his sisters. Not faring well there, he returned to Nessholt to live with another sister, but the restless teenager could not tolerate her husband. He tried working in Lancashire for a year, then returned once again to Nessholt only to find that he "could not make it seem like home." Determined to go to sea, he signed on to a ship in Liverpool bound for Virginia, but it wreaked so badly of tobacco that even his olfactory system that had spent years in coal mines could not bear it; it sickened him before he even left port, and he abandoned his maritime aspirations. Back to the mines he went, for a while in Lancashire, then to a stint in Staffordshire, and then on to find fortune in the city.[1]

In Wolverhampton, Watson found his future, if not his fortune. He met up with a recruiting party from the 23rd Regiment of Foot, the Royal Welch Fusiliers. They were raising men to bring the regiment up to full strength, for soon they would sail to New York, where they expected to stay for several years, relieving another regiment, part of a routine rotation of troops manning overseas garrisons. Watson wrote that he was "persuaded" to enlist, but his itinerant path during the five years since his mother's death suggests he was an easy mark for a profession that offered an enlistment bounty, steady income, camaraderie, and travel to distant lands. By April 1773, the twenty-year-old recruit was embarking with his regiment at Plymouth Dock.[2] He later reported that "he liked the profession of a soldier so much better than the trade he had been brought up to, that he would not have taken his discharge, if it had been offered to him."[3]

With the hardships and dangers that a soldier's life offered, one wonders why men would join the army. Thomas Watson's enlistment provides an excellent example of the difficulties in determining why—if he had not left an account, there would be no way to guess his motivations. He had a profession, such as it was, and had been consistently able to find work when he chose to. He enlisted far from where he was born and raised. He joined a regiment with no regional ties to his place of birth or enlistment. He had no family ties or other connections to the military. What he did have was a disrupted family situation, discontent with his profession, and a roving disposition that compelled him to leave home and jobs, return and leave again, a disposition that could have been caused by his troubles or have caused those troubles. No analysis of information such as birthplace, age, trade, economic conditions, family size, recruiting practices, or other data would lead to an accurate conclusion about why this individual enlisted. He demonstrates the impossibility of attempting to determine reasons for enlistment based on indirect information rather than on each man's own words.[4]

The challenge of understanding why soldiers enlisted during times of peace is that few men left their own words. Thousands joined the army during Britain's peaceful years in the late 1760s and early 1770s, but only a handful recorded their reasons. Of that handful, not a single one presents a rationale that would be predicted by analytical techniques, calling into question any conclusions derived from such analysis. The data tell us what happened—men enlisted—but they do not tell us why.

Among the soldiers who enlisted during this era was Valentine Duckett, who left home and joined the 65th Regiment, probably knowing it was soon to sail for North America, because "my step-mother and I could not agree."[5] In 1772, Alexander Andrew "came into the army in place of a brother of mine, who was cunning enough to persuade me, young and foolish enough, to go in his place"[6] in the 44th Regiment. Wiltshire native Richard Taylor had four years of schooling, then took an apprenticeship with a plasterer at age fourteen. After over five years in that line of work, he ran away and joined the 63rd Regiment; his reason is not recorded, but it clearly wasn't lack of employment.[7] Dubliner Roger Lamb lost all of his money to gambling in 1773 when he was seventeen, and sought out a recruiter in the 9th Regiment of Foot. Although this suggests the army was an economic refuge, Lamb was well educated and had a working family to fall back on; his real impetus was that he was "afraid to return and tell my father of my indiscretions, who would have rebuked and forgiven me."[8] Not a single man who left a record of his rationale gave unemployment or impoverishment as a reason for becoming a soldier between 1765 and 1775. With only about a dozen first-hand accounts, no possibility can be discounted, but neither can any be assumed.

A number of men who did not record why they enlisted clearly chose the military over other opportunities. Jacob Margas was twenty-four, working in the family business as an optician in Dublin, where they had moved from London a decade before, when his father died in 1767. Rather than take over the business, Margas enlisted in the 54th Regiment, where he spent the next twenty-three years.[9] Thomas Machin supposedly left work with canal-builder James Brindley to join the 23rd Regiment shortly before it sailed for America, jeweler Joseph Dunckerly left the family business in London to enlist in the 38th Regiment, and Andrew Brown, supposedly a graduate of Trinity College in Dublin, enlisted in the 47th Regiment in 1774 when it was already on service in America. All three deserted from Boston at different times, and all three had the education and charisma to become officers in the Continental army; Machin became a successful military engineer, Dunckerly a portrait painter, and Brown a publisher.[10] Why men with such capacity chose to enlist as private soldiers remains a mystery, but they were not alone in the ranks of British regiments.

A 1775 advertisement placed by the 33rd Regiment sought "any able-bodied young man . . . who is fired with ambition, has a roving disposition, and whose spirit soars above the dull sameness of staying at home."[11] In the early 1770s, a recruiting officer for the 42nd (Royal Highland) Regiment posted a notice in Gaelic appealing to highland Scotsmen, proclaiming, "I have come to seek men in whom there is spirit and bravery, who are willing and able to stand in the place of those who went before them and to win honour and fame for your native land," going so far as to "give him an absolute guarantee that every distinction will fall upon him and that he will acquire that elevation of status to be expected from the people of his country and from his own fellow soldiers." The regiment was quartered in northern Ireland at the time, and the officer took care to point out that recruits would "get a hearty welcome from your fellow countrymen and affection from the Irish lassies."[12] Almost all those 1760s and 1770s enlistees who wrote down their motives were targets of this colorful language, and they gave reasons for enlisting that were aspirational rather than pragmatic. Irishman William Crawford for years spent the money he earned as a stonecutter on drinking, gambling, brawling, and womanizing, "but I soon after raised my views and laid aside my shillelah for a sword. The splendid uniform and glittering epaulettes, the beauty of the horses and grandeur of the parade, and above all, the king's golden guineas in form o' a bounty, won my heart, and I enlisted in the Prince of Wales' regiment of light dragoons."[13] Edward Hall, who joined the 43rd Regiment in 1770, related "that his Family being in very independent Circumstances he first entered into the Service not from Want, but Inclination."[14] Thomas Sullivan signed on with the 49th Regiment in early 1775, explaining, "My chief intention . . . being to travel and traverse a stretch of the Seas, occasioned my inlisting, thinking by that means that I would be enabled to satisfy an inclination, so strongly bent upon rambling; especially by entering into a Regiment that was going abroad, and not likely to return home for some years to either England or Ireland."[15] William Cobbett, who enlisted in 1784 just after the American war ended, left his home town of Farnham, Surrey, "to seek adventures." After trying a couple of jobs in London that didn't hold his interest, "a change was what he now wanted," and although he "was not so ignorant as to be the dupe of this morsel of military bombast" on a recruiting poster in St. James' Park, he intended to join in the marines but enlisted in the 54th Regiment of Foot by mistake.[16] William Burke's succinct reason for leaving a steady and comfortable clerk's job in Ireland in 1775 to enlist in the 45th Regiment is perhaps the most common of all, unstated but understood by thousands of young men drawn from other pursuits and professions by the army's adventurous allure: "I had a wish to become a soldier."

There were financial incentives. The immediate temptation was an enlistment bounty, a sum given (or credited) to the recruit immediately. In the late 1760s and early 1770s, this was usually twenty-one shillings (one pound one shilling), the value of the widely circulated gold guinea coin. A savvy candidate could bargain for more, or the recruiter could offer more to a promising prospect; one writer advised officers to offer no more than one pound eleven shillings and sixpence, consistent with the "no more than a guinea and a half" offered by the 17th Regiment of Foot in 1767.[17] This was about a month's pay for typical working-class people—not a life-changing sum but quite an enticement for a young man with an adventurous spirit stuck in a monotonous laboring life. For the long-term thinker, the army offered assurance of steady income in a world of itinerant labor. There was even the prospect of a pension after long service, a perquisite offered by no other profession, which will be discussed in detail in the closing chapters of this book. Without first-hand accounts, it is impossible to guess how many chose a career in the army with this future benefit in mind, but there were pensioners all over Great Britain with stories of foreign adventures to supplement the silken words of recruiters.

To entice men "strongly bent upon rambling," recruiting parties fanned out across the British Isles, frequenting market towns, county fairs, manufacturing centers, and any places where likely enlistees might be found. Not every man was suited to be a soldier. Service in the infantry meant marching mile upon mile for months on end, sleeping on hard ground for part of each year, toiling at labors from felling trees to raising fortifications, all the while maintaining body, clothing, and equipment in serviceable condition. Each regiment did its own recruiting, following guidelines provided by commanding officers that reflected a combination of corporate knowledge passed down through the regiment, institutional wisdom collected in books authored by ambitious army officers (some of which were widely used but none of which were endorsed by the War Office or any overarching authority), the laws at the time, and the commanding officer's own judgment. A few sets of recruiting instructions from the 1760s and 1770s survive, in addition to the books that may have influenced them.

"You are to enlist no man under the age of 17, nor above 25, unless he has served in the army," asserted author Thomas Simes in 1768, and his fellow author Bennett Cuthbertson described the rationale: "Young, active Men, from seventeen to twenty-five years of age, make the most tractable Soldiers."[18] Simes's recruiting instructions, included in his popular guidebook and reprinted in another volume eight years later, were

Years of Age	AGE from 18 & under to 55 Years & upwards. COMPANIES.										Total.
	Col° Robt Henr Clitherow	Lt Col° Thos Watson Powell	Major Jams McFarlane	Capt. Willm Hughes	Capt. Chas Brissac Molly	Capt. Wigney Carow	Capt. John Campbell	Capt. John Wynts	Capt. Jams Shepherd	Capt. John Edwards	
55				1							1
50		1	2			1		1			5
45		3	2	1	1	1		1	2	3	14
40	3	8	5	5	6	11	2	3	2	3	48
35	5	7	10	8	6	6	3	5	5	8	63
30	5	4	3	7	7	9	9	9	11	5	69
25	10	7	10	13	10	4	16	14	13	12	109
20	10	5	7	2	6	7	10	10	6	7	70
18	6	6	3	4	5	2	2		3	3	34
Total	39	41	42	41	41	41	42	43	42	41	413

Age distribution in the 53rd Regiment before they embarked for America. Detail from Inspection Return, 53rd Regiment of Foot, WO 27/35. (*The National Archives*) intended as a template, and instructions given by individual regiments did indeed depart from them. The 17th Regiment of Foot, in 1767, for example, directed recruiters not to take "any man upwards of twenty-five or under fifteen years of age." In 1775, the 33rd Regiment sought men between the ages of seventeen and twenty-two, while the same year the 7th Regiment of Foot gave no age range.[19] Age was less important than stature. "Inlist none under five feet seven and a half high, except growing lads whom you may take at five feet five inches" was the direction to officers of the 17th Regiment, while the 7th accepted "men of five feet six inches provided they are able bodied, Broad Shoulders well Limbed and not above Twenty Years of Age," even offering that "Young Lads of five feet High will be allowed of provided they are Well Limbed and Likely to Grow." Cuthbertson advised seeking no one under five feet six and a half inches, and "that the Lads under eighteen have stout thick joints (a certain indication of growth), and not too much the look of being set." After suggesting a maximum age of twenty-five for men who had no prior military service, Cuthbertson admonished "to depend more on a Man's looks, for determining his age, than on what he calls himself; the common people are in general so ignorant in this point, that it is absurd to take a peasant's word, for being only twenty-five, when his appearance probably bespeaks him to be many years advanced beyond that age."[20]

Recruiters for the 7th Regiment were told to "take particular care that such men as you inlist are free from Ruptures, Scabbed Head, Sore or Crooked legs, In-knees, or any other deformity."[21] Simes wrote, "A man who is subject to fits, or has any appearance of a rupture, broken bones, sore legs, scald head, ulcers or running sores, on any part of his body, old wounds ill cured, or any infirmity in body or limb, will not be approved of."[22] According to Cuthbertson, "In-kneed, or splay-footed Men should never be enlisted, being, from the formation of their limbs, unable to undergo the fatigue of tedious Marches: those with round shoulders, or past thirty years of age, are also to be avoided, the first never acquiring an upright carriage, and the others from the stiffness of their joints, seldom learning to handle their Arms with dexterity."[23] Admonitions such as these, however obvious, were spelled out for the benefit of inexperienced or hasty recruiting officers.

The prospective recruit's character was as important as his physique. "It is desired that none will apply who cannot have an honest character, as those men only will be taken who promise to be a credit to their officers, and an honor to their country," announced the 33rd Regiment's advertisement, leaving some allowance by saying "cannot have" instead of "do not have." Although a man with prior service would be considered regardless of age, it was important to learn why he was no longer in the army. Unless the candidate "produces an Honourable Discharge" to show that he was "dismissed at the desire of his Friends, or . . . the Corps he belonged to was entirely disbanded," it might be assumed that he "has been whipped or drummed out," "though he positively denies it," necessitating "some pretence should be made for looking at his naked back" to reveal scars of corporal punishment.[24] It was important to measure each man in stocking feet, "taking care, that nothing is concealed between his feet and stockings, to help his stature." And "an Officer should not be too ready at entertaining men, whose characters are not attested by some person of Credit in the neighbourhood,"[25] as the army was an expedient exit for those with something to run from.

Records giving the enlistment age and height of individual soldiers are scant, but those that exist demonstrate the recommendations being put into practice, in terms of both the overall guidelines and the occasional exceptions. It is clear that recruiters used judgment rather than strict rules. A description list of Captain Walter Home's company in the 7th Regiment of Foot prepared in November 1772 contains information about thirty-eight sergeants, corporals, drummers, and private soldiers, arrayed neatly between five feet six and five feet ten and three-quarter inches tall. Two men were slightly shorter, between five feet five and five feet six; one of the two was forty years old and had been in the regiment for sixteen years, the other twenty-four with fewer than two years in the regiment—in other words, neither could be expected to grow taller. Of the thirty-three men for whom both age and year of enlistment are legible, two had enlisted when under age seventeen (one sixteen, one thirteen), and three above age twenty-five (two twenty-six and one twenty-seven). Eighteen men were from seventeen to nineteen years old when they enlisted, and the remaining twelve from twenty to twenty-five.[26] A survey of 385 soldiers' discharge papers, which give each man's age and years of service, shows that the average enlistment age of peacetime recruits was between twenty-one and twenty-two—not surprising, given the desired range of seventeen to twenty-five. But the distribution is not equal across that age range; 25 were below age sixteen, and 20 to 30 were at each of the ages seventeen, eighteen, and nineteen. Over a quarter of the total, 101, were twenty or twenty-one years old. Between 35 and 45 were at each of the ages twenty-two and twenty-three. Fifty-five were twenty-four or twenty-five, while 45 were from twenty-six to thirty-four. Overall, recruiters were following the age guidelines, but almost 20 percent of the men were either older or younger than the suggested age range when enlisted.[27]

Some men had a predisposition toward soldiering. They were not just from military families, but were "born in the regiment" or "born in the army," in the nomenclature used by pension examiners. With their characters and capabilities well known, boys born in the army were good risks "because such boys, from being bred in the regiment from their infancy, have a natural affection and attachment to it, and are seldom induced to desert, having no other place to take shelter at." They could begin military work at a young age as fifers, "as their duty is not very laborious, it matters not how young they are taken, when strong enough to Fife, without endangering their constitutions." Drumming was somewhat more challenging, requiring "active, ingenious lads, with supple joints," preferably under the age of fourteen because "few, when past fourteen years of age, attain to any great perfection on the Drum." Size and strength were especially important: "Boys much under fourteen, unless they are remarkably stout, are rather an encumbrance to a regiment (especially on service) as they are in general unable to bear fatigue, or even carry their Drums on a march." "If proper boys can be selected in the regiment, it will answer best," but although "the soldiers' children in most regiments can afford a sufficient supply," "otherwise pains must be taken to search the country for them."[28]

How many soldiers' children followed their fathers' paths cannot be determined. Muster rolls, the only surviving documents for most regiments that record all of the men in the ranks, give neither ages nor relationships. Was Edward Clarke, added to the rolls of the 35th Regiment as a drummer or fifer in 1768, the son of one of the several men named Clark or Clarke in the regiment? We can only guess.[29] Pension admission records, which give each man's age and years of service, reveal some who enlisted at around twelve; muster rolls often show that they served as drummers and that long-serving men with the same surname were also in the regiment. Between August 1774 and April 1785, between 13,000 and 14,000 men went before the pension examiners, of whom 33 were explicitly denoted as having been born in the army,[30] but there were more than just these few. Alexander Major, for example, was listed in the pension examination book as having been born in Chamblee, Canada, but his discharge clarified that he was "an old soldier's son that was killed in the service."[31] Knowing that birthplaces were listed for some men born

Size	\[S I Z E \] from 5-6 & under to 6-2 & upwards. Companies as above.										Total
Feet Inch											
6-2			/					/			2
6-1½											
6-1			/								1
6-.½											
6-.			3								3
5-11½		1	3		1						5
5-11			1	5							6
5-10½		2		12							14
5-10			2	8		1	2		1		14
5-9½	2	1		5		1	6	3	3	1	22
5-9	3	3	6	3		2	2	3	1	4	27
5-8½	6	6	6			6	3	6	5	8	46
5-8	8	6	5		2	7	5	5	5	12	55
5-7½	6	5	6	1	1	6	8	6	8	3	53
5-7	6	4	5		13	5	6	6	4	6	55
5-6½	3	3	3		8	2	2	2	4	2	29
5-6 under	3	2	2		8	4	3	3	4	4	33
5-6	3	2	3	2	10	3	2	4	5		34
Total	40	38	39	44	42	38	39	39	40	40	399

Size (height) distribution in each of the 37th Regiment's ten companies before they embarked for America. The grenadier company, typically composed of the regiment's tallest men, is fourth from the left; the light infantry, typically composed of the smallest men, is fifth from the left. Detail from Inspection Return, 37th Regiment of Foot, WO 27/35. (*The National Archives*) in the army means there is no way to determine how many soldiers had been literally bred to military life.

"You are not to suffer your party to use any Villainies or low practices" to entice men to enlist, recruiters for the 17th Regiment were warned. During this era, enlistment was strictly voluntary—there was no conscription, impressment, or other mandatory service in the British army. To guard against "low practices," recruiting parties were constrained by a number of laws governing when and where they could operate; in effect, they needed permission to recruit in a given town. Within four days of agreeing to enlist, the recruit was required to go before a magistrate to attest that he had enlisted voluntarily. This time interval gave an opportunity for the recruit to rethink his decision—or to sober up, if necessary—and for the recruiting party to check up on the man if they so chose. Whether recruited in Great Britain or the colonies, the legalities were the same, including that enlistees did not have a fixed duration of service and "their attestations are to be regularly taken, and kept, as well as registered in the Regimental Books."[32] With these restrictions, it was up to recruiters to find likely men and persuade them to volunteer if they did not come forward of their own volition. An officer of the 60th (Royal American) Regiment, which enlisted primarily non-British-born men, "had a snug, economical method of his own. He generally dispensed with the noisy ceremony of the recruiting coterie," instead relying on his own "knowledge of mankind, of low life especially; and he seldom scented a subject that he did not, in the end, make his prey. He knew his man, and could immediately discover a fish that would bite." This recruiter "familiarly held his booby by the button, his small, black, piercing eyes, which derived additional animation from the intervention of a sarcastic, upturned nose, penetrated to the fellow's soul, and gave him distinct intelligence of what was passing there."[33]

There is no way to verify whether every soldier enlisted voluntarily and was properly attested, but trial records of men who deserted suggest that the laws were followed well. With attestation being a legal requirement, a man who was not attested would have legal grounds to dispute his enlistment. When Luke Murphy of the 38th Regiment stood trial for desertion in Boston in 1774, his attestation was read to the court, "by which it appears he was duly enlisted to serve his Majesty as a Soldier."[34] John Man volunteered to join the 47th Regiment in New York in September 1774, but on the way to a magistrate to be attested he revealed

A fifer depicted in the frontispiece of a British fife instruction book, dressed in conformance with the clothing regulations of the 1770s and 1780s. In the near background is a tent that is shaped like a bell tent for storing arms, albeit rendered much too large. Five-man soldiers' tents appear in rows in the background. *Entire New and Compleat Instructions for the Fife* (London: John Preston, no date).

himself as a deserter from the 64th Regiment; when he was brought to trial in Boston, his attestation was shown to the court to prove he had enlisted in the 64th on February 9, 1768.[35] Charles Toomey enlisted in Boston on April 3, 1775, but "never was attested to serve His Majesty, for being a Soldier's Son, the Recruiting party of the 59th Regiment with whom he enlisted, thought it unnecessary." This might have given him legal grounds had he brought it up immediately, but he served for three years before deserting.[36] If significant numbers of men were enlisted by illegal practices, some of them surely would have stated their cases when on trial for the capital crime of desertion, but none did.[37]

Desertion was a common problem among recruits, which is why recruiting parties were cautioned to be so careful in discerning the character of their quarries. The numbers are countless because records for recruiting parties are rare, but the reasons can be deduced as falling into three general categories: men who regretted their decision to enlist, either because it was made in haste or because they quickly learned that army life was not for them; men who took the enlistment bounty with every intention of deserting with it, including some who made a regular practice of it; and those incorrigible characters who joined the army to get away from something, and absconded to get away from something else. An army that appealed to wanderlust was liable to get those who wandered away, as well as those who wandered in.[38]

It was the practice of the age to place newspaper advertisements seeking the return of people who left employment obligations of all sorts, including servants, apprentices, slaves, sailors, and of course soldiers. Not all deserters were advertised, at least not in newspapers—handbills or word of mouth could also be used—but newspapers of the era abound with notices of deserters among the other advertising. A substantial portion of these were for recruits, although long-serving soldiers also appeared. The ads contain a brief description of each man in the hope he would be recognizable, usually giving his age, height, hair and eye colors, place of birth, and sometimes the clothing he was thought to be wearing. Often included were other distinguishing features such as complexion, visage (facial shape, such as round, square, oval, or long), trade, and recognizable traits such as scars or speech patterns. The ads occasionally yield clues about the reason for desertion, such as the ad for nineteen-year-old John Smith from Yorkshire, a recruit for the 17th Regiment; the fair-skinned, blue-eyed laborer enlisted in Carlisle on June 29, 1772, but within four weeks deserted after stealing forty shillings from a comrade.[39] At around the same time, David Keeny absconded from the 69th Regiment's recruiting party in Kelso, Scotland, less than three weeks after enlisting; the twenty-two year-old weaver from Montrose had "a brown complexion, his face marked with the small pox, black eyes, and short black curled hair," and the recruiting sergeant's hat for which he probably hoped to get some good money.[40] William Newton, "17 years of age, 5 feet 8 inches and a half high, slender made, brown complection, light brown hair tied behind, born at Ryton, in the county of Durham, by trade a labourer," fled from recruiters of the 32nd Regiment in Penrith (Penrydd), Wales, on August 15, 1773, and was "suspected to be a deserter from some regiment in Ireland."[41]

These three advertisements, a small sample of the hundreds like them, show that men were enlisting far from their hometowns—in spite of one writer's warning, "An Officer must be cautious of enlisting a man, who is not an inhabitant in or near his recruiting quarters, especially if he insists on too much money, as it may be almost certain, his intention is to desert the very first opportunity which offers."[42] The advertisements taken in isolation suggest that men who enlisted far from their hometowns were likely to desert, but the advertisements show us only deserters; few other documents survive giving both places of birth and places of enlistment, leaving no way to measure the proportion of men who deserted compared to where they enlisted. Valentine Duckett and Thomas Watson, mentioned at the beginning of this chapter, are examples of men who enlisted far from home and did not desert as recruits. In Captain Home's company of the 7th Regiment in November 1772, of the men for whom both the place of birth and place of enlistment are given and legible, thirty out of thirty-four enlisted within fifty miles or so of their birthplace.

Enlistment close to home did not mean that regiments were homogeneous in their demographics. Captain Home's company included men from all over Great Britain: twenty-three from England, six from Scotland, and one each from Ireland and Wales. Ten English and three Scottish counties are represented. What is clear from deserter advertisements, pension records, regimental inspection returns and other sources is that most British regiments recruited from every corner of the British Isles. When the 17th Regiment of Foot was inspected in 1774, its ranks included 292 English, 58 Scottish, and 58 Irish soldiers; in the 55th Regiment the same year were 146 English, 207 Scottish, and 69 Irish, while the 49th had 201 English, 89 Scots, 115 Irish, and 1 foreign-born man.[43] In the 22nd Regiment in 1775, 172 men whose places of birth are known came from 64 counties in Great Britain.[44] The infantry regiments in the early 1770s were truly British in that each was composed of men from counties all over England, Scotland, Ireland, and Wales.[45]

With the exception of the 42nd (Royal Highland) Regiment, which was composed almost exclusively of men from Scotland, British regiments did not recruit exclusively in particular counties or regions. That said, the value of focusing on areas where recruiting officers had influence, or from which the regiment already had many soldiers, was recognized. In 1768, military writer Bennett Cuthbertson advised, "Regiments, which confine themselves to recruit in particular counties, have generally the best success, young Men being most desirous of enlisting into a corps, where they are certain of meeting many countrymen, and perhaps relations."[46] Standing orders for the 37th Regiment echoed a further recommendation by Cuthbertson, that brothers or friends who enlisted together be put in the same company if they desired.[47] A captain in the 33rd Regiment several times mentioned his "Herefordshire Recruits" in letters home, sometimes mentioning the activities of individual soldiers he had enlisted in his home county.[48]

The regiments encamped in Boston as tensions grew through 1774 and into 1775 were a thoroughly British mixture, none predominately from any particular region, with variations depending on where each had recently been. The 59th, 64th, and 65th Regiments included a smattering of North American-born men in their ranks, having been in Nova Scotia and Boston since the 1760s, as did the 10th, 18th, and 52nd, which had served at various posts in North America since 1767. An advertisement for deserters from the 18th in November 1771 listed five men, two born in Ireland, one in Germany, one in England, and one in Philadelphia; the German, the Englishman, and the Philadelphian had all enlisted in America.[49] The 23rd and 47th had done some recruiting since their arrival in the colonies in 1773.[50] The 4th, 5th, 38th, and 43rd all came from the British Isles in 1774 but nonetheless included the occasional "foreign" soldier in their ranks. Insufficient information survives for any of these regiments to know exactly where each man came from, but the portion that eventually received pensions suggests that none had any particular favored location for recruiting.[51]

The great demographic mixture of men introduced the challenge of language: not all recruits spoke English, or spoke it well. In 1770, a soldier named Rudolph Buckhouse deserted from the 68th Regiment, then in Philadelphia, and was described as "a Dutchman, speaks bad English."[52] Leonard Printzell, the German who deserted from the 18th Regiment

Country	NUMBER of each Country. COMPANIES.										Total.
	Col. Robt. Wm Elphinstone	Lt Col. Hon. William Prescott	Major James McFarlane	Capt. William Hughes	Capt. Chas. Braongant Myer	Capt. Wilmy Green	Capt. John Campbell	Capt. John Wright	Capt. Jam. Proprietors	Capt. John Edwards	
English	4	26	27	26	32	25	26	22	31	27	259
Scotch	4	7	12	5	5	9	12	10	7	6	93
Irish	2	5	3	7	4	7	4	11	4	8	61
Foreigners											–
Total	39	11	12	41	41	41	12	13	12	41	413

Nationalities in the 28th Regiment before they embarked for America. Detail from Inspection Return, 28th Regiment of Foot, WO 27/35. (*The National Archives*)

in November 1771, spoke "but little English," which may have contributed to his "seemingly very quiet" disposition.[53] When a man deserted
from the 45th Regiment in Limerick, Ireland, in early 1775, Galway-
born recruit William Burke was included in the search party because "the
corporal and the other three had but little knowledge of the customs and
manners of the Catholic Irish, but I was well versed in their language,
and well acquainted with their customs."[54] The 42nd Regiment, unusual
in that it recruited almost exclusively in highland Scotland, advertised
for recruits in the regional language; upon joining the regiment, Lieutenant William Leslie, although Scottish himself, sought instruction "to
learn me Earse," as Gaelic was called by the English.[55] The ability to
manage recruits of different national and linguistic backgrounds would
serve the army well in the coming conflict.

In 1770, an apprentice named William Nicholls enlisted in the 38th Regiment of Foot. His master demanded he be discharged and returned to
his apprenticeship, which brought several legal questions to the Privy
Council of Ireland: was it legal for the regiment to enlist an apprentice,
could a master demand the apprentice back, and was the enlistee in violation of any military law and therefore subject to court-martial? Privy
Council member Philip Tisdall reviewed the applicable laws and ruled
that the enlistment was legal, the apprentice had broken no law, and the
master had no claim. The regiment could, as a favor, release the man back
to his apprenticeship if someone—anyone—repaid the enlistment bounty
and any other money the regiment had spent.[56] No records survive to
suggest how many apprentices left their contracts to join the army. There
were large numbers of tradesmen in the ranks, anywhere from half to
three-quarters of soldiers giving something other than "labourer" as their
trade. Most men enlisted between ages twenty and twenty-five, however,
suggesting that most had completed apprenticeships and worked for a
while before enlisting.

From all over the British Isles and from other British possessions, men
joined the army perhaps for adventure, perhaps for stability, often simply
for "a wish to become a soldier." They enlisted into regiments, first joining
recruiting parties, then companies of their corps, starting their military
education from the moment they joined and continuing for years and
decades. For many encamped on Boston Common and garrisoning posts
in Canada and the Caribbean in 1774 and 1775, their time in America
was just a portion, sometimes a small portion, of a long military career.

CHAPTER 3

Closeness and Smartness in Everything He Does

TRAINING AND DUTIES

W<small>HEN THE</small> 43<small>RD</small> R<small>EGIMENT OF</small> F<small>OOT</small> sailed from England in early 1774, Robert Andrews stayed behind. The forty-seven-year-old had been a private soldier for more than half his life, twenty-seven years. He was done. No longer fit for miles of marching and sleeping in damp encampments, he was, in the language used on his discharge, "worn out."[1] A career like this was not unusual; in general, soldiers who enlisted during times of peace did not enlist for any fixed duration, but joined the army as a career, to serve until their health no longer allowed it. As will be seen, wartime enlistees could be discharged after a term of service, but they often reenlisted and continued until no longer fit for service. Unless cut short by illness, injury, or death, marching to infirmity as a private soldier was the most common career that the army offered.

The infantry offered only four nonofficer ranks: private, drummer (or fifer), corporal, and sergeant. Within those ranks there were no pay grades, specialties, or other subclassifications; a private was that and nothing more, no matter how long he served. The frequency of men reenlisting after being discharged, and returning when given opportunities to abscond, shows that soldiering was a reasonably attractive career compared to the era's other options. Advancement was unlikely; 20 to 25 percent became corporals or sergeants, and not all retained those ranks for the remainder of their careers. Twenty, thirty, or even forty years at the same rank and base pay seems like a lot to endure, but other avocations offered similar prospects, some without the stability that the army offered. And there was more to military compensation than just base pay.

"From the eight pence per day which is issued for the pay of a soldier, when all deductions are made," read a pamphlet published in London in 1775, "there is not sufficient overplus for healthful subsistence; and as to the little enjoyments and recreations . . . the brave, the honorable, the veteran soldier, must not aspire to."[2] This was not wholly untrue, but also falls far short of describing the earning potential of a private soldier in the 1770s and 1780s. The base pay—the amount guaranteed to a private in an infantry regiment—was indeed eight pence per day or one pound sterling in a thirty-day month. Privates in the Foot Guards, cavalry, and artillery earned a little more. Deductions from pay covered the cost of the soldier's clothing, food, and other expected expenses. When troops were posted in Ireland, their pay was reduced by a penny (one pence) a day, because food was cheaper there.[3] But no matter the location, with variable food prices there could be little or no money left over for discretionary spending. This scant pay, however, was in a nonconsumer society where the material possessions of any laboring-class individual were few. A worker at any trade had clothing and food as expenses, and perhaps lodging as well; the difference for the soldier was that clothing and food were paid for through deductions rather than directly. The soldier was not required to pay for lodging. Moreover, the common British soldier could earn additional money throughout his career, often by doing work that the army required.

An example can be found in the Scottish highlands in summer 1772. A detachment from the 22nd Regiment of Foot, probably about thirty men, was tasked with repairing a seventy-five-mile roadway from Campbeltown, adjacent to the regiment's quarters at Fort George, to Braemar on the river Dee. Led by a sergeant, they had three months to remove loose stones, unclog drains and build new ones where needed, fill erosion around bridge piers, repair surfaces, and generally see to the road's overall condition. For this work each man received sixpence per day over and above his base pay.[4] They were to spend no more than ninety-two days on the job. Assuming that the base pay of eight pence per day was covering each man's basic expenses as designed, these men employed at military work earned over two pounds in spending money, an ample sum for "little enjoyments and recreations."

Opportunities for extra work like this existed everywhere that the army maintained garrisons. There were fortifications and barracks to maintain, firewood to be cut, supplies and stores of all sorts to transport. "A working party consisting of a Corporal and ten men, to parade without arms every morning at 6; they will be employed in arranging the wood yard, and will be paid for that labour agreeable to the Established regulation," read general orders for the garrison in Boston on August 18, 1774.[5] Working parties, including not just laborers but also soldiers who had, prior to joining the army, been trained as sawyers, masons, carpenters, smiths, and other trades, had been employed for some months in maintaining Boston's fortifications and constructing new ones, for which "the troops will be paid according to the rates" specified in standing orders.[6] In October, "If two or three men can be found capable of driving teams they are to attend Mr. Goldthwait to morrow morning; and will be paid for the work they do."[7] Fitting up winter barracks for the garrison required soldier labor: "When the work is finished, the gratification promised to encourage the men to carry on the work with spirit, will be paid to each Regiment in proportion to the work done."[8] After the fort at Crown Point on Lake Champlain burned in 1773, privates employed in cutting through the collapsed gate were paid the standard rate of sixpence (half a shilling) per day, corporals seven and a half pence, and sergeants one shilling. The work took sixteen days, earning each soldier an extra eight shillings.[9]

What is lacking, unfortunately, is any record of the earnings of individual soldiers over the course of a typical year for labor. The pay rate was sixpence per day, and in some cases the sizes of work parties are known, but not the individuals in the party, nor how often an individual was a member of a work party. When the 22nd Regiment was maintaining roads in Scotland in 1773, a total of 116 privates were recorded on the muster rolls as being "on party," but the semiannual rolls do not say which parties, what they were doing, or how long they lasted.[10]

The officer charged with repairing Castle William, the island installation in Boston Harbor that quartered the 14th Regiment of Foot in September 1770, showcased the diversity of military work when he complained that he could get only forty men for working parties; the remainder were either on guard, sick, or "supplying the Garrison with Fuel, Straw & Provisions, from the Barrack master & Contractors, together with servants, cooks, Bargemen, Boatmen and on furlough, sentinels, regimental fatigues, Taylors, &c. &c."[11] He did not give the numbers employed in each of these roles but did mention about seventy-five men sick. With a total strength of about three hundred private soldiers, of whom about a third who were not sick might be posted as guards and sentinels on any given day, having only forty available for working parties suggests over one hundred employed in the several other rolls, all earning money over and above base pay—and the men on guard one day might be employed at other work on other days.

Between 3 and 5 percent of the men in a regiment had learned the trade of tailoring before enlisting, providing plenty to continue that work in the army.[12] At least one man in each of an infantry regiment's ten companies was needed to fit regimental coats received annually from contractors, to make or fit new regimental waistcoats and breeches each year, to make supplemental clothing when needed, and to keep all of these garments in repair, "As the custom of the Army has established it part of the Duty of a Soldier, who is a Taylor, to work for his brother-soldiers."[13] No record has been found of a single tailor's earnings, but recommended rates for the routine work of making and fitting annually issued regimental clothing suggests annual peacetime earnings of between thirteen and fourteen pounds. Other clothing was needed besides the annual regimentals, and regimental tailors also did work for officers,[14] suggesting that tailors earned two to three times their base pay each year. Although they were expected to be soldiers first and tailors second, the demand for clothing meant that these skilled tradesmen were often excused from routine duties.[15]

Shoemakers were in the ranks in similar numbers to tailors, with one employed at this work in each company, but it is not clear that they spent as much time off duty for work as tailors did.[16] In a detachment of the 18th Regiment, for example, they were ordered to make shoes for the company only "when off duty."[17] No records of shoemakers' earnings have been found. Harness makers and shoemakers mended leather accoutrements, and gunsmiths maintained firearms, but probably only one or two of each were employed as such within a regiment.[18]

Soldiers employed as officers' servants earned a shilling each week, if paid according to recommendations in popular military texts of the era.[19] Some earned more, like John Irish of the 18th Regiment who was paid fifteen pence (one shilling three pence) per week by the captain he served in 1774.[20] At full strength, an infantry regiment in 1774 had three officers in each of its ten companies. The commanding officer of each company was entitled to employ two private soldiers as servants, while the two junior officers could each employ one, resulting in forty soldiers working as servants, each earning at least a third more than his base pay.

For a soldier not employed in his regiment as a servant, tailor, or tradesman and not needed for labor on roads, fortifications, and other projects, there was work outside of the army when time permitted. There are even fewer records of this than there are of military work, making it impossible to know how many soldiers found such employment, or how frequently. It was common enough, however, that one popular military writer devoted an entire chapter to the subject, giving commonsense recommendations: work should not interfere with duty, work should not be done in regimental clothing, no soldier should "engage in works of drudgery, such as carrying coals, removing dirt, or any other thing, which may reflect dishonour on the Regiment, or lessen that character which every Soldier of spirit should endeavour by his conduct to establish in the opinion of the public," and so forth. The writer recommended that company officers receive the pay for outside work and maintain each soldiers' account, paying out only what was due after the individual's expenses were met; not only did this cover the cost of extra wear on the soldier's shirts, shoes, and stockings, it helped keep men out of the temptations that might ensue from having too much cash.[21] It wasn't always predictable which men to trust with their money. William King, a soldier of the 14th Regiment at Dover Castle in England, was hired for the harvest in 1773 and, according to his employer, "behaved Soberly, honestly, and in every respect to his Satisfaction." Not long after, however, he "went down to the pier to see if he could get any laboring work," went into a house, bought beer, and got drunk, starting a chain of events that led to him being tried for desertion.[22]

On occasion, a soldier's pay was supplemented by a reward for some special action or service. William Burke of the 45th Regiment was sent with a party from Limerick, Ireland, into the Irish-speaking west country to apprehend a deserter; they succeeded, and the commanding officer "thanked us for our faithfulness, and when he understood from all the party that young Burke was the sole means of taking the prisoner, he told me he would not forget me, and then put his hand into his pocket, and gave me a guinea," a reward equivalent to just over a month's pay.[23] In Boston in August 1774, Robert Begant of the 43rd Regiment was cited in general orders after he "gave a very proper and laudable instance of Fidelity and attention to his duty, in apprehending a soldier of another Corps who last night was attempting to desert in disguise." The commander of Begant's brigade thanked him publicly "for his manly and good behavior" and promised to "take care that he is properly rewarded."[24]

In the 1760s, the 5th Regiment of Foot instituted a medal of merit, a brass medallion awarded to men who had served seven years without being brought before a regimental court-martial. The medal, hung from a ribbon, was worn on the left lapel; one side bore an image of St. George and the dragon with the regiment's motto, *Quo fata vocant!* (wither fates call, or wherever destiny takes me); the other side was inscribed "Vth Foot. Merit." A similar medal, in silver, was awarded to those with fourteen years of meritorious service, and another silver variant for twenty-one years. Awarded in a ceremony at the head of the regiment, the medal could be revoked in a ceremonious manner if the soldier misbehaved.[25] "It is not to be express'd the good effect which this Reward has upon the Men," wrote an officer from Ireland in 1769, "the Anxiety they shew when Competitors to be admitted is wonderful & so careful are these medal Men of keeping their little Corps unsullied, that the other Day on a Man's being promised one, who had serv'd 7 years without being punish'd, they found out somehow that he had been try'd by a Court Martial 6 years ago (which the Officers had forgot) tho' not punish'd. Upon which they came in a body to beg he might not be admitted, as they must look upon him as a Stain to their Order."[26] The 37th Regiment adopted a similar medal in the early 1770s, and other regiments began to follow suit in the 1780s.[27] This type of award, although not monetary, had considerable prestige value during and after a soldier's career.

Military writers recommended that a recruit not be allowed to work outside of the army "until he is at least a year in the Regiment, and is thoroughly acquainted with every part of his duty as a Soldier."[28] There is no way to verify the extent to which this suggestion was followed, nor whether recruits were restricted from doing military work; when men of the 22nd Regiment were working on roads in Scotland in 1772, none of those "on party" had been in the regiment for less than a year, suggesting that recruits focused on training before having opportunities to earn extra money.[29] Recruits had to learn about their finances, and their rights. Roger Lamb, who joined the 9th Regiment in Ireland in 1773, wrote of his hardships as a new soldier:

> The non commissioned officer who had us in charge received our pay every Saturday, and squandered the better part of it in paying the expences of his weekly score at the public house, by which means, we had to subsist upon a very scanty allowance, although at that time,

provisions were very cheap in Waterford. We often complained in private among ourselves, but whenever we remonstrated with him he menaced us with confinement in the guard-house, and such was our inexperience, and apprehension of being punished by his interference against us, that we submitted in silence. If we had boldly stated our grievances to the officer commanding, we most certainly had been redressed. No doubt such an effect would have resulted from our complaints properly made.[30]

In time, Lamb's sergeant relented and withheld less, fearing the consequences of his behavior being discovered. Lamb, meanwhile, found another source of revenue: being well educated, he "was employed by a serjeant and his wife to teach their son writing and arithmetic," for which they paid him in money and food. He earned still more because he "had also plenty of writing to do for the various serjeants and corporals, in making out their reports, &c."[31]

Lamb's skill at reading and writing was not unusual, but the prevalence of literacy among British soldiers is difficult to quantify. Far too few soldiers left writings to form a statistical sample. There are nonetheless some clues to the proportion of literate soldiers. Military writer Bennett Cuthbertson pointed out that a sergeant or corporal could not "be called thoroughly qualified, who does not read and write in a tolerable manner."[32] Between 20 and 25 percent of soldiers spent some part of their careers as sergeants or corporals, suggesting that at least that portion could read and write. Among the trades listed on soldiers' discharges are a smattering that certainly required literacy—writing clerk, scrivener, printer, writer, schoolmaster, and so forth—but there are also men known to have been well educated, like Alexander Andrew of the 44th and Roger Lamb of the 9th, who are listed as "labourer" because they had not pursued a trade.[33]

Cuthbertson wrote, "From the common people (the English in particular) employing their children very early, in works of labour, their education becomes totally neglected, and as the Soldiery is in general from that class, many of them . . . can neither read nor write."[34] And yet over half of soldiers who received pensions signed their discharge forms.[35] It may be that Cuthbertson overstated his case, but the army also provided opportunities for illiterate men to improve themselves. Thomas Watson, who enlisted in the 23rd Regiment at age twenty after working in coal mines since he was seven wrote, "I found that I had bettered myself in regard to bad company" and "my education, while young, at the coal

mines, was far worse than in the army." He learned to read and write during the five years between enlistment in 1773 and desertion in 1778.[36]
Some regiments facilitated their men's education by following Cuthbertson's advice that "it would be of infinite improvement, if . . . every Regiment was to establish a school, under the management of an old Soldier
qualified for such an undertaking." His thoughts were echoed by another
military writer: "A Serjeant, or Corporal, whose sobriety, honesty, and
good conduct, can be depended upon, and who is capable to teach writing, reading, and arithmetic, should be employed to act in the capacity
of school-master."[37] Standing orders for the 37th Regiment, presumably
written before 1774, directed "The Regimental School now Established
to be kept up in all Quarters and duly attended," overseen by a sergeant
who was to prepare bimonthly returns of the soldiers who attended, their
studies "whether to Read or write &c. and the progress they make." Those
who were "bad behaved, Remiss or Irregular" would be reported, while,
"If they are any way remarkably well behaved," the commanding officer
would "Notice them."[38] The 32nd Regiment was directed to instruct
"younger Men in Writing & Arithmatick 2 Hours in the Forenoon &
2 in the Afternoon" in Ireland in 1776; the regiment provided paper. A
school for army children was established in Halifax, Nova Scotia, in 1776
with directions to include catechism in the course of study, and in the
71st Regiment in America, the chaplain was ordered to "pay a charitable
regard to the School of the Battalion."[39] As with basic literacy, there is
insufficient information to know the prevalence of regimental schools or
access to other means of education in the army as a whole.

Before being concerned with earning extra money or improving his education, the soldier required training. Sometimes there was a standing
order that no recruit be taken as a servant, excused from duty, or employed except as a soldier until he had served for a year.[40] Training began
upon enlistment with instruction in basics of hygiene and care for clothing, fundamentals critical to a soldier's health that might not have been
part of his upbringing. Regular combing of hair, washing of shirts, attention to the condition of shoes and stockings and other aspects of cleanliness were discussed by military writers and mentioned in orderly books.
The recruit received a knapsack, several shirts, pairs of stockings, and a
pair of shoes, all paid for by deductions from his enlistment bounty
money and pay, providing an incentive to keep track of them and make
them last as long as possible.[41] These clothing items, which wore out fre-

quently, were called "necessaries" or "necessary items" and were provided, as the name implies, as often as necessary,[42] always at the soldiers' expense. The accounts were managed initially by the recruiting officer and then handed off to a company officer when the recruit joined the regiment. In any other profession, the man would be paid and then have to purchase his own clothing, so the army was not taking unfair advantage but instead managing the recruit's budget and ensuring that money was spent on what was most important to the man's fitness. In addition to the basics of cleanliness, the enlistee may have started some of his martial training with the recruiting party; it certainly began in earnest when he joined the regiment.

"I joined the regiment, and was put into the hands of a drill serjeant, and taught to walk and step out like a soldier. This at first was a disagreeable task to me. During twenty one days I was thus drilled four hours each day."[43] Such was the experience of Roger Lamb and, as far as we know, peacetime recruits in general. Men like Lamb, whose middle-class Dublin education had even included swordsmanship, were brought together with men like Thomas Watson, who had worked in coal mines and other toilsome jobs since age seven. Training within recruiting parties and regiments may have varied considerably from regiment to regiment, governed by the corporate knowledge of the officer corps rather than any central authority. A number of commercially published books were widely used to impart some uniformity to the process. Author Bennett Cuthbertson provided the most detailed discussion of recruits' military education:

> The first thing to be done in training of young Soldiers, is to give them a free and easy carriage; to set them well upon their limbs, and totally expel the clown from their Gait and air: it must be rendered familiar to every man to hold up his head; to stand quite upright and motionless; to cast his eyes to the right, without the least appearance of a formal stiffness, and to turn out his Toes, to march firm upon his Feet, keeping his Knees stiff, turning out and pointing his Toes at the same time, to keep his body straight without leaning backwards, or pushing out his belly; to bring forward his chest; and to draw his shoulders back: to face to the right and left, and quite about, both standing and marching; to wheel in a proper manner, and to march in slow and quick time: in all of which, Recruits should be perfectly instructed and well trained, before they are allowed to touch a Firelock.[44]

In short, learn to stand and march before learning to handle a weapon. Standing orders for the 37th Regiment echoed Cuthbertson's recommendation, directing that "Obedience, Attention and Steadiness are the main Articles in which he must be most thoroughly grounded, and having first learned his position to Walk &c he may then be put under Arms."[45] In the 9th Regiment, Lamb, after twenty-one days, "having at last rectified the most prominent appearance of my awkwardness . . . received a set of accoutrements, and a firelock, and was marched every morning from the barrack to the bowling green, near the water side, to be instructed in the manual exercise."[46]

Equipped with a firelock (musket), a waist belt holding a small cartridge box and "frog" for a bayonet and scabbard, and a larger cartridge pouch slung over the left shoulder, the infantry soldier learned a carefully prescribed sequence of movements and positions for handling the firelock. This manual exercise, or manual of arms, had been published and distributed throughout the army in 1764 and contained the firelock positions and marching movements every soldier was expected to master.[47] Regiments may have had their own variations of detail, and additional movements were widely practiced in the army.[48] The commanding officer of the 37th Regiment directed:

> Great Attention is to be given to make him stand properly shouldered and to carry the firelock in that position perfectly easy and well, moving & Marching, and till this is attained, the Non Commissioned Officer must not go on with him. A thorough Exactness must be taught and required from him in the doing of every motion. He must be taught a closeness & smartness in every thing he does. The placing of a thumb or finger must not be neglected. He must not be hurried on too fast, but be perfectly grounded in one Movement or Motion, ere he is shewn another.[49]

The movements associated with loading and firing were accomplished by replacing the flint that provided the flintlock musket's ignition spark with a similarly shaped piece of wood called a driver, allowing the trigger to be pulled without spark or damage.[50] Cavalry and artillery recruits followed other training regimens specific to their branches of service.

The pace of training was managed with care. "As it is at the drill, that every soldier receives the first impressions of his duty & the Service, & first Impressions are generally the strongest and are those which are most apt to give a Cast to the whole Character of the Man, the utmost care, caution, Assiduity, temper and perseverance are expected from those who at any time may be appointed to Conduct it," stated the standing orders of the 37th Regiment. "Men even of lively & willing dispositions, are in their first attempts to learn any profession or art, however simple in its nature, frequently so Aukward & untoward as often to appear stupid and perverse."[51] Wrote Cuthbertson, "The Serjeants and Corporals, who are appointed to instruct Recruits, must not use too much severity with them, lest they should become disgusted with the Service: it requires a great share of temper and coolness to lead them on, and break them of their aukward clownish ways."[52] Noncommissioned officers in the 35th Regiment were expected "to treat the soldiers with mildness and good humour, when they behave well. . . . If any non-commissioned officer is known to use bad language to the soldiers, or to treat them unbecoming that character, he will be reduced for the same."[53] In spite of these admonitions, "some of the old drill serjeants were unnecessarily, if not wantonly severe," according to Roger Lamb.[54] Too few firsthand accounts survive to judge whether "wantonly severe" treatment was unusual or commonplace.

Only when the recruit was, in Cuthbertson's words, "master of all the motions in the Manual and Platoon-Exercise," including all aspects of handling the firelock and moving in formation with his fellow soldiers, was he taught the use of live ammunition. A musket cartridge consisted of a paper tube with a spherical lead bullet (a ball) and a measured amount of black powder (gunpowder). These were made by the regiments themselves, and blanks simply omitted the ball. Replacing the wooden driver with a gun flint rendered the firelock effective so that the recruit could be "trained to the use of Powder, to which most of them have at first that aversion, which may reasonably be expected in ignorant unexperienced peasants, whose heads are filled with the dreadful apprehensions of its effects, from the stories told them out of fun, by the old Soldiers."[55] They learned to fire with ball, although peacetime economy allowed firing with ball only a few times each year.[56] Throughout this martial training, "his attention must be frequently tried, in an unexpected manner, which will by degrees be sure to fix it in him, and this is a point of the greatest Consequence in a Soldier. Without it you can do nothing with him, with it, everything."[57]

Infantry regiments had ten companies in the 1770s, each with a maximum peacetime strength of thirty-six private soldiers. Two companies were composed only of selected, experienced soldiers, leaving the remaining eight companies, called the battalion, to receive new recruits. A given regiment in Britain might have anywhere from two dozen to one hundred recruits—men with less than a year in the regiment—at any given time, but about fifty was typical.[58] Most regiments distributed these men equally among the eight battalion companies, meaning six or seven in each company of thirty to thirty-six; between 15 and 25 percent of each battalion company might be recently enlisted soldiers. These numbers and proportions would change when war began, as will be seen.

Within the company, each soldier belonged to two other organizations, a mess and a squad of inspection. The mess was primarily for ensuring that each soldier had "a regular and well-chosen diet."[59] Rather than each man procuring his own food, groups of five to ten men drew provisions, cooked, and ate together.[60] On campaign, messes consisted of five men who shared a tent and a tin-plated kettle similar in shape to a pail.[61] They procured fresh food locally; every few days, a man from each mess went to the market—in a group, under supervision of an officer or noncommissioned officer—to "buy a proper quantity of good and wholesome meat (either beef, mutton, or pork) and also of vegetables, salt and oatmeal, to serve each mess, until the next day for receiving pay; and, if not in the Field, they ought to buy a sufficiency of bread too, at the same time."[62] On foreign service, difficulties in procuring local foodstuffs necessitated the use of packed, preserved provisions shipped from Great Britain. Salt being the principle preservative, a distinction was made between fresh provisions and salt provisions. In Boston in 1774, orders directed that "A Ration of fresh meat consists of one pound of Beef and one pound of flour per day; and salt meat, four pounds of Pork, three pints of pease, six ounces of Butter, half a pint of Rice, and seven pounds of flour or bread per week."[63] By necessity the soldier's diet varied with seasons, locations, and myriad situational constraints.

Squads of inspection, each under the authority of a noncommissioned officer, were unrelated to messes and facilitated order and discipline within each company. The noncommissioned officer was responsible for the clothing, equipment, and behavior of a portion of the men. Some writers recommended that each noncommissioned officer, five in a peacetime company, oversee an equal portion of the company's thirty-six privates, resulting in squads of seven or eight men when at full strength; another suggested a squad for each rank (row of men) when the company was in formation, resulting in three squads of twelve.[64] In spite of a recommendation that within squads "an equal proportion must be given to each of sober, good men, and those of a contrary turn," a surviving squad roll shows the men divided alphabetically into three squads, with no other apparent consideration.[65] The noncommissioned officer saw that his squad's clothing was clean and properly worn; leather and brass were polished; hair was clean, combed, and cut according to the regiment's style; weapons and accoutrements were in good working order; and all manner of military minutia was attended to.[66] It was from the noncommissioned officers of squads that men learned "the respect and obedience they are to pay to their superiors."[67]

Officers of the 37th Regiment were instructed to "find out and distinguish the men who have the best capacities, and are most diligent and obedient; that the regiment may be supplied with able non-commissioned officers."[68] Each infantry company had three corporals and two sergeants to manage thirty-six privates. Becoming a corporal meant a pay increase of 50 percent, from eight pence to one shilling per day in the infantry,[69] and considerable additional responsibility. There was no prescribed timeline for advancement; it was rare for peacetime enlistees to be appointed to corporal with less than five years in the army, with eight to twelve years being common and in some instances fifteen years or more.[70] The 37th Regiment of Foot maintained a standing order that when a private soldier was appointed to a noncommissioned rank, he was placed in a different company—presumably to prevent too much familiarity with the men over whom he now had authority—but muster rolls show that not all regiments followed this practice.[71]

In addition to the likelihood of overseeing a squad of inspection, corporals marched soldiers to and from sentry posts, directing the procedure of relieving each sentry at the appointed time. There was more to this than mere ritual; it was the corporal's responsibility to "instill into their heads and hearts, that the security of the post depends upon their courage and diligence."[72] Recruiting, carrying messages, and leading small parties on special duties were all common responsibilities for corporals. In 1769, a party sent out from New York to seek deserters was led by a corporal of the 16th Regiment; "they proceeded to New Rochelle, where the Corporal procured them colour'd cloaths and divided the party in two different roads, with orders to meet at the Kings Arms on the White Plains," showing the level of trust placed in these junior noncommissioned officers, and their initiative.[73]

Not all men were up to setting a constant example and performing duties of higher responsibility. Corporals deficient in their duties could be reduced to private soldiers and replaced by other likely men. This turnover meant that the odds of being appointed corporal were somewhat higher than the proportion of three per company would suggest, but nonetheless the possibility of rising above the rank of private soldier remained less than 25 percent. "Eye servants will be tried for neglect of duty," warned standing orders for the 35th Regiment about men who attended to their duty only when being watched,[74] and court-martial records of four regiments in Ireland between 1774 and 1777 bear this out. With around two hundred corporals altogether in these regiments during this period, there were seventy-six reductions. Charges included generalities such as "neglect of duty" and "disobedience of orders" but were usually more specific. Aspects of personal misconduct such as "being drunk on duty"; being "absent" from parade, roll call, barracks or quarters (often with "being drunk" as an additional charge); and many variations of drunken behavior, such as "being Drunk and Making a Noise in his Barrack Room" and "being Drunk and Dirty in the Streets," were frequent, with occasional more-calculated crimes such as theft from townspeople and soldiers, "Selling his Necessarys," "embezzleing part of the Recruits Necessarys when on the March," embezzling pay or provisions, and "abusing an Inhabitant." Other charges referred to the corporal's duties and responsibilities: "Suspicion of taking off a Centry without Leave," "suffering a Recruit to Desert and not striving to hinder him," making false reports or false charges," "suffering two men to go out of the Barracks at an unseasonable hour," "Encourageing the Men to Quarrell," "encouraging two Soldiers to be Riotous," "allowing a Deserter to escape from the Guard House," "suffering prisoners to Gamble," and so forth. In these four regiments over a four-year period, corporals were brought to trial 93 times (some individuals were tried more than once), compared to 824 trials of private soldiers. This proportion of about one in ten trials being of a corporal, compared to there being one corporal for every twelve privates, reveals the higher disciplinary standard that these "most diligent and obedient" men were expected to maintain. In eleven trials the corporals were acquitted, but for those found guilty, reduction was the sentence in all but three cases where the man was suspended (temporarily relieved of duty) instead. Three men sentenced to reduction had their sentences mitigated.[75]

No regimental court records exist for most regiments. Muster rolls do not give reasons for reduction but do show that reductions were as frequent as in the four regiments discussed above, so we can assume that most were disciplinary actions. There were, however, other reasons for reduction. In particular, infirmity from long service or injury could render a man unable to do a corporal's duty, resulting in temporary or permanent reduction. This appears to have been the case for Samuel Graves of the

22nd Regiment, who was reduced in November 1776 after several years as a corporal and died the following April, presumably from extended ill-ness.[76] Some men asked to be reduced, including a corporal of the 4th Regiment of Foot who was confined because he "ill treated an Inhabitant" in Boston in November 1774; feeling that he was the one being ill treated, the corporal "begged leave to resign his Knott, as in the character of a private Soldier he shou'd be less exposed to Complaints."[77] Bryan Kelly of the 63rd Regiment spent a mere four days as a corporal before being replaced in accordance with his "wishes to return to his former Duty."[78]

In most cases, however, we know only the dates of appointment and reduction, with no information about the reasoning behind them. In the 22nd Regiment, Joseph Harrison was appointed corporal eighteen years after he enlisted at age nineteen; he was reduced five years later, appointed again two years after that, reduced two years later, then discharged as a private soldier after twenty-nine years of service, including seven as a cor-poral.[79] In the same regiment, James Grant was appointed only two years after his enlistment at age twenty-four, reduced after three years, ap-pointed again within a year and a half, then reduced only six months later; he served five more years as a private soldier.[80]

Corporals who did well were eventually appointed to sergeant, but with only two sergeants in a peacetime infantry company, only two-thirds of the corporals stood a chance of advancement when a sergeant's vacancy opened. The advance might come within just a year or two, or after a decade or more as a corporal, even after one or two reductions and reap-pointments.[81] The base pay of an infantry sergeant was sixpence more per day than a corporal, one shilling sixpence.[82] Reading, writing, and ac-counting were essential skills for sergeants, and they were expected to be "careful, sober, honest and exact in all dealings; diligent, active and res-olute upon all duties," expert at handling arms and perfect in all aspects of dress and discipline.[83] Each sergeant oversaw a squad of inspection and had additional responsibilities. One sergeant in each company acted as paymaster or "pay sergeant,"[84] managing each soldier's accounts and distributing money when required, always answerable to the company commanding officer for proper management of funds. One sergeant was the company's orderly sergeant, tasked with preparing morning reports and other periodic returns; he also received and recorded the day's orders from headquarters, then disseminated them appropriately. It is not clear whether the role of orderly sergeant was taken by a different sergeant each day or held by one man for an extended period; if the former, then the paymaster sergeant also was sometimes an orderly sergeant. Sergeants led guard detachments, recruiting parties, work details, and innumerable other small commands. When men were missing from roll call, it was usually a sergeant who went to the man's tent or quarters to see whether his belongings were still present and testified under oath if the offending soldier was tried for desertion.[85]

As managers of their men's day-to-day finances, it was sergeants who saw to the purchase or procurement of provisions. Honest sergeants spoke out on behalf of their men, as did four sergeants of the 60th Regiment on the island of Antigua. They petitioned that "what we have been able to buy for our support from time to time was not fit for men to eat. . . . Provisions of the very worst kind bore such exorbitant prices that our pay was not sufficient to purchase enough to support nature." They pleaded that "our pay is little enough to furnish us with bread, so that we must bid adieu to meat of any kind, besides as every kind of provisions gets scarcer and dearer daily it seems as if we should be left here to starve."[86] Sergeants who took the opposite tack and defrauded their men faced court-martial and reduction on charges such as "embezzling part of the Mess Money belonging to the Men of the Mess under his Command," "Embezzling the Company's Money," and "Embezzling his partys money."[87] As Roger Lamb noted when he was defrauded by his sergeant, soldiers could go to their officers if their sergeant was cheating them, if they were confident enough to do so.[88] Sergeants also policed each other, as when Sergeant Thomas Lang of the 37th Regiment charged his fellow sergeant, James Banbury, of "having Defrauded the men of part of their provisions." In this case, a court of inquiry found the accusation to be "both frivolous and groundless and that Serjt Lang should make a Publick submition to Serjt Banbury."[89]

The same four regiments that tried ninety-three corporals over a four-year period also tried thirty-six sergeants, showing that sergeants were brought to trial much less frequently than corporals, especially considering that these regiments were on a wartime establishment of three sergeants per company for eighteen months of that four-year period. Charges included generalities like "neglect of duty" and "Repeated Irregularity," drunkenness in combination with other infractions, absence from one thing or another, "selling his old Coat without leave," "parading for Guard with dirty Arms," "Sconcing an Inhabitant" of a sum of money (that is, leaving without paying his bill), and "Rioting in the street."[90] There were failures "to be strictly careful and honest in all money matters"[91] including "allowing the Soldiers to contract a Debt with him," "drawing money on Account of the Regiment, and not accounting for it," receiving money that he knew a recruit "did not come Justly by," "Embezleing the Subsistence" of an officer's recruiting party and saying the officer "was indebted to him half a Guinea for every Recruit the Party Inlisted," and "contracting debts, drawing Bills on the Regiment when Recruiting." "Being Frequently in Liquor and encouraging the Recruits to follow his Example," and other types of "misbehaviour" were also charged.[92] Sergeants were acquitted at a similar rate as corporals, with four acquittals in thirty-six trials. But sergeants were much more likely than corporals to be suspended (nine out of thirty-two, compared to three out of eighty-two convicted corporals) rather than reduced (twenty-three out of thirty-two, compared to seventy-six out of eighty-two convicted corporals), with suspensions lasting one to three months.[93] Sergeants also were reduced when no longer fit for the role. Thomas Miller of the 22nd Regiment, for example, who had enlisted at age twenty-eight in 1766, spent sixteen months as a sergeant before being reduced in April 1777; a year later he was discharged and sent home "quite emaciated" and afflicted with rheumatism.[94]

Among the twenty sergeants in a peacetime regiment was one who served as quartermaster sergeant and one who served as sergeant major. Although their base pay was the same as for all sergeants, their duties brought additional compensation. The quartermaster sergeant was an assistant to one of the regiment's officers, the quartermaster; together, these two men were responsible for ensuring that the regiment had everything required for habitation, whether it was finding ground and laying out an encampment, ensuring that barracks were properly outfitted, or securing quarters from innkeepers and local residents in Britain (in America, the Quartering Act restricted troops to vacant buildings, outbuildings, or public buildings in places that had no barracks).[95] Besides finding suitable accommodations, the quartermaster procured fuel (firewood or coal), bedding (hay or straw), candles, and other consumables, and procured or maintained barrack furniture such as fire irons, blankets, kettles, and cooking implements. If barracks or quarters were deficient in any way, the quartermaster saw to correction of the problems and conducted regular inspections to ensure they were being maintained by the soldiers. Besides marking where tents were pitched for encampments, the quartermaster oversaw the clearing of brush, trees, and other obstructions; located and directed the digging of kitchens (circular trenches with fire pits dug into the inside wall) and necessaries (latrines); and tended to any other material requirements. The quartermasters procured and managed wagons to carry the regiment's baggage on the march. They found a suitable location for the regimental hospital, usually some sort of building near the encampment or quarters, and saw that material needs of the hospital were met. In all of these activities, the quartermaster sergeant played an integral role, keeping "a just and exact entry of every thing," running the errands, conducting the inspections, directing the labor.[96]

The sergeant major assisted another officer, the adjutant, in every aspect of the regiment's administration. This single highest noncommissioned rank required "a man of real merit, a complete serjeant, and a good scholar." Collecting reports from company orderly sergeants, collating and tabulating that information, managing duty rosters, issuing passes and furloughs, preparing muster rolls, filling out discharge forms, and all manner of other paperwork required him to be "ready at your pen." He oversaw formations, being "skilled at telling off the regiment by files, platoons, sub or grand divisions, wings, columns, squares, or in any other form required," "present at all parades of the regiment, either for guard-mounting, piquets, detachments, and punishments, &c. to see that the number of men ordered from each company, for duty, are brought; that they are perfectly sober, clean, and uniformly dressed according to the order of the regiment; that their arms and accoutrements are in perfect order," and so forth.[97]

Since there were only two sergeants in each peacetime company, it is not clear who took over the ordinary company responsibilities of the sergeants serving as quartermaster sergeant and sergeant major. Court-martial records occasionally include men with the title of lance (or "launce") corporal or acting corporal, and lance sergeant or acting sergeant,[98] but it is not clear whether these men were filling in for sergeants who were absent, incapacitated, or acting in elevated roles; they may also have been temporary appointments in detachments where there were not enough noncommissioned officers available. A detachment of three companies of the 18th (Royal Irish) Regiment of Foot in Boston tried for a time to get by with one man as both sergeant major and quartermaster sergeant but found it was "too much for one Man at present to do." They restored the more conventional arrangement of one sergeant in each of these two important roles.[99]

James Anderson, a native of Oldmeldrum in Aberdeenshire, enlisted in 1770 at age seventeen, was appointed corporal after four years, sergeant four years later, and spent fourteen years at that rank, including nine years as quartermaster sergeant.[100] Hiram Murphy, from Fort Augustus on the banks of Loch Ness, also enlisted at seventeen but spent eleven years as a private before becoming a corporal; he spent four years as corporal, then nine years as sergeant in two regiments, including eighteen months as quartermaster sergeant.[101] For John Wilson of Kilpatrick, county Dunbarton, it took eight years as a private and five as a corporal before he spent sixteen years as sergeant, including two as sergeant major, again in two regiments.[102] Donald Forbes was twenty-eight when he joined the 22nd Regiment in 1772; he spent eight years as a private, five as corporal, and fourteen as sergeant before joining another regiment, where he spent two more years as sergeant and three as quartermaster sergeant.[103]

Here and there, muster rolls indicate that men rose extraordinarily quickly, becoming sergeants after very little service or even upon enlistment. The few cases where more information is available show that these were not ordinary recruits who happened to stand out; rather, they were men whose education and social background qualified them to be officers but who lacked the means and influence to obtain a commission. One such man was Scotsman Ranald McDonell, who joined the army in America as a gentleman "when very young" during the French and Indian War. It was typical of young men aspiring to be officers to join as volunteers in this way, but the conflict ended and his regiment was disbanded before McDonell obtained a commission. "He was left without the least inclination to follow any other than the Military profession," but "his finances were so low in a strange Country that he had no other resource than to enlist as a private man" in the 52nd Regiment of Foot, which had arrived in Quebec in 1767. His background and experience served him well, and he was soon appointed corporal and then sergeant, but this was as much as the peacetime regiment's officers could do for a man who might otherwise be an officer.[104] Some men recorded on muster rolls as private soldiers were "promoted" to commissioned officers within a year of enlistment, clearly indicating that they were in the ranks only as a way to learn their profession while awaiting a vacant commission.

In the early 1770s, each British infantry regiment had one drummer per company. The grenadier company also had two fifers, for a total of twelve drummers and fifers. This book will collectively call them "drummers"; there was a different group called musicians, discussed below. Drummers earned the same pay as corporals, although the standing orders of the 37th Regiment stipulated that they were to receive a private's pay until "perfectly taught."[105] Their instruments communicated signals that could

be heard throughout an encampment or garrison town. Every martial activity, from reveille in the morning to tattoo (or "taptoo") at night, had a
distinct drum signal: assembly, noncommissioned officers call, fatigue
parties, roll call, wood or water detachments, and others. There were
drum signals for marching and maneuvering: left and right face, march,
wheel, charge, halt, cease firing, and so on. It was also the drummers' duty
to administer lashes, the army's most common corporal punishment,
which will be discussed in greater detail below.

Playing the drum was a specialty requiring practice to be perfect, followed by discipline and punctuality to be in the right place at the right
time to convey signals that moved regiments. Many were like William
Pudner, who enlisted in the 22nd Regiment at twenty-two and drummed
for almost twenty years, [106] and Thomas Huggans, who left work as a
bricklayer to join the 44th Regiment as a drummer when he was seventeen and continued for twenty-five years.[107] Presumably they knew how
to play the instrument when they joined the army. Some who started as
drummers at a young age became private soldiers when they were older.
A popular military text recommended that "lads for drummers and fifers"
be put into the ranks when "the Commanding-officer shall think proper,"
but this transition did not entitle them to additional bounty money.[108]

John Hardman of the 22nd Regiment enlisted as a drummer at age
twelve in 1755, when William Hardman, probably his father, was a sergeant.[109] Showing the truth of one text's guidance that "from this little
nursery, if proper attention is shewn to their morals and education, there
is the greatest reason to hope, that some excellent non-commissioned officers may one day or other be produced,"[110] John Hardman eventually
became a sergeant and devoted an impressive fifty-one years to the army
before finally leaving the service in 1806.[111] A number of sergeants had
similar career paths, starting as drummers in their early teens and remaining in the service for decades. Others who began as children stayed
with the drum for their entire careers, like Flanders-born John Hogg,
who started drumming at fourteen in 1760 and continued for thirty-one
years in three regiments.[112] The ten drummers in a peacetime regiment
might range in age from twelve to somewhere in the forties or fifties; not
enough data survives to reveal any typical distribution, each regiment
having an assortment of drummers of various ages.

In the early 1760s, the 29th Regiment's drummers were men of
African descent brought into the regiment from the West Indies. Some,
like James Sharlow (or Charloe) and John Bacchus, served into the 1780s,
Sharlow being discharged at age sixty-one after drumming for twenty-

nine years, and Bacchus at fifty-four after twenty years.[113] As new drummers were needed, men like nineteen-year-old Thomas Smith, born in "Bengal, East Indies," enlisted; he stayed in the regiment for twelve years and in the army for over twenty.[114] When the regiment was in Boston from 1768 into 1770, these men caused some consternation when the populace saw them whipping white men at regimental punishments. "To behold Britons scourged by negro drummers was a new and very disagreeable spectacle," reported a newspaper,[115] while drummer Thomas Walker was assaulted and called a "black rascal" by Bostonians during an altercation just three days before the Boston Massacre in 1770.[116]

Although the regimental establishment allowed for only two fifers, nominally part of the grenadier company, anecdotal evidence suggests that boys still too young to handle a cumbersome drum instead played the fife; with no indication of them on muster rolls, there is no way to know how many were in any regiment. Standing orders for the 37th Regiment directed "every Drummer to be taught the fife, and every fifer the Drum,"[117] suggesting that the annotation of drummer or fifer on muster rolls may not always strictly define the man's role. The career paths of those annotated as fifers were similar to drummers. In the 22nd Regiment, Michael Clarke and William McLeod were fifers for the entire war in America; Clarke, a Londoner, enlisted at age twenty in 1766 and fifed for nineteen years,[118] while McLeod, born in Quebec when the regiment was posted there in 1760, was put on the muster rolls at ten and continued as a fifer for twenty-two years.[119]

One of the regiment's drummers was the drum major, responsible for the drummers' order and discipline in the same way a sergeant was responsible for a squad of inspection. Base pay was the same as for other drummers—except when posted in Ireland, where he earned an extra shilling per day[120]—but his role brought additional compensation. He instructed new drummers "in a cool and intelligent manner, adapted to the early age of those he is to teach,"[121] for which he was paid by deductions from the pay of the students.[122] He ensured that drums were properly maintained, and he appointed duty drummers punctually (in the 22nd Regiment, officers contributed to the purchase of a watch for the drum major).[123] He delivered the regiment's mail, a task for which the 37th Regiment had required payment to him of a halfpenny by each letter's recipient until that fee was abolished in an undated standing order.[124] Military texts also refer to a fife major; since neither of these roles is explicitly denoted on muster rolls, it is not clear whether every regiment had one of each, or if in some the same man filled both roles. In December 1774, a sergeant in the 18th Regiment of Foot was ordered to "act as Fife Major till further Orders," showing an example of a nonfifer filling the role and suggesting that this individual began his career with the fife.[125] The fife major's role was similar to that of the drum major, "instructing his pupils, with temper and coolness," maintaining instruments and music books; and keeping the regiment up to date by striving "to find out the most-admired tunes and pieces of music suited to the fife."[126] To maintain the proper authority over their charges, the drum and fife major were expected to "associate with the non-commission-officers" so they would "not to be looked on altogether in the light of a Drummer."[127]

Drums and fifes lent an air of pageantry to peacetime military activities, but their purpose was primarily pragmatic, providing cadence and communication. For entertainment, many regiments also maintained a band of music, six to ten men proficient with instruments such as the French horn, hautbois (oboe), and clarinet. With no provision for a band in the regimental structure, the musicians, distinct from drummers and fifers, were carried on the muster rolls as private soldiers. This makes them difficult to identify without other documents, and detailed information on musicians is available for only a few regiments. Six out of ten band members of the 22nd Regiment can be identified,[128] of whom five spent most of their careers as private soldiers while one was a drummer.[129] Two of them enlisted in their early twenties, two were shoemakers before joining the army, one was a "labourer," and James Harvey, a Devon native who enlisted at sixteen, spent twenty-five years in the army as a private, corporal, and drummer, then listed his trade as "musician" when he was discharged.[130]

Standing orders for the 37th Regiment called for teaching "the Musicians different Instruments that the full harmony of the band, may at all times be preserved,"[131] and a few descriptions of musicians who deserted speak to their versatility. John Humphries of the 17th Regiment played "well on the French horn and fife"; John Whitfield of the 19th played well "on many musical Instruments"; Matthew Carroll of the 71st played "on the bagpipe, fiddle, and fife"; Nathanael Lock of the 64th played "on the bassoon, hautboy and flute"; and William Simpson of the 29th played "well on the Flute and Fife, and . . . a little on the Violin and French Horn."[132] Some regiments hired professional musicians to lead their bands, such as the 17th Regiment of Foot's "Frederick Jordan, engaged as Musick Master, in the said Regiment, for the Space of three

Years, commencing in September, 1768. He is a Native of Hanover, speaks broken English, and bad French, limps in walking, from having had his Leg broken, about five Feet, nine Inches high, has a good Address, and plays remarkably well on the Clarinet."[133] The 28th Regiment's "Henry Piscadore, Musician, about twenty years of age, five feet ten inches high, fresh complexion, round visage, grey eyes, dark brown hair, born at Brussells and Parish of St. Singore, was inlisted by Lord Townshend as Master of a Band for said Regiment the 12th of July 1773. He went off in a scarlet frock, laced, with buttons the number of the Regiment, laced hat, white cloth breeches and waistcoat, speaks tolerable good English."[134] In July 1775, the drum major of the 37th Regiment was "appointed to take charge of the Band," and another drummer took over the duties of drum major.[135]

Presumably the band members were soldiers first and musicians second, devoting themselves to their instruments only when conditions allowed for such a luxury. There is little evidence that bands played when regiments marched; most mentions of their performances are in the context of public or private functions. A visitor to a Scottish town garrisoned by the 37th Regiment in 1773 enjoyed "a dinner of two complete courses, variety of wines, and the regimental band of music playing in the square before the windows after it."[136] The 1771 commencement of the College of Philadelphia included "the Band of Music belonging to the Twenty first Regiment (or Royal North British Fuzileers) playing during the whole Procession,"[137] and that band played a few months later at "a Concert of Music, Vocal and Instrumental" in Philadelphia that concluded "with an Overture, composed (for the Occasion) by Philip Roth, Master of the Band."[138] In 1773, the College of Philadelphia's commencement ceremonies included "the Band belonging to the 18th or Royal Irish Regiment, which the Commander of that Regiment, with his usual Politeness, was pleased to lend on that Occasion,"[139] and in Boston in April 1774, there was "a Grand Concert of Vocal and Instrumental Music assisted by the Band of the 64th Regiment."[140]

Ten soldiers, one in each company, were designated as pioneers and equipped with an axe and saw. The title had a rugged glamor, but the duty, usually under the direction of the quartermaster, was laborious and menial: clearing vegetation in and around encampments, digging and filling latrines and drainage ditches, burying the dead, shoveling snow, and similar tasks.[141] It was a role rather than a rank; muster rolls do not designate pioneers, nor do any other surviving documents correlate the role with individual men, leaving it unknown whether it was a rotating or long-term assignment.

Regardless of rank or role, soldiers were required to conform to military regulations. When William Ferguson, a private in the 10th Regiment, was brought to trial in Boston for desertion in 1774, the first witness, a sergeant in the regiment, deposed that "the Prisoner has heard the Articles of War read against Mutiny and Desertion."[142] The Articles of War governed discipline. Published regularly throughout Great Britain and the colonies, 111 articles grouped in twenty sections described the expectations of officers and soldiers, what constituted breaches of military law, penalties for offenses, precedence of officers, rights and entitlements.[143] The Articles of War laid out procedures for enlisting and mustering soldiers, granting furloughs and discharges, filing returns, redressing wrongs, procuring carriages and quarters, holding military courts, disposing of the effects of the dead, granting licenses to purveyors of provisions, and managing of captured stores. Not all articles applied to noncommissioned officers and private soldiers. Those that did, particularly those pertaining to desertion and mutiny (a term applied to any willful disobedience of orders), were read out loud to soldiers regularly.

Minor infractions like drunkenness, losing or selling clothing, theft from other soldiers, failure to attend roll call, dirtiness, disorderly conduct, and so forth were tried by a regimental court-martial, a board of several officers from within the regiment that heard depositions for the prosecution and defense, judged guilt, and set punishment. There was no need for records of these trials to be preserved outside of the regiment; as a result, few such records survive, making it difficult to reach specific conclusions about discipline issues within individual regiments and in the army as a whole. Regimental courts could set corporal punishment and nonbodily punishments such as pay stoppages (for theft, to repay the debt), fatigue duty, confinement to barracks or a windowless "black hole," and occasional exotic punishments like being ordered "To Wear a black Strap for a Week," or "His coat turn'd, chaind to a Bombshell for 2 Months & confined to the Barracks." By far the most common punishment was lashes, applied to the bare back with a cat-o'-nine-tails.[144] With sentences ranging from twenty-five to five hundred lashes, these were severe beatings, but it was against the army's interests for these punishments to be fatal, and measures were taken to ensure men survived this brutal treatment.

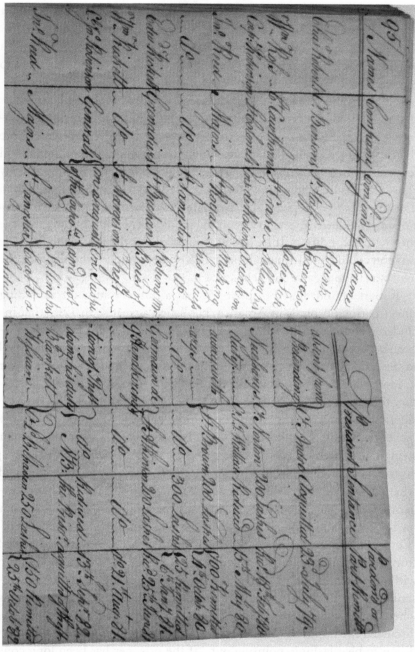

A page from the punishment book of the 44th Regiment of Foot, recording each man tried by a regimental court-martial, the charge, the date, the sentence, and the extent to which the sentence was carried out. (*MG 23 K6, Public Archives of Canada*)

Lashings were ritual affairs; because "Punishments were never meant only to affect Criminals, but also as Examples to the rest of Mankind,"[145] the regiment, garrison, or some portion of the soldiers at hand formed a square or circle to witness the proceedings. The accused was stripped to the waist or completely naked[146] and was tied to a frame (usually composed of several halberds—long-handled weapons carried by sergeants that resembled poleaxes—lashed into an A-frame). Drummers then administered the lashes, twenty-five per drummer.[147] Seldom were more than 250 lashes given at one time, which happens to equate to one round for each of the regiment's ten drummers, but the quantity was more likely chosen to ensure the victim's survival. If the total sentence was more than 250, the balance was given at a later date. It was crucial for the regiment's surgeon (medical officer) to attend the punishment and carefully observe the victim's condition. If he had any doubt about the man's survival, the surgeon could stop the punishment; he also determined when, if ever, the man was fit to receive the balance of it.

Robert Hamilton, who spent years as a military surgeon, including time in army hospitals in America, published a treatise in 1787 that included a chapter on "the Punishments of the Soldiery, as far as the Surgeon is concerned." He discussed at great length how men should be tied to the halberds to be neither so constrained as to hinder circulation nor so loose that lashes could not be applied with precision. "The arms neither too tight bound nor over stretched," "The thighs ought to be considerably tighter bound than the hands, because it more effectually prevents swinging," and, "If the cords be too loose, room is allowed for swinging, whereby it is out of the power of the Punisher to give [lashes] on the parts directed" were among his recommendations. He described what parts of the body were best suited to receive lashes without endangering vital organs, including, "Let their strokes fall on the shoulders, not on the neck," "To punish so low down as the ribs should be avoided," "Let as little new skin as possible be wounded" on men who had healed from recent lashes, and, "The posteriors, as well as the shoulders, can without much risque of danger, bear a moderate punishment." He described in great detail the musculature and circulatory system in areas where lashes should fall, and the effects lashes would have on them. He discussed the importance of the prisoner's muscles being in the best condition to bear lashing, pointing out, "If the prisoner has been long confined, the body will be relaxed and weakened," and, "Punishments should not be inflicted immediately after a march," when the heart rate was increased. He wrote of the effects of weather and air circulation on infection, noting, "In cold winter weather, the fibres are tense and rigid," "much less danger is to be apprehended from fever," "Autumn is the most sickly season," and, "Never suffer a prisoner to receive his punishment under cover." Hamilton recognized that, "Some are more robust, some of a more delicate make," and therefore had differing ability to bear punishment; "Men of red or fair hair, with ruddy complexions, or tall genteel shape, will be more affected by a given number of lashes, than a man of a hard dense fibre, with three times the number"; and, "The way of life, i.e. the trade they have been bred to, may add to this. Taylors, for instance, are more delicate and tender." Most important, he described physical signs that indicated when a punishment should be stopped because the damage was becoming too much to survive.[148]

How regimental surgeons handled punishments certainly varied. Before Hamilton's publication, it was institutional knowledge passed from surgeon to surgeon. Even the instrument of punishment, the cat-o'-nine-tails, or cat, was not standardized. Each regiment procured its own, and the few descriptions from this era suggest that they differed widely. A writer in 1786 described "a cat of nine tails, being a whip with nine lashes, of whip cord, each lash knotted with nine knots," while a man who joined the army as a drummer in 1797 wrote, "Those which I have seen and used were made of a thick and strong kind of whipcord; and in each lash, nine in number, and generally about two feet long, were tied three large knots."[149] At an 1802 trial concerning a 1789 punishment, a witness deposed, "The cat-o'-nine-tails is an instrument of punishment composed of small cords—the cords are nine in number; and they are generally whipped at the ends with threads that are turned up and twisted round with a bit of thread, in order to prevent their unfolding; the handle of this instrument is wood."[150] But a witness to an East India Company punishment in 1780 wrote "the adjutant brought a small whip made of cotton, which consisted of a number of strands and knotted at the ends; but these knots were all cut off by the adjutant before the drummer took it, which made it not worse than to have been whipped with cotton yarn."[151] Surgeon Hamilton recommended, "The cords should be small, by which means they will cut cleaner, and bruise less; nor should the same cat be long used at one punishment; for by the additional weight of blood, with which they are loaded, the severity of each stroke is greatly augmented."[152] Cats may have been replaced often, but no records survive to indicate how frequently they were acquired.

Regiments kept "punishment books" recording the date of every court-martial, the man tried, the charge, the sentence, and the extent to which the sentence was carried out. Only a few punishment books are known to exist. Those of four infantry regiments in Ireland from 1774 through 1777—the 3rd, 36th, 67th, and 68th Regiments of Foot—combined with their muster rolls, allow the effect of corporal punishment to be determined, at least to some extent. Of 480 men lashed in the four regiments during the four-year period, 320 are traceable in spite of gaps and inconsistencies in the muster rolls. Only three died within a year after being lashed; muster rolls give the date of death but not the cause, so it is only a guess that complications from punishment caused the fatality. Twenty-three men were discharged within a year of punishment, which could be either because they were too damaged to continue serving or their discipline was poor enough that the army no longer wanted them; indeed, sometimes the court sentenced lashing followed by being "drum'd Out."

Within a year of being punished, 53 men deserted, not surprising except that it shows they were healthy enough to do so. The remainder, 267, continued in the army for at least a year after punishment, some for long careers ending with pensions when they were discharged; 20 were fit enough to be drafted into other regiments for service in America. Punishments ranged from twenty-five to five hundred lashes, and many men were tried and punished more than once, with no correlation between the number of lashes and their ability to continue in the army.[153] The surgeons apparently were doing their duty "to prevent any danger to the life of the patient."[154]

The four regiments conducted 972 trials over four years, but only 723 individuals were tried, about one-fifth of the estimated total number of soldiers in these regiments. The precise number of men cannot be determined because of gaps in the surviving muster rolls, but it appears to be about 3,500. Based on this estimate, 80 percent of the men in these regiments committed no infractions significant enough to be brought to trial, at least not during this four-year period. A quarter of the trials were of repeat offenders: 109 men were tried twice, 33 three times, 14 four times, 7 five times, 3 six times, 1 seven times, and another an astonishing eight times. That man, Francis Downey of the 68th Regiment, faced all eight of his trials in the ten months from March 1776 through January 1777. He was lashed for all eight offenses, a total of 1,450 strokes, and he finally deserted in September 1777. There were 334 desertions among the 3,500 men who served in these regiments during this period; of the 355 men who were lashed, 53 deserted, indicating, unsurprisingly, that men who had been punished were somewhat more likely than others to desert.

Not all trials resulted in guilty verdicts, and not all men convicted were sentenced to corporal punishment. Ninety-three trials were of corporals, who were usually reduced in rank if convicted and only occasionally lashed as well. Thirty-six sergeants were tried, and none were given corporal punishment. When men were sentenced to receive lashes, the sentence was sometimes pardoned (or remitted, or mitigated; terminology varied by regiment) in part or in full. Punishment books record pardons but do not give the reasons. Partial mitigations may represent the judgment of the surgeon, but in many cases the entire punishment was pardoned. When full pardons are taken into account, 355 men were lashed during the four-year period, some several times, representing about 10 percent of the estimated total strength of these four regiments.

Since the end of the French and Indian War in 1763, British troops stationed in America when no major war was in progress were quartered in barracks, forts, and frontier posts and fed at the expense of colonial governments in accordance with the Quartering Act of 1765. By 1774, tensions surrounding taxation policies and other parliamentary attempts to modernize British governmental authority over the colonies resulted in six regiments being posted in the middle of Boston. Concerts and pageantry could not quell public resentment over this perceived oppression. The British soldiers encamped on Boston Common recognized immediately that they were in hostile territory and immediately began preparing for the very conflict their presence was designed to prevent.

CHAPTER 4

Working Hard at the Firelock

PREPARING FOR WAR

"THE DRILL SERJEANTS AND CORPORALS of the several Regiments, will be under arms at six o'Clock this evening, on some convenient spot in the rear of the Camp on the common, which the field Officer of the day will fix upon."[1] Orderly sergeants conveyed these directions from headquarters to the appropriate men in the six regiments encamped in Boston on August 4, 1774. Having arrived piecemeal from England and Ireland during the previous three months, they were now formed into a "little army," formidable but nonetheless in need of training.[2] Within each regiment were plenty of experienced soldiers, the majority with anywhere from three to ten years in the army,[3] but peacetime routine in England, Ireland, and Scotland often saw them distributed, a few companies here and there, when in garrison for the winter, and encamped as single regiments outside of cities and towns for the summer.[4] Having six regiments encamped together, in the confines of a peninsular city, against the wishes of many of the inhabitants, demanded a high level of regularity and discipline. They were also preparing for the possibility of war.

Encamped soldiers lived in tents, pitched on Boston Common as soon as the ground was dry enough in June. One infantry tent held each mess of five men, a row of seven or eight housing one company, with one on the end turned sideways for the sergeants. Two such rows facing each other composed a "street," so that an infantry regiment's camp consisted of five parallel streets for its ten companies. At the end of each street, in front of the sergeants' tents, were conical tents called bell tents in which muskets were stored, readily accessible when the regiment formed on its parade ground that stretched the width of the camp in front of the bell tents. At the opposite end of the streets were tents for the officers; even farther back, safely away from flammable hemp canvas tents and straw bedding, were kitchens—circular ditches with fire boxes for each mess dug into the interior perimeter, the earth heaped into the center of the circle.[5] A tent or two was pitched well in front of the parade for a quarter guard, and another some distance in back as a rear guard, "to the best advantage the ground will admit." In early June, while the newly arrived regiments were still on transport ships, their quartermasters, assisted by soldiers on duty in a role called camp-color men, marked out the ground to show soldiers where to pitch tents in orderly streets, allowing them to be "ready for action the moment they are called upon," as well as "having as little intercourse or Conversation with the Inhabitants as possible."[6]

Health was necessary for readiness. Combing hair; wearing clean shirts and stockings; keeping breeches, waistcoats, and coats mended; and other facets of basic hygiene were routine for soldiers.[7] Seaside Boston afforded opportunities to "bathe either in the Morning or Evening," but not "between the hours of seven in the morning, and six in the evening."[8] Tents were "opened and aired for some time every day,"[9] weather permitting; streets were swept every day; "necessary houses" had "fresh earth thrown into them every morning" and were "filled up every seventh day and new ones made."[10] Men were cautioned that "lying on the ground or sleeping in the sun" was "particularly hurtfull" in America.[11]

When cold autumn winds blew into Boston from the bay, the army moved from encampments into barracks. In October, each regiment sent soldiers skilled as carpenters, sawyers, masons, and other trades to fit up vacant buildings as barracks. By mid-November, the regiments "marched into Winter Quarters, leaving the tents standing under the care of a small guard, that they might dry before they were pack'd up, as it had been wet weather for two days."[12] Regiments' pioneers were directed to "cover their wells, pull up their tent pegs, and level the earth on the ground they respectively occupied in their several encampments."[13]

Barracks, whether purpose-built or improvised, presented their own challenges to health and sanitation, as the 23rd Regiment experienced arriving in New York from England in June 1773, "when the heats just set in, by which means, and by improper bedding, and the construction of the barracks, most of our men were immediately attacked with Dysenteries, and we lost several."[14] In December 1774, sickness broke out in the companies of the 18th Regiment in Boston. Initially it was thought that "the ill health of the Men is in some respects attributed to the Womens washing and drying their Cloaths in the Mens Rooms," and the practice was prohibited.[15] Soon after, the detachment left their barracks and "embark'd on board their transports, a malignant spotted fever having broke out among them, which carried off several Men in a short time. The Surgeons are of opinion the disorder was occasion'd by a quantity of stagnated Water in a reservoir under the floor of their Barracks, which was a still House before they got it for their Barracks."[16] A week later, the illness continuing to spread in spite of the detachment's isolation, "the Doctors who inspected the Sick yesterday Attribute the Increase of the Disorder to the Neglect of the Non Commissioned Officers, who do not report their Sick in a proper time to the Doctor, and not as was imagined to its being Infectious." The regiment's commander gave orders to send men to the hospital as soon as they showed fever symptoms.[17] The 43rd Regiment had issues with the same illness; Corporal Thomas Miles and private soldier Benjamin Miles (possibly related) died of it,[18] and soon after, when removing the foul pools beneath the barracks, "many of the Men drop down in fits while they are pumping."[19] Over the next three months, "as the sickness amongst the soldiery has been attributed to the use of the stoves several have been removed & stacks of Chimnies built in lieu particularly the 5th Regiment" and there were "Ventilators of wood made to some of the barracks & a sliding pane made to the windows of the whole," as it was well recognized that fresh air was crucial to preservation of health. To help restore the stricken, a number of adaptations were made, including "an hospital fitted up in Cole Lane for the 43d independent of their former one, for want of room," "an Hospital fitted up in Green's Lane for the 23d on account of a malignant fever this independently of the one adjoining their Barracks," and "Cradles in numbers made for the several hospitals on account of the uncommon sickness."[20]

"Nothing remarkable but the drunkenness among the Soldiers, which is now got to a very great pitch, owing to the cheapness of the liquor, a Man may get drunk for a Copper or two."[21] In crowded conditions and weather to which they were not acclimated, soldiers turned to the cheap, poor-quality liquor that was all too readily available in Boston. Each regiment licensed a few sutlers, vendors who set up tents, booths, or stalls

No detailed images exist of British encampments in Boston. This picture of a camp in England in 1780 shows a typical arrangement, rows of soldiers' tents forming streets, sergeants' tents turned sideways, conical bell tents for weapons, and officers' tents a short distance away. This camp shows some adaptations to suit the local ground, such as the broad avenue up the middle of the camp. Encampment of the 2nd West Yorkshire Militia, London, by Samuel Hieronymus Grimm, 1780. (*Royal Collections Trust*)

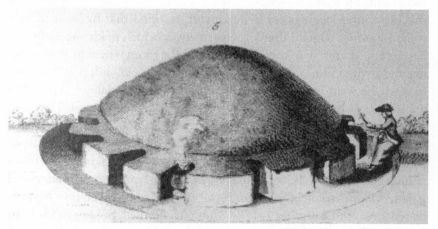

A camp kitchen. Earth from the circular trench is piled in the middle, with fire boxes dug into the inside wall of the trench. Detail from Francis Grose, *Military Antiquities*, volume 2.

behind the camp so soldiers could purchase niceties like tobacco, soap, and chocolate when off duty.[22] The nicety that most soldiers sought was alcoholic beverages, so that was the primary commodity offered by sutlers. Licensing the sellers and putting cash into the hands only of soldiers who would spend it responsibly was expected to prevent problems with drunkenness, but it failed to do so in this new environment. Problems started almost immediately after the camp was established in summer 1774. As early as July 6, an order directed "No person to be allowed to sell spiritous liquors within the bounds of the Camp." Just five days later, "If any people set up stalls out of the line of Encampment, to entice the soldiers there to get spiritous liquors, the Quarter Guard near which such stalls are erected, will post Centinels to prevent any Soldiers going to them." Two weeks later, orders stated, "No soldier or soldiers wives are on any account allowed to go into the Barn in the front of the 38th Regiment as they have been found selling spiritous liquors there contrary to repeated orders."[23]

Soldiers nonetheless found ways to overindulge. Alcohol factored in most of the general courts-martial held in Boston for which records survive. Luke Murphy of the 38th Regiment "drank pretty freely" with friends when off duty in camp one night, until "he did not know his own Tent"; two soldiers of the 43rd were tempted out of Boston when they "were heated with Liquor"; and William Nicholson of the same regiment "was carried out of the town of Boston to a Place called Mystick, by four men whilst he was in liquor."[24] William Ferguson, a tailor in the 10th Regiment, on trial for deserting when he was supposed to be at work making winter leggings for his regiment, testified that he "sent out for some Liquor of which I drank pretty freely, & which made me incline to have more." Later on a "townsman" visited the room where he was working and invited him out to "drink a Dram," which he did; now too tipsy to work, he went into town, where he "met with two Sailors, they asked me if I won'd have a dram & to which I unluckily consented. They had a bottle of Rum which they gave me & of which I drank out of the Bottle, they pressed me to drink again, which I did & got entirely insensible of what I was about or where I was going to, so staggered along, sometimes falling, sometimes walking, until stopped by the Sentries at the advanced Lines."[25] Some soldiers were not lucky enough to be taken into custody by sentries. On December 1, 1774, "John McDonald, Soldier in the light Infantry of the King's Own, was found dead this morning; he mounted Guard at the Lines yesterday, and last night about 10 oclock was seen exceedingly drunk, but not being confined wander'd into the rear of the

Works, where he was found early this morning dead. He was some distance below High Water Mark, and the tide had washed over him; but as his forehead was much bruised, it is supposed that a fall among the stones on the beach had seconded the Yanky rum in his death."[26]

Problems with intoxication were not unique to Boston; in May 1774 in Quebec, "John Dunn, a soldier of the 7th Regiment was found dead, lying on his face in a puddle on the Road between St. Roch and Mr Grant's Windmill. It is imagined being intoxicated he had fallen in the Mud whereby he was unfortunately suffocated, as there was but very little water where he lay."[27] Quantitative data on drunkenness in the army is sparse. In summaries of 1,400 regimental trials in thirteen infantry and cavalry regiments in Ireland from 1774 through 1777, drunkenness was an explicit charge (often in combination with other charges) in 26 percent; only four of the regiments were infantry, but being much larger than the cavalry regiments, they accounted for 983 trials, among which 28 percent included drunkenness in the charges. Alcohol was a factor in a number of other charges, such as "Selling Liquor to Prisoners" and "breeding a Riot in a beer house." It may have been a factor in cases where men were charged with "being Dirty at Morning Parade," "indecent behaviour in the Barrack Yard," "being Insolent and speaking very Disrespectfull Words" to an officer, "lighting a Fire on the Guard bed," and an assortment of other disorderly activities.[28]

Detailed records from Boston are too few to draw broad conclusions, but what exists suggests that alcohol was a much greater problem there than in Ireland. Detachments of the 18th and 65th Regiments—three companies of the 18th and two of the 65th—operated together in Boston; composite corps like this were called battalions and operated in the same manner as regiments regardless of size. From October 1774 through May 1775, ninety-two trials were held in this corps, with drunkenness explicitly stated as part of the charges in fifty-seven of them, 62 percent.[29] Perhaps the behavior in this battalion was significantly worse than other regiments—or perhaps the stresses of garrisoning Boston, combined with plentiful cheap liquor, played havoc with the army as a whole.

William Fanthorp, a grenadier in the 5th Regiment of Foot, was tried on September 5, 1774, "for being drunk when on picquet, and for attempting to take his arms from Corporal Cheene, who was ordered to disarm him, and take him prisoner to the quarter guard." Fanthorp was found guilty and sentenced to two hundred lashes "in the usual manner by the drummers of the regiment," but was spared by the military justice system. The sentence of a court-martial required review and approval by a superior officer. The 5th's commander deemed two hundred lashes "altogether inadequate to crimes of so very heinous a nature, and tending rather to encourage in, than to deter the men from, the committing of such dangerous and atrocious offences," and being "unwilling, that so very improper and inadequate a sentence should be read in the presence of the men," he did not approve the sentence. Fanthorp could not be tried or sentenced again for the same crime, so he was released and returned to duty.[30]

Hand in hand with drunkenness went desertion. Robert Vaughan of the 52nd Regiment, on trial for desertion after he exchanged words with sentries who stopped him and then "placed himself against a Post, and soon dropt down as if Dead, and did not say any thing more," told the court that "he was unfortunately so much in Liquor, that he has not the least remembrance of what he was about."[31] Worse, as described in chapter 1, inhabitants routinely plied soldiers with alcohol to persuade them to desert or outright kidnap them. To prevent desertion, or to give a missing man less time to get away, rolls were called four times each day; if a soldier was absent, his tent or barrack room was inspected to see if his spare clothing was missing, and a search begun.[32] If the man was found quickly, or in circumstances that aroused no suspicion, he might be charged by a regimental court with being "absent at evening roll calling" or something similar, as were eight men in the detachments of the 18th and 65th Regiments.[33]

An officer wrote home in December 1774, "You have heard much of the Desertions. I have seen a return of them, the whole is but 91. I dare say such an army would have lost more men in England."[34] His count of ninety-one desertions appears accurate when compared to available muster rolls, but he wildly overstated the experience of regiments in England. The 23rd Regiment of Foot suffered twenty-two desertions in England from 1771 through its embarkation for America in 1773, and twenty-nine between arriving in New York that summer and the outbreak of hostilities in Boston in April 1775, including two who enlisted in America after the regiment arrived.[35] The 43rd lost only five men during two years in England before embarking for America in 1774, but eighteen between arriving in Boston in June 1774 and the outbreak of hostilities.[36]

Illness, alcohol, and desertion did not stop the little army in Boston from training; it was a peacetime army preparing for the possibility of armed conflict, if not open war. "Commanding Officers of Corps may have their Regiments out to Exercise as often as they think proper" was the order given on July 18, 1774.[37] "Exercise" in this context referred to practicing at arms, which improved health as well. Standing orders for the 37th Regiment (still in Ireland at this time) addressed the importance of year-round discipline rather than just practicing for the annual reviews customary in Great Britain: "It is not the screwing up the Battalion for the appearance of one hour in the twelve Months that speaks either to the merit of its Officers or the Discipline of the Corps"; instead, the purpose of the review was to show how a regiment always behaved. Without frequent practice, a regiment would "lose some part of its smartness in the article of tossing the firelock."[38] The regiments in Boston set about regaining that smartness. In August came orders that, "The Picquets for the future to be drawn out an hour before sunset, and to be joined in the rear of the Camp, and there exercised by the field officer, or Adjutant of the day. The whole will take their motions from the flugal man of the Royal Welch Fusileers, who will take care to give distinct time between the motions, but in performing them, he cannot be too quick, and more particularly so, in the Priming and loading."[39] The fugleman (also written "flugel man," "fugel man," or, as above, "flugal man") selected from the 23rd Regiment of Foot was an experienced soldier who stood where the practicing men could copy his movements.[40] Exercising the pickets—men on guard duty posted at intervals around the periphery of the camp—was a way of working with smaller groups of men when they were on duty anyway.

An officer of the 4th Regiment of Foot wrote, "we work very hard every morning at the firelock."[41] Emphasis was not on ceremonial procedures but on the practical aspects of the manual of arms required for war fighting: loading, firing, and maintaining formation during rapid movements. "When the Regiments go out to fire at marks or otherwise, they are not to be kept long standing to go through their Manual, but may go through their loading motions for a short time. The General has only the following particulars to recommend; first that the men be taught to take good aim, which if they do they will always level well. Secondly that there should be no superfluous motions in the Platoon exercise, but to be performed with the greatest quickness possible. Thirdly that wheelings, and all movements whatever be performed with the utmost rapidity without running, which would create confusion. If the Regiments can get any places in their barracks or elsewhere under cover, young and inexpert soldiers may be there perfected in the Manual."[42] The term "wheeling" referred to a rank (row) of soldiers turning from one direction to another while maintaining a straight front, like the spoke of a wheel, essential for maintaining cohesive formations. The manual of arms was quite specific in its instructions on taking aim when preparing to fire. "Raise up the Butt so high upon the right Shoulder, that you may not be obliged to stoop too much with the Head, the right Cheek to be close to the Butt, and the left Eye shut, and look along the Barrel with the right Eye from the Breech Pin to the Muzzel,"[43] it instructed, and the era's most prolific military writer emphasized, "Great attention must be had in the instructing of recruits how to take aim, and that they properly adjust their ball."[44] The firelock had a sight at the muzzle, which, although also used for attaching a bayonet, was clearly labeled "sight" in military texts.[45]

Firing with live ammunition could be a rare peacetime occurrence,[46] but proficiency was soon acquired in the Boston garrison. As early as June 26, 1774, orders directed, "If the Commanding Officers find it necessary to practice their men in firing ball, they may do it: reserving at least 36 or 40 rounds in case of accidents: the men to be marched to a proper place for such practice."[47] Martial practice continued after going into barracks: "The Regiments to Exercise every fine day; and to be frequently practised in firing ball, singly, by squads, and platoons (particularly the young soldiers) in all directions."[48] An officer commented sarcastically, "It's obvious to the most inattentive Observer that the American Winters must be particularly favorable to parade Duties," but the garrison practiced throughout the cold months. On December 3, there was "Remarkable fine weather some days past, some of the Regiments out firing at Targets &c."[49] The detachment of the 18th and 65th practiced firing with live ammunition eight times between December 1, 1774, and April 15, 1775, firing eight, ten, or fifteen rounds each time, a total of eighty-four rounds for each man, even carefully ensuring, "Those men who were not in the Field this day will be under Arms to Morrow at one o'Clock in order to fire the same Number of Rounds as were fired this day."[50]

An officer of the 23rd described his own regiment's procedure as it took advantage of "a proper place for such practice":

> The Regiments are frequently practiced at firing ball at marks. Six rounds pr man at each time is usually allotted for this practice. As our

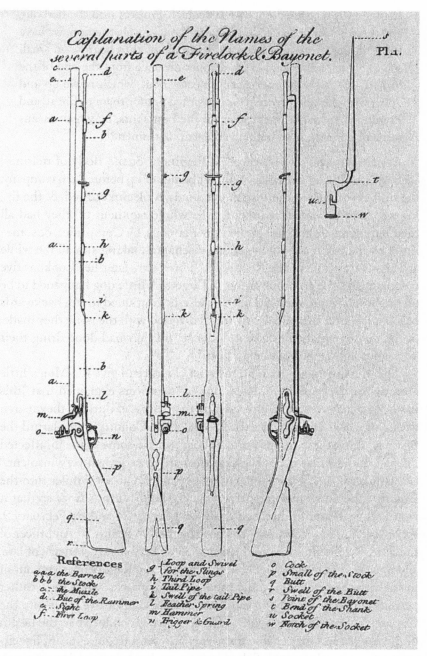

Explanation of the Names of the several parts of a Firelock & Bayonet. Pl.1.

References

aaa the Barrell
bbb the Stock
c. the Muzzle
d. But of the Rammer
e. Sight
f. First Loop

g. Loop and Swivel for the Slings
h. Third Loop
i. Tail Pipe
k. Swell of the tail Pipe
l. Feather Spring
m. Hammer
n. Trigger & Guard

o. Cock
p. Small of the Stock
q. Butt
r. Swell of the Butt
s. Point of the Bayonet
t. Bend of the Shank
u. Socket
w. Notch of the Socket

Diagram of a musket showing the names of different parts; note the sight at the muzzle. From William Windham, *A Plan of Discipline composed for the use of the Militia of County of Norfolk* (London: J. Shuckburgh, 1759).

Regiment is quartered on a Wharf which Projects into the harbour, and there is very considerable range without any obstruction, we have fixed figures of men as large as life, made of thin boards, on small stages, which are anchored at a proper distance from the end of the Wharf, at which the men fire. Objects afloat, which move up and down with the tide, are frequently pointed out for them to fire at, and Premiums are sometimes given for the best shots, by which means some of our men have become excellent marksmen.[51]

A visitor to the city observed "a Regiment & the Body of marines, each by itself, firing at marks. A Target being set up before each company, the soldiers of the regiment stept out singly, took aim & fired, & the firing was kept up in this manner by the whole regiment till they had all fired ten rounds. The Marines fired by Platoons, by Companies, & sometimes by files, & made some general discharges, taking aim all the while at Targets the same as the Regiment." Three days later he "Lookt at five companies on the common firing at Targets. A little dog happened to be on the beach where the balls fell thickest, & continued to run backwards & forwards after the balls, being much diverted with the noise they made, & the dirt flying about; & kept doing so, till they had done firing their 10 rounds apiece without being hurt."[52]

The 4th Regiment "march'd into the Country to give the Men a little exercise" on December 16, 1774; one of its officers explained that "this has been practised several days past by the Corps off duty; as they march with Knapsacks and Colours the People of the Country were alarm'd the first day; think these troops were sent out to seize some of the disaffected People; finding that is not the case they are since grown very insolent." On January 3, 1775, the same regiment "march'd about 5 miles into the Country, the Snow in some parts was very deep, but was froze so that it wou'd all bear," and it marched again on January 24 and on February 9, six or seven miles each time, "to keep the men in health."[53] An officer of the 23rd Regiment wrote on February 3, "It has been customary of late, and approved of by The General, for some of the Regiments to go out of town, with their Arms, Accoutrements, and knapsacks, when the weather permits and they are off duty, and march three four or five miles into the Country." He added presciently, "This practice is conducive to the health of the troops, and may enable the General to send Regiments or Detachments to particular parts of the Country without occasioning so much alarm as would otherwise take place. Our Regiment marched out this day towards Cambridge."[54] His regiment marched out again on February 8.[55]

The 18th Regiment went out on December 15, 1774, "under Arms and in marching Order," "careful that the mens Knapsacks are done up well and compact." They went out again, "guards, sick and taylors excepted," on December 20, January 22, February 1 (instead of January 30 due to bad weather), February 9, and February 28. In mid-February they were cautioned, "If any of the Men is detected in carrying Rum in their Knapsack when they are ordered to march into the Country, they will be punished for disobedience of Orders."[56] In March, "Whenever the weather is fine, some of the Regiments off duty continue the practice of marching into the Country to the distance of from 4 to 8 Miles, with Arms, Knapsacks, &c, and return before dinner."[57] At the end of that month it was the 4th, 23rd, 47th, and marines that marched out to maneuver together for five hours,[58] and on April 10, the 38th and 52nd "marched out this Morning as far as Watertown, and did not return to Boston till 5 oClock in the Afternoon," a round trip of between fifteen and twenty miles.[59]

This was the British army in America in spring 1775, the peacetime army charged with suppressing a belligerent but so-far-peaceful rebellion begun two years before. Mostly men in their twenties, thirties, and forties, a few younger and older; mostly from the British Isles, with a few from other places; all volunteers, in the army as a career, having joined in search of adventure or stability or objectives unknown perhaps even to them; some in the army barely a year, some veterans of decades of service, most with more than one and fewer than ten years in uniform; in a land of English-speaking British subjects who seemed in some ways foreign and in most ways hostile. For nine months they had trained for eventualities that they hoped to prevent by their presence. While some may have come to expect a fight, none could have predicted how long or how extensive it would be, or how it would affect their training, their careers, their lives, and their nation.

PART II

THE WARTIME ARMY

CHAPTER 5

Evident Superiority
Even in Woods

ADAPTING TO WARFARE IN AMERICA

"Our troops are as keen as we could wish them, but I can't say much for their discipline. This winter, however, will improve them much in that respect, as General Howe is very strict,"[1] wrote a British officer in Boston in January 1776 about the commander in chief in America, Lieutenant General William Howe. The army that came to America to forcibly prevent war instead found itself embattled and under siege. From summer 1774 into the following spring, an ever-growing force that finally included ten regiments, elements of two others, a battalion of marines, and a corps of artillery had trained hard, marching long distances and firing at targets. In some ways this practice paid off well; on April 19, 1775, twenty companies, about a fifth of the entire Boston garrison, were able to march nearly twenty miles inland to Concord, then make the return march while engaged in a running firefight for two-thirds of the way, all in less than twenty-four hours, even though the journey began "after getting over the Marsh where we were wet up to the knees."[2] It was, however, a far-from-smooth operation.

The troops on this expedition were the light infantry and grenadiers, ten companies of each, detached from their regiments the day before and formed into two battalions. For a peacetime operation, this was a sensible choice—the lights and grenadiers were selected for their fitness and trained in fast marches and skirmishing. Forming them into battalions had been successful during the French and Indian War in America. As long as the countryside remained peaceful, these were the right men for the task, seizing warlike stores secreted in Concord. When fighting broke out, problems arose immediately among disparate companies of thirty to thirty-five men each that had not trained or operated together before that day. They were also heavily outnumbered.

In Lexington, early in the morning, after a shot rang out from an unknown source, light infantrymen fired into dispersing militiamen and then rushed at them with bayonets. Only with some effort did their officers regain control. This lapse in discipline may have been the result of pent-up rage from the treatment soldiers had endured from Massachusetts inhabitants for the last ten months, or confusion from working with unfamiliar officers.[3] In the middle of the day, a clash occurred at the North Bridge in Concord, where three light infantry companies skirmished with a larger force of militia. It was after leaving Concord in the afternoon that fighting began in earnest, with militia companies from far and wide swarming around the flanks and rear of the redcoat column bent on returning to Boston. While the column stayed on the road to achieve the best speed, flanking parties went out to drive sniping militiamen from the cover of walls and woods; assailants were easily driven off but simply disappeared into the countryside, and every mile of roadway brought new foes. For most of the seven miles from Concord to Lexington, where four fresh and well-managed regiments from Boston provided relief, the grenadiers and light infantry kept up this running fight, exhausting both ammunition and men.

In this battle that was unlike any other that would occur during the war, British soldiers "shew'd no want of courage, yet were so wild and irregular, that there was no keeping 'em in any order; by their eagerness and inattention they kill'd many of our own People," according to a British officer who was on the expedition.[4] The latter part of this remark could mean that some British soldiers fell victim to friendly fire, or that some died unnecessarily due to poor discipline. General orders expressed a similar thought, that the soldiers, "tho' they behaved with much courage and spirit, shewed great inattention and neglect to the commands of their Officers, which if they had observed fewer of them would have been hurt."[5] Considering the circumstances, it is difficult to see where better training would have significantly improved British performance that day. A more cohesive column would still not have known that war would break out, would have marched the same distance, would have made the best time by staying on the road, and would have been heavily outnumbered by hordes of angry militia sniping from distant cover. Better training and discipline may have reduced casualties somewhat, but it would have been a bad day for the redcoats nonetheless.

The next eight weeks brought a host of operational challenges. The little professional army in Boston immediately found itself hemmed in by much greater numbers, initially from New England and soon by troops from other colonies. This demanded a defensive posture. Eight new regiments on the way from Great Britain would nearly double the size of the garrison, possibly allowing offensive operations. Until they arrived, the soldiers in Boston improved the security of their peninsular post. Working parties of several hundred men toiled at fortifications and artillery batteries, taking their arms with them to work in case of alarm. Men on working parties received "two Gills of Rum per day; one to be given them in the morning, the other in the evening."[6] Rolls were called more frequently, and an officer slept in each barracks. Every regiment prepared sixty rounds of ammunition per soldier, enough to fill a shoulder-slung cartridge pouch and waist-belt-mounted cartridge box, the leftovers "carefully packed in dozens, and wrapped up in bladder, if it is to be had, or in leather, in the best manner they can."[7] As the weather improved, the troops moved from barracks into encampments; to protect against springtime dampness, boards from barracks berths became flooring in tents.[8] One barracks was allocated for soldiers' wives and children rather than accommodating them in the encampments.[9] With many heavy cannons defending the city but not enough gunners to serve them all, "Five Serjeants, five Corporals, and a hundred privates with their arms and ammunition" were "sent to do duty with the Royal Regiment of Artillery, till further orders. They are to be such men as have been instructed, and are most expert in the use of the great guns."[10] It was not yet clear that this was a full-blown war, but it certainly was a warlike emergency.

Late in May and continuing into June, transports with troops trickled in to Boston Harbor, each ship carrying a few companies of the 35th, 49th, and 63rd Regiments, troops of the 17th Light Dragoons (cavalry regiments were divided into troops rather than companies, different terminology for operationally similar entities). New men arrived for regiments already in Boston, a mixture of new recruits and experienced men drawn—drafted—from regiments not on overseas service. There were about the same number of drafts as recruits, each regiment receiving some of each: twelve recruits and twenty-three drafts for the 10th Regiment, thirteen recruits and twenty-nine drafts for the 23rd, twenty-one recruits and twenty drafts for the 38th, and so on.[11] This ensured that less than 10 percent of each regiment was composed of new recruits. The drafts, while unfamiliar with their new regiments, were trained in the basics of soldiering, with at least a year in the army and most with considerably more.[12] The recruits had been enlisted by regimental officers, but the drafts were assigned to individual regiments by lottery.[13] The 10th Regiment's drafts came from thirteen regiments, the 23rd's from twenty regiments, and others in kind. Since each soldier owned his clothing, drafts arrived wearing uniforms from their old regiments; their new regiments would outfit them as time permitted, but the first order of business was training. The emphasis was on combat, just as it had been in Boston since the previous year. Officers strove to "drill their Recruits and Drafts, without a days delay after receiving them, beginning with the Platoon exercise, and teaching them to fire ball; proper marksmen to instruct them in taking aim, and the position in which they ought to stand in firing, and to do this man by man, before they are suffered to fire together."[14]

Light infantry and grenadier companies returned to their regiments immediately after April 19. At the beginning of June, they were embodied into a light infantry battalion and a grenadier battalion, establishing their own camps, with a commanding officer appointed to each.[15] Casualties from April 19 were replaced by transferring suitable men from their regiments' battalion companies, while those no longer fit to serve as light infantry or grenadiers were transferred back to the regiments.[16] Within each regiment's eight battalion companies, men were moved from one to another to balance their strength, and most regiments distributed recruits and drafts evenly among these companies.[17] This kept the light infantry and grenadier battalions at full strength and composed of fit, experienced men, while the liability of recruits and drafts was spread evenly, leaving no single company deficient, new men surrounded as much as possible by older hands.

By June 16, enough new troops had arrived to expand the area under British control. Northeast of Boston, over about a half-mile of water, was another peninsular eminence with two high points, Breed's Hill facing Boston and Bunker Hill facing the rebel lines. Occupying this ground would further secure the city and provide a second land route for further offensive operations. The besieging American army, however, learned of British plans and occupied the hills first, erecting an earthen redoubt on Breed's Hill during the night of June 16-17. A fence extended to the right, as viewed from Boston—down to bluffs overlooking the beach, and

American troops reinforced this line as well. When the hostile fortifications were discovered at dawn on June 17, a plan of assault was quickly devised. Boats ferried the grenadiers, light infantry, and six regiments to the peninsula in two waves, landing out of range of opposing positions. Planning to hold the ground after seizing it, but needing to remain light and agile, the soldiers marched off equipped as they would be on most subsequent American campaigns, carrying a blanket and a haversack with provisions in addition to arms and ammunition, but leaving heavy knapsacks behind.[18] It took hours to ferry the troops, so it was midafternoon when they advanced. The light infantry trotted in column along the beach to the right, intending to outflank the American fence line. The grenadiers advanced in line toward the fencing, slowed and disordered by other fences they had to climb over, brick kilns, and other obstructions. The remaining regiments feinted in front of the redoubt, menacing but safely out of range.

The neat plan unraveled when the light infantry column ran headlong into a fusillade from a barricade that, unbeknownst to them, had been erected across the beach. The narrow column could not assault it, and with water on its right and bluffs on its left, could only retreat. The light infantrymen retired to rising ground near where they landed, from which they had a clear view of the enemy lines and the grenadiers struggling to advance over obstructed ground and under heavy fire. With zeal perhaps inflamed by their setback, some light infantrymen fired at extreme range, inadvertently hitting several grenadiers, including the battalion's commander.[19] The plan had fallen apart. Only after a great struggle and horrendous casualties—nearly half the attacking force was killed or wounded—did British troops force their way into the redoubt and drive the defenders from the peninsula.

The Battle of Bunker Hill was a victory in that the objective was taken, but a defeat by any other measure. Culpability for the disaster quickly became a topic of discussion, and continues to be to this day. While one officer at the scene wrote that "the oldest soldiers here say that it was the hottest fire they ever saw not even the battle of Minden [during the Seven Years' War] which was reckoned one of the greatest actions ever gained by British Troops was equal to it. And for the honour of the British Troops, many of whom had never seen a Ball fired, they behaved with the greatest courage," another asserted, "our confidence in our own troops is much lessened since the 17th of June. Some of them did, indeed, behave with infinite courage, but others behaved as remarkably ill. We have great want of discipline both amongst officer and men."[20] There were errors unrelated to the soldiers, including failure to discern the existence of the beach barricade and lack of artillery support because of incorrect ammunition brought to the field. But the pseudovictory was a severe blow to British confidence.

Elsewhere in America, peacetime soldiers struggled with the onset of hostilities. In New York, the modest garrison of a detachment of the 18th Regiment was driven out of town by angry mobs. They sought refuge on board British warships in the harbor but lost some of their arms, baggage, and a few deserters. In Virginia in December 1775, the 14th Regiment's grenadier company, veterans of harassment in Boston in 1769 and bush warfare against rebellious Caribbean natives in 1773, made an overconfident bayonet charge against a rebel position at Great Bridge and were driven off in a hail of gunfire that inflicted heavy casualties. The small garrison at Fort Ticonderoga surrendered in May 1775, unaware that the conflict in Boston had spread to them. Later that year, most of the 7th and 26th Regiments were captured at posts between Lake Champlain and Montreal, in some cases after valiant resistance against overwhelming odds.

Back in Boston, the garrison was secure but continued to suffer the tribulations of shifting from peace to war. Troops on the lines at Boston Neck responded to an alarm in late June with "a general fire of small arms," which an officer of the 23rd Regiment attributed partially to "the hurry & inattention natural to young troops, most of our Regt here being composed of recruits & Drafts, who never having seen service, foolishly imagine that when danger is feard, they secure themselves by discharging their muskets, with or without aim. Nothing but examples & custom can break them of it, and these are no where to be met with on parades. Theory is nothing without practice, & it requires one Campaign at least, to make a good soldier."[21] Officers exerted themselves to restrain soldiers who showed zeal but not discipline. Duty on newly captured Bunker Hill was hard as the soldiers there recovered from the shock of the battle, toiled over construction of new fortifications, and stood sentry in the face of skulking snipers. "Yet believe me, each duty is carried on with the greatest chearfulness," wrote an officer on June 19. "This, in a great measure, is to be ascribed to the unremitting attention of General Howe, who has never left us since the action of the 17th instant, and shares our fatigue as much as his situation will admit, a line of conduct which has rendered him very popular here."[22] Orders on August 10 warned, "The

Brigadiers having represented that the duty of the Garrison in general, is done in a very careless and unSoldier like manner; Officers of all ranks are required to be more attentive and diligent to their duty. The Officers Commanding Guards and detachments, will be made answerable for all neglects or unsoldierlike behavior discovered either in the guards or Sentries under their command, and for all accidents that may happen through such neglects and want of discipline."[23]

Converting career soldiers who were well-trained in fundamentals into a force fit for fighting an all-out war would take time. As fate would have it, time was available. Lacking sufficient strength to oust their besiegers, the army in Boston waited out the winter and, faced with bombardment on their little peninsula, made a hasty evacuation in March 1776. They removed to Halifax, Nova Scotia, a port not threatened by rebellion, arriving at the end of the month. Immediately, preparations began for an active military campaign. From the second week in April, each day that weather permitted, a portion of the army went to the heights overlooking the town for training—not as individual regiments, but as tactical commands that would execute a new campaign in this new war. The light infantry and grenadiers exercised under an officer who, starting with eight light infantry companies at a time,[24] then moving on to the grenadiers, taught them to operate together.

There are no records of the exact training undertaken, but it can be inferred. General William Howe, commanding the army, was a proponent and innovator of tactics for light infantry. In 1774, as a major general, he had led a special exercise in England, taking light infantry companies from ten regiments and instructing them in maneuvers he developed. They learned to form in two ranks, that is, two rows of men one behind the other. Instead of standing shoulder to shoulder, men stood two feet apart, and they learned to extend that interval to four feet, and to ten feet. Advancing and retreating in lines while maintaining these intervals was not easy, but light infantry companies were composed of men who had already mastered close-order work and showed aptitude for adaptability. They learned to collapse their lines into a column two-men wide by having the men at the center of the line move forward while those to the left and right fell in behind them; they practiced forming on the left or the right rather than on the center. Using similar techniques, the line could be reformed facing to the left or the right of its current direction. All these maneuvers were practiced at a marching pace, at a quick

march, and at a run. The result was fluid, fast movement that could be
accomplished over uneven or obstructed ground while maintaining the
linear or columnar integrity of each company and of larger formations.[25]
These maneuvers created in 1774 were probably similar, if not identical,
to those taught at Halifax in 1776. On May 11, each regiment transferred
men to bring their grenadier and light infantry companies up to full
strength of thirty-six private soldiers.[26] On the fourteenth, these companies were arranged into new battalions: the 1st and 2nd Battalion of Light
Infantry, each consisting of nine companies; and the 1st and 2nd Battalion of Grenadiers, each with ten companies.[27] These battalions, although
their composition varied, remained intact for much of the war.

Detaching the flank companies—the light infantry and grenadiers—
left each regiment with eight remaining companies, the battalion companies. They were grouped into brigades of three regiments each, and
every fair day one brigade went to the heights and learned to operate together.[28] Here, too, what was instructed was not recorded. A year before
in Boston they had abandoned the standard three-rank formation in favor
of two longer ranks.[29] Now they were ordered back into three ranks, but
with eighteen inches between men.[30] Presumably, they learned the efficient movements of the light infantry, although perhaps not at the extreme intervals.

Other campaign preparations proceeded apace. Firing at marks—target practice—continued at the discretion of regimental commanders.
Each regiment provided two armorers to repair muskets and bayonets for
the army; regiments sent batches of ten guns at a time until all were serviceable. Older muskets with wooden ramrods were replaced with more
modern ones with iron ramrods.[31] Some regiments were armed with the
pattern of musket first used in 1756, with barrels forty-six inches long,
while others had a newer model released in 1769 with a forty-two-inch
barrel. In Halifax, grenadier companies with the shorter guns were
reequipped with the earlier, longer weapons, so that the grenadier battalions were uniformly armed[32] (the light infantry companies, having been
created and equipped in 1771, all had the shorter guns).[33] Unserviceable
arms were replaced.[34] Initially two, then four, and finally nine men from
each regiment went to the artillery laboratory, where ammunition was
prepared, to make thousands of musket cartridges. Three gun flints were
issued to each battalion company soldier; grenadiers and light infantry
received four, with a caution to "take the greatest care of as they are of a
better sort."[35]

Eight weeks of hard work made the army ready for war. It sailed out of Halifax and landed unopposed on Staten Island, at the mouth of New York Harbor, at the beginning of June. There it continued preparing, training, readying for a campaign to seize the city of New York. More regiments arrived and were integrated into the army by increasing each of the six brigades from three regiments to four. Three more flank battalions were created, two of grenadiers and one of light infantry. A brigade composed of about one thousand volunteers from the three regiments of Foot Guards that protected the royal family and their properties arrived to bolster the army in America, as did the 42nd Royal Highland Regiment and the newly raised 71st Regiment, also highlanders. Several regiments of German soldiers, collectively known as Hessians even though they came from several German states, joined the army. Knowing that their opponents had built extensive fortifications to defend the city, regiments were asked which men had experience "carrying on works by sap," the techniques of using trenches to approach fortified places.[36] Most significantly, "The Infantry of the Army without exception" was "ordered upon all occasions to form two Deep, with the Files at 18 Inches Interval till further orders,"[37] an indication that the entire army adopted the rapid, efficient maneuvers introduced by General Howe in England in 1774.

The campaign that followed proved the worth of those maneuvers. At the end of August, the bulk of the American army was nearly destroyed on Long Island. While several regiments demonstrated along the American front, the main British force, led by light infantry, marched for miles through the night around the flank. Taking the enemy by surprise, they swept all before them. No walls or woods or other obstructions could shelter the rebel army from the redcoat onslaught that continued throughout the day in spite of the all-night march. The victory "was entirely owing to our Men attacking them the proper Way. The moment the Rebels fired our Men rushed on them with their Bayonets & never gave them Time to load again. Our Men behaved themselves like British Troops fighting for a good cause," wrote the general who had trained the brigades in Halifax.[38] The commander of the 57th Regiment's light infantry company recorded, "The Light Infantry who were first engaged dashed in as fast as foot could carry. The scoundrels were driven into the wood and out of the wood, where they had supposed that we would never venture to engage them," and boasted, "It requires better troops than even the Virginia riflemen who make much opposition on one side when they know that their retreat is cut off on the other."[39]

This fast-moving attack became the hallmark of British operations for the remainder of the war.[40] Leaving heavy baggage like tents and knapsacks behind, troops took only their arms, accoutrements, blankets, and haversacks with one to four days of provisions, allowing them to cover long distances quickly, taking breaks every few days to rest and allow tents and baggage to catch up. Training and discipline allowed lines of battle to be maintained in spite of the intervals between men, and soldiers accustomed to hard work and long marches during times of peace could muster the energy for vigorous attacks even after hours and miles of marching. Two weeks after the victory on Long Island, preparing to land on Manhattan and take the city of New York, British troops were "reminded of their evident Superiority on the 27th August last by charging the Rebels with their Bayonets even in Woods where they thought themselves invincible, they now place their security in Slight Breastworks of the weakest construction & which are to be carried with little loss by the same high Spirited mode of Attack. The General therefore recommends to the Troops an entire dependence on their Bayonets with which they will ever command that Success which their bravery so well deserves."[41] The standardized maneuvers learned at Halifax and Staten Island did not prohibit officers from innovating and soldiers from taking initiative. Wrote one light infantry officer of a colleague's work in September:

> Johnson and his Company behaved amazingly, he goes thro his manavers by a whistle for which he has often been laughed at, they either form to right or left or squat or rise by a particular whistle which his men are as well acquainted with as the Battalion with the word of Command, he being used to Woods fighting and having a quick Eye had his Company down in the moment of the Enemies present & up again at the advantegious moment for their fire, killed several and had not one of his Company hurt during the whole time he drove the Enemy before him.[42]

Another light company officer described fighting at Pell's Point in October:

> [A]t Frogneck I was engaged (having mine own and another company under my command) with 150 or 200 riflemen for upwards of seven hours at their favorite distance about 200 yards, they were better cover'd than we were having a house a hill and a wall we had only trees, they got the first fire at us before I saw them, I bid my

men cover themselves with trees and rocks and turn out volunteers among the soldiers to go to the nearest trees to the riflemen and keep up the fire with the Hessian riflemen who came to us but did not stay above an hour, I continued the popping fire at them and they at us and we had the satisfaction of knocking several of them down and not a man hurt.[43]

During a fight in New Jersey in February 1777, "The fire was prodigiously heavy at one time but per favour of some pretty large trees, which by a good deal of practise we have learnt to make a proper use of, my Company suffered very little," according to a light infantry company commander.[44] Two months later, another gave a more vivid description of similar fighting:

[T]he Light Infantry are in the most danger, that is of being wounded in the Arms for we have learn'd from the Rebels to cover our Bodies if theres a Tree or a Rail near us. I faced two hundred of the Rebels with my Company only in a Wood, for two minuits, myself not twenty Yards from some of them and received all their fire . . . had only one man wounded in the Arm . . . I was so near as to call to them 'by God my Lads we have you now' in hopes they wou'd be bullied to surrender but that wou'd not do they answer'd me with a heavy fire, however when I got my men to the Trees round about me and the other Company coming up to my Support, I bullied them another way, seeing them snug behind the Trees and showing no disposition to run, and too many of them to charge as we were rather too thin I cried as loud as I cou'd hollow that they might be sure to hear me 'my God Soldiers they run, have at them my brave Boys' which had the desired effect, one thought the other run and they all set off as if the Devil drove them.[45]

A grenadier officer recalled supporting another corps engaged in the woods in May: "The Company's turn'd out to their support & dash'd into the Wood upon the enemy."[46]

In Canada, an aggressive American advance in late 1775 seized every British post between Lake Champlain and the St. Lawrence River but stalled at Quebec. A powerful British reinforcement of ten regiments arrived in late spring 1776 and promptly pushed their adversaries all the way back to the lake. German regiments reinforced this northern army, and one of their officers described tactics similar to those used in the New York area: "Here we have a special way of waging war which departs utterly from our system. Our infantry can only operate two deep, and a man must have eighteen inches space either side to be able to march in line through woods and brush."[47] Preparing for a campaign from Canada to Albany in 1777, Lieutenant General John Burgoyne established "a Constant rule in or near Woods to place Advance Centries where they may have a Tree or some other defence to prevent their being taken off by single Marksmen." His orders for attacking echoed those General Howe had given the previous September:

"The Officers will take all proper Opportunities and especially at the beginning of the Campaign to inculcate in the mens mind, a reliance upon the Bayonet. Men of half their bodily Strength and even Cowards may be their match in firing, but the onset of bayonets in the Hands of the Valiant is irresistable. The Enemy Convinced of this truth, place their whole dependence in Entrenchments and rifle pieces. It will be our Glory and preservation to Storm where possible."[48]

His soldiers heeded his orders well. Advancing on Fort Ticonderoga in July, "the Enemy that prided themselves in the Woods, were taught to know that even there the British Bayonet will ever make it's Way."[49] Soon after, the Battle of Hubbardton "did our troops the greater honour, as the enemy were vastly superior in numbers, and it was perform'd in a thick wood, in the very style that the Americans think themselves superior to regular troops."[50] Even as the campaign bogged down near Saratoga in September, British troops skirmished skillfully against superior numbers. At the Battle of Freeman's Farm, "The 24th Battalion received orders to file off by the left, they took the wood before them firing after their own manner from behind Trees."[51]

An American officer discovered just how difficult it was to fight the well-trained and tenacious British regulars when his force attempted to surprise a party of the 23rd Regiment only one-third its size in August 1777 near Head of Elk, Maryland:

[W]e discovered a few of the Welch fusileers cooking at a barn in the middle of a large field of Indian Corn. Capt. Dark resolved to take them if possible, on which account he divided his men into 6 parties of 25 each, under the command of a Lieutenant and 2 Serjeants. The party on the left to which I belonged, he ordered to surround the field, which we did, but were discovered by those we thought to surprise, who were only a few of a party consisting of

British light infantry soldier on campaign near Philadelphia, late 1777. This detail from a cartoon published by Matthew Darley was almost certainly based on a sketch by Lt. Richard St. George Mansergh of the 52nd Regiment, and shows the utilitarian adaptations often made to uniforms for this and other campaigns. Detail from *A View in America*, Matthew Darly, 1778. (*Library of Congress*)

fifty that were out foraging. They drew up immediately and marched out of the field; upon which our Lieut and 4 of his men fired upon them, which they returned with a whole volley, and plyed us very warmly from among the trees, for some considerable time, untill the other parties came up and attacked them in the rear; whom they also gallantly repulsed and put to flight.[52]

Weeks later, a German officer described the British attack on the American flank at Brandywine after a march of some seventeen miles: "The English, and especially the English grenadiers, advanced fearlessly and very quickly; fired a volley, and then ran furiously at the rebels with fixed bayonets without firing a shot, in spite of the fact that the rebel fire was heavy."[53] Days before Philadelphia was seized without opposition, a British artillery officer wrote, "The rebels fly before us; they run whenever we advance. They say we are mad or drunk or we would never dash in among them as we do. Our light infantry are the finest set of fellows in the world for this mode of fighting."[54] In the June 1778 Battle of Monmouth, New Jersey, "The 3d Brigade came up after a very quick & fatiguing march of six or 7 miles, and leaving their Packs at the edge of the wood on their right, they dash'd thro' that wood & a deep swamp, and came upon a Scatter'd Body of Rebels," wrote a grenadier battalion officer.[55]

As late as 1780, by which time the American army had matured significantly, British troops continued to prevail against superior numbers by using zealous speed and steadiness. An officer recalled the 1780 Battle of Camden, South Carolina:

I must request your indulgence while I relate the Gallant Services performed on that important day, by your Old Mindonian Regiment the Royal Welch; being drawn up on the right of the exposed line & assending the rising ground, described in their front, to within forty Yards of the Rebel line (drawn up four deep, shoulder to shoulder) & we only two deep, with open files, so as to occupy as great a front as opposed to us, gave them three Huzza's, received their fire, then gave ours, & immediately rushed in upon them with our Bayonett's before they cou'd load a second time, which made such an impression upon them, that they fled precipitately into Swamps and thick brush wood, lightning themselves with the loss of their Arms & Packs, which they threw away as they run along.[56]

Occasional variations to the two-rank, open-order formation were used when local commanders saw fit. For his expedition to the Virginia

Tidewater region in April 1781, for example, Major General William Phillips gave orders to "Practice forming from two, to three and to four deep, and that they should be accustomed to Charge in all those Orders, in the latter order of 3 & 4 deep the files will of course be closer, so as to render a charge of the greatest force . . . one division of a Battalion attacking in the common open order of 2 Deep, to be supported by the other division as a second line, in the charging order of 3 or 4 deep."[57] An American officer noticed these formations at the Battle of Green Spring on July 6, where he "Saw the British light infantry, distinctly, advancing at arms-length distance, and their second line in close order, with shouldered musket, just in front of their camp."[58] Another American noted, "The British advanc'd in open order at arm's length & aiming very low kept up a deadly fire."[59]

Battles like Long Island in 1776, Brandywine in 1777, and Guilford Courthouse in 1781 were fought after all-night marches. Other attacks had different physical demands. Assaulting Fort Washington at the northern end of Manhattan in November 1776, the British light infantry "had a very steep and rough mountain to ascend, where the enemy was covered by the rocks and trees; but they were soon driven by the unparalleled activity and bravery of the Light Infantry, who bid defiance to all opposition, and gave time for landing the rest of the troops."[60] Four days later, a much larger force scaled the Palisades that loomed over five hundred feet above the Hudson River's western shore, "having discover'd a Path that would admit but two Men a Breast. They Climb'd up a very steep & difficult Precipice," achieving surprise by using a place "considered as inaccessible for any body of troops,"[61] then marched several miles to take Fort Lee, achieving full control of the region around the city of New York.

Many marches included wading through rivers and swamps, sometimes on the way to a fight, sometimes directly into a fight. Advancing on Philadelphia on September 6, 1777, "The Army march'd at 4 O'Clock in ye evening towards Lancaster and the Light Infantry after a very disagreeable march, thru swamps, and rivers, in many places up to ye middle; and after several halts, took post on a hill, at 2 O'Clock in the morning, about three miles from ye ground we had left."[62] At the Battle of Brandywine five days later, troops pressed on their opponents despite a drenching: "As soon at the Attack commenc'd with the left, the Order was given to pass the River. The 4th & 5th Regiments leading the Column & wading up to the middle forc'd their way over & storming the work bayonetted the Rebels loading the guns."[63] Another participant recounted, "The water was breast high and we were obliged to carry our muskets in one hand and our ammunition in the other, the grape shot from the enemies battery playing upon us the whole time. Many poor fellows fell in the river and were swept away with the current."[64] More dramatic was the 1781 crossing of the rain-swollen Catawba River, "up to their breast in a rapid stream, their knapsacks on their back, sixty or seventy rounds of powder and ball in each pouch, tied at the pole of their necks, their firelocks with bayonets, fixed on their shoulders,"[65] while under heavy fire. An officer described the treacherous crossing:

> It is impossible to conceive a more awfull appearance than the many very formidable obstacles that opposed themselves to us in the Passage of the Catawba: a Broad, Deep and Rapid Water, full of very large Rocks, the opposite shore exceedingly high and steep, cover'd with the largest Timber, and from the number of Camp Fires, it might be presumed, a large Corps was posted there. The Spirit of the Officers and Men upon that occasion, deserve the highest praise, under every possible disadvantage, contending against a powerful current that carried many of the strongest Men down the stream, under a very heavy Fire. They were never thrown into the smallest confusion or fired a single Shot, 'till they landed on the opposite shore (which with difficulty they were so exhausted they could ascend) where they attacked and immediately dispersed the Enemy, formed upon the Heights.[66]

Lieutenant General Charles, Earl Cornwallis, praised his men, "for a constant fire from the enemy in a ford upwards of 500 yards wide, in many places up to their middle with a rocky bottom and strong current, made no impression on their cool and determined valour nor checked their passage."[67]

Although the British army, "by the vigor, firmness & discipline of its advanced Corps [had] gain'd that superiority in the woods over the Rebels which they once claim'd,"[68] there were nonetheless issues with tactical discipline among eager soldiers, particularly after the dramatic victories of August and September 1776 against an enemy they regarded as "an Undisciplined Rabble."[69] Advanced pickets sometimes wasted ammunition by taking unauthorized shots at real or imagined opponents, leading to admonishing orders in the New York area on October 15, 1776: "As nothing can mark the unsteadiness of Troops more than the frequent & useless firing of the Advanced Posts, the Commander in Chief flatters himself it is unnecessary to remind the Army of the Superiority they must have in discipline over the Enemy oppos'd to them."[70] More dangerous was unbridled impetuosity on the battlefield, where frequent victory sometimes invoked overconfidence. The day after routing American defenders and seizing the city of New York, the British advance was checked at Brooklyn Heights when "the Light Infantry in pursuing farther than was intended lost many Men by a party of Rebels in Ambush."[71] The next day, Howe scolded them in general orders, "the commander in chief . . . finds himself under a necessity of disapproving of the want of attention in the light infantry companies, who pursued the Rebels without the caution to be observed when there are not troops to support."[72]

Victories after long marches had the unintended consequence of leaving soldiers exhausted. "Our light infantry being employ'd to flank, Scour the Country & Skirmish with every body that interrupts the way before a Serious attack & afterwards push'd in the front of the attack itself, are generally too exhausted to be able to pursue with effect," wrote an officer in 1778.[73] A light infantry officer described a day-long action in New Jersey in February 1777, after which, "You may believe by this time the men were pretty much fatigued; it is impossible to conceive what life and spirits was communicated to the breasts of every one upon the first appearance of the attack. . . . We had marched at least 28 or 30 miles over fences woods and ditches every step up to the ankles in mud or snow, and some part of it at run. My Company in particular had not halted a single instant since we left the parade, et qui pis étuit we had not had a morsel that day."[74] On September 5, 1778, the 1st Battalion of Grenadiers was part of a large force that raided the region around New Bedford, Massachusetts, during which, "The Troops march'd I suppose near 20 miles." Three weeks later they were engaged in a foraging expedition in New Jersey that saw them "pretty much fatigued, marching & halting far above 20 hours & little to eat or drink."[75]

The Battle of Brandywine on September 11, 1777, is one in particular where a rapid pursuit the following day could have consolidated an already-stunning victory. But pursuit was impossible. The attack was late in the day after a march of many miles, after which the troops "were by this time much fatigued."[76] Recalled one officer, "Marching above Sixteen Miles, which We was from Day break to three o Clock in the Afternoon a doing owing greatly to the badness of the Roads which did not allow the Cannon to get on faster, by that time you must imagine our men were pretty much fatigued, having had nothing to Eat or drink, since the Day before, but when they formed at 3 o'Clock the enemy so close, the March and fatigue was all forgot, its impossible for Men ever to go into the field, with more spirit and determined resolution then they did."[77] But "having marched seventeen miles of very dusty road" before the battle took a toll on the soldiers; "it growing dark, together with the vast fatigue the first column had gone through, prevented any farther pursuits."[78] "The Rebels were driven back by the superior fire of the Troops, but these were too much exhausted to be able to charge or pursue."[79] The aggressive advances that made victory possible required recovery time, often allowing a vanquished foe to escape total destruction and fight another day.

British senior officers, particularly General Howe, are often criticized for not pursuing after overwhelming victories, but they knew the limits of their soldiers. Attempting to sustain fast-paced operations without sufficient respite or resupply could wear down an army to the point of ineffectiveness. This was demonstrated by General Cornwallis's relentless 1781 campaign in the Carolinas that gained tactical victories but failed to achieve strategic goals. Cornwallis wrote enthusiastically to the secretary at war:

> The conduct and actions of the officers and soldiers that compose this little army will do more justice to their merit than I can by words. Their persevering intrepidity in action, their invincible patience in the hardships and fatigues of a march of above 600 miles in which they have forded several large rivers and numberless creeks, many of which would be reckoned large rivers in any other country in the world, without tents or covering against the climate, and often without provisions, will sufficiently manifest their ardent zeal for the honour and interests of their Sovereign and their country.[80]

But one of his subordinate generals, while praising the soldiers' fortitude, had a different view of the campaign, writing, "what remains are so completely worn out, by the excessive Fatigues of the Campaign in a march of above a Thousand Miles, most of them barefoot, naked and for days together living upon Carrion, which they had often not time to dress, and three or four ounces of unground Indian Corn has totally distroy'd this Army—entre nous, the Spirit of our little Army has evaporated a good deal. No zeal or courage is equal to the constant exertions we are making."[81]

Exhaustion manifested in many ways. Duncan Robertson of the 71st Regiment went missing on the night of August 30, 1777, in Maryland while searching for some cattle that had escaped and was discovered the next day lying on his blanket in the woods. Brought before a court-martial for desertion, he testified of "being fatigued and his feet sore and blistered with wandering about all night in search of the Cattle."[82] Heat added to the soreness and blisters of long marches, sometimes with fatal results. "The Day was so remarkably Hot—sev'ral Men fell Dead," wrote an officer about fighting in New Jersey on June 26, 1777.[83] Another noted, "One man raved with a coup de soleil and fired at our own flankers."[84] At the Battle of Brandywine, "The fatigues of this Day were excessive: some of our best of men were obliged to yield, one of 33rd dropped dead."[85] An officer commented that "the fatigue of the day having been very great & the Men encumbered with their Blankets &c. it soon became necessary to halt."[86] Even repositioning four thousand men about fifteen miles on Long Island in August 1778 took its toll because the weather was "amazingly hot. Thermometer in the night 88 degrees. The Troops for the intended Expedition marched from Bedford to Flushing. The heat was such that 9 fell dead in this march and 63 left behind with sickness. . . . Thermometer at mid-day 94 degrees."[87] Worst was the Battle of Monmouth on June 28, 1778, where substantial numbers on both sides fell due to the heat; almost sixty British soldiers, half of the total who died in the battle, succumbed to the sultry conditions.[88] "Having pursued with great ardor five or six miles during the extreme heat of the day, sev'ral men dropped down dead, and the rest were too much exhausted for further action," wrote one officer,[89] while another observed, "These several Maneuvers & rapid marches with the excessive heat & the difficult passes they met with had so fatigued & knock'd up the men that a great number of the several Corps died upon the Spot."[90] But this was the nature of campaigning when "their Discipline is that of light infantry, which is the only Method of proceeding in this Country."[91]

Foot soldiers sometimes took on roles that were very different from light infantry. Every place the British army occupied for more than a short while was soon brimming with cannons, not the lightweight brass guns that fired three- or six-pound balls, mounted on field carriages designed to support infantry on campaign, but larger, heavier bronze or iron guns for defensive works that fired solid shot weighing twelve, eighteen, twenty-four, and even thirty-two pounds. These guns were the domain of the Royal Artillery, a force in general well trained but undermanned in America. Soldiers from infantry regiments often augmented the artillery, usually in garrisoned cities. Those selected, usually ten to twenty men per regiment, were to be "well behaved men, and the most expert in the use of the great Guns."[92] Those without knowledge of gunnery received the necessary training.[93] Usually a noncommissioned officer went as well, and although under direction of the Royal Artillery, they were paid and clothed by their own regiments.[94] An unnamed additional gunner from the 4th Regiment was wounded in the knee by rebel artillery in Boston on September 17, 1775, requiring the amputation of his leg.[95] On August 5, 1777, a raid on Rhode Island was driven off in part because, "The greatest alacrity was shewn by the troops in assisting at the battery on Windmill hill."[96] The powerful British force that laid siege to Charleston, South Carolina, in 1780 brought massive thirty-two pounders to pummel the city's fortifications. These guns, weighing over two tons each, were hauled over land and into place by the infantry. It was punishing work. Thirty-two-year-old Donald McDonald of Kilmarnock, in the 74th Regiment's grenadier company, "contracted a violent Pain in his Breast, and spilling of blood" from "an over-exertion in drawing Cannon at the Siege of Charlestown." Inverness native John McIntosh of the 71st, also thirty-two, complained of "spraining his Back and a violent pain in his Breast caused by a zealous over-exertion in pulling up Cannon at the Siege of Charlestown; he cannot Bend his Back without excruciating pain."[97] Once the guns were in place, infantrymen helped crew them, including "the 64th regiment being well practiced in that service."[98]

In the massive military buildup of 1775 and 1776, only two light cavalry regiments went to America. Unlike the European continent, the colonies had few broad, unobstructed expanses to deploy horse soldiers in battle. During the early years of the war, the 16th and 17th Regiments of Light Dragoons worked mostly as scouts and messengers, occasionally making successful incursions deep behind hostile lines. There were, however, times when horses were useful for the infantry. Before war broke out, soldiers sometimes went on horseback, disguised in civilian clothing, into the country around Boston to look for deserters.[99] As the war progressed, horses began to transport infantry. In September 1778, the 2nd Battalion of Light Infantry, part of a major foraging operation, surprised an American dragoon regiment in what came to be called the Baylor massacre; an officer recorded, "The greatest part of the Light Infantry were mounted behind Dragoons, and marched after it was dark, but the Light Infantry soon tired of riding" and continued on foot since they "preferred marching." After the raid, however, "We all returned to camp on horseback, mounted on the horses that had been taken."[100] Around this time, the light infantry embodied its own mounted troop; former cavalrymen in the battalions joined it,[101] including ten men recently transferred from the 16th Light Dragoons into the 17th Regiment of Foot light infantry company.[102] By April 1779, there was just one light infantry battalion on Long Island, which had two corporals, two drummers, and thirty-five privates "in the Troop," including two men each from most of the battalion's fifteen companies, the drummers no doubt using the hunting horns favored by light infantry.[103] Few details of their activities are known, other than their success in tracking down deserters on at least two occasions in July and August.[104] William Hudson and William Rowland, two of the former 16th Light Dragoons now in the 17th Foot, were posted as videts—pickets on horseback—on July 16 in the same area near the New York-Connecticut border that the deserters were caught. They took advantage of their horses' speed to abscond, and were last seen "riding very fast, and enquiring the Road to Horse Neck." Two years later, Hudson turned up among American prisoners of war and was sentenced to death for "Desertion and bearing Arms in the Rebel Service."[105] The troop was still embodied in January 1781, and appears to have been used primarily for scouting and pursuing deserters.[106]

It was in the south, where small numbers of soldiers were responsible for vast expanses of sparsely inhabited land, that mounted infantry came into its own, but their utility was not recognized soon enough. Around September 1780, the 63rd Regiment of Foot was "mounted on indifferent horses of the country for the purpose of reducing and disarming the Cheraws" and then went to help secure the post at Ninety Six in South Carolina. As mounted infantry, they rode to the battle at Blackstocks Farm in November but upon arrival "dismounted and kill'd and wounded about seventy of the rebels."[107] Although they usually fought on foot, General Cornwallis went so far as to call them the 63rd Dragoons, and on November 30 he offered "the officers and soldiers of the 63rd my acknowledgements for the spirit with which they have supported the very fatiguing service on which they have been employed for these last three months."[108] Portions of the 80th Regiment were mounted in Virginia in

April 1781, seventy men of the 23rd on horseback took part in a raid on Charlottesville that June, and the 76th fielded some mounted men at Suffolk, Virginia, in July.[109] Overall, there were simply not enough British soldiers in the south to secure the vast territory, and rushing foot soldiers from place to place on horseback, while tactically effective, was not enough to fill the gaps caused by insufficient troop strength.

On occasion, soldiers fought from ships. They journeyed from Britain to America on transports, privately owned vessels operating under contract to the British government.[110] These ships of many sizes usually carried one to five companies each. Crews were small, so soldiers assisted in fending off threats, and war meant threats were frequent. From 1776 on, transports left Great Britain in convoys escorted by a few warships, but Atlantic weather often dispersed these fleets, leaving transports to arrive piecemeal off the American coast. On April 24, 1776, the transport *Golden Rule* carrying two companies of the 33rd Regiment came upon an American merchant sloop; rather than shy away, *Golden Rule* gave chase and captured the sloop and its cargo of chocolate, coffee, candles, and other goods, commodities useful to the army.[111] The following month, several transports carrying portions of the 42nd and 71st Regiments made their way toward Boston, not knowing that the British had evacuated the city. The *Oxford* and *Crawford* transports surrendered at sea to a powerful American privateer, while the *Ann* and *Lord Howe* were captured near the entrance to Boston Harbor. The *George* and *Annabella* were met at the harbor mouth by a swarm of armed vessels that they fought off for two days, all the while believing Boston to be a safe haven, before finally capitulating when the senior officer "thought it my duty not to sacrifice the lives of gallant men wantonly in the arduous attempt of an evident impossibility."[112] A dozen soldiers of the 71st died, a similar number were wounded, and over six hundred of the 42nd and 71st went into a long captivity. In a few subsequent incidents, transports laden with soldiers had better success fending off privateers. Three soldiers on the *Bristol* transport were wounded fighting a privateer schooner in late July 1776, and in November a transport carrying two companies of the 6th Regiment sparred with two privateers off Sandy Hook before getting safely into New York.[113] A year later a transport with three young officers and about eighty recruits for the 60th Regiment was accosted by a rebel schooner off the coast of east Florida; the attackers attempted to board the transport, but a hail of musket fire forced them to surrender, and the schooner sailed into British-held St. Augustine commanded by a British army officer.[114]

Fighting on warships was usually the purview of the marines, the sea soldiers of the Royal Navy, but exigencies of war occasionally put the army's infantry on Royal Navy ships. A common practice during the era, the first instance in the American war occurred far from the ocean, on the fresh waters of Lake Champlain. In October 1776, eighty-five men of the 29th Regiment went on board a makeshift fleet of vessels that sailed from the Canadian border toward Crown Point and Fort Ticonderoga.[115] They encountered a rebel fleet sheltered behind Valcour Island on October 11, and a lengthy battle ensued. Wind and water conditions prevented most of the larger British vessels from engaging, but the topsail schooner *Carleton* managed to get into the fray. A drummer and three soldiers of the 29th were killed, including Alexander Orr and Robert Airs, career soldiers who were in the regiment in Boston in 1770 when their comrades were involved in the Boston Massacre.[116]

Summer 1778 saw the first real threat to British dominance on the American coast since the evacuation of Boston. France had joined the war and sent a powerful fleet to operate off New York. The British warships in New York Harbor were slightly outnumbered and, lacking sufficient marines, asked for three hundred men from the army to supplement their complements. "The Army not forgetful of the many services it had experienced from the fleet embraced with ardor this opportunity of shewing their sense of it," wrote a light infantry officer.[117] On July 12, "Eight Companies from the Light Infantry and Grenadiers were distributed on board the ships of war. The Companies were chosen by lot and the whole drew at their own request."[118] A week later, however, those men were replaced by the entire 23rd Regiment of Foot,[119] perhaps to maintain the strength of the flank battalions ashore. The two fleets faced off for battle in mid-August, but before they could engage, a hurricane-force storm dispersed them, damaging many ships. Individual vessels made their way to rallying points once the weather calmed, here and there encountering enemy ships. A celebrated engagement occurred when the fifty-gun ship *Isis* encountered and defeated a much larger French ship on August 16, owing in part to the valiant fighting of the 23rd's light infantry company.[120] John Fowler, in the regiment over fourteen years and appointed corporal in early 1777, was killed in the action.[121]

In 1781, some of the largest embarkations of soldiers onto warships occurred. In October, in a belated bid to relieve a besieged British army at Yorktown, Virginia, a fleet assembled in New York. Soldiers initially went on transports but were soon shifted to warships in anticipation of engaging a French fleet off the Virginia coast. "We got under way & came to along side the *London* & by means of a rope from each end haul'd close to her, & the troops went on board by seniority of Companys, & were dispos'd of on the middle and lower decks, 6 to a mess between the Guns," explained a grenadier officer of his battalion's disposition on a ninety-gun man-of-war. For battle, three grenadier companies were to serve "along with the Sailors at the great Guns," "7 to each Gun officers included," while another company retained their muskets to fight on deck.[122] But no battle came. By the time the fleet got to sea, the army at Yorktown had surrendered, and the tardy relief fleet returned to New York.

The close-order parade-ground formations taught in training had produced professional soldiers so well versed in handling their weapons and following orders that they were able to adapt to dramatically different methods of fighting in America, usually with outstanding tactical results. Once it was recognized as a real war requiring a determined military commitment, British soldiers were seldom bested on the battlefield, even in the face of much greater numbers. Many small defeats were due to overzealousness, while the major defeats occurred after encirclement and besiegement by armies three or more times larger. The ultimate loss of the American colonies was not caused by inability of British soldiers to adapt to warfare in America but to challenges of logistics, manpower, and especially the lack of a clear strategic vision of how to win a war against a popular insurgency. Wrote an officer of his soldiers' willing exertions on an expedition in 1779, "The silence, perseverance and cheerfulness, the soul of Enterprise with which the Troops Supported the Greatest fatigue of the Long march through uncommon Bad Road and Part unfavourable weather, excites both his praise and thanks."[123]

CHAPTER 6

Gone Volunteer to America

RECRUITING FOR THE AMERICAN WAR

THE WAR IN AMERICA REQUIRED MORE MEN TO FIGHT IT, and William Morgan answered the call. It was April 1776; the war had been going on for a year, and Britain was sending fresh regiments from England, Ireland, and Scotland to overwhelm the "unnatural rebellion." Each corps preparing for deployment needed to come up to fighting strength quickly. Morgan volunteered to join the 53rd Regiment of Foot, one of nine preparing to relieve the besieged city of Quebec. It was a bold move for the twenty-three-year-old from Sligo, Ireland, whose career paid better than that of an infantryman. Perhaps he was drawn by patriotic fervor, or the opportunity to travel from his native land. He was well suited for overseas military service—he was a trooper in the 5th Regiment of Dragoons, a British cavalry regiment serving in Ireland. He had enlisted five years before and had seen two dozen troopers volunteer for American service the previous year, and thirty-five this year, from his regiment alone. All told, over three hundred cavalrymen volunteered to leave their regiments and join others bound for the American war, over two hundred leaving horses behind to serve in the infantry.[1]

In the terminology of the era, William Morgan was drafted—pulled or transferred from one regiment to another. It was a common practice in the British army, used in times of peace to keep experienced soldiers where they were needed. When regiments on foreign service prepared to return to the British Isles, men still fit for foreign service were often drafted into regiments still serving abroad, keeping those regiments up to strength without the burden of recruiting and training new soldiers. When war broke out, drafting was used in another way: experienced soldiers were drafted from regiments staying home into regiments being deployed, ensuring that the deploying regiments had enough experienced men in the ranks. Although the regiments at home needed to make up the loss, they were already in the best place for recruiting and training.

Drafting from regiments in Britain began in early 1775 as part of the military buildup that would, it was hoped, prevent war. Three infantry regiments embarked from Ireland for North America in April. To get each one up to full peacetime strength of thirty-six private soldiers in each of ten companies, about sixty men were drafted from other regiments in Ireland, twenty for each embarking regiment. The 17th Light Dragoons, a cavalry regiment, also embarked in April. Its peacetime strength was only eighteen privates in each of six troops; for American service, that number was doubled partly by recruits and partly by drafting sixty men from the 12th and 15th Dragoons.[2] All four embarking regiments also took on about the same number of recruits as drafts, ensuring that less than 10 percent of each regiment was newly enlisted. Accompanying this first wave of one cavalry and three infantry regiments were drafts and recruits for the regiments already in Boston, even though news of the casualties sustained on April 19 had not yet reached England.[3]

The next wave of four regiments, embarking in May at peacetime strength, each received twenty drafts in addition to recruiting. The 44th Regiment, for example, enlisted forty-eight new men from the beginning of January until embarkation in May, accounting for about 13 percent of its 360 private soldiers; if it had added more recruits instead of twenty drafts, the proportion would have been 19 percent. As discussed previously, most regiments already in Boston received more drafts than recruits.[4] The British army had dealt with emergencies before, and the War Office knew the importance of having trained men in the corps it deployed.

When the emergency became a full-blown war, more regiments were deployed and more drafts drawn to fill them. The established size of each regiment was increased by 180 private soldiers, requiring greater numbers of drafts to balance increased numbers of recruits. The 55th Regiment sailed for Boston in September with about fifty drafts in its ranks, including a few cavalrymen who volunteered for the infantry. With them came the 17th and 27th Regiments, with an unspecified number of drafts that included at least ten cavalry volunteers.[5] In early 1776, seven regiments sailed for the Carolinas with at least two dozen drafts each.[6] Soon after, nine regiments embarked for Canada; among them, the 9th, 20th, 53rd, and 62nd each received eighty drafts from the 32nd, 67th, 36th, and 11th Regiments respectively.[7] This was the first time each regiment giving drafts sent all of them to the same receiving regiment; in all previous cases, drafts were distributed more or less evenly to the embarking regiments. One final draft occurred in 1776 from regiments on home service, when the two battalions of the 1st Regiment of Foot, a corps considerably larger than most infantry regiments, sent forty men who were distributed among regiments already in America. They joined recruits that arrived in October in New York, by then in British hands.[8]

Drafting orders spelled out the requirements for a man to be drafted. "No man to have been less than one year in the Service not under 5 feet 6 Inches high nor more than 35 years of age," were the directions for the draft in September 1775.[9] Orders for the 32nd Regiment to send eighty men to the 9th were more lenient, giving no limit on age or size and requiring only four months' service rather than a full year. "They must have bodily strength for immediate service, & they must have been suffishently trained to the use of arms, to be fit for the common duty of a soldier. They are to have no bodily impediment." Moreover, "Volunteers for the American Service are to have the preference to others."[10] Drafting orders for the 1st Regiment of Foot similarly specified "Volunteers, if so many offer," restricted, of course, to "sound and able Men" with at least a year in the army.[11] Some men may have volunteered because the "roving disposition" that inclined them to enlist in the first place was not satisfied by home service, but there was a financial incentive as well: when a man was drafted, he received a bounty of a guinea and a half (one pound, eleven shillings, and sixpence), almost two months' pay.

There is no record of which infantry drafts were volunteers and which were not. Robert Young, who left the 2nd Regiment of Foot after nearly ten years to join the 33rd in 1776, stated he "joined them as a volunteer."[12] Drafts from the cavalry to the infantry were certainly volunteers, as evidenced indirectly by the varying numbers contributed by each regiment and directly by annotations on muster rolls such as "went Volunteer to the Infantry" and "Gone Volunteer to America."[13] William Morgan, who left the 5th Dragoons to join the 53rd Regiment, responded to "an order being issued for volunteers to serve in America."[14] John Barry of the 46th was "a very large, big man, not only tall, but well set, and had a hoarse strong voice" who "had served nine years as a soldier in the second Reg-

iment of Horse, and turn'd out as a Volunteer to come to America."
Robert Mack came "as a Volunteer from a regiment of Horse to the 62nd
Regiment."[15] Most cavalry drafts went into grenadier companies of the
receiving regiments, prestigious service in the infantry that nonetheless
paid about a third less than the cavalry, not to mention the daunting
prospect of crossing the Atlantic and going into a war zone.[16] A senior
army officer wrote, "What is this Mystery of the willingness of Troopers,
to serve as private Grenadiers? I can't Decypher it: however it's done."[17]

Modern writers often describe drafting as "bitterly disliked," using a
few incidents to conclude that the practice was generally unpopular and
bad for individual and army-wide morale.[18] There were some problems,
primarily later in the war, but they were rare considering how commonplace drafting was. Tracing the long careers of large numbers of soldiers
reveals that roughly half served in more than one regiment, some in three,
four, or more.[19] Looking at just a few examples, the 3rd Regiment of Foot
sent drafts for American service in 1775. John Jolly and Samuel Rawley
went to the 45th Regiment and William Stimpson to the 10th; when
those corps were sent home in 1778, each man was drafted again and remained in North America.[20] Their comrade Richard Cotton joined the
59th Regiment, which was sent home only a few months later; he then
joined the 38th.[21] John Merrick of the 67th moved into the 20th and
sailed to Canada in early 1776; captured in 1777, he spent eighteen
months as a prisoner of war before escaping, at which time he joined the
7th Regiment of Foot, was captured again in 1780, and finally returned
to Great Britain with his regiment at the end of the war and continued
his career—hardly the behavior of a man discontented by being drafted.[22]

The careers of drafted men demonstrate that for the most part, they
served as long and as reliably as any others. For example, the 22nd Regiment of Foot received six drafts from the 1st Regiment of Foot in 1776.
Robert Harrie, from county Banff in Scotland, was thirty-seven when
drafted from the 1st into the 22nd and served five more years, twenty-
seven in all, before being discharged and pensioned. James Gibson, a
Scotsman from Kelso a year younger than Harrie, had twelve years in the
army when he was drafted from the 1st to the 22nd, and he remained in
the 22nd until 1784, when he received a pension after twenty years in
the army. And Jacob Holts, a carpenter from Dunham in Cheshire who
was the same age as Gibson, had enlisted in the 30th Regiment when
that corps was in Gibraltar in 1768. When it left Gibraltar in 1770, he
was drafted into the 1st Regiment, and then into the 22nd in 1776. He
was discharged in 1783, but he later enlisted into the 84th Regiment, fi-

Soldier drafted from the 12th Light Dragoons into the 20th Regiment of Foot, 1776. Drafts typically retained their clothing when they went to a new regiment until the next annual clothing issue. This man wears the coat from his cavalry regiment, and a hat, waistbelt, and pouch from his new infantry regiment. Drawing by Eric H. Schnitzer.

nally leaving the service in 1799 at age fifty-nine, having spent twenty-eight years as a soldier. John Bocking enlisted in the 19th Regiment in 1763 and was drafted into the 1st in 1770 before being drafted into the 22nd; he was discharged in 1779. Nehimiah Ellis enlisted in the 1st Regiment in 1771 and was discharged from the 22nd in 1784. Only one of the six drafts from the 1st to the 22nd showed any sign of discontent: Andrew Anderson, who enlisted in the 1st Regiment in 1771, eventually deserted, but only after spending three years in the 22nd Regiment. [23]

Drafting may seem like a handy way for a regiment to get rid of undesirable men, but there was a protection against that: the receiving regiment had the right to refuse unwanted men. Some were refused. The 53rd Regiment rejected five drafts sent by the 36th in early 1776, for example. [24] That April, the commanding officer of the 69th wrote glowingly of the men he had picked for drafts: "They expressed the greatest joy in going; and in answer to a speech I made them before the Regt. expressed the greatest regard for me, acknowledged their being pitched on as a favour, and said it should be their study by their behaviour to be a credit to the Regt. they were draughted from." [25] He nonetheless requested an escort for them when they marched away, being "apprehensive of some irregularity." [26] It soon became clear why: "By all accounts, I understand that your Drafts were not very fit for any Corps, as to their Morals," wrote the army's adjutant general to the 69th's commander. "I hope that you have not so many Sad Dogs left in the 69th." He further admonished, "By their Accounts, they were Drafts, not Volunteers. This was not quite consistent with the orders." [27]

There were bad ones like John Pearce, who was in the 3rd Regiment of Foot for twelve years and was lashed a total of seven hundred times for three separate offenses in the six months before being drafted into the 22nd Regiment in 1775, from which he deserted within two months of arriving in America. [28] And Arthur Petty, drafted from the 13th to the 20th in 1776, and then to the 53rd in 1778. In 1782, an officer of the 53rd described him as "an incorrigible Thief" who had been given "repeated punishments in the severest manner to no purpose." Being "about forty five years of age, not a very Stout man," rather than being punished yet again he was discharged to local authorities in Quebec in the hope "he might perhaps be of some use to His Majesty's Service as a marine, or, in Africa." [29] Overall, however, there is no correlation between drafting and desertion or other ill behavior; drafts got into trouble in similar proportions to men who were not drafted. The 38th Regiment, for example, received 194 drafts during the course of the war, of whom twelve deserted and 1 never returned from being a prisoner of war.[30] The 23rd received 175 drafts and lost 12 to desertion and 8 who never returned from captivity,[31] while the 22nd lost 19 of 144 drafts to desertion and 3 who did not return from captivity. These rates are similar to the desertion rate of men who were not drafted.

All America-bound regiments recruited to attain and maintain their numbers. In August 1775, recognizing that a significant military buildup was required and that the peacetime strength of infantry regiments would not be sufficient to sustain the likely attrition, the strength of each deployed regiment, and each one subsequently deployed, was increased by 50 percent, from 360 private soldiers to 540; ten sergeants and ten drummers were also added, one to each company.[32] Drafting made up part of these new numbers. Recruits made up the rest, and more would be needed as the war continued. Regiments on overseas service normally left a few officers and men behind to recruit in the homeland, but in 1775, a formal recruiting establishment was authorized. To each regiment were added six officers, six sergeants, four drummers, and funding for 112 private men to be raised as recruits. This was the strength of two companies, and the term "additional companies" was applied, but it was really a budgetary measure so that regiments could fund their recruiting. The money allotted allowed the officers, noncommissioned officers, and drummers to fan out all over the British Isles, establishing recruiting posts wherever they thought they could get volunteers, and pay recruits during their training. Some officers went to their hometowns or principal cities in their home counties, where they knew the families and the goings-on; others went to market towns at harvest time or industrial centers where men might be seeking work. If results were poor in one place, they went to another.

The handful of wartime enlistees who recorded why they joined the army gave similar reasons as peacetime enlistees, reasons that once again could never be discerned analytically. Thomas Cranfield fled an abusive employer in 1777, encountered a recruiting party from the 39th Regiment, "and was by them induced to enlist into the king's service." His circumstances were desperate not because he was unemployed but because he could not bear the treatment of the tailor to whom was apprenticed.[33] Weaver William Stell, whose work for his father was critical in supporting their family, nonetheless enlisted in the 12th Regiment of Foot in "an unguarded moment," abetted by "his simplicity & guileless heart."[34] Twenty-one-year-old Andrew Scott, a farm worker from Bowden in the Scottish county of Roxburghshire who had enjoyed reading and writing poetry since he was twelve, recorded no motive for enlisting in the 80th Regiment in April 1778 other than that he "was tall enough for the service," but added that the army "afforded me an opportunity of seeing the world to an extent which, in another situation, I might never have had an opportunity of doing."[35] That June, Scottish schoolmaster John MacDonald, age twenty-six, was on his way to start a new job when he encountered an officer he knew in a fencible regiment and "determined to go with him let the consequence be what it would." He shunned advice not to join, and even the officer himself "expostulated with me so much as he could to deter me from enlisting, but all availed nothing." A year later, he convinced his officers to discharge him from the fencibles—who would never leave Scotland—so he could join the 73rd Regiment bound for overseas service.[36] In 1779, farm laborer William Pell took some time off from his job to visit his family and met a soldier of the Foot Guards on the road who entertained him with tales of a military life. Pell wrote, "I myself, tho' I did not discover it [that is, reveal it], had a secret inclination that I should like to go with that man."[37] The same year, Jeremiah Clinton booked a passage on a boat from his native Ireland to Bristol, England, from where he intended to sail to New York, but lost his baggage and money. "In this situation I had no other resource to accomplish my design, as well as for present Subsistence, than Enlisting in the 47th Regt.," he wrote, "thinking the present Crisis of National Affairs, would be a means of sending me in that situation, to the place I had so great a desire of going to."[38] James Andrew, an Irishman working in Scotland as a linen weaver, was married with two children, but because "the connexion was unlucky" for him, he enlisted to be "freed from the clamours of a wife."[39]

As a teenager in Yorkshire, John Robertshaw rebelled: he did not want to work at the family weaving business, he argued with his stepmother, he hung with friends who goaded him into misdeeds—in other words, he behaved like a teenager. He ran away, he returned, and he ran away again after his father told him "that if I did not finish my last week's work, when he came home he would give me a trimming." During this second elopement, "the dread of paternal chastisement and the ridicule of my acquaintances, to which I must be exposed in case I came back the second time, banished all thoughts of domestic concerns and firmly fixed my resolution of enlisting as a king's soldier."[40] Not one person who left a reason mentioned unemployment as a motive for pursuing a military career; instead, they all suggest the impulsive, roving disposition that seems to have been, based on the few available accounts, the prevailing reason that men became soldiers. A farm worker identified only as W. Griffith, fully employed but discontent, elucidated what may have been on the minds of most enlistees: "One day, while musing in my mind what to do, I thought I would go for a soldier," he wrote. "I could not resist it, though I could give no particular reason."[41]

The August 1775 order establishing two additional companies for recruiting directed that one operate in England and one in Ireland. This meant rapidly filling posts for six new officers, six new sergeants, six new corporals, and four new drummers, for each of twenty-three regiments serving in North America. Some officers came out of retirement, young men awaiting vacancies were commissioned, and officers were sent home to recruit both their health and their regiments; many had been wounded fighting on the road from Concord in April and Bunker Hill in June and went home to recover, perhaps not providing the best motivation to prospective recruits. To fill the all-important noncommissioned officer posts, sergeants for the English companies were appointed from among men already in England, and sergeants and corporals were sent from America for the companies in Ireland.[42] Drummers were in short supply, so rather than send any home, "they should find them in England in the best manner they can."[43] The orders given by the War Office in August did not reach Boston until October, and it was early December before men assigned to recruiting duty were actually on board ship for the voyage home. To effect recruiting in the meantime, in August 1775, twenty-three sergeants from the regiments of Foot Guards in London were "loaned" to the recruiting parties in Ireland, one for each regiment in America, each one given a uniform for the regiment he would recruit for.[44]

Recruiting proceeded with vigor and mixed results. Demand for recruits in Ireland was particularly great, because regiments stationed there had given up drafts and were striving to restore their peacetime strength at the same time that recruiting parties from regiments in America, and from regiments in England preparing for embarkation, were seeking to attain wartime numbers. The adjutant general of the army wrote in July, "What can be the meaning of recruiting going on so slow in Ireland? The Regiments in Britain have 17 partys in that Country, & only 24 Recruits are got on one Week, 29 in another, & 10 in another. This will not do. This Country is but in a middling situation, if men are so scarce."[45]

The mayor of Limerick accompanied recruiting parties in August 1775, urging citizens to "engage in the public service . . . at a time, when the enemies of the King and our glorious constitution have been so basely insulted by a set of American Rebels, who wish unnaturally to shake off their Mother Country and obedience to the laws of the land."[46] The *Freeman's Journal*, a Dublin newspaper with a name proclaiming its liberal leanings, suggested that the Irish populace had a different view. "We hear from Bandon," began a report from county Cork in August 1775, "that a recruiting party being lately there to enlist men, to fill up the regiments, the serjeant was ordered by the people of the town to withdraw from thence, as he should not get a single man as a soldier, to draw a sword against their virtuous American brethren; but if his Majesty wanted their assistance against a foreign enemy, they were ready and willing to defend his crown and dignity with their lives and fortunes." The same issue reported that "Saturday a recruiting party of the 53d regt. beat up for volunteers at Blarney, and brought away only one recruit," and in Waterford, "A recruiting party of the 19th regt. is now beating up in this city for volunteers, but meets with extremely bad success, owing to the general dislike of being transported to America for the purpose of slaughtering our oppressed fellow subjects."[47] In September, a newspaper announcement assured recruits they would not be sent to America with any of the regiments embarking that month, "notwithstanding the invidious reports to that purpose spread by the enemies of Government, to discourage the recruiting service."[48]

Recruiting officers saw things differently. An officer of the 29th Regiment complained that his efforts were "in some measure retarded" because local magistrates refused to provide accommodations for recruiting parties, interpreting the law to require quarters only for regiments on a march or during times of civil unrest.[49] Others found many a man eager to take the enlistment bounty but far fewer willing to serve any longer than it took to pocket the cash and abscond. "It is not possible for your Lordship to conceive the difficulty there is in getting Men in Ireland," complained an officer to the secretary at war. "Besides they are the very Scum of the Earth, and do their utmost to desert, the moment they are Cloathed."[50] An officer of the 23rd, writing from Strabane, explained that he had raised fourteen "fine Recruits" in just eight days, but could not send them to England, where they would begin training and be less likely to desert, because the officer charged with inspecting them was out of town. The recruiter felt obliged to reject "men who voluntarily offered themselves" because "I fear it will be absolutely impossible to keep recruits long together whilst surrounded by their Friends & Relations who employ every allurement to prevail on them to desert." If allowed to inspect his own men, he could "raise many good men for the Regt provided a method is fixed upon to take them from this part of the Country where they make a trade of Desertion & too often with impunity." He proposed sending them by sea either to England or to Kinsale on Ireland's south coast rather than having them go by land, since experience had shown "that on long Marches through this Kingdom at least one half of the men rais'd are generally lost by desertion."[51]

Recruiting wasn't easy, and recruits did desert, but regiments nonetheless managed to raise the numbers they needed. No muster rolls or other comprehensive records survive for the additional companies—the administrative bodies doing the recruiting—for this early period in the war, but regiments still in Ireland preparing for overseas service give telling information. These corps were required to reach the increased size of fifty-four privates per company and so faced the same demand for recruits as the regiments overseas. In summer 1775, the 17th Regiment of Foot was distributed among several towns around Galway Bay on the west coast of Ireland. From July 1 until they embarked at Cork in the third week of September, they raised forty-five recruits, of which only five deserted.[52] The 55th Regiment, in Dublin during the summer, had similar results during the same period, enlisting fifty-six new men and losing sixteen to desertion, resulting in exactly the same number of recruits as the 17th had, forty.[53] Both regiments received some drafts but embarked well short of their target strength, having had too little time to raise more. The 9th and 24th Regiments fared better between October 1 and December 31 as they prepared for deployment. The 9th, in the Dublin area, took on 71 new men and lost only 5 to desertion, while the 24th enlisted 107 and lost 17.[54] Bolstered by similar numbers of drafts as recruits, both embarked in early 1776 close to their new wartime strength of 540 private soldiers.

On December 16, 1775, the War Office enacted two significant new enlistment incentives. Rather than joining the army as a lifelong career, men who enlisted as of that date would be entitled to their discharge "at the end of three years, or at the end of said Rebellion, at the option of His Majesty." The policy was to be in effect until the end of the rebellion.[55] This may have provided the necessary encouragement to men with roving dispositions who were unsure of making a lifelong commitment. In addition, men enlisted under these terms who chose discharge at the end of hostilities could settle in America on a grant of land, a remarkable incentive for tenant farmers and laborers with no other prospect of owning their own land. There is no way to directly measure the effect of this new policy, other than that regiments continued to enlist enough men to achieve full strength. Sparse records reveal that recruiting in Ireland remained successful albeit difficult. The Irish additional company of the 22nd Regiment of Foot reported on January 5, 1776, having brought in 160 men, of which 39 deserted.[56] A detailed return of recruits for the 46th Regiment describes seventy-one men raised in Dublin and Tipperary between December 23, 1775, and February 4, 1776, including fourteen who subsequently deserted.[57] Although the height requirement was relaxed for wartime, only fourteen of these recruits were below the peacetime standard of five foot six; three of those were below five foot five, and none was below five foot four.[58]

Recruiting also proceeded apace in England. The 54th Regiment, for example, sent officers and sergeants to towns all across Norfolk and put an advertisement in the *Norfolk Chronicle* appealing to "All Gentleman Volunteers who are willing and able to serve his Majesty." The ad promised one guinea in advance "and a crown to drink his Majesty's Health," as well as clothing, arms, and accoutrements (the latter two items being a bit of a stretch, since they were not the property of the soldier). The ad listed nine public houses—inns or taverns—in Norfolk towns where recruiters were waiting. "Any person who brings a recruit," the ad promised, "shall be amply rewarded for their Trouble." The ad also included the text of the December 16 proclamation about discharge at the end of the rebellion or after three years.[59]

The 21st Regiment of Foot, the Royal North British Fusiliers, was stationed in England at the beginning of 1775 but sent its recruiting officers to the Scottish highlands. "On Wednesday, no less than 70 fine young recruits, for the Royal North British Fuzileers, went from Glasgow to Greenock, in order to take shipping for Bristol," boasted an Edinburgh newspaper account. "And 80 highland recruits, within these few days, embarked at Dumfries for the aforesaid regiment."[60] In 1776, a recruiting officer for the 26th Regiment brokered an agreement with officials in the town of Cupar, Fifeshire, to pay a guinea to each recruit in addition to the usual bounty money.[61]

The 42nd Regiment, traditionally a highland corps that had recently taken to accepting "English & Irish without distinction,"[62] found itself in competition with other regiments for Scottish recruits. The regiment's colonel wrote to the secretary at war that his recruiting instructions stip-ulated "no men are to be inlisted under five feet Six Inches high without Shoes, except under Eighteen if likely to grow," but because "other Corps takes them much lower, will it be agreeable to your Lordship, I give orders to lower the Size one inch." He pointed out that "the Highlanders in general are not tall but Strong, and well made, and in my humble opinion, every way as fitt for Service & fatigue as those of a higher Size."[63] To fur-ther the regiment's connection with the highlands, the 42nd added a bag-piper for each company, in addition to drummers. Seeking to fill these new positions, an advertisement ran in the *Edinburgh Advertiser* in Oc-tober 1775 seeking "able bodied Highlanders, who are well skilled in playing Pibrochs." Not only would they receive drummers' pay and "a pair of new pipes with flags, and other advantages," but the enlistment bounty was three guineas for this specialized role. "He that is the best piper, and regularly bred at the colleges in the Isles of Skye and Mull, will be appointed piper major."[64]

Then there were the Germans. Europeans, more accurately, for among them were a smattering of Swedes, French, Swiss, Poles, Hungarians, Danes, and others. But almost all came from German states, and British writers at the time usually called them German recruits. The British gov-ernment negotiated with several German states to send existing German regiments to America, but they also contracted with a Hanoverian army officer, Lieutenant Colonel Georg Heinrich Albrecht von Scheither, to raise two thousand men in the electorate of Hanover as recruits for British regiments. Von Scheither set to work in late 1775, sending recruits in groups of a few hundred at a time to board transports for England. Although they enlisted in Hanover, a state ruled by the king of England, the recruits came from many German states—Brunswick, Saxony, Silesia, Bohemia, Waldeck, and others—as well as a smattering of other Euro-pean countries. They ranged in age from late teens to mid-thirties. About a third had previous army experience[65]—just like the men raised in Britain, they were not all new to military service—but those who were new did not receive the same sort of training with recruiting parties that British recruits did. The army's adjutant general called them "a Wild Multitude, & very bad & expensive plan."[66]

The two thousand or so German recruits were handled quite differ-ently than men recruited in the British Isles. Transports took them from German ports—Stade on the river Elbe, Bremen on the Weser—to

Portsmouth in England or Cork in Ireland, where they were assigned to British regiments. Those whose regiments were already overseas were issued a pair of shoes, two pairs of stockings, two shirts of checked linen, and a black neck stock, as well as "slop clothing" consisting of red jackets, white waistcoats, and breeches, cheaply made and without regimental distinctions.[67] Some never went ashore but instead transferred directly from the ships that brought them across the English Channel, upon which they had been "very much crowded on board,"[68] to those that would carry them across the Atlantic. Rather than being integrated immediately into their new regiments, or at least with other recruits for those regiments, they were often transported separately. In April 1776, 450 Germans assigned to regiments that had recently sailed for Canada were put onto three transports, with eighty British privates and eight noncommissioned officers also distributed among those ships, and three British commissioned officers assigned to each vessel. They stayed entirely too long on the ships, getting little exercise and training. A German artillery officer wrote from Portsmouth on June 20:

> A large number of recruits raised by Scheiter are lying here in the roadstead, ready to sail. There are many from Hanau and even more from Hesse among them. These men were equipped quickly and are quite poorly maintained. Their complaints are astonishing. I was on board one of their ships with my ship's captain yesterday, but in order no longer to hear their complaints, I hastened to leave the ship. . . . A part of these ships have lain here in the roadstead for eighteen to twenty weeks.[69]

These recruits finally arrived in Canada in September.[70] In May, three transports were allocated for 410 German recruits, with three British officers and twenty British drafts—experienced soldiers rather than recruits—on each ship.[71] The convoy carrying them and a large number of British recruits and drafts sailed first to Cork in Ireland and did not leave that port until August. It was October before they arrived in America.

Besides strengthening existing regiments with drafts and recruits, the War Office created an entire new regiment for the war in America composed of men from the highlands of Scotland. Simon Fraser, a veteran officer, was authorized in 1775 to raise two thousand men for the 71st Regiment of Foot, consisting of two battalions of ten companies each, with four sergeants, four corporals, two drummers, and one hundred private soldiers in each company—a total of some 2,200 men. "No price will be grudged for good men," proclaimed a leaflet circulated in Dundee in January 1776. "The advantages that will arise to those who inlist into this corps, are very great." It promised to discharge each "gentleman Volunteer" after three years—going so far as to clarify, "that is in 1779"—or at the end of the rebellion, and explained that with an army of fifty thousand men in the colonies in the coming year, "it cannot, in all human probability, fail to be entirely quelled, next summer." Then came the real enticement for tenant farmers: "Then, gentlemen, will be your harvest, and the best one too you ever cropt. You will, each of you, by visiting this new world, become the founders of families. The lands of the rebels will be divided amongst you, and every one of you become lairds." It pointed out that "no old regiment" would have this benefit, since their men would not be discharged at war's end (those enlisted before December 16, 1775, that is). If this wasn't enough, the flyer closed with an appeal designed to make every reader consider his present circumstances:

> Is not this better than starving at home in these poor times? and will a man of spirit sit unmoved, and hear such proffered terms? Ye who are now dreading the sentence of stool-meal, who are drudging like slaves under a cruel or harsh task-master. Any of you who have got a termagant or cross wife, or who smart under the displeasure of an ungracious parent, come all to Ensign Thomas Hamilton, and he will ease your fears, and make you at once free and happy.[72]

Plenty of men in the highlands responded to these attractive terms. Some were veterans willing to reenlist, ensuring that this new regiment was not composed solely of raw recruits. Men like Allan Roy Cameron from Ardnamurchan, Argyllshire, had served from 1756 through 1761 in the 42nd Regiment and joined the 71st at age forty-eight. Donald McPhee from Kilmallie near Fort William enlisted at forty-four, having served three years during the Seven Years' War "and was severely wounded on the Head by the splinter of a Bombshell" in Germany. Men over three decades old with no prior service also joined the ranks. Archibald McMillan enlisted at thirty-one, leaving his home in Inverness to answer the call to arms, as did thirty-year-old Kilmallie resident Hugh Duncan. On the other end of the spectrum were John Bogg, a sixteen-year-old nail maker from Rutherglen, Lanarkshire, and nineteen-year-old weaver Hugh Cameron from Lochaber, Inverness-shire. The war in America and the subsequent reward of land offered an exit from "a cruel or harsh task-master," "a termagant or cross wife," or "an ungracious parent."[73]

A British militia sergeant engaged to recruit for the 71st received orders to limit his efforts to men at least five feet, four inches tall, no more than thirty years old, and with no prior military service (either exceptions were made to the age and service criteria, or other recruiters were given different instructions). There were the usual stipulations about physical condition—"straight and well made, Broad Shouldered, a good face and in every respect fit for his Majesty's Service," no evidence of "Rupture, Broken bones, Kings evil Running Sores on any part of His Body, Falling sickness or ffits, and in a word any Infirmity in Body or Limbs." No apprentices were to be enlisted, since they were already under another form of service contract. And of course no "Stroller, Vagabond or Sailor."[74] When the new regiment arrived at Greenock to embark for America, an officer of the 42nd Regiment called them "Stout, raw & irregular."[75]

Throughout 1775, 1776, and 1777, recruiting continued. Regiments in Britain refilled ranks depleted by drafts, and additional companies of regiments in America gathered men to replenish wartime attrition. The recruits learned to keep themselves clean and walk like soldiers, to march in formation and eventually to handle and maintain a firearm. Once or twice each year, when enough recruits were ready, an additional company officer took them onto a transport for the voyage to America, for many, their first time off their native soil, the adventure of a lifetime, from which they might never return.

CHAPTER 7

Barracks and Barns,
Transports and Tents,
Wigwams and Blankets

"I WOULD HAVE GIVEN THE WHOLE WORLD that I could be on shore, but I had made my own bed and felt that I must lie on it," recalled William Burke, a twenty-three-year-old Irishman in the 45th Regiment of Foot, of a two-day storm at sea.[1] Having enlisted only the previous year, he was making the Atlantic crossing that every British soldier who served in America—except for the smattering born in the colonies—made at least once, some several times. Most experienced at least one storm during each voyage. Dangerous though it was, the crews of warships and transports had a seafaring heritage to draw on, and fatalities during the passage were rare.

For transatlantic voyages, transport ships carrying soldiers were apportioned at the rate of two tons of shipping per man, such that two hundred men were put on board a four hundred ton vessel, and so forth; for shorter voyages along the Atlantic coast, one and a half tons was typical, sometimes even less if shipping was in short supply.[2] Transports were private vessels operating under contract to the Royal Navy, and there was no standard size or design.[3] Most transports carried two or three of a regiment's ten companies, that is, one hundred to three hundred men, while a few were big enough to carry an entire regiment at peacetime strength, about five hundred men. Tonnage was allocated for six soldiers' wives per company, although more might actually be on board depending upon how well embarkation orders were enforced,[4] and a number of children might also be on board with no tonnage allotted for them. Officers traveled on the same ships. When parties of recruits and drafts boarded transports, at least one army officer was on board each vessel; a transport might carry recruits for more than one regiment, and the accompanying officer might not be from the same regiment as any of them.[5] Soon after war broke out, transports carrying provisions and other stores took on parties of recruits, usually twenty to forty under the care of an officer, for protection against enemy ships.[6]

The officers oversaw the men's health and welfare by enforcing a set of orders to be observed while on board ship, orders propagated either through the regiment or through army officials at the port of embarkation. A few sets of these orders survive, and while no two are the same, the gist is similar. Provisions for the voyage were furnished by the master of the transport, who was reimbursed by the government, and charged to the men at a rate of three pence per day, half the cost of subsistence on land. Bedding or hammocks were brought on deck to dry and air every day that weather permitted, and berthing areas belowdecks were ventilated as well as possible, swept regularly, and occasionally sprinkled with vinegar for cleanliness. No smoking was allowed belowdecks, nor candles without lanterns; gambling was prohibited.[7] Whenever possible, men went on deck for fresh air and exercise. Above all, "The greatest Harmony is to be kept up with the Master of the Vessel & those under him."[8]

In case of encounters with privateers, sixty rounds of ammunition per man were kept available and inspected periodically. Recruits on their way to join regiments were issued arms out of ordnance stores for use during the voyage that were returned to army stores upon arrival in America, since their regiments would issue arms to them.[9] Men were divided into watches, usually three, and assigned duty stations in case of alarm. Some transports carried a few cannons, which some soldiers helped man while others fought with muskets; activities were practiced periodically during the voyage. An officer of the 42nd Regiment had his men practice using mattresses as defensive cover along the ship's railings in case of attack.[10] Recruits continued their training: "priming, loading, and leveling and firing well at a mark are the principal objects to be attended to in this kind of exercise."[11] Target practice was effected by having "a target fixed to the end of the fore-yard-arm, which the troops are to be exercised every day in firing at with a single ball, in order to perfect them in shooting."[12] And of course, "In case of attack the Officer is to make the best defence he possibly can with his Detachment. A Judicious Gallant Behaviour on such an Occasion must recommend an Officer very Essentially."[13]

"The six Regiments who go from here are in the highest spirits, and I can with pleasure say and without vanity that we are by far the finest Regiment of the whole, both in figure and discipline," boasted an officer of the 9th Regiment of Foot as his corps embarked at Cork in April 1776.[14] The prospect of a sea voyage was exciting, the actual experience tedious and dangerous. "I stood on deck eying my native country with indescribable emotions, as the land was disappearing from my view," wrote Roger Lamb of the same regiment as his transport headed for Quebec.[15] Being at sea was new to many if not most soldiers, with the expected initial effects. "The Soldiers are mighty Sick," wrote a young officer of his twenty recruits for the 8th Regiment of Foot in May 1776, five days out of the Thames estuary on a ship called the *Canadian* carrying four hundred barrels of gunpowder to Quebec. Within two days, however, they were all "quite recovered" and "amused ourselves fishing for Macarel."[16] When men were not busy standing watch and practicing with arms, there were new and wondrous sights to behold: flying fish, sharks, sea turtles, seals, and icebergs. Occasionally ships from other places came within speaking distance, bringing much-sought-after news, as when the recruits for the 8th heard "the account of the troops quitting Boston" two months after it occurred.[17] The approach of an unidentified vessel caused a ship "to be clear'd & man'd, 12 rounds given to the men." Nothing came of the encounter, and "the men order'd to draw their charge & clean their firelocks."[18]

Boredom and cramped quarters took their toll. Thomas Sullivan of the 49th described a dispute that broke out on his transport in May 1775, after several weeks at sea, between soldiers and sailors; officers broke it up "after some struggle and a few blows between them," but then the sailors refused to work the ship, and there were too few soldiers with nautical knowledge to take their place. It took a visit from the regiment's commanding officer, coming in a small boat from another transport, to put things right.[19]

Roger Lamb recounted three men on his transport intentionally jumping overboard. On April 20, 1776, William Brooks "leaped off the forecastle into the ocean; the vessel in a moment made her way over him, and he arose at the stern. He immediately with all his might, swam from the ship." The vessel came about and launched a boat crew that managed, with some difficulty, to haul Brooks in. "The fear of punishment was the cause of this desperate action, as the day before he had stolen a shirt from one of his messmates knapsacks." On April 30, "a serjeant had an altercation with his wife while they were sitting at breakfast, in consequence of which he got up in a rage, leaped overboard and was seen no more," and three days later "one of the recruits stationed on the forecastle was so provoked by his comrades, that in a fit of rage he jumped over board, uttering at the same time dreadful curses upon them. He was swallowed up by the great deep in a moment!"[20]

"A man of the 22d Light Company fell over board, and was drownded," noted an officer on August 19, 1777, in Chesapeake Bay, referring to Andrew Handley, who had served in the regiment for over a dozen years.[21] Muster rolls confirm other deaths at sea but give no cause, leaving it a mystery how many died of illness and how many went overboard by design or by accident.

Storms seldom sunk ships but caused havoc on board. "We are tossed about terribly & broke most of plates & Glasses," recalled an officer, adding as the storm persisted five days later, "we Are all in bad Spirits, as we Cant amuse ourselves at Cards or reading, as the Hatches are all Shut down & we are quite in darkness." Another recalled, "it blowing pretty hard & a rough sea, there was much tumbling about in the cabin . . . some broken ribs & other bruises." "The Transports, with the poor Soldiers, were tossed about exceedingly, & exposed at times to much Danger in running foul of each other." Robert Reeves of the 31st Regiment and James McKilligan of the 37th each had leg bones broken while on transports, and James McPherson of the 82nd manned pumps in his leaking ship for three weeks before falling down a hatch and being injured in the chest. Henry Brown, whose career took him through three regiments, had the misfortune of being "bruised in the side & privates by a fall of a cask of rum" on a ship, "since which he cannot retain his water."[22] Most men, however, got through their voyages unscathed. As soon as safe land was near, soldiers were often allowed ashore for a few hours at a time, "more by way of exercise to the Troops, than to gain any other advantage than procuring some fresh provisions."[23]

The duration of voyages varied greatly. William Burke and the 45th Regiment made it in from Cork to Boston in seven weeks in May and June 1775,[24] while later in the year, contrary winds kept the *Grand Duke of Russia*, carrying six companies of the 55th, at sea twice as long, sailing on September 22, arriving on December 30, and finally disembarking on January 4, 1776. The troops of the 55th made the long journey "without having one sick person on board or loseing any Life in the Voyage," but a transport carrying six companies of the 17th Regiment that was near them the entire time "landed with us here very sickly"; no reason was

Soldiers crossed the Atlantic, and sailed along the American coast, in private vessels contracted by the Royal Navy. Ships of all shapes and sizes were used as transports, typically carrying one to four companies depending on size. These ships were drawn by a British officer on the voyage from Nova Scotia to New York in 1776. Sketch by Archibald Robinson. (*New York Public Library*)

This room in a postwar British cavalry barracks is probably more commodious than most wartime infantry barracks in America, but conveys the social aspects of soldiers living with their wives and children in garrison towns. *English Barracks*, Thomas Rowlandson, circa 1788. (*Anne S. K. Brown Collection, Brown University Library*)

given for the disparate conditions on the two ships.[25] The time on board was lengthened by the time between embarkation and setting sail—often protracted by unfavorable winds or waiting for other ships to be ready—and between arrival and disembarkation, often delayed while awaiting availability of shore accommodations. Roger Lamb embarked at Cork on April 3, 1776, and was watching the coast of Ireland slip away only five days later, whereas John Robertshaw, a recruit in the 33rd, boarded in Portsmouth on January 11, 1778, waited four weeks to sail, and made an eight-week stopover in Cork while a convoy assembled before finally sailing on April 7.[26] Troops bound for Quebec faced an extra week or two working their way up the St. Lawrence River, respited by calm if not slow sailing and extensive views of the countryside. Among the longest voyages was that of German recruits who embarked at Stade on the Elbe River on May 25, 1776, sailed to Spithead to join a convoy, then to Cork to increase the convoy, and finally to New York, arriving on October 20. After five months on transports, it is no wonder they were "very sickly during the passage."[27]

For the most part, efforts to maintain cleanliness and nutrition were effective, and troops arrived in America in reasonably good health. Disease did sometimes break out, such as on the way from New York to Charleston in January 1780, when there were "ten or eleven of the 38th ill of a fever supposed to be contracted from the wetness of their births, but it does not appear to be infectious," according to an officer on their transport; "the 42d only 5 sick. 3 of the flux & 2 of the ague." The reason for the wet berths was clear: "the men complain much for some time past of the water come thro' the deck upon them, the seams open from the working of the Boats."[28] In one extreme exception to the usual safe albeit harrowing passage, recruits landed in New York at the end of August 1779 after a "voyage of four months and ten days from the time we embarked."[29] Disease, which may have boarded with the troops, ran rampant on this trip, exacerbated by the length of time in cramped quarters. Of 1,325 recruits in the convoy, 43 died during the voyage and 285 were sick when they arrived in New York.[30]

Once securely on land, British soldiers in America found shelter in accommodations ranging from purpose-built military barracks to blankets on the ground, depending on what was available in garrison or on campaign. The city of New York had a barracks built in the 1760s, as did Trenton, Philadelphia, and Lancaster. Boston had Castle William on an island in the harbor. All housed British troops when under British control but were far too small to shelter wartime force levels. Even outposts like Fort Niagara in western New York became crowded when locally raised Loyalist corps increased the size of garrisons and civilian refugees sought safety from a war that polarized the population.

In cities, available buildings, some abandoned, some appropriated, were converted to barracks. Wartime exigencies took precedence over the peacetime Quartering Acts, but the army nonetheless avoided putting soldiers into private homes unless other options were not available. "From the number of houses at this Moment habitable in this town, and the number of troops to be quartered in it," wrote an officer in Newport, Rhode Island, in 1778 as winter approached, "it would not appear by any means difficult to quarter the troops with great convenience . . . but the method of quartering troops in America, is in every particular totally different from what I have ever seen. From the circumstances of affairs at Boston, there was a necessity of providing empty houses, Stores, and such other places as could be hired, for the use of the troops, since when the same method seems in great measure to be followed tho' the circumstances are totally changed."[31] The year before in Philadelphia, an officer recorded, "The Light Infantry goes into the Barracks, the Grenadiers into the House of Employment."[32] A resident of Greenwich, a village on Manhattan, complained at the end of the war, "In the Year 1781 her House was converted into a Barrack for the 42nd Regt.—about 40 Common Soldiers, & 3 Officers being quartered in the different Rooms of it. By this means a great part of the remaining fence of the Farm was destroyed."[33] Buildings converted into barracks varied widely, from churches to warehouses on wharves, size being the only common factor. Around garrisoned cities, barrack buildings were constructed near fortifications guarding strategic locations like Bristol Ferry in Rhode Island and Kingsbridge in New York. Unlike the permanent structures built in the 1760s, these were probably lighter and more economically built, needed only for the duration of the war, which was expected to be short. Plans survive for the prewar barracks, and the one in Trenton has been meticulously restored, but little detail exists on the construction and quality of wartime barracks. Regardless of the building, however, there were common elements of barracks life.

By the standards of working-class living in the 1770s and 1780s, barracks were comfortable. The purpose-built peacetime barracks held twelve to sixteen men in each room; those built during the war were likely similar, while retrofitted buildings probably varied. Bunks built of boards lined the walls. In some cases, each berth held more than one man; preparing for winter in Rhode Island in 1777, for example, meant "The houses allotted for the Winter Quarters, to be repaired as soon as possible, and in such Rooms as are large, and convenient, the births to be made for three Men."[34] The army provided barrack bedding and furniture such as palliasses (linen bags filled with straw to serve as mattresses), sheets, coarse blankets called rugs, barrack blankets (separate from the soldiers' own blankets), iron pots, trammels, firedogs, tongs, fire shovels, fire grates, candlesticks, tables, bowls, trenchers (plates), spoons, ladles, and whatever other odds and ends might be needed for the specific building.[35] Each room was fitted with a stove or fireplace, and the men received an allowance of straw (for the palliasses), firewood (or sometimes coal), and candles. Each garrison appointed an officer as barrack master whose responsibilities included inventorying and periodic inspection of the barrack furniture. Losses or damage were charged to the regiment, and ultimately to the soldiers responsible.[36] When a regiment left a barracks, it returned bedding and furniture to stores or turned them over to new occupants.

Cleanliness and ventilation were essential to maintain health. "Every day when the Weather permits the Mens Bedding and Blankets to be taken out of the Barrack Rooms thoroughly shaked and Air'd, the Windows thrown open and the rooms kept as Clean as possible."[37] Noncommissioned officers slept in the same rooms as the private soldiers and ensured that everything was kept in good order, while officers might have separate rooms in the same building or lodgings nearby. Rooms were to be swept regularly, as were the "yards, with all the avenues leading to the Barracks," ensuring that no "dirt or nastiness" prevented them from being "always sweet and healthy."[38] Chimneys were swept periodically— monthly in Boston; every six weeks in Rhode Island.[39] A couple of towels in each room, changed regularly, reduced the likelihood of men wiping their hands on bedding.[40] Pegs or nails afforded places to conveniently hang hats, knapsacks, and accoutrements.[41] Weapons and accoutrements were "so placed that they may get at them in the Dark, so that in Case of Alarm they may turn Out without Confusion."[42]

Maintaining army property in good order required constant reminders to opportunistic soldiers. "Complaint having been made that some of the Regiments make an improper use of their sheets, by carrying bread in them, it is the Commander in Chief's orders that no part of the barrack furniture is applied to any other purpose but such as it is designed for, nor taken out of the barracks on any account whatever,"[43] troops were told in Boston during winter 1774–1775. "The troops on no account to carry coals, bread, or any other thing in their Sheets, or Blankets," was the direction given in Rhode Island in February 1777.[44] "Information having been given to Major Genl Pattison that the Pump belonging to the Barrack occupied by the Light Infantry of the Guards during last Winter was taken away, and the Well upon their leaving the Town filled up with Rubbish" in New York in 1779, an inquiry eventually led to the recovery of the pump, which an inhabitant had purchased from a Foot Guards sergeant.[45]

Married soldiers were "indulged with liberty" of living with their wives outside the barracks, as long as they found suitable quarters nearby.[46] This indulgence could invite opportunism, as it did for Thomas McMahon of the 43rd Regiment and his wife, Isabella. They lived in a house in Boston in December 1775; three soldiers from the 59th, whom they knew, came by one night and asked to store some bundles of clothing and fabric at the house, claiming they had found the goods in an abandoned building. The McMahons agreed to store the goods, help divvy them up, and sell some things off. The goods were in reality stolen from a local shopkeeper, a theft for which a military court convicted the men of the 59th and sentenced Thomas and Isabella McMahon to lashing for receiving stolen goods.[47] In New York in January 1777, the commander of the 15th Regiment gave orders that "married men who are allowed to lie out of the barracks" were not to be in the streets after 9 PM, and a week later that married men were not to be absent from formation during an alarm; violators of either order would "not only be confined but not be allowed to lie out of the barrack thereafter."[48]

It took more than barracks to quarter a wartime army. Even if enough suitable buildings were available, which was not the case in war-torn New York, location was a factor: troops needed to be quartered where they could be brought quickly to action. Boards and other building materials were in high demand for platforms and other components of fortifications, limiting the number of new barracks that could be built close to the lines. Huts were the solution, structures built into hillsides to take advantage of the earth's natural protection, the dug-out material used to complete side walls. Limited supplies of boards, doors, and windows walled off the open ends, with thatching for roofs. Fireplaces were easily built into the dugout end wall. Arranged in rows along south-facing hillsides to admit the most sunlight and keep the north wind out, with huts

for officers behind and above those of the soldiers, brigade-sized cantonments of huts sprang up on Long Island and Manhattan beginning with
the onset of winter in 1776. For the next seven years, cantonments were
occupied each winter, with huts renovated and new cantonments built,
such that almost every British soldier in the region spent at least one winter huddled in a hut.

Huts had been used in other wars and other places. Soldiers of the
6th Regiment suffered in poorly made huts on the island of St. Vincent
during the Carib War in 1773:

> The Regiment has above one hundred and fifty men constantly
> upon duty, one captain and two subalterns about twelve miles, an-
> other above twenty advanced into the Carib Country, who lodge in
> huts made of wild Canes, Houses so little adapted to this climate,
> that in the end the soldier must suffer extreamly, during the Heat
> they can scarcely breathe in them, and in the Rains which are most
> excessive for at least six months of the year, they are in danger some-
> times of drowning. I have often been above the ancle in Water in
> going into the soldiers Huts, in spite of all precautions.[49]

With carpenters, masons, thatchers, glaziers, nailers, and legions of
laborers in each regiment's ranks, there was plenty of skill and brawn to
build huts. Captain John Peebles, commander of the grenadier company
of the 42nd Regiment, devoted many lines of his diary to the process of
building huts for the 1st Battalion of Grenadiers outside the town of Jamaica on Long Island in November 1778. On the eighth, an engineering
officer brought workmen and tools "to give directions & assist in making
Hutts for the men." Two days later, "The Ground for the huts being
mark'd out in the morning on the South side of the hill north of Town,
the men with a few tools they had, broke ground & fell to work to make
huts for their abode in Winter, each hutt 24 feet by 12 to contain 12 men
the wall partly dug in the face of the hill, & the rest made up of sod, the
roof to be covered with cedar branches & straw or thin sod." Four huts
could accommodate most grenadier companies at attrition-reduced
strength, while the double-sized companies of the 42nd and 71st Regiments required six or seven. Throughout the week the grenadiers worked
at their huts; on the eighteenth, Captain Peebles visited the cantonment
site of the 42nd Regiment's battalion companies and discovered "they are
more forward than we are." The next day he lamented of "the huts coming on but slowly, it is almost time now for the men to be under better
shelter than an old tent."[50]

Two weeks into the process, materials became an issue. On November 23, "the work on the Hutts at a stand for want of Nails & straw," Peebles wrote. "All the wagons here about gone to the Eastward for boards to make doors, windows & Beds, which should have been provided before, but there seems to be a want of that care of & attention to the Troops that is necessary, & that we used to experience." Four days later, Peebles "sent to flushing fly for Thatch for the Hutts, no more straw to be had." By November 28, the roofs were done and berths were being built inside, and finally on the thirtieth, the soldiers could occupy their new abodes. On December 2, they were still working on the huts, "trimming them in the inside & getting doors & windows made—one pane of glass in each hutt."[51]

The following winter, things were easier for the grenadier battalion: they returned to the same huts. Having been vacant all summer, they required repair, which the soldiers set to in spite of having no tools. But within two weeks, by mid-November, they were lodged once again, having only the hut for the company officers to complete.[52] That same November 1779, the Brigade of Guards set about building a cantonment at Kingsbridge on the north end of Manhattan. The work took even longer than it had for the grenadiers in 1778, hampered by harsh weather and significant shortages of materials:

> Upon our going down we encamped on the hills until we learnt that we were to winter there, when we set about building huts, which, however, from the vast scarcity of materials we could not get finished until after Christmas, during which time we had a great deal of snow and bad weather. When we began building our huts we were obliged to send without the lines to get wood, all the trees having been cut down when the works at this post were erected. . . . Sometimes the weather was so extremely severe that the men could not work.[53]

In 1780, the two British grenadier battalions had to build new huts, this time outside of Newtown on Long Island. Again they faced shortages, this time being "told at the parade to begin our Hutts with such tools as we can borrow in the Neighbourhood, till we get others from N: York." These huts were twice the size of the previous ones, so that the 42nd's grenadier company required "three Hutts of two Rooms, each 14 feet Square, 24 men in each hutt." In spite of an early start in mid-September, by November 2, Peebles complained, "The late bad weather retards our Hutts & this cold weather makes it necessary to get them finish'd soon." The grenadier company of the 43rd had managed to finish its huts the previous week. The 42nd's finally had roofs by the fourth, and interiors completed a week later.[54]

When new huts were built, sometimes new techniques were tried, and sometimes things went wrong. To build chimney tops in the Newtown huts, soldiers drew on skills they had learned in the army. They wove cylinders from saplings and brush, frameworks called gabions that were normally filled with earth to quickly assemble field fortifications. For chimney tops, they applied clay and straw to the gabions to make a sort of terra-cotta tube. The unfortunate drawback was recorded by Captain Peebles on December 3: "one of our huts catched fire in the top of the Chimney, the consequence of a great mistake in the fabrication, they being top'd with Gabion work plaster'd with cut Straw & Clay, which we now find is subject to take fire, so may expect more accidents of that kind, & perhaps be entirely burnt out before winter is over, some of the Mens own faults who advised this kind of tops to the Chimneys." This was not the first time a hut had caught fire. In November 1779, a hut of the 33rd Regiment's light infantry company burned, forcing the occupants into tents until it was rebuilt. On September 27, 1780, while the grenadier battalions worked on their new huts, "an old Hutt at New Town burnt & a Corporal of the 43d in it."[55] There is no record of a man of the 43rd dying on this date, suggesting that the corporal survived the ordeal.

Bedding and furniture for huts came from the barrack master's department just as it did for barracks, delivered as soon as the huts were ready for occupancy. When fair weather meant it was time to leave the huts behind, bedding and blankets were returned. Captain Peebles noted in June 1781, "Barrack bedding given in & like fools we did not keep good blankets."[56] He may have realized it would have been easier to keep the blankets and pay for them than to find others, or he may have had inferior blankets to turn in instead of those his men had drawn from the barrack master; although he followed proper procedure, he recognized the missed chance to better take care of his men, albeit at the army's expense.

"We are in hopes the Ground will soon be dry enough to encamp without much risk to the Health of the Army, at all Events I am afraid it will add to the Sick List, used as our Soldiers have been for these five Months in hot Stoves,"[57] wrote an aide-de-camp from Montreal in spring 1777. Comfortable though barracks and cantonments were, summer months in garrison were passed in encampments. Around the end of May or early June, the army laid out encampments on ground chosen for proximity to key locations, drainage, and overall security. Rows of five-man tents, about ten sheltering a typical company, faced each other to form streets, with parallel streets forming a regiment's camp; in America, grenadier and light infantry companies were usually detached, so four streets were enough.[58] If the lay of the land didn't allow this arrangement, alternatives were used such as long rows of tents similar to the hut arrangements in cantonments. The regiment could form at the head of the streets; officers' tents were to the rear, and behind them, kitchens. Conical bell tents stored firelocks upright with the butts on the ground, dry and ready, at the front of each street, but it is not clear whether these tents were always used.

Each year camp equipage arrived from Great Britain in time for the summer season. Each infantry regiment received its proportion: for each five-man mess, a tent six feet wide and seven feet tall, its canvas staked down at each side and draped over a ridge pole six feet above the ground to form a canvas A-frame; two wooden standard (vertical) poles and a ridge (horizontal) pole; a tin-plated kettle with a lid and a bag to carry it; and two hatchets. Each man received a tin-plated canteen and a linen canvas haversack to sling over one shoulder to hold three or four days' worth of provisions.[59] In wartime America, each man had a blanket, a luxury compared to the two blankets for five men issued during peaceful years in Britain.[60] Locally procured fresh straw, anywhere from five to thirty-five pounds per tent, provided fresh bedding every few weeks.[61]

The army in Boston, not yet on a war footing, had tents that were old and worn out, not up to the job of protecting the army into the late months of 1775. "The weather for some time has been very wet and dis-agreeable, and what still renders it more so, our tents do not keep out the rain," wrote an officer from Bunker Hill in mid-October.[62] A month later, another officer described his own corps' temporary solution that lasted until the second week of December: "Those Regiments who have De-camp't have Supplied us with Tents to double our mens, which were ex-tremely cold without."[63] Wrote a third officer, "We came into winter quarters two days ago. It was full time, for our tents were so shattered that we might as well almost have lain in the open field."[64] For the most part, new tents arrived each subsequent year in time for the encampment season, although occasionally tents were sent to one place while the reg-iment was in another.[65]

A navy official visiting Staten Island in August 1776 saw encampment life as harsh, writing, "'Tis a hard unpleasant Life this of Soldier's, which is passed in a little paltry Tent which will neither keep out Wind, or Rain, or Vermin, and which seems to have little other Solace on this dusty Is-land than the Association of multitudes in the same Condition. The Ship is a House or a Palace compared with the Accommodations of the mili-tary."[66] Of an encampment near Quebec in July of the same year, an of-ficer of the 53rd Regiment related, "the weather was then intensely hot, scarce bearable in a camp, where the tents rather increased than dimin-ished it, and the great number of men in so small a space made it very disagreeable, though we all went as thinly clothed as possible, wearing large loose trousers to prevent the bite of the moscheto, a small fly which was then very troublesome." Although this suggested that sickness would prevail, he continued, "Our men in general were very healthy, and not much troubled with fevers and fluxes, so common when encamped in a warm climate, and lying nights on the ground under a heavy dew."[67]

Severe weather could be too much even for new tents, anchored to the ground by a dozen or so wooden pegs around the perimeter. At least three times in 1777 and 1778, tents in Rhode Island were uprooted by storms, including an August 1778 hurricane after which an officer recorded, "Most of the tents are blown down and torn to pieces . . . the troops are at present in a most uncomfortable situation . . . every thing belonging to the men being perfectly soaked with the rain."[68] Even when tents remained standing and watertight in heavy rains, if drainage was insufficient a camp could be "overflow'd," as was the Long Island camp of the 1st Battalion of Grenadiers in August 1779: "the ground being of a close clay soil bears the water on its surface for a long time."[69] In cold weather, soldiers sometimes supplemented tents by building A-frame shelters of brush or boughs over them, or small earthen walls around the edges.[70] Delays in readiness of barracks that left men in tents late in the year caused soldiers to "suffer a good deal from the severity of the weather."[71] When weather was fine, however, encampments on well-cho-sen ground were comfortable, safe, and easy to move when necessary. When camps stayed in one place, soldiers added what amenities they could. "The Men employed in making Bowers before their Tents," wrote an officer on Long Island in June 1781, referring to shades made of boughs that provided a sort of porch for the soldiers' canvas homes.[72]

The principle benefit of encampments was, of course, mobility. Around garrisons, camps could be moved quickly to ground that was fresher, healthier, more strategic, or safer.[73] Tents also provided shelter on campaign, when armies were on the move. Orders given on campaigns illustrate different considerations for placement and preparation of encampments, accounting for terrain, vegetation, and hostile threats. Early in the march from Canada toward Albany in 1777, a brigade in General Burgoyne's army was ordered to encamp "in double Rows" about a dozen yards apart, with thirty yards between each of the brigade's three regiments, on ground "fronting the Wood and as near the Lake as the Land will permit for the benefit of the Air, the whole being nearly in a line." Quarter guards were placed "well advanced into the Wood," kitchens in the rear, necessary houses "in the front beyond the Quarter Guards, with Centrys over them from each of those Guards."[74] For sanitation, "Great attention to be paid to the cleanliness of the Camp, Garbage and Nastiness of all kinds to be immediately buried."[75] While encampments around the city of New York and in Rhode Island could be conveniently placed in fields prevalent in those agrarian regions, Burgoyne's army moved through relative wilderness that often required clearing to make room for an orderly encampment:

> The Camp will always be extended as widely as the Ground will Admit For the Sake of Cleanliness and of Health, but as it must often happen that the extent will be insufficient for the Line to form in the front of the Encampment According to the present Established Rule of open Files and Two Deep, the Quarter Master General will therefore Mark at every new Camp the portion of Ground each Battalion is to clear, over and above its own Front in Order to make the Work equal. To clear this Ground must be the immediate business after Arriving in Camp and in this Country, it may often be necessary to have an alarm post cleared in the Rear as well as in the Front. By clearing is meant the Removal of such obstructions as might prevent the ready forming of the Troops to receive or advance upon the Enemy. It is not necessary to cut the large Trees for that purpose, except where they may afford Shelter for the Enemy.[76]

Whether at the end of a summer encampment or when pulling up stakes on campaign, tents, each clearly marked with the regiment and company to which it belonged, were folded and rolled up so the markings were visible, "in order to prevent any confusion in future in delivering them."[77] Ideally, they were carried on baggage wagons, but when those vehicles were in short supply, as they often were in America, horses, called batt horses, hauled tents and baggage.[78] Occasionally, soldiers carried the tent poles so as not to overload wagons or horses.[79]

For armies on the move and moving quickly, wagons and batt horses were an impediment rather than a convenience, and time was much too precious to spend clearing ground, pitching tents, and digging kitchens, only to pack up and move on the next day. So British troops campaigning in America often did without, bedding down with blankets in an assortment of improvised shelters.

"Most of us lye in Barns upon a blanket," wrote a light infantry officer from Staten Island in July 1776.[80] His regiment had just arrived there, and camp equipage was not yet unloaded from transports; their time in barns was an expedient until tents came ashore. Toward the end of August, though, in preparation for a few months of campaigning, explicit orders came: "The Light Infantry are not to have Tents as they expect to be in constant motion."[81] Even though other troops nominally retained tents, the speed of campaigns left them unused for days at a time. Wagons moved them into place only every few days when a rest and regroup was required. Soldiers of the 22nd, 43rd, 54th, and 63rd Regiments spent their first night on Manhattan in September 1776 in "houses and Barns on each side of the road from the 3 mile stone, to within a short distance of a redoubt the Enemy made at the North end of the Town." Two weeks later, "The Light Infantry cantoned in the farm houses and Barns near Bloomingdale."[82] By the end of November, the army was in New Jersey, where, "We marched to Newark & were there cantoned, the enemy had evacuated it only in the morning & had left their quarters in great haste; we found the rooms in the houses very unclean from the filth and dirt of the rebel troops."[83]

And so it went on every campaign. The army that marched through New Jersey in November and December 1776 and halted at Trenton, blocked by the Delaware River and the onset of winter from further advance. Quartered in buildings, soldiers in the 17th Regiment of Foot were told, "As no Straw Can be got the men are to Make use of Watchcoats and Blankets by Way of Bedding." Rooms were to be swept each day, kept "as cool as possible" by opening windows. Fires were allowed only outside, and an officer was to visit each evening and call the rolls. The regiment turned out for parade each morning at ten, and at other times, "The officers are to take Care that the mens Arms and Accoutrements be so placed that they may get at them in the Dark, so that in Case of Alarm they may turn Out without Confusion."[84] When troops landed in Portsmouth, Rhode Island, on December 8, 1776, they spent their first night in "Houses & barns some of which were inhabited and others not," and remained for a few weeks while barracks were prepared, enduring "Clinking hard frost & very cold for the poor soldiers in the barn."[85] A German officer in Canada noted in September 1776 that his "troops were quartered in a barn, in which they all lay together, by his regiment. This is done by all the English and Germans here in Canada."[86] On campaign, barns and outbuildings were a convenience for one or a few days until the army moved to its next stop; in garrison, they provided interim shelter while preparing barracks or huts.[87] Sometimes the barrack bedding was delivered while the troops were still in barns, affording a bit more comfort in the temporary lodgings.

One of the most difficult winters was the first in America for many of the troops that experienced it, spread out across New Jersey in houses, barns, and whatever other space could be had. "The light infantry were always in front of the army, and not allowed tents," wrote an officer of the 52nd Regiment's light infantry company about living in New Jersey in early 1777. "We generally quartered our men in farmhouses and barns, or made huts when houses were not conveniently situated, and we were always so near to the enemy that the men never pulled off their accoutrements, and were always ready to turn out at a minute's warning."[88] Another light infantry officer described conditions in Brunswick, New Jersey, where he was "miserably ill lodged; my whole company, which consists of 53 men, are obliged to live in one small room, and I am in a pigeon hole, with 11 officers, where we eat, drink, and sleep."[89] Similar conditions were endured in Hillsborough, Raritan, Woodbridge, Amboy, Elizabeth, and other towns.[90] Being spread out at posts miles apart "Incouraged the Enemy to Attack us Frequently," wrote an officer of the 42nd Regiment, "But by being very Vigilant, and neither officer nor Soldier Throwing off his Cloaths During the Winter, We never were surprised."[91] A light infantry officer echoed the danger and vigilance: "I don't believe a man of this army ... have had their clothes off; for my part, except one fortnight, I have not been uncased these ten months."[92]

Describing a foraging expedition outside of Philadelphia in late December 1778, a German staff officer wrote, "Our men constructed temporary cover as well as they could. We did not have tents with us, as we almost never did during this whole campaign."[93] He could have been describing almost every campaign in America from the operations in New York and New Jersey in 1776 to the march through North Carolina in 1781. The army typically moved at a rapid pace for three or four days, leaving baggage behind, then halted for a day or two, resting and allowing baggage, including tents, to catch up. Buildings of any sort were often too few for masses of soldiers stretched in columns or spread across a wide front. An officer of the 40th Regiment, two days after landing on Manhattan in September 1776, summed up many days on many campaigns throughout the war: "No tents, built wigwams."[94]

Writing on the same day, a staff officer provided more detail about how the army was sheltered: "The Camp Equipage and Baggage of the Army has not yet been brought over from Long Island, owing to the difficulty of transporting so many Waggons and horses. Most of the troops therefore remain without tents, but they have made wigwams or other shelter for themselves. Some Corps lie in Barns which are near their posts."[95] Campaigning in Pennsylvania a year later, the 2nd Battalion of Light Infantry received orders "to make Wigwams as fast as possible."[96] Foraging in New Jersey in November 1778, an officer of the 63rd recalled, "the 26th, 33d 63d and a Company of Guards remained here three nights in wigwams" while demolishing a recently abandoned enemy fortification.[97] Writing from Portsmouth, Virginia, at the end of March 1781, General William Phillips informed his superior that "the weather has been and continues this morning so extremely stormy and raining that it will prevent any arrangements being made for the troops, and indeed it will require time to prepare huts and wigwams."[98]

Wigwams were an American contrivance, so much so that a British military dictionary defined the term simply as "a hut used in America."[99] Very different from the sod-walled huts dug into garrison slopes, wigwams were temporary shelters built of boughs and branches. They were seldom described in any detail, and while the few images depicting them show A-frame structures similar in shape to tents, they may have taken whatever shape soldiers could quickly construct with scavenged materials. An officer of the 76th Regiment recalled campaigning in Virginia, where "Our encampments were always chosen on the banks of a stream, and were extremely picturesque, as we had no tents, and were obliged to construct wigwams of fresh boughs to keep off the rays of the sun during the day. At night, the blazing fires which we made of fence-rails illuminated the surrounding scenery, which, in this part of America, is of the most magnificent description."[100]

"On the first shots being fired at our piquet the battalion was out and under arms in a minute," wrote an officer about the surprise of his light infantry encampment at Germantown in October 1777. The British light infantry had only recently surprised General Anthony Wayne's brigade of American troops at Paoli, and "so much had they in recollection Wayne's affair that many of them rushed out of the back part of the huts."[101] This suggests that their wigwams—or whatever shelters they were using—were open at both ends, or that the soldiers simply broke through whatever closure there was. Wigwams were probably seldom sufficient cover in severe weather, as evidenced by a grenadier battalion's experience at Verplanck's Point on the Hudson River in June 1779: "a good deal of rain last night which wet us in our Wigwams."[102] At Flat Rock Point on the shores of Lake Champlain in late October 1778, William Bardin of the 29th Regiment met a lamentable fate for a soldier who had served over two years in America when "a very unlucky Accident happened by one of our Men Cutting down a Tree carelessly which fell on a Wigwam where there were several Sitting, by which three men were hurt. One died of his wound the Same Morning another was obliged to return to Canada, the third was hardly worth mentioning as he was able to do his duty again in a day or two."[103]

Without barracks there were barns, without barns there were tents, without tents there were wigwams, but sometimes there was nothing. On the war's very first foray outside of a garrison, after British troops stormed a rebel redoubt where their "blankets had been flung away during the engagement,"[104] victorious soldiers on Bunker Hill "lay on their arms, on this ground" for the night. The next day tents came from Boston.[105] It was the first of many times soldiers lay on the ground with only blankets, if they had any covering at all. The regiments that intended to take Charleston, South Carolina, spent June and part of July 1776 on an island named Long Island, just up the coast from the city. "We sleep upon the sea shore, nothing to shelter us from the violent rains, but our coats or miserable paltry blankets. There is nothing that grows upon this island, it being a mere sand bank, and a few bushes which harbour millions of musketoes, a greater plague than there can be in hell itself,"[106] wrote an officer to his brother. They sailed north and joined the army that soon seized the verdant New York island of the same name. But that campaign, too, began in Spartan conditions. "It is now a fortnight we have lain on the Ground wrapt in our Blankets," an officer of the 17th Regiment wrote in early September.[107] The following month, the night after the Battle of White Plains, he related, "after dark at 10 oClock we received orders to be ready for a General Engagement next morning at break of Day, it rained excessive hard the whole night so that we who lay in the open air had most of our ammunition spoil'd & ourselves driping wet notwithstanding which the men were in high spirits eager for the attack."[108]

The night of landing on Rhode Island on December 8, 1776, some troops found barns and houses, but much of the army was "obliged to lie without any shelter, on a bleak hill, much exposed to the severity of the weather."[109] The next day they "pitched Tents but such a snow fall that it was with great difficulty the Troops kept themselves warm, tho' great fires were made."[110] Conditions were similar after landing at Head of Elk, Maryland, in August 1777; on the first night, "The whole lay under arms all night, which proved a very bad one," and the next night "was exceedingly bad. The army still untented."[111] Four days after landing, tents finally came ashore.[112] In February 1780, after landing in South Carolina on the campaign that would capture Charleston, "some went a stray in the night 2 Companys of Light Infantry & 4 of Grenadiers lost their way," wrote one of the company officers, and "after splashing thro' the mud & rain till near 10 o'clock we halted in a wood & made fires & staid there all night."[113]

Often on short expeditions no tents were taken, such as the force that left New York in August 1778 to relieve the besieged garrison in Rhode Island. Although they arrived to find the siege already lifted, they subsequently spent two days ashore in New Bedford, and again on Martha's Vineyard.[114] An expedition into New Jersey in June 1780 was expected to last only a few days, and soldiers carried nothing more than a blanket, an extra shirt, and several days of food.[115] They were actually out for nearly three weeks. John Allen, a veteran soldier drafted into the 43rd Regiment from the 65th in 1776 and taken prisoner on this expedition, pointed out the resourcefulness of soldiers encamped weeks longer than expected: "They have put up their Blankets by way of covering which appears like Tents at a distance. None of the British have any Knapsacks or any kind of Baggage with them, except one shirt."[116] A raid on the towns of Bristol and Warren, Rhode Island, was a day-long affair, so not even blankets were taken, but landing in hostile territory at dawn meant marching out of garrison the night before. "It began to rain at the time the troops marched from town, and continued, with some intermissions till near 12. As the troops had no blankets, and waited near an hour on the beach for the boats, they were all thoroughly wetted."[117]

In spite of efforts to minimize soldiers' burden on the march by moving knapsacks, tents, camp kettles, and other heavy baggage on wagons or boats, sometimes no such transport was available. "The load a soldier generally carries during a campaign, consisting of a knapsack, a blanket, a haversack that contains his provisions, a canteen for water, a hatchet and a proportion of the equipage belonging to his tent, these articles (and for such a march there cannot be less than four days provisions), added to his accoutrements, arms and sixty rounds of ammunition, make an enormous bulk, weighing about sixty pounds," recalled General Burgoyne of his men's plight in the latter stages of his 1777 campaign near Saratoga when few wagons were available.[118] Three and half years later, Roger Lamb, who had been on Burgoyne's expedition, was on another of the army's most difficult campaigns, ranging through the Carolinas in 1781, again hauling knapsacks, because baggage wagons had been burned to streamline the march. The troops on this campaign experienced some of the greatest deprivation of food and shelter of the entire war. In January an officer in the Brigade of Guards wrote from "camp near Camden" that "Our Army cannot afford to carry tents, so we are obliged to live in the Woods & make the best Shifts we can, but this will be attended with the worst consequences to our men's health when the rainy season comes on."[119] Lamb left the most vivid description of British troops on campaign, not specifying whether it was Burgoyne's or Cornwallis's. His paragraph titled "The Bivouack of an Army" may relate elements common to both:

> It is a pleasing sight to see a column arrive at its halting ground. The Camp is generally marked out, if circumstances allow of it, on the edge of some wood, and near a river or stream. The troops are halted in open columns and arms piled, pickets and guards paraded and posted, and in two minutes all appear at home. Some fetch large stones to form fire places; others hurry off with canteens and kettles for water while the wood resounds with the blows of the tomahawk. Dispersed under the more distant trees you see the officers, some dressing, some arranging a few boughs to shelter them by night, others kindling their own fires. How often under some spreading pine tree which afforded shade, shelter and fuel have I taken up my lodging for the night. Sitting in the midst of my comrades, men whom I loved and esteemed partaking of a coarse but wholesome meal, seasoned by hunger and cheerfulness. Wrapt up in a blanket, the head reclining on a stone or a knapsack covered with the dews of the night or drenched perhaps by the thunder shower sleeps many a hardy veteran. A bivouack in heavy weather does not I allow present a very comfortable appearance. The offi-

cers sit shivering in their wet tents idle and angry. The men with
their forage caps drawn over their ears huddle together under the
trees or crowd round cheerless smoky fires—complaining of their
commissaries, the rain and the Americans.[120]

CHAPTER 8

Beef and Bread,
Fever and Flux,
Swimming and Sack Races

John Hopwood, hailing from Hutton in Yorkshire, was thirty-five when he was wounded in the war. In the garrison of Rhode Island in 1778, his regiment, the 54th, fended off nighttime rebel incursions, conducted raids on enemy towns, endured a three-week siege, and fought in one of the war's largest battles. The loss of two fingers on his right hand, however, was "occasioned by an accident when killing cattle for the use of the army in 1778."[1] He was a butcher, working at his trade while a professional soldier, doing his part to keep his comrades fed.

"A Ration of fresh meat consists of one pound of Beef and one pound of flour per day," directed orders in Boston in June 1774. With no refrigeration, fresh meat came only from butchering cattle and distributing the meat quickly, affording ready employment for men like Hopwood. More convenient but less desirable were salt rations, which the Boston orders called "salt meat," consisting of "four pounds of Pork, three pints of pease, six ounces of Butter, half a pint of Rice, and seven pounds of flour or bread per week."[2] With terminology like "ration of fresh meat" referring to a portion of meat and flour, and some rations being described per day and others per week, it is no wonder that many writers get confused when discussing the diet of British soldiers in America. Compounding the confusion is that the components of fresh and salt rations changed: salt beef instead of salt pork, oil instead of butter, oats instead of rice, and so forth.

Like so many aspects of the soldier's life, diet varied with time and place; food was sometimes scarce and sometimes plentiful. Quantities of food were allocated and tabulated on a per-man basis but were not issued that way; in the same way that shipping was allotted at two tons per man but each man did not get his own two tons of the ship, food was procured at so many pounds per man but was issued out in bulk to the mess groups. Benjamin Williams of the 55th Regiment, for example, retrieved provisions for seven of the regiment's mess groups, bringing the food-stuffs to their quarters where they were divided into seven portions for cooking.[3]

"It is customary with the Regiments to make an agreement with some baker, who being paid 1d [one pence] for each man per week for baking, gives nine pounds of bread for seven pounds of flour,"[4] recorded orders in Boston in June 1774, not meaning that each loaf weighed nine pounds but expressing the overall ratio of bread to flour. Flour was sometimes scarce, such as in winter 1778–1779 in Rhode Island. "The bread which is at present served out to the troops, is made of equal parts of Ground Rice and flour, and is very good," wrote an officer of that garrison on Christmas day about measures taken to remediate the shortage; relief arrived a few weeks later in a supply convoy from New York.[5] Long storage could affect the quality of flour; a commissary in New York explained that bread issued to troops during winter 1776–1777 had "a blue mould in the heart of it," and that the flour was "coarse, dead, & other wise deficient," not fit for making soft bread without mixing in "prize flour" obtained from captured maritime cargoes.[6]

On campaign, armies usually stopped every three or four days to re-group, refresh, repair, and replenish provisions. Building ovens for baking bread was part of the normal routine but not always possible. Sometimes troops were issued flour and told to "make it into Cakes and Bake it if possible," while others mastered "the Art of making flour Cakes without Ovens which are equally wholesome and rellishing with the best bread," a useful technique when moving "too quick to admit a possibility of con-structing Ovens."[7] Another substitute for baked bread was biscuit, hard bread made from flour and water and baked twice to remove moisture, allowing it to keep for long periods. Called hardtack in later eras, biscuit was a common maritime staple sometimes sent on campaign when ovens were not expected to be available. The army that landed in Quebec in 1776 took "Biscuit to furnish the Troops for about 5 or 6 weeks" in case the city was in enemy hands and there was no place for baking. A War Office official noted, however, that flour would otherwise be preferable, "as Biscuit takes up so much room, comparatively with Flour."[8] Like meat saturated with salt to preserve it, biscuit was not intended to be eaten without soaking or boiling first.

"Four days bread . . . one days salt provision and 3 days fresh meat" was issued out to the army campaigning near the city of New York on November 14, 1776; on November 27, it was "four days flour" and "four days fresh meat, with one ounce of salt each man."[9] Provisions like these were typical on campaign, doled out and cooked up every few days, the proportion of fresh or salt meat, bread or flour varying with the availability of cattle for the one, ovens for the other. In camp or on campaign, the meat was boiled, an officer making the rounds to see that it was done regularly.[10] Admonitions were given against frying, "being prejudicial to the mens health."[11] When shortages hit besieged Boston in January 1776, the weekly ration of salt provisions changed: what had been four pounds of pork was now three pounds of pork and either a pound of dried codfish or nine ounces of salt pork; instead of three pints of peas it was three pints of meal or peas; six ounces of butter became one ounce of oil and five ounces of butter; half a pint of rice changed to eight ounces of rice, apparently meaning the same amount. To make up for the missing seven ounces of pork, an additional pound and fourteen ounces of flour was added to the seven pounds already in the ration.[12] Within weeks, relief came on ships from Halifax, Nova Scotia, "freighted with fresh beef"; it was, however, "so much frozen, that if you strike the beef with a chopper it flies into pieces, nearly as if you struck a piece of glass. Put it to the fire in this state, it becomes so tough as not to be edible," recalled an officer, who then described the successful preparation of this unusual commodity: "we therefore steep it for several hours in salt water; it then dresses well, and has a flavor superior to any I ever eat in Europe, though not so large, nor yet so fat."[13] In autumn 1778, the garrison in Rhode Island was served fresh meat one day each week, provided from several thousand sheep rounded up on Martha's Vineyard that September.[14] By December, food supplies were running low, causing a gill and a half of oil to replace the six ounces of butter in the usual ration.[15]

On campaign, where rations consisted solely of meat and bread, it was vital to supplement the diet with foraged vegetables. Operating in New Jersey in June 1777, the 40th Regiment received orders to "provide greens or contrive to have something warm every day."[16] In Rhode Island that July, Thomas Cook of the 54th told a court-martial that he had left his

encampment "to gather some greens."[17] When the army marched from
Head of Elk, Maryland, at the end of August 1777, soldiers carried two
days of salt provisions and four days of rum, "depending upon two days'
fresh provisions to be got in the country."[18] At Verplanck's Point in June
1779, Benjamin Reynard, a grenadier in the 37th Regiment, gathered
"wild docks and other greens that grew in the fields" for his mess.[19] The
following month, two light infantrymen of the 23rd "went to gather some
Vegetables, and lost their way" in the nighttime.[20] In Germantown, Pennsylvania, in December 1777, two soldiers talked of going to a house to
buy onions; the following February, a Philadelphia shopkeeper recalled
several times selling onions to John Walker of the 10th Regiment.[21] On
campaign near the city of New York in October 1776, the 17th Regiment
sent out a "rooting party" to gather crops; the next month they had potatoes available for "those Companies that Chuse."[22] In December 1777,
near Philadelphia, a soldier of the Brigade of Guards remembered "roast-
ing Potatoes by the fire."[23] In September 1777 near Saratoga, New York,
"A party of the Enemy came within a few hundred yards of Camp and
fired upon some men gathering potatoes."[24]

An officer on Long Island wrote in September 1776, "The Army ordered to draw two days fresh provisions tomorrow, which they are to use
that day and the next, and keep their Salt provisions ready dressed."[25]
"Ready dressed" meant cooked and ready to carry on a march, but exactly
what this cooked food was like is not stated. Bread or fire cakes were easy
enough to carry, but a couple of pounds of cooked salt beef or salt pork
seems like a messy load for a linen canvas haversack. Perhaps the meat
was stuffed into the bread; no known document goes into such detail.
On April 19, 1775, men of the 18th Regiment in Boston were issued
three quarters of a pound of cheese instead of their daily ration of pork,
in case they were required to march out to join the battle that had begun
on the road to Concord that day.[26] But that October, Thomas Parker of
the 23rd mentioned that "when he went on guard he put a pair of regimental breeches, a waistcoat and some pork in his haversack," a curious
mixture of clothing and cooked meat.[27] The regiments encamped on the
coast near Charleston, South Carolina, in June 1776 were told to "cook
their Pork this night and reserve it Cold, if the Army does not move tomorrow they will dress their peas and flower and Content themselves to
make a Banyan day keeping their meat in Case of Immergencie," using
a vernacular expression for a day of meals without meat.[28] On the day of
the Battle of Brandywine in September 1777, an officer recalled a break
"to sitt down and refresh ourselves with some cold Pork and Grogg."[29]

Another officer remembered of a 1778 campaign in the West Indies, "though we were without the means to dress our pork, this was not the first time we had eaten it raw, or sliced and broiled upon the end of a bayonet, with yams and plantains, of which we found abundance upon the post, affording to a hungry man no despicable meal."[30]

Never stated as part of the rations but frequently fed to soldiers was sauerkraut—cabbage pickled in vinegar and packed in puncheons that preserved the vitamin-rich vegetable for extended periods. When the army was in Halifax, Nova Scotia, in April and May 1776, sauerkraut was issued at a rate of three pounds per man per week.[31] The expedition that landed on the Carolina coast that March was unable to obtain fresh provisions from the countryside and was forced to subsist almost entirely on salt pork and sauerkraut until it went to Staten Island during the summer.[32] When the Brigade of Guards arrived on Staten Island that August from England, they received "a fresh Supply of Sour Crout," and in winter 1777, a puncheon of it was delivered to each regiment in Rhode Island each week, as "the troops are very fond of it."[33]

Three soldiers of the 18th Regiment of Foot, barracked in New Jersey the year before war broke out, took advantage of the region's fruitful orchards and attempted to gather apples but were themselves gathered up by antimilitary citizens who kidnapped them.[34] The army that descended on Long Island in August 1776, however, far outnumbered the orchard-owning residents; "the Soldiers & Sailors seemed as merry as in a Holiday, and regaled themselves with the fine apples, which hung every where upon the Trees in great abundance."[35] An officer wrote home that "Peaches & Nectarines grow upon Hedges, so plenty that even all the Soldiery were not able to consume them."[36] In July 1780, Corporal Henry White of the 54th Regiment went out from the post at Paulus Hook, New Jersey, with a party of men to "gather greens for the soldiers" but strayed into the woods when he "went to the top of the Hill to get some Cherrys."[37] That August an officer summed up the impact his soldiers would have on a Long Island widow's apple crop when they camped in her orchard: "Camp in the Widow Fields orchard who won't make much Cyder this year."[38]

The seasons and fortunes of war conspired to ensure that the military diet was highly variable. On Staten Island in July 1776, residents seemed "very glad at our coming amongst them, & supply us with provisions at reasonable rates."[39] Six months later, a setback at Trenton, New Jersey, caused local citizens to cease support of the British army, causing a "want of fresh provisions, which the country people tho well paid would not bring in" and forcing the army to subsist on salt provisions.[40] It was well known that fresh food prevented health problems, even if the underlying biological mechanisms were not understood. "Our Troops have been attacked with severe fluxes & many have died for want of fresh provisions," wrote an officer in Boston in August 1775; another ascribed the high mortality rate among the wounded in the months after the Battle of Bunker Hill to the lack of fresh provisions, "even after they have been in a manner healed."[41] In Boston, New York, and Rhode Island, soldiers garrisoned for lengthy periods tended gardens that provided fresh produce that was no longer available from the countryside. The gardens yielded turnips, potatoes, cabbages, onions, and perhaps other vegetables not recorded, which were distributed primarily to regimental and army hospitals.[42] Preference was also given to the sick when sauerkraut was in short supply.[43]

The 1775–1776 wartime winter in Boston was perhaps the least healthy, as an army unprepared for prolonged war settled into a besieged garrison reliant almost entirely upon preserved provisions sent from overseas. "Fluxes, agues, and other disorders proceeding from the damp and cold" began to take their toll as days grew short and windblown rain soaked the tents of an army largely still encamped.[44] "Nothing but a desire of Scourging the Insolent Rebels of our Country keep up the Soldier's Spirit," commented an officer that December.[45] Over the next eight years, illness broke out from time to time, but British soldiers remained mostly healthy—that is, once they had gotten their land legs. When James McFarlane of the 55th Regiment was questioned by American officers after deserting in July 1776, he told of men "so weak that they cannot march twelve miles a day to save their lives."[46] Much of the British army that he left on Staten Island had recently arrived from Great Britain either directly or by way of the Carolinas, the remainder from Nova Scotia. Even if McFarlane's report was true, most of the army recovered sufficiently by the following month to launch a dramatically successful campaign.

As with many facets of the British military during this era, quantitative information on diseases is sparse. Numerous returns give the number of sick in various regiments at various times, without listing specific illnesses; they show the impact of sickness on the army but not the causes or the rates at which individuals were stricken and recovered. Army hospital returns from New York list the numbers too severely afflicted to be treated at regimental hospitals but again lack details of the illnesses.[47] Regimental muster rolls record deaths but not causes and annotate which individuals were "sick" at the time each roll was prepared, but this terminology is too vague to be useful.[48] With conditions varying widely from place to place and year to year, generalities are risky. Thomas Reide, surgeon for the 29th Regiment of Foot, maintained detailed records for the regiment's eight battalion companies from late 1777 through 1786.[49] The 29th was stationed in Canada, with a climate different from New York, Philadelphia, the Carolinas, or especially the West Indies, so Reide's data is not representative of the British army as a whole. Reide's details about one regiment are nonetheless useful for interpreting anecdotal material from other places.

Prevalent among the diseases recorded by Reide are fevers that, he explained, other medical authors subdivided into many types with a variety of names. This varied nomenclature makes it difficult to determine causes, but Reide used two general categories based on symptoms: remitting fevers and inflammatory fevers. As the name suggests, remitting fevers recurred every day or every other day; many writers used the term "ague," meaning malarial fever, even if malaria was not always the cause. Reide called remitting fever "the most common disease that mankind is attacked with,"[50] and his experience in Canada bears this out. From 1778 through 1782, each year about a quarter of all illnesses in the regiment were remitting fevers, although the portion of men afflicted each year varied from as low as 8 percent to as high as 31 percent. After British forces captured Fort Ticonderoga in 1777, a medical officer requested medicines for the garrison "as intermitting and remitting fevers are so very epidemic in that position, that strange to tell it, scarce one of fifty of the troops has escaped that disease for twelve months in any one period."[51] Although rarely fatal to those who received proper treatment— the 29th Regiment lost only five men to remitting fevers in five years—incapacitation could have dire consequences. In September 1777, an American raid attacked several posts near Ticonderoga; an officer of the 53rd Regiment commanding a detachment of fifty men recorded that "they were so ill of the ague, that we had not 25 fit for duty,"[52] contributing to the entire detachment's capture.

In the 29th in Canada, remitting fevers were restricted almost exclusively to warmer months, April through November, with the majority of cases during the summer, but a devastating outbreak that began in August ravaged British troops in New York throughout the waning months of 1779. The fever may have originated in England. In late March, just over

1,300 recruits embarked in Portsmouth, England, along with four British regiments and a number of recruits for German regiments.[53] They sailed in April, but the transports soon dropped anchor in Torbay while their escorting warships went to help fend off a French attempt to seize the islands of Jersey and Guernsey. It was a month before the convoy was underway again, finally arriving in New York in late August.[54] The troops had been on ships for nearly five months, and 800 were sick, including almost 300 British recruits; 43 of those recruits had died during the passage.[55] The admiral commanding the convoy was confident that the malady was "principally scurvy" and that most would "soon recover," but they did not. Of 63 recruits for the 22nd Regiment, 26 died within a year; for the 38th, 34 of 106 died. They may have brought pestilence with them, or been vulnerable after their long sea voyage.

Other troops in the New York garrison began falling ill in August. Captain Peebles of the 42nd Regiment's grenadier company made the first of many diary entries about the fevers on August 31, writing, "The Men growing very sickly within these few days, a general complaint over the whole army, they are mostly taken with headache & universal pain a chill & feverishness, which for the most part turns into a quotidian or tertian intermittent." He noted twelve men, about an eighth of his company (which was twice the size of most infantry companies), were sick that day, including "six fellows down in the last 24 hours." He observed that many local residents on Manhattan and Long Island were sick, "owing probably to the great deal of rainy weather we had lately, more than any body remembers, with little or no thunder."[56] A week later about two hundred were sick in the grenadier battalion, nearly a quarter of its strength.[57] The end of September brought northerly winds that Peebles hoped would "be of service to the sick & check the progress of the disease, which is still seizing on new subjects & but very few of the old recovering." Still more were sick in October with the "undistinct remitting & intermitting fever, with & without more or less of an ague," and recovery was hindered by the sheer numbers that overtaxed hospital staff.[58] Only by mid-November did the numbers of sick gradually decrease, with men recovering slowly and continuing to suffer relapses. Peebles made his last comment on the fever outbreak, which the British commander in chief called "malignant jail fever,"[59] during the first week of December, when the number of sick was still decreasing.[60] His company fared well in the long run, with only three deaths during the time of fever.[61]

The 37th Regiment, which saw nearly every man in its eight battalion companies become sick, lost thirty-five men from August through December, including fifteen newly arrived recruits and drafts.[62] The 54th, encamped on Long Island, fared even worse, with sixty-six deaths in the seven companies for which muster rolls survive.[63] A board of army doctors concluded that the "Intermittent, Bilious Fever, & Dysenteries" that swept through the army were caused by "the frequent heavy rains, succeeded by unusual, calm, sultry Weather, with the defect of Thunder, and Lightning Common to the Climate," but also noted that "the chief Mortality in the Hospitals has been amongst the Troops which arriv'd from England on the 25th August owing to a contagious Fever that they brought with them."[64]

In spite of orders and admonitions, soldiers unaccustomed to campaigning were liable to carelessly undermine their own health. After the Battle of Brandywine on September 11, 1777, a British officer complained to an American doctor that "his soldiers were infants that required constant attendance, and said as a proof of it that although they had blankets tied to their backs, yet such was their laziness that they would sleep in the dew and cold without them rather than have the trouble of untying and opening them. He said his business every night before he slept was to see that no soldier in his company laid down without a blanket."[65] Soldiers wiser than this could nonetheless be endangered by the placement of camps, determined by military necessity even though healthfulness was a consideration. An encampment on Harlem Heights, where the 37th Regiment was ravaged by fever in 1779, was known to be "a very sickly camp" even though the ground was high and dry.[66] A year earlier, an army surgeon who visited the nearby encampment at Kingsbridge occupied by the 71st Regiment noticed that even though "the immediate situation was dry, and of considerable elevation," there was a swampy area not far to the right of it, and it was on that side of the camp that "disease raged with violence."[67]

The climate in the Carolinas hindered British operations in 1780, reducing strength in a region that already had far too few soldiers to meet operational needs. "Our troops are in general sickly," wrote General Cornwallis to his superior in August, "the 71st so much so that the two battalions have not more than 274 men under arms," a far cry from the 1,600 that this regiment's two battalions would have at full strength.[68] A remitting fever had caught hold in the regiment, such that "two thirds of both officers and men were unable to march."[69] The approach of enemy forces caused the post to be evacuated rather than defended, but there were not enough wagons to carry the infirm. Some were sent instead by water but were captured in transit, resulting in the loss of some ninety men.[70] By late September, even though many had nominally recovered, "a great number of their men who had missed the fever for some time were still too weak to march," and "the 63rd Regiment arrived at Camden in a very sickly state," rendering it "totally hors de combat and unfit for any active service."[71] Cornwallis moved the sickly regiments to healthy locations where they recovered their fitness, but precious time and momentum was lost in this important region at a critical stage of the war.

Surgeon Reide's monthly tallies for the 29th Regiment indicate that dysentery was as prevalent as remitting fevers, but the distribution of cases was very different; over thirty-four months from October 1779 through July 1782, 370 cases of remitting fever occurred exclusively in warm months, while 368 cases of dysentery were spread out almost evenly, between one and a dozen every month, with only occasional months having as many as 20 and one month, August 1780, having 44. Seeming to contradict his own figures, Reide wrote that there was a high correlation between dysentery and remitting fevers, so much so that "some late writers suppose it is the same," and "it arises from the same causes."[72] Apparently he listed patients as having dysentery only when it was not accompanied by remitting fevers, thereby insuring that each sick man was counted only once. Dysentery was the leading cause of fatalities in Reide's regiment, accounting for seventeen deaths from 1778 through 1782.

Inflammatory fevers, the nonrecurring type, were third on Reide's list and were a winter phenomenon, occurring exclusively from November through April and in numbers only about half those of the warm months' remitting fevers. Scurvy kept a few men in the hospital most months but seldom more than five, and it was never fatal; there were eighty-eight cases in thirty-four months. Rheumatism was similar, with ninety-two cases but never more than seven in the same month, and no fatalities. Consumption, an archaic term for tuberculosis, occurred less frequently, with only fifty-seven cases, never more than four at a time, but with nine deaths. Other maladies recorded by Reide were sore throats, jaundice, cholera morbus, epilepsy, sore eyes, earache, venereal diseases, inflammation of the bladder, cough, erysipelas, worms, stomach complaints, vertigo, cutaneous eruptions, hemorrhoids, pain in the side, scrofula, headaches, dropsy, asthma, stones, gravel, colic, palsy, and "chronic complaints of old age." During the five years from the beginning of 1778 to the end of 1782, Reide recorded 2,186 individual cases of illness among

586 soldiers in eight companies of the 29th Regiment. Only forty-five patients died, a fatality rate of just 2 percent, a respectable reflection on the quality of military health care during this era.[73] The regiment's muster rolls record fifty-six deaths during these years, eleven more than died of illness. Two are known to have died of gunshot wounds and one by a falling tree. Presumably the other eight also died of wounds or accidents.[74]

The northern regions where the 29th served were less liable to fatal illness than the area that included Rhode Island, New York, New Jersey, and Pennsylvania. An officer in the Brigade of Guards kept a careful record of deaths in this corps from May 1776 through December 1779 when they were exclusively in that region. There were 182 deaths from "sickness" among the 1,335 men in the brigade during those years, a fatality rate of almost 14 percent. There were one to three sickness deaths most months; besides an outbreak from January through March 1777 that claimed forty-three guardsmen, only four months had more than five sickness deaths, with a high of eleven in January 1778. In addition, one man died of "accidental wounds," two by drowning, and one died "suddenly."

Over forty-five months, the Brigade of Guards suffered forty deaths due to combat, including twenty-two killed in battle and eighteen who died of wounds, a mere 3 percent of those who served. Significant is the low number that died of wounds, a testament to the quality of treatment of that particular malady. Similar recovery rates are discernible for other corps by comparing casualty figures to muster rolls; the rolls seldom record the cause of death, but they do record the date. After the Battle of Rhode Island on August 29, 1778, the commander of the 22nd Regiment reported eleven men killed and fifty wounded; another officer recorded fifty-six wounded. Only five men died in the four months following the battle; one certainly died of wounds, as reported in a casualty return, and one succumbed to exposure in a December snowstorm. The causes of the other three deaths are not known, but it is clear that fewer than 10 percent of the wounded men died of their wounds, at least within four months of the battle.[75] The 52nd, 57th, and 63rd Regiments each sent their eight battalion companies into battle on October 6, 1777, storming Fort Clinton and Fort Montgomery on the Hudson River. The three regiments suffered sixty-one men wounded, but by the end of the month only eleven had died of any causes; by the end of the year, twenty-two others had died of all causes, mostly in December, suggesting they fell to sickness rather than wounds.[76] It appears that the chances of a wounded soldier surviving were quite good.

On Long Island in September 1776, an officer commanding a grenadier battalion, concerned about the number of sick men in the corps, ordered his men to bathe or wash their feet three times each week.[77] Cleanliness was critical to maintaining the army's health, and regular orders promoted good hygiene. A brigade in New Jersey in June 1777 received orders that "such men as choose" could bathe in the Raritan River, but only in the early morning or evening.[78] Similar orders were given that month to the grenadier battalion in General Burgoyne's army in Canada and to the garrison in Rhode Island, the former specifically prohibiting bathing between ten in the morning and five in the afternoon, and the latter allowing it only before nine in the morning.[79] In all cases, soldiers were permitted to bathe, but not required to.

Each soldier ideally owned a few shirts, typically three or four, although on some campaigns only one spare shirt was carried, the others remaining with the regiment's baggage. A brigade in New Jersey in June 1777 was directed to change their "linens" three times a week, certainly referring to shirts and perhaps to trousers or overalls—garments made by regiments in America of linen for summer and wool for winter. Shirts were washed regularly by the soldiers themselves or by soldiers' wives working as washer women, a routine activity seldom mentioned except in court-martial testimonies, which reveal diverse practices. In Germantown near Philadelphia in September 1777, George McCulloch of the 49th Regiment told a court that "he had been washing with many other soldiers" and sought to buy soap at a nearby house, "and being unwilling to go into the house naked, he put on a check shirt, which he found by the water side, which he thought might be his own."[80] Also in Germantown, John Walton of the 46th went in search of a tub to wash his trousers, while his comrade John Connell searched for a brush for the same purpose.[81] John Connolly of the 64th washed a shirt and hung it to dry on Long Island in July 1778, but "laying down fell asleep," and "whilst he was sleeping his shirt was stolen."[82] Joseph Taylor of the Brigade of Guards washed his own trousers in August 1778, but the same day also got a clean shirt from "his washing woman," and his fellow soldier Thomas Clarke told a court that "his shirt being dirty, he went to his washing woman's and got a clean one."[83] And so forth, as men included washing in their alibis when on trial for plundering, desertion, and other crimes.

On July 27, 1776, the adjutant general of the British army at the War Office in London wrote, "The King has lately expressed his intentions that the hair of all infantry should be tied behind in one uniform manner, & that the mode which is commonly called Clubbed should be observed."[84] This "intention" may not have applied to troops overseas, and even if it did, it was too late for some soldiers in America. That September an American doctor wrote of a prisoner from the 23rd Regiment with hair "cut short all round by Genl. Howe's orders," noting that a popular military writer had recommended this style to save time and prevent both lice and the dangers of dampness from rain.[85] No such order by Howe has been found,[86] but anecdotal evidence suggests that the regiments that evacuated Boston cut their hair short, perhaps only an inch or so all around, before sailing from Halifax to Staten Island. A soldier from one of those regiments, John Manning of the 40th, had hair described ambiguously as "short" when he escaped from prison in Connecticut in May 1777 after being captured at the Battle of Princeton in January; Manning was a recruit who had arrived in America only in October 1776, so his hair may have been short when he enlisted, or it may have been cut to conform to the rest of his regiment when he joined it in New York.[87] Henry Mitchell of the 10th had also joined the army in America in the second half of 1776, and deserted in June 1777. One month later he was described as having "short black hair, tied behind."[88] If his hair had been cut to an inch in length the previous summer, it would have grown out enough by July 1777 to fit the description.

Other than those in Halifax in 1776, for which information is inconclusive, there is no evidence that regiments cut their hair short nor that short hair was worn later in the war except when it was growing out after having been cut short, or on recruits whose hair had not yet grown long. Grenadiers of the 42nd and 71st joined the army on Staten Island in summer 1776 and were ordered on August 24 to "comb their hair" before appearing on parade, suggesting fairly long hair.[89] In Canada that summer, men of the Royal Artillery were to "wear their hair always queued," but also cut "at the top and sides quite close."[90] In January 1778, artillerymen in Philadelphia were directed to "wear their Hair tied up and Clubb'd," with the further instruction that "such of the men whose hair is now too Short to tie up, do let it grow from this time forward," followed by the warning, "Anyone who shall presume to cut it Short behind in disobedience of this order may depend upon being severely punished."[91]

John Clements, a grenadier in the 38th Regiment, shaved two of his comrades on September 11, 1778, and "tied the hair" of one of them; all three had been with the army in Halifax, but if their hair had ever been cut it was long again by this time.[92]

"We are at present indeed remarkably healthy for which we are indebted to the sea breeze which never fails to moderate the intense heat of the atmosphere," wrote an officer of the 57th Regiment. They were encamped in South Carolina in July 1776, the effects of a harsh climate mitigated by a well-chosen location.[93] A fellow officer agreed but added that "it likewise proceeds from our taking a degree of moderate exercise, which I fancy is necessary in every climate," resulting in "fewer sick altogether than might have been expected in country quarters in England."[94] Regular exercise afforded movement and fresh air, both recognized as healthful. When the army that left Boston in March 1776 arrived at Halifax on overcrowded transports, portions were "landed & exercised on the Hill above Halifax in turn." When quarters in town became available, there were enough for only a third of the troops, so a portion of the army stayed ashore for one week at a time, then returned to their ships so others could come ashore.[95] The 42nd Regiment, part of the force that landed on Rhode Island in December 1776, practiced field maneuvers on the twenty-third and again on the thirtieth in spite of it being "rather too cold for field business."[96] The 40th paraded for exercise in early June 1777 without muskets,[97] and the following March regiments in Philadelphia were out "every good day at exercise."[98] The 1st Battalion of Grenadiers "took a walk for an hour or so" in February 1779, followed by a march of "a few miles" and field maneuvers in March, two or more hours of marching and maneuvering twice in April, and ten rounds per man of target practice that same month.[99] In May the following year, the 37th and 43rd Regiments, supported by four brass field cannons from the Royal Artillery, demonstrated "evolutions, firings, and marchings, with their accustomed adroitness" for senior officers of the New York garrison and "thousands of spectators assembled on the ground."[100] Activities like these kept soldiers fit and prepared.

"The British troops," commented an officer in New York in May 1777, "have been Remarkably healthy from the great Attention pay'd them. They Swim in the Sea most mornings & in the Evenings have foot Races & other manly Exercises."[101] This is one of but few mentions of how British soldiers spent leisure time. In January 1782 on Long Island, the 54th Regiment held a field day that included a horse race, a sack race, and a grinning match—a contest to make the most ridiculous facial expression. The garrison at Fort Niagara in 1787 amused themselves with competitions that included "a race of four men in sacks." An 1801 account of sack races in England said men were "tied up in sacks, every part of them being enclosed except their heads, who are in this manner to make the best of their way to some given distance, where he who first arrives obtains the prize."[102] The Niagara garrison also played the following game:

> A space of Forty yards square was measured out and enclosed with Ropes into which Thirteen men were placed twelve of whom were Blindfold. The thirteenth was not but had in his hand a small Bell which he was to keep ringing and endeavouring to elude the twelve others who on their part were to strive to catch him. The Bet was wither or no they would be able to accomplish it within an hour. The Match from the very begining appeard to be unequal, as the exercise of evading so many within so small distance was to much for one man. The man who undertook it was both strong and active and did more than any one could have expected he would after the first five minutes notwithstanding which he was taken in about a half an hour.[103]

In Boston, a boxing match between two soldiers of the 64th Regiment went wrong when one of the pugilists, William Elliot, "received an unlucky Blow, which put an End to the Combat, and soon after to his Life."[104] Patrick Henry, formerly sergeant of the 17th Regiment of Foot who became an officer in a Loyalist regiment, drew criticism for "playing at knock-chops" with a private soldier, apparently a game in which two people sat on a fence and tried to knock each other's hats off.[105] Sergeant Thomas Burk of the 55th recalled being "in the college yard, stripped, with our coats and hats off, playing ball" in Princeton on the morning of January 3, 1777, when an American attack resulted in their capture.[106] Because "many disorders of Drinking, Gaming & Quarrelling" arose among men of the 37th Regiment in Dublin a few months before embarking for America "from the mens playing in the fives Court or at Ball play," they were "strictly forbid to play at the above mention'd game, upon pain of being brought to a Courtmartial for disobedience of Orders."[107] Similarly, recruits at Chatham Barracks near London in 1780 were told, "Any Soldiers found in future playing at Ball Against the Board of Orders in the Barrack Yard will be severely punished for the same."[108]

It is mostly court-martial testimony that contains casual references to the casual activities of soldiers at leisure. Malcolm Campbell of the 38th invited fellow soldier Luke Murphy "to accompany him to see a friend of his in the 5th Regiment" where "they drank some Grogg" in the friend's tent on Boston Common in 1774. Michael Connolly and John Corrigan of the 40th smoked pipes together in the barn where they were quartered on Staten Island in 1776. John Lusty of the 57th asked fellow soldier John Dunn to take a walk with him to a house to buy cider on Long Island that September. Duncan Robinson's sergeant in the 71st Regiment described him as usually "very merry singing and telling stories." After going to bed in a Philadelphia barracks in May 1778, men of the Brigade of Guards "were talking as usual, but making no noise." A year later in New York, two other guardsmen were "taking a walk together, after the evening parade." Richard Hallum of the 22nd Regiment went fishing in Rhode Island in June 1779. Robert McDonald of the 76th remembered "that one day when on Board the *Kingston* Transport he was looking over a Corporal's Shoulder who was reading."[109] Thomas Sullivan found that service as a private in the 49th Regiment afforded "many hours in which I could divert myself in Reading and Writing; which Exercise I practiced from my Youth."[110] An unnamed sergeant in the 98th Regiment kept "a daily Journal or Diary of every thing that happened, besides many curious things agreeable to his own Ideas," but what became of this work is not known.[111]

The son of Sergeant John Hunter of the 26th Regiment recalled spending time in a French prison after being captured by a privateer while returning to England in 1779. He wrote:

> [O]ur only amusement was story telling, which was generally kept
> up until a late hour of the night by some of the prisoners, several
> of whom distinguished themselves by this talent. But I recollect
> more particularly, an old soldier who was preeminent in his line.
> Indeed, he exceeded any person I have ever heard. No sooner had
> the prisoners retired to bed, but by general consent he was called
> upon for a story, and well he repaid the attention that we bestowed
> upon him. He appeared to have gotten the whole of Arabian Tales
> by heart, and could relate them as circumstantially as if he had the
> book before him.[112]

During almost five years in America, poet Andrew Scott of the 80th Regiment "wrote as many pieces as would have completed a small volume; some of them founded upon the varied scenery of the country, some on the manners and customs of the people, but most related to the incidents of military life, being wrote both from and to the feelings of soldiers." He said his work "produced the good effect of securing me the favour of a number of my fellow-soldiers," but only two pieces survived because they were songs that "I particularly used to sing among my comrades, consequently preserved them in my memory."[113] An officer of the 60th Regiment wrote of a skirmish in Georgia in early 1778 after which a corporal named West "who distinguished himself in the action had his left arm amputated, and composed a song next morning."[114]

When Edward Moran of the 35th Regiment arrived in Boston from Ireland just as the war began in 1775, he brought a letter for a soldier in the 65th.[115] The letter is long lost, as are most letters from and to British soldiers in America; only a handful survive, far too few to estimate the number of soldiers who were both literate and had cause to write home. Alexander Grant, a corporal in the 22nd Regiment, wrote to his father in Scotland from Boston shortly after landing there, asking "to be forgiven for my ungreatfullness in not sending you any word these 3 years Last." He reported that the war was "Turing out A greater War than ever was in Europe or America Before" but that he was "in Expectation of Overthrowing the Enemy and then the Country is our own."[116] Thomas Plumb, a long-serving soldier in the same regiment, wrote a one-paragraph letter to his brother in Cornwall from Rhode Island in February 1777, telling of hard duty within sight of rebels "as numerous as motes." "The cowardly rascals will not stand their ground," he wrote, "But watching all Oppertunitys by lying in Ambush behind some trees which is the cause of us looseing so many men but thank God where we loose 10 they loose 100." He was confident in ultimate victory but did acknowledge that "had they the heart as we Britoners have we should stand no chance with them." He closed his letter by offering "kind respects" to his "loveing Wife & Child," other family members, and "all Enquireing friends."[117] The letter was never delivered, being in a packet that was intercepted, and it is not known whether Plumb wrote again to his family before he was killed in battle in Rhode Island on August 29, 1778.[118]

Duncan Grant of the 21st Regiment wrote to his father from Montreal in September 1777, relating the whereabouts of relatives and acquaintances serving in America, including "My step mothers Brothers son is in General Hows Army but for his sister I do not know what place she is in." He wrote proudly that "my wife is Bigg with child at present

expecting to ly in every day," and that "happy was the day that ever I got
such a good wife for she keeps me more like a gentleman than a Soldier.
... I do not want both gold and silver and good Cloaths by her industry."
He signed the letter from himself and his wife, Margaret.[119] Five months
after being captured in New Jersey in June 1780, Sergeant Richard
Williams of the 22nd Regiment wrote to his wife, Rosanna, in New York,
asking her to come to Philadelphia where he was held in jail and to bring
warm clothing. He explained how she should get a pass and that he was
"sorry that you never sent me a Letter to let me know how you are and
where you Lived which gives me great uneasyness of not hearing from
you." The letter was never delivered by the American commissary of prisoners, and Williams died in captivity two months later.[120]

   Soldiers also occasionally wrote letters for official purposes. Owen
Smith of the 63rd Regiment deserted in Ireland before the war and wrote
to his commanding officer asking for a pardon so he could return to the
army.[121] Two corporals of the 14th Regiment of Foot, Charles Hay and
John Elborn, wrote detailed letters in support of the officer commanding
their detachment after an altercation between soldiers and the crew of
their transport in August 1776.[122] Sergeant James Buchanan of the 9th
Regiment, "a man of decent education," wrote letters "full of religious
contrition" while in jail in Worcester, Massachusetts, in 1778.[123] A year
later, William Naylor of the Royal Artillery wrote a long and eloquent
letter to General Henry Clinton in New York, "reflecting on the miserable state into which the Brigade of Royal Artillery is at present reduced"
and describing in detail what he perceived as mismanagement and injus-
tice during the past two years. His letter earned him a court-martial for
presenting "a false, Scandalous, and Mutinous Libel" and "tending to create unjust suspicions and dissatisfaction among the Soldiers." He was
found guilty and sentenced to a thousand lashes, after which he was to
be "drummed through the town with a rope about his neck, and every
other mark of infamy," then held in jail until the commander in chief de-
cided what to do with him.[124]

   As discussed in chapter 3, the army valued literacy so much that regiments were encouraged to establish schools for soldiers requiring basic
education. With reading and writing crucial for the duties of noncommissioned officers, it was essential to have enough literate men to fill
those roles. There are, however, too few writings of soldiers to draw conclusions about literacy rates within their population. What exists in large
numbers are signatures. Soldiers discharged from the army signed a form
stating they had been legally released from their service obligation, and

several thousand of these forms survive. Some men signed their names, and others made an "X" with the annotation, "his mark." A sample of these for soldiers who served in the American war yields 57 percent bearing signatures and 43 percent with marks. This percentage remains similar for each country when the sample is subdivided into English (including Welsh), Scottish, and Irish. When Scotland is divided into highland and lowland counties, men from the highlands signed only 45 percent of the forms, while lowlanders signed 71 percent.[125] However, whether the ability to sign a name is an indication of literacy is debatable.

Top, signature of John Mayell, musician in the 22nd Regiment, from his petition to the pension board, WO 121/140/158. Bottom, mark of Anthony Townshend, 29th Regiment, on his discharge, WO 121/13/171. (*The National Archives*)

Corporal John Graham watched as the captain commanding his company in the 18th Regiment of Foot was rowed from ship to shore in a small boat. Graham took a Bible out of his pocket and "wished in the most solemn manner that the boat that took Capt. Payne on shore might sink, as they would then get rid of a tyrant." When questioned about this, Graham did not deny the sentiment but clarified that "he commonly read the bible every day, and did not take it out of his pocket purposely for the wish relative to Capt. Payne."[126] It is a rare indication of religiosity among British soldiers. Orders routinely required "The men to parade for church" on Sunday mornings in garrisons,[127] or to hear a "sermon in camp."[128] Before the war, recruiters were to "enlist no man who is not a

Protestant,"[129] but the rule was relaxed in 1775 to allow recruitment of Irish Catholics.[130] Among the German recruits were Catholics, Lutherans, and Reformed Protestants.[131] William Burke, a young soldier from county Galway in Ireland who joined the 45th Regiment, wrote that he "had been taught to pray in the Catholic manner from a child, and always kept a prayer book." An officer of the 18th Regiment berated soldier John Harrison as "a swadling rascal, a Presbeterian rascal, and a Jesuit," and asserted that he "would go to a church and receive the Sacrament, and then come back and swear a false oath for a shilling."[132] In 1797, a letter published in a British religious magazine, purportedly from a British soldier mortally wounded at the Battle of Bunker Hill, described his awakening to Christianity and Methodism under the tutelage of a corporal in his regiment, but neither the soldier's nor the corporal's name appear on the muster rolls of any regiment engaged in that battle, calling the letter's authenticity into question.[133]

The British soldiers who fought the war in America cannot be characterized as a pious population, regardless of reported religious affiliations, orders to attend services, and the practices of individuals. A religious tract for sailors reported that a member of Parliament proclaimed, "What signifies the religion of soldiers? They have no more religion than my horses," while Methodist leader John Wesley wrote in his journal, "The English Soldiers of this age have nothing to do with God!"[134] Recalled Thomas Sullivan of his experience in the 49th Regiment, "The Army in General was a Repository for all manner of Vice," and any "endeavour to maintain and Practice his duty towards God" resulted in a soldier's being "derided and laughed at, and hated by some, while others load him with reproaches."[135]

A British officer penned an oft-repeated passage in a letter home about the landing at Kip's Bay, New York, on September 15, 1776, when British and German troops were ferried in longboats across the East River: "The Hessians, who were not used to this water business, and who conceived that it must be exceedingly uncomfortable to be shot at whilst they were quite defenceless and jammed together so close, began to sing hymns immediately. Our men expressed their feelings as strongly, though in a different manner, by damning themselves and the enemy indiscriminately with wonderful fervency."[136] He may have exaggerated to amuse the letter's recipients, but other soldiers made explicit mention of their lack of reverence. Thomas Watson of the 23rd Regiment wrote that "he was at the height of his wickedness" while serving in America, perhaps with some hyperbole as he described his path to Quaker convincement.[137]

Roger Lamb, who served in the 9th and 23rd, recalled years after his own religious conversion that while a soldier, "I was a most extraordinary sinner. I had almost filled up the measure of my iniquities. Behold my picture. There was nothing I had but the devil had dominion over it; he ruled the whole man; my eyes were blinded."[138] William Crawford, who started his military career in the cavalry before volunteering to join the 20th Regiment of Foot for the American war, wrote:

> In all my adventures and services in his majesty's army, though I possessed no religion in my heart, I found it convenient to carry my prayer book about my person, because appearances of religion I have found to have great efficacy in the affairs of the world, by giving consequence to its owner and astounding the vulgar and ignorant, with the splendor of a jewel which they can never hope to own, and with the sublimity of a thing which they can never understand—besides, between the leaves of my prayer book I found a safe depositary for my money, which I won in battle by rifling the dead and wounded, or took from prisoners or got by any other fall speculation.

As an escaped prisoner of war, Crawford used the prayer book to force a guide to swear an oath not to fight against Great Britain.[139]

"The Garrison drinks and games very much," lamented an officer of the 7th Regiment of Foot in Quebec in January 1774, summarizing the principal pastime of British soldiers in America throughout the 1770s and 1780s.[140] Rum, not part of the soldier's normal rations but authorized regularly on campaign and when duty was hard, was issued at a rate of an eighth of a quart per man per day, intended to be mixed with half a quart of water.[141] The resulting grog was too weak to intoxicate, but liquor was plentiful in urban America, and soldiers had a knack for finding it. The problems in Boston described in chapter 4 continued throughout the war. On Long Island in March 1781, a grenadier officer lamented about soldiers drunk on parade, "no keeping them sober when [they] get money."[142] Trial testimony is replete with passing mentions of social drinking, often resulting in the infractions that led to the trial. "He was drinking in a Hessian canteen.... [T]he prisoner came in, and called for half a pint of rum and drank it himself but did not join their company"; "was in a house ... where the prisoner with three other British soldiers were drinking"; "they went to the Hessian huts and drank some"; "some days ago as he went into a dram shop in York he saw the prisoner dressed as a sailor";[143] and so forth.

A fellow soldier recalled that Evan Evans of the 52nd Regiment was "so drunk at one o'Clock on Saturday afternoon last, that he could not drink his own Grog." John Sullivan of the 5th "appeared very stupid from having drunk too much" when he was apprehended for desertion, and a sergeant testified that "when in Liquor he is differently affected by it from any man Deponent ever saw—Being quite Mad."[144] During the fever outbreak in 1779, a New York resident wrote that "the Season has been very unhealthy, 2/3 of the Army have been sick, the Guards excepted, who are almost constantly drunk."[145] Wrote a grenadier officer during the 1780 siege of Charleston, "Some of the men will get in liquor now & then notwithstanding all I can say to them."[146]

For the most part, British soldiers in America prevailed over inconsistencies in diet, dangers of illness, and temptations of alcohol, and bore remarkable fatigues willfully and well. "The army travelled over a great extent of country," wrote a doctor attached to the 71st Regiment about campaigning in the Carolinas in 1781, "but I have the satisfaction to add, that notwithstanding occasional forced marches, wading of rivers, exposure to rain, accidental scarcity of bread, and no great profusion of beef, with the total want of rum, the troops enjoyed in general a most perfect state of health."[147] His observations could apply to any campaign in America. Even in the waning campaigns of a long and unpopular war with little hope of ultimate victory, the British soldier in America remained able to "chearfully suffer any hardship, to acquire glory, in doing his duty to his King and country."[148]

CHAPTER 9

The Plunder Problem

"I CANNOT COMMEND THE BEHAVIOUR OF Our Soldiers on their retreat," wrote a British staff officer from Boston soon after hostilities broke out on April 19, 1775, "As they began to plunder & payed no obedience to their Officers."[1] A colleague elaborated, writing, "many houses were plundered by the Soldiers notwithstanding the efforts of the officers to prevent it. Many who staid too long in the houses, were killed by the Enemy in the very act of plundering."[2] The commander in chief took notice and admonished the soldiers in general orders, first acknowledging that they had "behaved with much courage and spirit" but pointing out that they "shewed great inattention and neglect to the commands of their Officers, which if they had observed fewer of them would have been hurt. The General expects on any future occasion, that they will behave with more discipline, and in a more soldierlike manner, and it is his most positive orders, that no man quit his ranks to plunder or Pillage, or to enter a house unless ordered so to do, under pain of death, and each officer will be made answerable for the Platoon under his Command."[3] Taking advantage of a chaotic situation to plunder may have been attributable to the same lack of wartime experience that caused other breakdowns of discipline in the first few months of fighting. But while steadiness and obedience to orders under fire was rapidly trained into the army, no amount of orders, training, discipline, or punishment curtailed the British army's proclivity toward plunder. High-spirited soldiers who adapted quickly to fighting in woods and wilderness, made rapid marches over all manner of terrain, and improvised shelter wherever they went, could not be deterred from taking what they wanted, at every opportunity.

The plunder problem was pervasive on every British campaign and in every British garrison throughout the American war. It was the army's Achilles' heel. The best military efforts to suppress rebellion by defeating hostile armies on the battlefield and protecting loyal citizens in secure areas were undermined by opportunistic soldiers. There was the immediate operational impact of losing men who, by straying from their camps or routes of march, were killed or captured. This was exacerbated by men who, fearing punishment for plundering, deserted. An army of career soldiers could scarce afford to lose men in whom years of training had been invested, or even the wartime recruits raised in Britain and brought to America at considerable expense. More severe was the impact on the American population, the hearts and minds that the British government sought to retain or win over. Distrust of standing armies was a major factor in fomenting the rebellion in the first place; when armies sent to subdue rebellion brought deprivation to all in their path, inhabitants inclined to loyalty or indifference instead chose opposition. Even though armies on both sides plundered, soldiers from overseas bore the brunt of the animosity it caused.

"The frequent depredations committed by the Soldiers, in pulling down fences and houses, in defiance of repeated orders, has induced The Commander in Chief to direct The Provost to go his rounds attended by the Executioner, with orders to hang upon the spot, the first man he shall detect in the fact, without waiting for further proof by trial,"[4] read orders in Boston on December 5, 1775, illustrating perhaps the most prevalent form of plunder throughout the war. Large armies required great quantities of wood for fuel—firing, in the parlance of the era—and although America had extensive woodlands, war made those woods largely inaccessible to coast-bound British forces. The result was frequent short allowances and outright shortages, which soldiers sought to supplement by any means available. Fence rails, initially abundant in agrarian areas around cities where soldiers pitched their camps or built their cantonments, were easy prey for scavenging soldiers, already cut in sizes easy to spirit away. During the first twelve months that British troops garrisoned Rhode Island, orders were given six times "to prevent their men from burning the rails" or otherwise destroying fences.[5] The winter quarters wood allotment was half a cord per week for twelve soldiers; for summer encampments, it was just two cords per week for each regiment.[6] It wasn't enough, and soldiers routinely ravaged whatever sources of wood they could find. Sheds and other outbuildings were dismantled board by board, either over time or all at once, as were abandoned houses. During times of great scarcity, like winter 1778–1779 in Rhode Island, pulling down abandoned buildings, wharves, and other structures was authorized to supplement inadequate wood supplies.[7] Soldiers nonetheless continued to scavenge on their own, indiscriminately.

Theft of wood was one thing, and arguably excusable for shivering soldiers, but the problem extended far beyond fuel. Soldiers preyed on anything that could be eaten or sold, from livestock to clothing, whenever it could be readily grabbed. The day after British troops landed on Long Island on August 22, 1776, orders warned of "no mercy to any man found Guilty of Marauding" and brigade commanders were directed to "take every step they shall judge necessary toward Suppressing such Scandalous & infamous behavior." Just three days later, though, the commander in chief observed that "Plundering is become so excessive that Commanding Officers of Corps must be responsible that the Soldiers do not quit their Encampments unless upon Duty in which case the Officer Commanding must be answerable for the behavior of his Men."[8] On September 6, the "great irregularities" committed in previous weeks prompted orders for the provost marshal—the equivalent of a military police chief—"to execute upon the spot" soldiers found "guilty of Marauding." Rolls were to be called frequently, and any soldier found more than a mile from his post would be confined, because "the present licentious behavior of the Troops is a disgrace to the Country they belong to."[9] How many soldiers were caught marauding is not known; only four were brought to trial by general court-martial for "pillage and plundering," that fall on Long Island, with only one conviction, John Kelly of the 27th Regiment, sentenced to receive one thousand lashes.[10]

Days after the city of New York was taken, orders appealed to soldiers' sense of duty as protectors of the populace: "Soldiers whose valor has freed a people from the worst kind of Slavery, will be careful that no act of theirs prevent the enjoyment of all the blessings that attend British liberty. No person is to take anything that does not belong to him, under pretence that it is Rebel property."[11] But the city offered too much bounty and opportunity. During the first week of October, John Owen of the 63rd Regiment was charged with plundering, John Murphy and

Thomas Chapman of the 43rd with breaking into a shop, and Bryan Sweeny and James Gardner of the 22nd for breaking into a house. Twenty-six-year-old Cork native Sweeny, drafted from the 50th only months before, and Gardner, a recruit enlisted in 1775 shortly before the regiment embarked for America, broke into the house's cellar. A man who discovered them described what he saw: "one of them hid away behind a Cask of bottled wine, and the other leaning over it, and the Cellar floor very wet, and many empty bottles broke and laying about; Gardiner, he thinks, had a bottle in his hand or between his legs; they were both very drunk, and one was vomiting."[12] Lashes were the punishment for these crimes, but their deterrent effect was no match for temptations in town and country.

Unlike the war's first year in Boston, by late 1776, the army in America was no longer all British. Needing more professional, campaign-ready troops than could be spared from Britain or raised and trained rapidly, the British government augmented the army with regiments from German states. Collectively called Hessians even though regiments came not only from Hessen-Kassel and Hessen-Hanau but also Braunschweig-Lüneburg, Anspach-Bayreuth, Waldeck, and other states, these troops also had an appetite for plunder—and it was on them that many British officers laid the bulk of the blame. Major Stephen Kemble, an American-born officer serving as deputy adjutant general, confided several complaints to his journal in 1776. "The Ravages committed by the Hessians, and all Ranks of the Army, on the poor Inhabitants of the Country, make their case deplorable; the Hessians destroy all the fruits of the Earth without regard to Loyalists or Rebels, the property of both being equally a prey to them, in which our Troops are too ready to follow their Example, and are but too much Licensed in it," he wrote on October 3. A month later, he repeated the lament: "The Country all this time unmercifully Pillaged by our Troops, Hessians in particular, no wonder if the Country People refuse to join us." And a week later, "Scandalous behavior for British Troops; and the Hessians Outrageously Licentious, and Cruel to such a degree as to threaten with death all such as dare obstruct them in their depredations."[13] The Germans, with no sense of attachment to America as their nation's colony, behaved as European troops normally did in an enemy country, despite receiving the same orders and admonitions as their British allies.[14] British troops, although seen by Kemble as following the German example, were much more likely putting their immediate interests first, fueled by the hateful treatment they had received from colonists before the war began, whether they had experienced it directly or learned of it from their comrades.

Aggravating, and perhaps to some extent inciting, the plunder problem was the need to acquire some materiel locally: firewood, straw, and fresh provisions. This was true in peace as well as war, and was supposed to follow a system of requisition and payment: supervised parties of soldiers collecting goods from local sources and putting them into army stores to be issued out uniformly, property owners receiving vouchers redeemable for cash. In friendly, peaceful places this worked well. Orders to a brigade settling in for the winter in Princeton, New Jersey, on December 15, 1776, described the process:

> As soon as the Brigade shall arrive in its Cantonments, the Commanding officers at each Farm House will require from the Farmer an Exact Account of his Wheat, Oates, Indian Corn . . . of his Horses, Sheep, Oxen and waggons, so that a Return may be given in when Called for. . . . Whatever is taken from the Inhabitants must be paid for at a fair Market price, so that the Farmer may have no just Cause of Complaint. When the Officers require from the Farmer an Account of their Grain and Stock, they are to Assure them that it is not meant to take any thing from them but what will be paid for by the Commissary at a fair price, which will be Settled by General Howe in a few days.[15]

This was only effective if the army stayed long enough for inhabitants to settle their accounts. In this case, British troops were ousted from Princeton before year's end, never to return. By this time, some officers were showing, at least in their private writings, resignation toward unauthorized foraging. Captain Peebles of the 42nd Regiment wrote to his diary the day after landing in Rhode Island, "less moroding than usual only a few pigs etc. suffer," while an officer of the 52nd's light infantry company years later characterized his men's exploits in New Jersey in early 1777: "The 52nd Light Infantry were famous providers. They were good hands at a Grab. Grab was a favourite expression among the Light Infantry, and meant any plunder taken by force; a Lob when you got it without any opposition, and I am very certain there never was a more expert set than the Light Infantry at either grab, lob, or gutting a house."[16] In June 1777, four men of the 5th Regiment were caught plundering a house, but the commander in chief had them tried by a regimental rather than a general court-martial—a court that did not have the authority to issue death sentences, even though the articles of war allowed capital punishment for the crime. "The spirit of depredation was but too prevalent on these marches," commented an officer to his journal.[17]

On the very first day of hostilities, militiamen from Woburn, Massachusetts, entered a house during the retreat from Concord to Boston and found Sergeant Matthew Hayes of the 52nd Regiment's grenadier company "plundering within."[18] Thirty-year-old Hayes, in whose possession was found a pair of silver shoe buckles belonging to a local resident,[19] became one of the conflict's first prisoners of war, and one of the first to demonstrate the cost in manpower of plundering. In addition to the loss of personnel, the army stood to suffer from information that prisoners might offer to the enemy. In early November 1776, a staff officer wrote that several soldiers campaigning around New York went outside British lines to plunder, were captured, and "ordered to the Congress for Examination."[20] Although a popular military writer cautioned, "The intelligence of deserters is, for the most part, not much more to be depended on. A soldier knows very well what is going forward in his own regiment, but nothing farther,"[21] information aggregated from a number of prisoners could reveal useful details. Richard Shea had been in the army about eighteen months when he swam from Staten Island to Perth Amboy, New Jersey, in the first week of August 1776. He gave a deposition to his captors, including the following:

> There are in the Fortieth Regiment three hundred and thirty-six rank and file. Supposed to have fourteen thousand on the Island. Two new Highland regiments very sickly. The Forty-Second Regiment of Highlanders. Expect some Hessians, but none come. The Fortieth Regiment opposite the Blazing-Star, in barns. Stretch two miles and a quarter on the right and left of the Old Blazing-Star. . . . Five days ago, ordered the officers' heavy baggage, and women of the Army, on board the fleet. As far as he heard, he believes they will not attack New-York, unless reinforced by the foreigners. He has seen in orders for working party at Billop's Point, where they are numerous, and have thrown up intrenchments. No works near the Blazing-Star. One company at the Old Blazing-Star. Don't know who is at the New Blazing-Star.[22]

Even though the Continental army was in no position to mount a full-fledged attack, knowing how many men were posted in one redoubt could have facilitated a raid. The intelligence was sent to General George Washington with the accurate assessment, "His account that the heavy baggage of the troops was ordered on board shows an intended movement of the troops from Staten-Island."[23] Hundreds of other depositions by prisoners and deserters provided details that, when assimilated, helped American commanders monitor the condition of the British army throughout the war.

Marching from Fort Ticonderoga toward Albany in 1777, General Burgoyne's army was dwindling from losses due to many causes, and it frustrated him that straggling and unauthorized foraging contributed significantly. On September 18, four months into the campaign and stalled tantalizingly close to their objective, Burgoyne expressed exasperation in general orders:

> To the great Reproach of Discipline & of the Common Sense of the Soldiers who have been made Prisoners, the Service has sustained a loss within Ten Days that might have cost the Lives of some hundreds of the Enemy to have brought upon it in Action. The Lt. General will no longer bear to lose Men for the pitiful consideration of Potatoes or Forage. The Life of the Soldier is the Property of the King, and since neither friendly Admonitions, repeated Injunctions nor corporal Punishments have effect, after what has happened the Army is now to be informed (& it is not doubted that the Commanding Officers will do it solemnly) that the first Soldier caught beyond the Advanced Centry of the Army will be instantly Hanged.[24]

In the same season, General Howe landed a large army at Head of Elk, Maryland, to move overland to Philadelphia. Problems began the first day troops went ashore. They landed in the usual manner without tents on August 25, and the next day, "There was a good deal of plunder committed by the Troops, notwithstanding the strictest prohibitions. No method was as yet fixed upon for supplying the Troops with fresh provisions in a regular manner. The soldiers slaughtered a great deal of cattle clandestinely."[25] Orders said to call rolls, examine knapsacks and haversacks, and "on no account to suffer any men to straggle beyond their out Sentries,"[26] but an artillery officer confided to his journal what had been learned so well in a year of American campaigning: "it is not in anyone's power to prevent this where there is so large an army and such a mixture of troops."[27] Four days after landing, orders came to "execute upon the spot" any soldier or follower found straggling or plundering.[28] Although some once again believed the Germans to be the principal perpetrators,[29] British soldiers were brought to trial as early as August 29. From that date through the end of January 1778, twenty-eight British soldiers in Howe's army went before general courts-martial on charges of plundering, and five more for robbery, during the campaign that secured Philadelphia.[30]

The first was William Johnstone, a soldier in the 43rd Regiment's light infantry company that was part of the 2nd Battalion of Light Infantry. On August 27, an officer noticed him walking away from the army toward an outpost carrying a bundle wrapped in a blue-and-white curtain, and apprehended him. Guards examined the bundle and found it contained "a Woman's gown, a small piece of Cloth, of the same colour as the Curtain, and a small white earthen pot, containing butter." Brought to see the goods, a local resident who had complained of being robbed identified them all as his (except the gown, about which he was uncertain), but he could not identify Johnstone as the man who had taken them. On trial on August 30, Johnstone claimed to have met a party of grenadiers returning from a foraging party, one of whom called to him, "Light Infantry man will you take this," and explained that the bundle contained "something which would be of service to him when he went to Camp." With no direct evidence that Johnstone was the thief, the court acquitted him.[31]

The next day, another court tried four men for "disobedience of orders by straggling beyond the posts of the Army and Plundering Sundry Articles." Three soldiers of the 23rd Regiment, Abraham Pike, William Houston, and John Smith, who had arrived as recruits the previous year, were caught coming into British lines, one on horseback, carrying fowls; one also had a spyglass. They explained that the horse was a stray they had caught when posted as advanced pickets, and they had found the fowls and spyglass in an abandoned house within British lines. The court found them guilty of both charges and sentenced them to receive one thousand lashes each. Drummer William King of the 27th was drunk when he was found "loaded with seven or eight Canteens and earthen jars, containing Whisky," a coverlet, and another piece of cloth. He told the court he was carrying an officer's equipment, including the coverlet. He had gone to fetch water but met several soldiers who gave him the liquor. An officer of his regiment verified that on campaign, King carried things for another officer and offered that "during six years that he had

Soldier of the 9th Regiment of Foot on campaign, 1777. Regiments in Canada did not receive new clothing in time for the 1777 campaign, so coats and hats from the previous year were cut down and trousers were made from old tents or other linen canvas. Drawing by Eric H. Schnitzer.

known him, he had always behaved well except being a little addicted to liquor," adding, "his general character in the 27th Regiment, in which he has served 23 years is a good one." King was found guilty of being outside the lines and sentenced to five hundred lashes, but was acquitted of plunder.[32]

General Howe reviewed the proceedings of these plundering trials and disagreed with the verdict for Johnstone and with the sentence for the three men of the 23rd. Military law stipulated that they could not be tried again for the same crime, nor could the commander in chief change the verdict or sentencing. This left Howe no choice but to have all four men released to rejoin their regiments. He stated his disapproval in orders on September 2, giving no reason about Johnstone (presumably he thought the soldier guilty), but declaring "the Punishment inadequate to their Crimes" for the three found guilty. Plundering was far too prevalent for corporal punishment to be a sufficient deterrent.[33] In the meantime, a few hapless marauders did suffer death for their misadventures, but not at the hands of military justice. An officer recorded on August 31, "Two soldiers of the 71st regiment were found a little way from the camp with their throats cut. It is supposed they were plundering and were set upon by some lurking rebels."[34] Another officer wrote of that incident and noted another: "2 Grenadiers hang'd by the Rebels with their plunder on their backs."[35]

An officer in the Brigade of Guards penned a letter to his sister-in-law on September 1 from "Camp, near the head of Elk River," mentioning an especially heinous incident: "A soldier of ours was yesterday taken by the enemy beyond our lines, who had chopped off an unfortunate woman's fingers in order to plunder her of her rings." He went on, "I really think the return of this army to England is to be dreaded by the peaceable inhabitants, and will occasion a prodigious increase of business for Sr. J. Fielding and Jack Ketch,"[36] referring to a real British magistrate and a figurative executioner. No other writer, though, corroborated this event, leaving it unknown whether the soldier was British, German, or Loyalist, or if the event itself was an exaggeration.

As the army moved through the countryside over the next several days, problems continued unabated. On the evening of September 10, Howe finally resorted to the extreme measure threatened eleven days before, ordering the "immediate execution" of Andrew Lauder, a soldier drafted from the 1st Regiment of Foot into the 10th Regiment in 1776.[37] Lauder was "guilty of the crime of Marauding and detected with plunder upon him," apparently caught in the act, as there was no trial. A summary execution would surely put an end to wanton behavior. But, unaccountably, the execution never took place. The army was on the move that very night in an operation that culminated in a dramatic victory at the Battle of Brandywine. Perhaps this put Andrew Lauder's case out of mind; reprieves were normally recorded in general orders, but there was no further mention of him. He continued to serve though September 1778, when he was drafted into the 49th Regiment, and was still on the rolls of that corps in the West Indies in April 1780.[38] For reasons unknown, the general who had deemed corporal punishment inadequate to the crime of plunder failed to follow through on his own orders for capital punishment.

A week later, Robert Hicks and Thomas Burrows of the Brigade of Guards were discovered coming toward their encampment intoxicated and carrying bundles of clothing on their shoulders after being absent from morning roll call. On trial, they claimed to have been out searching for fence rails, presumably for firewood, when some light infantrymen came by and dropped the bundles, which the guardsmen picked up, not knowing what they contained. The guardsmen also claimed to have "found some bread and liquor, the latter of which they drank." Burrows pointed to his twenty years of unblemished service as an indication of his credibility. The two were found guilty and sentenced to receive five hundred lashes each, once again in spite of the threat of capital punishment. Thomas Burford, also of the Guards, was tried by the same court along with two comrades after they tried to sell several pieces of silver tableware to a German soldier. Burford, who spoke a little German, claimed they were in the woods looking for boughs to cover their shelter when they noticed some freshly disturbed earth and found a buried box containing silver and pewter. Having heard that "the Hessian Grenadiers would buy anything," they tried to sell their treasure, only to be reported by their prospective customers. The three were acquitted. Edward Riley of the 15th Regiment was tried for plundering and acquitted, but the proceedings of his trial have not survived. All of these verdicts were confirmed by the commander in chief.[39]

Having secured Philadelphia, the British army encamped north of the city at Germantown. More plundering ensued, more trials, more convictions, a few corporal punishments, and unabated marauding and opportunistic theft. An area plantation owner wrote on September 28 that some light dragoons "broke open the house, 2 desks, 1 Book Case and 1 closet besides several drawers and other things, and ransacked them all." The next day he visited another owner who had "3 closets being broke open, 6 doz. wine taken, some silver spoons, the Bedcloathes taken off 4 Beds, 1 rip'd open, the Tick being taken off, and other Destruction."[40] Two soldiers of the 46th Regiment, John Walton and John Connell, were tried that day for the latter plundering; Walton was sentenced to six hundred lashes, while Connell was acquitted.[41]

Less fortunate was George McCulloch of the 49th, who had joined the army some time before 1775. He, along with fellow 49th soldier Thomas Jones, Benjamin Allen of the Guards, and two others unnamed, went to a Germantown house in September 1777 ostensibly to buy onions and soap. A safe guard placed at the house for protection, being an invalid soldier, fled the scene on the pretense of being afraid of capture by rebels. McCulloch and the others offered to protect the house in return for whatever goods they asked for. The homeowners refused, upon which the soldiers helped themselves, bundling up clothing and throwing it out upstairs windows to colleagues outside, breaking open locked drawers, forcing the owners to open locked chests, and generally ransacking the house in search of valuables. McCulloch was brazen enough to put on a checked shirt belonging to the homeowner in the course of looting. The arrival of a British and a German sergeant put a stop to the destruction and resulted in a court-martial for the three soldiers who were inside the house.

The perpetrators claimed that when they arrived at the house to make their purchases, the homeowners invited them upstairs "where the onions were," and that they found the place already in a shambles, the clothing already bundled up, having been plundered by other soldiers. The homeowners gave them the bundles, they said. McCulloch claimed to have been washing his own shirts earlier in the day, needed soap, and put on the checked shirt at the washing place believing it to be his own. None of these stories stood up to the testimony of the homeowners and other witnesses, and all three were found guilty. Jones was sentenced to one thousand lashes, but McCulloch and Allen were sentenced to be "hanged by the neck until they are dead." The court, "in consideration of the youth of Benjamin Allen," recommended mercy for him. The sentence was approved and directed to be carried out two days after the trial, October 7, "between the hours of ten and twelve in the forenoon, at the head of the Artillery Park." Allen was reprieved, only to be killed in battle two years later. McCulloch received no reprieve. Muster rolls record his death on the appointed day, one month and plenty of plundering after General Howe had ordered the immediate execution of perpetrators.[42]

And so it continued, campaign after campaign. Rampant plunder, a few men caught, a few trials, a few lashings, an occasional execution, and continued rampant plunder. It was not just British soldiers, of course, but also German and Loyalist soldiers, army wives, civilians employed as wagon drivers and artificers, and other followers of the army. Patrick Ferguson, an ambitious young officer, spent time in November 1779 doing what many ambitious young officers did: putting ideas and recommendations on paper to send to his commanding officer. His "Proposed Plan for bringing the Army under strict discipline with regard to marauding" said what regimental officers seem to have known from the start—that it was "necessary for the comfort, refreshment, & encouragement of the Troops in the field, that they be allowed to help themselves in some degree." Most plundering was theft of crops, cattle, and foodstuffs to supplement or replace the salted meat and flour of campaign rations. Because of that, "some latitude is allowed with regard to Poultry, Pigs, Fruits, Roots, &c." On the other hand, there was no excusing "the plundering of houses, destruction of fixtures, wanton carnage of cattle, and other outrages." He pointed to the present state of affairs, where "most of the houses are thoroughly & indiscriminately plundered, the beds cut up, the furniture & windows broke to pieces, the men rob'd of their watches, shoe buckles, & money, whilst their wives & daughters have their pockets and clothes torn from their bodies; and the Father or Husband who does not survey all this with a placid countenance is beat, or branded with the name of traitor and rebel, & the Cattle, either drove off by the inhabitants, or secretly kill'd in different corners by particular advanc'd Corps & the greatest part left to the crows." He somehow believed, however, that all of this could be put to a stop "almost entirely in forty eight hours with very little severity or trouble," even though some of his recommendations had already been tried and consistently proven ineffective. He recommended executing a few offenders as examples and giving strict orders against entering houses, measures that had failed to discourage soldiers since April 1775. He asserted that "the Women, Officers, servants, Drummers and Negroes" caused more "distress" to inhabitants than the rest of the army, which was perhaps true, but his suggestion that they be restricted from "quitting the line of march" had also been tried and proven impossible to enforce. He went on to describe different methods the army's commissaries could use to better collect and distribute cattle, grain, and other stores acquired along the march, naively believing farmers would not look so poorly on the army because they "would in general only lose their small stock, forage, garden stuff, and fire wood, which the necessity of our wants would reconcile them to as unavoidable."[43]

Ferguson focused his long-winded plan on preventing campaign plunder, but garrisons suffered too. The encampments and cantonments of Rhode Island, Long Island, and upper Manhattan were inhabited by soldiers with a voracious appetite for firewood, livestock, poultry, and vegetables. There may have been less overt destruction around garrisons, where it was easier to place guards and the odds of perpetrators being identified by residents was better, but premeditated robbery became a problem of its own. Three cases in Rhode Island characterize the types of crimes.

One night in September 1777, six soldiers of the 22nd Regiment of Foot, assisted by a dog, stole thirteen sheep from a local farm; one man took the dog into the sheep pen, killed the animals, and tossed each one to the others waiting outside the pen. They hauled their kills to a safe location, butchered them, and distributed the carcasses among themselves. Each man got one and three-quarters of a sheep, and they gave one to a soldier's wife in return for rum (their math doesn't seem to have been very good). They hid some carcasses in their own tents and some in the camp picket tent, neither of which were very secure since tent mates and men on picket duty might find them. Carcasses were in fact discovered the next day, and men known to have been absent the night before were singled out of their tents. The commander ordered a court-martial for some "notorious offenders."[44] One man involved in the theft deserted, and two others turned King's evidence—that is, they agreed to testify against their fellows. The three remaining men stood trial, and they as well as those testifying for the prosecution unanimously pointed to the deserter as the ringleader who organized the operation and killed the sheep. That man had joined the regiment in Rhode Island in May that year—whether he arrived from Britain or was enlisted in Rhode Island is not clear—and his desertion made him an easy scapegoat. The three accused were found guilty. One was sentenced to one thousand lashes, while the other two called on officers and sergeants to attest to their overall good behavior. Since one had "always behaved himself well" and the other's character had been "that of a Good Man," they were sentenced to only eight hundred lashes each.[45]

In February 1779, a Rhode Island resident recorded that his house was robbed of silver tableware, buckles, clothing, and money; he suspected soldiers of the 38th Regiment. He later wrote that Corporal John Edwards of the 38th was found in possession of a pair of his silver knee buckles and was tried by a court-martial.[46] No trial record survives, but Edwards was reduced to private soldier around this time, suggesting conviction either of theft or possession of stolen goods. This didn't derail the career of the thirty-two-year-old thirteen-year veteran; a year later he was appointed sergeant and in 1783 was discharged and received a pension.[47] Neither the homeowner nor military documents make any further mention of the theft, which seems to have been simple burglary rather than the ransacking plunder of campaigns.

In September 1778, three grenadiers of the 38th were charged in connection with a violent home invasion in Rhode Island. A soldier came to the door of a country house one night aggressively demanding to search for "rebel stores." The homeowner turned him away with some difficulty, then went to get a couple of Loyalist soldiers to protect his house. But the searching soldier also went for help. Around 11 at night, several soldiers burst into the home, seized the arms of the Loyalist guards, and took the men outside, held the men and women of the house at bayonet point, and robbed the place of an assortment of goods. One assailant even used a ruse, telling the Loyalists that "he had the honor to be a Lieutenant in the Pennsylvania Troops, and that they were resolved to make him suffer for the Cruelties exercised on their Men." Put on trial, the three soldiers of the 38th asserted that they had no knowledge of the crime and called on comrades to testify to their whereabouts on the night of the break-in. Two officers testified to their good character. Even though the homeowners and Loyalist soldiers identified the three, they were acquitted based on the testimony of their fellow soldiers and officers.[48]

This case shows the difficulties the army faced in convicting marauders. Crimes committed in darkness by bands of roving soldiers were difficult to pin on individuals, with uncertain identification by witnesses and alibis supported by comrades. From the early days of the war, safe guards (also spelled "sauve guards") were assigned to protect homes along routes of march and in garrison areas, but these were not absolute deterrents. At the Germantown home invasion by George McCulloch of the 49th and two comrades in September 1777, described above, the safe guard was "lame," probably chosen for the duty because he was unable to march long distances, and he fled when he feared danger. The two safe guards in the September 1778 Rhode Island break-in were easily overwhelmed by slightly superior numbers. Posting safe guards was surely more effective than having none, as many more crimes probably would have occurred without them, but their actions are seldom discussed unless there was trouble.

When Rhode Island was occupied in December 1776, safe guards were immediately assigned to protect farms but were challenged by the extent of the properties and the determination of marauders.[49] Safe guard Thomas Edwards of the 22nd Regiment was dragged through the fields one night by German soldiers who refused to heed his authority; the next day, he sought and received permission to fire on future invaders. The following night he charged his musket with shot made from cut-up musket balls and took position behind a haystack. When German troops descended on the farm, he fired one shot that killed one and wounded another. Put on trial for "Maliciously Firing a Musket, wounding two Hessian Soldiers," Edwards described the abuses he had suffered, and officers testified that he had permission to protect himself and the property. He was acquitted because his actions were "in the discharge of his Duty as a Sauve Guard."[50]

On a march, safe guards were posted where needed when the army arrived and removed again when it departed, sometimes switching off regiment by regiment as elements of the army passed by.[51] In garrison, a safe guard might spend weeks or more posted at a given property. Such was the case with John Smith of the Brigade of Guards, posted at a New York home in August 1778; a fellow soldier brought him "his shirt and his grog for a week."[52] John Hamilton of the 44th pitched a tent in the yard of a Long Island house and spent more than a month there, including over three weeks fending off soldiers of the 64th "who had come there to gather Peaches." After midnight on October 8, 1778, he heard noise among the poultry. He spotted two men, one of whom immediately ran. Hamilton fired at the fugitive then ran at the other, John Sutherland of the 64th, but came face to face with an aimed musket. Twenty-seven-year-old Hamilton, however, had spent his entire three-and-a-half-year career as a soldier in the light infantry; after braving several American campaigns, he wasn't about to let a poultry thief intimidate him. He told Sutherland "that if he offered to make any resistance he would kill him." Sutherland let the gun down, and Hamilton grabbed the muzzle, but Sutherland refused to relinquish the weapon and instead attempted to point it once again. Hamilton had a bayonet fixed on his own firelock and quickly put the point to Sutherland's breast. Sutherland then took the odd step of going to the house, where two musicians from the 33rd Regiment happened to be quartered. Hamilton and the musicians managed to break Sutherland's firelock, upon which he finally submitted.[53]

Tried on a charge of forcing a safe guard, Sutherland claimed to have been so intoxicated that he didn't know what he was doing. The court acquitted him, perhaps because he had utterly failed to actually force the guard. Within three weeks, the spirited Hamilton was appointed corporal in a battalion company, and he was a sergeant by the end of the war.[54] Sutherland, on the other hand, wandered away from his regiment nine months later, again intoxicated; the "poor silly creature" was brought in as a deserter, tried, sentenced to death, and pardoned on the gallows.[55] He was but one of countless soldiers who diverted themselves with liquor during inactive months and who helped themselves—or tried to—to local produce and livestock.

A few sought more than food and firewood. In mid-February 1779, a corporal and five privates, grenadiers of the 71st Regiment, left their quarters at Sag Harbor during the night. They blackened their faces, went to an area home, and asked for water at around midnight. The home-owners directed them to the well, but they forced their way in, the corporal dutifully staying outside to keep watch while the others beat the man of the house and stole an assortment of clothing, bedding, some sides of leather, and a gun. They returned to their quarters and divvied up their spoils. One of them later agreed to testify against the others, and a court-martial found the perpetrators guilty of being absent from quarters and of robbery. One of the privates, Allan Boyd, who broke down the door for the others, was sentenced to death; the remaining men were sentenced to 1,500 lashes and to "make reparation as far as their Abilities will admit."[56] The recruiting officers who had promised the highlanders that "The lands of the rebels will be divided amongst you" certainly never anticipated this.[57]

The same court-martial that convicted the 71st's grenadiers tried four light infantrymen of the 43rd for "being concerned in killing an Ox the property of an Inhabitant," and a grenadier of the 37th for "Killing and secreting a Cow the property of Henry Post an Inhabitant."[58] While that court was in session in the Long Island town of Southampton in March 1779, another court-martial convened in nearby Jamaica to try six grenadiers of the 26th and 37th for "an attempt to maraud the Property of Phillip Platt in the night of 4th instant, and also beating the said Platt in a most inhuman manner."[59] These trials did not end the troubles; within three weeks several grenadiers were apprehended and punished for being "out in the Country with arms no doubt for the purpose of mauroding"; a grenadier battalion officer commented that "some of the rascals deserve to be shot." The following month, "the 57th Light Company march'd from Jamaica to join their Regt for ill behavior & obstinate perseverance in it," but the specific nature of the "ill behavior" was not recorded.[60]

Summer brought some measure of reprieve to the region when a substantial portion of the troops moved to front-line locations, spending the summer vying for the best position should a major engagement occur. None did. By late October, the grenadier battalions moved back to winter quarters on Long Island, earlier in the season than usual, where they "saw some old acquaintances who I believe are sorry to see the Grenadiers return . . . for which indeed they have reason, for they suffer'd a good deal last winter from the depradation & tricks of some sad rascals." Within a month, trials commenced once again and punishments were meted out "to put a stop to this infamous practice."[61] From fall 1779 into the following spring, only four British soldiers were tried by general courts for crimes against Long Island inhabitants, including a trooper of the 17th Light Dragoons for housebreaking and three men of the 17th Regiment of Foot for robbery.[62] During the same period, six Loyalist soldiers of the Queen's Rangers were tried by general courts for similar crimes.[63] Probably more British and Loyalists were tried by lower courts for which no records survive.

In all, twenty-one British soldiers were tried by general courts for crimes committed against Long Island inhabitants from fall 1778 through summer 1782. Many infractions involved theft of livestock, but some were for housebreaking, robbery, harm to homeowners who tried to defend themselves, and even one murder. Twenty-five others, Loyalist soldiers or civilian inhabitants, were also tried during this period by general courts for crimes against Long Island residents, and there may have been additional trials for which there are no records.[64] Certainly there were crimes for which the perpetrators were not caught and for which no trials occurred.

There were also soldiers who went out of their way to protect inhabitants. Sergeant Donald McCraw of the 42nd Regiment's grenadier company, a French and Indian War veteran who had been in the regiment for twenty-two years,[65] was quartered in a farmhouse in Jamaica on Long Island. The forty-four-year-old Perthshire native, suffering from an abdominal hernia,[66] stayed behind when the grenadier battalion went on campaign early in 1780, and "from the good treatment of the People of the House, he considered himself as a Safe Guard." One night, a band of

Loyalist soldiers with blackened faces, one with a gun, forced their way into the home and demanded valuables from the homeowner. McCraw attacked them with his broadsword, parrying the musket with his bare hand, and wounded two assailants before they all fled. His bold action led to the conviction of nine Loyalist soldiers who had robbed at least five houses over a six-week period.[67]

The regimental punishment books surveyed in chapter 3 demonstrate that a minority of soldiers committed the majority of crimes. While no data survives to prove that this was true on Long Island, or in any garrison or campaign, it was probably the case. A grenadier of the 42nd Regiment, Alexander McDonald, stood trial twice in a nine-month period. The first time, in late November 1780, he and another soldier tried to steal a cow from a farm a mile from their cantonment, but two alert black farmhands caught them, shooting McDonald's accomplice dead. For this "infamous business," the "rascal McDonald" was tried and sentenced to one thousand lashes, and his company commander tried "to get him turned over to the Navy or somewhere else."[68] That he was already considered a "rascal" suggests that this wasn't McDonald's first brush with military discipline. Corporal punishment, to which he may have been no stranger, did not deter him, nor could his captain foist him off on the navy. Half a year later, he killed a hog belonging to a Long Island widow, and when a neighbor challenged him, he attacked the man with his hatchet, wounding him in the head. Now called a "notorious scoundrel," he again stood trial and was sentenced to another one thousand lashes.[69] He died the following year, in summer 1782, of unknown causes.[70] It would be easy to assume he died of complications from the punishment, but it is just as likely he was killed fighting with inhabitants in another late-night livestock raid.

Alexander McDonald's marauding was stopped not by punishment but by his death. Plundering by British soldiers in general was stopped not by punishment but by the war's end and the army's departure. The army that had been sent to America to keep peace and maintain order destroyed all hope of gaining the trust of a population that resented its presence and was suspicious of its intent from the outset.[71] There is no way to determine the number of soldiers who took liberties with the property and persons of the colonists they were supposed to treat as fellow British citizens, or the proportion of marauders that were British regulars, German auxiliaries, or Loyalist troops. But some were British, and even a few was enough. Probably there were a few incorrigible characters in each regiment who committed most of the crimes, and some portion that occasionally took advantage of an opportunistic situation, while the remainder—probably the majority—adhered to the Articles of War and general principles of decent behavior, at least most of the time. No matter the numbers, the plunder problem was severe enough, and went on long enough, to taint the army's reputation with inhabitants of the American colonies-cum-states during the war, and in histories of the war ever since.

CHAPTER 10

Bringers Handsomely Rewarded

RECRUITING FOR GLOBAL WAR

"I'D BE A FINE LAD, IF I'D LEAVE MY MAMMY," wrote John Hawthorne of a recruiting sergeant's friendly goading. When the young prospect objected that he would "never draw a trigger of a gun" nor "be shot at, whilst I keep my senses," the sergeant scoffed and told him to go home "and bear your mother's lashes, loiter about, and live among the ashes," then "gave a snap to catch me by the nose," all to the entertainment of "the gaping, raw recruits" who looked on and laughed. But the sergeant offered more than humiliation. "I'll bring you right cheer, mountains of roast beef, and wells of beer, and bowls of punch at every inn we call, that a dragoon might swim in, horse and all; then when you have beat out a Frenchman's brains, a purse of good French gold rewards your pains." It was a pitch well designed to tempt a young wanderer to become a soldier.

Hawthorne's writing was fictional, but he knew his subject well. He was a trooper in the 6th Dragoons, having left his apprenticeship as a linen weaver in a small Irish town to enlist in 1778. He may have responded to words very much like those of the recruiting sergeant in his poem "The Journey and Observations of a Countryman," published just a year after he enlisted.[1] Being a soldier was a path to prosperity, at the expense of the French, for in Great Britain in 1778, France was on everyone's mind.

France's entry into the war changed the army's manpower demands drastically. Instead of an opponent an ocean away, Britain now faced an enemy whose land could be seen on a clear day. There was still a war to fight in America, but an adversary with colonial ambitions as extensive as Britain's was also a threat to valuable possessions in the West Indies, the Mediterranean, India—even the English coast. Defending those interests required a bigger army. This was attained in several ways. The size of deployed regiments was increased yet again, from the 54 private soldiers per company authorized in 1775 to 70 per company—an increase of 160 men for most infantry regiments. New regiments were authorized and raised—the 72nd through 83rd Regiments of Foot authorized in December 1777, the 85th through 95th in 1779, the 96th through 101st in 1780, the 102nd in 1781, the 103rd and 104th in 1782. The Royal Highland Emigrants, a Loyalist regiment raised in America, was put onto the regular establishment as the 84th Regiment. Militia regiments were mobilized and expanded in England, fencible regiments were raised in Scotland (similar to militias, for service only within Scotland), and a plethora of volunteer corps appeared throughout Ireland. Only a few of the new-raised regiments, and none of the militia or fencibles, served in the thirteen rebelling American colonies. The recruiting furor was, however, shared by all, and the intensive efforts to enlist men brought about some bad practices and abuses that have been subsequently cited as characteristic of recruiting practices in general during the 1770s and 1780s.[2]

For additional companies recruiting for regiments in America, the military buildup meant competition for recruits. The methods remained the same, but now men were accepted who were shorter, younger, older. A poster for the 22nd Regiment of Foot seeking volunteers gave no further criteria than "Young Men, not under five feet four inches and a half high," while the 52nd sought "Young Lads under Twenty Years of Age, five Feet five Inches high, and Men, under Twenty-eight, five Feet six." A poster for the 45th gave no criteria at all for "Gentlemen Volunteers . . . who have Courage enough to Fight for their Country." The enlistment bounty increased to three guineas and was explicitly mentioned on the posters of the 22nd and 45th; the 22nd offered an additional guinea to "All such Men who are fit for Grenadiers." Addressing the characters known to enlist, the 52nd Regiment invited "Young Men whose inclinations lead them to prefer a Military Life," promising that they would "experience every Indulgence due to their Merit" and receive "every thing they can wish or desire in Honesty to complete a Gentleman Soldier."[3]

New regiments added patriotic fervor to their promises of a generous bounty and adventurous life. The 22nd Light Dragoons, raised in 1779, began their recruiting poster pitch by addressing it to "All those who prefer the Glory of bearing Arms to any servile mean Employ," then heightened motivation by singling out those who "have Spirit to stand forth in Defence of their King and Country, against the treacherous Designs of France and Spain." Rather than mention money, there was the promise of being "handsomely Cloathed, most compleatly Accoutred, mounted on noble Hunters, and treated with Kindness and Generosity." The following year, the 88th Regiment of Foot, called the British Volunteers, filled their posters with flowery language that repeatedly invoked national pride. It began, "Arouse Britons for the Honour and Glory of Old England! Now is the Moment my noble-minded Countrymen, now is the Crisis of our Country's Fate!" It made a general appeal to join the army or the navy, for "By acting thus, Britons, you shall restore the native Resplendency of our Beloved Country, chastise the Perfidious French and Spaniards, and be again united to our Brethren in America, who have been so basely deluded from their Natural Allegiance by the sworn Enemies of All Englishmen." The regiment called not for just any volunteers, but for "All Real Volunteers whose Hearts are filled with Loyalty for the best of Kings, and Love for the Noblest of Constitutions, and who are willing to maintain the Honour of Old England in Defence of French and Spanish Treachery," offering them "now a noble Opportunity of obtaining immortal Renown." "The Sons of Freedom are alone worthy to support the Honour of Old England, and the Conduct of the Noble Regiment of British Volunteers, shall prove that Englishmen never wanted Courage to defend their Wives, their Sweethearts, or their Firesides."[4]

Recruiting expenses were offset in some areas by public subscriptions for raising new regiments. So it was that the 72nd Regiment of Foot was called the Royal Manchester Volunteers, the 79th the Royal Lancashire Volunteers, the 83rd the Royal Glasgow Volunteers, and so forth. The county of Warwick opened a subscription to raise a new regiment, but county officials chose instead to support the 6th Regiment of Foot, recruiting anew after returning from American service in 1778. The regiment became the Warwickshire Regiment, "in Honour of the Loyalty and Zeal manifested by the County in Support of Government, at this critical and important Junction of public Affairs." In April, regimental officers arrived in Birmingham, the county's principal city, and "made a public Procession through the Town, to encourage Volunteers to enlist. They were preceded by a blue Flag, a Band of martial Music, a large Piece of Roast Beef, several Loaves of Bread, and a Barrel of Beer, and were attended by a great Concourse of People."[5] The success of efforts like these set the precedent for a new system of county designations that would be introduced in 1782.

Regional recruiting and national identity were particularly important in Scotland. While additional companies continued to bring in significant numbers of Scottish recruits, the army authorized six new highland regiments, widely referred to by the names of the colonels charged with raising them—the 73rd (McLeod's), 74th (Campbell's, or Argyll Highlanders), 76th (McDonald's), 77th (Murray's, or Atholl Highlanders), 78th (Seaforth's), and 81st (Gordon's). Each was larger than typical British infantry regiments, with five sergeants, five corporals, and 100 private men per company; the 73rd had two battalions, doubling the number of companies from ten to twenty. Other regiments raised at this time, early 1778, also were of this increased size.

In Scotland, accepting men "of low size" was particularly advantageous. The 74th Regiment, which would be sent to America, filled its complement of almost 1,100 men in the four months from being authorized in December 1777 to being inspected in April 1778. They included 149 men under five feet, four inches tall. There were 77 sixteen- and seventeen-year-olds, and 192 men older than thirty, all of them "in general strong and stout." The inspecting officer considered about 800 of the men to be "exceeding good," while the others were "rather too young, but very stout promising Boys." About two-thirds were highlanders and one-third lowlanders, with a handful of English and Irish. Twelve men were rejected by the inspector for being too old and four for being too young.[6] The 76th, also bound for the American war, was inspected in Inverness in May 1778. This regiment had 241 men under five foot four, but the inspecting officer considered them "very fine little fellows." The 118 sixteen- and seventeen-year-olds were "promising lads," and the 148 men over thirty were "stout fellows." While a bit over two-thirds were highlanders, the remainder were equal numbers of lowlanders and Irishmen, over 100 of each, plus a handful of English. Forty-five were rejected, but overall the men were "very uniform as to size, not tall, but very strong men in General, and fit for any service, the Highlanders Remarkable fine young fellows."[7]

The 80th Regiment, inspected in Edinburgh in June, raised men who were "in general not very well looking, but seem all fit for Service, and none under the age of sixteen." They consisted of almost 700 lowlanders, just over 100 English, and just under 100 Irish, of whom 251 were over thirty years old. The grenadiers were "of a tolerable size, a good many Old men, but still fit for a few years service," while the light infantry were "very low, but neat little fellows, a few of them too young for that duty." Twenty-three were rejected.[8] The 82nd Regiment, the last of the new-raised regiments sent to the rebelling American colonies, had raised only six companies when they were inspected in April 1778. Of those 600 men, 148 were below five foot four. The 86 that were sixteen or seventeen years old were "promising young lads," and the 142 over thirty were "stout men." Most were lowlanders, with some highlanders, English, and Irish in the mix, in general considered "tolerable good men."[9] In an unusual move, these companies embarked for Halifax, Nova Scotia, that year rather than wait for the remainder of the regiment to be completed.

The "neat little fellows" of the highlands often did not speak English, having been bred in regions that spoke Scottish Gaelic, often called "Erse" by period writers. This was manageable for an army with a long tradition of recruiting native Scottish and Irish speakers. The 76th Regiment had an "excellent officer, who had served a long time in the 42d, was perfectly acquainted with the character of the Highlanders, and spoke the Gaelic language most fluently." This made the problem solvable, but not with ease. "It so happened that few of the non-commissioned officers who understood the drill were acquainted with the Gaelic language, and as all words of command are given in English, the major directed that neither officer nor non-commissioned officer ignorant of the former language should endeavour to learn it. The consequence was that the Highlanders were behindhand in being drilled, as they had, in addition to their other duties, to acquire the knowledge of a new language." Initially, only the lowlanders and Irishmen, about a third of the soldiers, were able to do routine duties, while the highlanders struggled to learn; "uncommon pains were taken by the major to explain to them the articles of war, and the nature of the duties required of them in Gaelic." Soon enough, the highlanders were fit for service "and evinced a natural talent for the profession of a soldier."[10]

Recruiting posters for the 22nd, 45th, 52nd, and 88th Regiments conclude with a line that hints of a potential darker side to the recruiting fervor. "Any Person who brings a good Man, shall be handsomely Rewarded," promised the 45th; "Bringers will be handsomely rewarded," touted the 52nd, and the 88th proclaimed, "Bringers of Recruits may depend on being most liberally rewarded." The 22nd was more explicit, offering to any man who brought a recruit "half a Guinea reward; if a Grenadier, One Guinea, to be paid with thanks."[11] The intent was innocent enough: a wandering lad might need help—or persuasion—to find a recruiter. But there were people who made a practice, if not a living, at inveigling men to join the East India Company, and warfare threatening Britain's very shores presented an opportunity to expand their trade. Crimps, as they were called, would not ordinarily be able to bring an unwilling man to the army because of the requirement for attestation before a magistrate.[12] James Miller, a young man from the lowlands of Scotland, was "singled out, by one of those worthies called crimps" and was glad for it, as he had always intended to enlist. "A soldier, in my idea, must be the first of mortals, being the guardian of his country," he wrote of his youthful zeal for the profession. His conversation with a crimp in 1756 initiated a career of almost twenty years in the 15th Regiment of Foot, followed by an officer's commission in a Loyalist regiment during the American Revolution.[13] But 1778 saw a new law enacted that allowed men to be brought into the army involuntarily: the Press Act.

Pressing men, something normally the purview of the navy to obtain seamen who were idle between voyages, was a wartime emergency measure "for the more easy and better recruiting of his Majesty's Land Forces." An army press act had been passed at the onset of the Seven Years' War for a very limited duration.[14] The act passed on May 28, 1778, was specific in scope, allowing men to be pressed only in "the City of London, The City and Liberties of Westminster, and . . . parts of the County of Middlesex" as well as in Scotland. Only men who were "able-bodied and idle," and those who were "disorderly" and "could not, upon Examination, prove themselves to exercise and industriously follow some lawful Trade or Employment" or other means of support could be pressed. Petty smugglers could be pressed, while harvest workers were exempt. Men needed to be fit, between seventeen and forty-five, and at least five feet, four inches tall. After five years they were entitled to be discharged. In February 1779, a new press act superseded the 1778 act, expanding the range of men subject to impressment. The new law widened the age rage to sixteen to fifty, and those sixteen to eighteen could be five foot three. Men who had abandoned their families could be pressed. The new act applied to all of Great Britain but was suspended throughout England and Wales from the end of May through the end of November, the London area excepted, so as not to interfere with farming.[15] In May 1780,

G. R.
YOUNG MEN

Whofe Inclinations lead them to prefer a Military Life, may have an Opportunity
of engaging in

His Majefty's 52d Regt. of Foot,

Commanded by

General T R A P A U D,

And will experience every Indulgence due to their Merit;
Let them repair to the Rendezvous, at

The PLOUGH,
In Plough-Yard, Shoreditch.

Where a proper Officer attends.

They fhall receive his Majefty's Royal Bounty, and have every thing they can wifh or defire
in Honefty to complete a Gentleman Soldier.   GOD fave the KING !

Young Lads under Twenty Years of Age, five Feet five Inches high, and Men, under
Twenty - eight, five Feet fix will be taken.

Bringers will be handfomely rewarded.

Recruiting poster for the 52nd Regiment of Foot, appealing to young men aspiring to become "Gentleman Soldiers." Courtesy Eric H. Schnitzer.

the press act was repealed, and impressment remained illegal for the remainder of the war.

The acts also provided incentive to those who enlisted voluntarily; indeed, their true purpose was to encourage men to volunteer rather than be pressed. The enlistment bounty was raised to three pounds by the 1778 act, and to three pounds three shillings by the 1779 act. Volunteers would be discharged at the end of the war if they had served three years, versus five years for pressed men, and under the 1779 act, men who volunteered once would never be called to serve again. Both acts lifted restrictions on where volunteers could practice trades after leaving the army, a good incentive for tradesmen.

A jailor at London's Savoy prison, where pressed men were held until the army could take them, observed, surely to no one's surprise, that "the whole of the impresst men seem determinately bent to get out." On the evening of November 21, 1778, a group of them attacked their jailors with "short bludgeons cut from the brooms that were given them for the cleaning of their apartments." A few got out of the confinement area and into the kitchen. Most were apprehended, but two men threw themselves out a window. One escaped, but the other, a Jewish man named Thomas Ralph bound for the 5th Regiment of Foot in the West Indies, landed on his head and died.[16]

In effect for under two years, limited in scope geographically for thirteen of twenty-three months, the press acts had only a small impact on the army that served in America from 1775 through 1783. There is no way to measure the number of volunteers the acts stimulated. What can be shown, at least in part, is the number of men pressed while the acts were in effect. Data is available for six months from March through October 1779, when the second press act was in effect in Scotland and the London area. During that time, 1,463 men were pressed in England and Wales, of whom 501 were discharged as being either unsuitable or ineligible, had died, or for other reasons never joined the army.[17] In Scotland, 67 men were pressed from March through June.[18] The eleven new regiments raised during that time, the 85th through 95th, each consisting of 700 private men, accounted for almost 8,000 recruits, and the other eighty-four infantry regiments, twenty-two cavalry regiments, artillery, Guards, and other corps were all recruiting during this period; at the very maximum, pressed men could not have made up more than 10 percent of army recruits during these six months of 1779.[19]

An embarkation return dated March 26, 1779, at Chatham Barracks, the training depot outside London, tabulates 1,329 recruits for each of fifteen regiments in America, including the numbers of impressed men.[20] Of the latter, there were only seventy, about 5 percent, all of whom were certainly pressed under the 1778 act (since the 1779 act had gone into effect only the previous month). An onlooker who watched these men march by in handcuffs under a guard of armed soldiers remarked that pressing them "proves the utility of the late act in making these men useful to the state who were before a nuisance to society, and lived chiefly by fraud and rapine."[21] Initially allocated to the 60th Regiment of Foot, a corps that served exclusively in North America, the seventy were instead distributed among only six of the fifteen regiments receiving recruits:

7th Regiment: 92 recruits, including 9 impressed men
23rd Regiment: 49 recruits, including 13 impressed men
37th Regiment: 89 recruits, including 15 impressed men
42nd Regiment: 45 recruits, including 6 impressed men
44th Regiment: 147 recruits, including 16 impressed men
63rd Regiment: 133 recruits, including 11 impressed men[22]

Three new-raised regiments preparing for their voyage to America received a further seventy-three impressed men in April 1779, distributed as follows:

76th Regiment: 24 impressed men
80th Regiment: 37 impressed men
82nd Regiment: 12 impressed men [23]

The first two regiments consisted of about 1,100 men each, and the 82nd's six companies of about 600; here again, the proportion of impressed men was negligible.

These are the only figures available, which suggest but do not prove that the overall number of men pressed into army service was small, and the number sent to serve in the American war trivial. The report giving numbers for March through October 1779 included a lengthy analysis of numbers of voluntary recruits during the same period, and for the same length of time beforehand, concluding that the existence of the press act had increased volunteerism by one-third.[24]

Whether or not the press acts actually increased volunteerism, they invited corruption. Both the 1778 and 1779 acts included a provision that "Any person whatever who shall discover to a Constable an able person, liable to be impressed under this Act, is entitled to 10 shillings reward."[25]

The secretary at war recognized when approving the acts that "it has been necessary to give Powers to the Commissioners, which, if abus'd, may occasion Acts of Cruelty and Oppression," and cautioned that no matter how badly soldiers were needed, "no necessity of the State can authorize their being got at the Expence of Justice and Humanity."[26] But abuses occurred. Throughout the time of the acts, pressed men plead their cases that they were not "within the meaning of the act"—the War Office sent out letters ordering the discharge of eight men during the third week of March 1779 alone,[27] and between that March and October, 138 were discharged "as not being Objects of the Act."[28] For some, relief did not come in time. A man named John Watkins was pressed into the 60th Regiment, then drafted into the additional company of the 37th Regiment and put on a transport for America. The War Office, finding he "was not at the time of his being impressed within the meaning of the Act," ordered him discharged, but his ship had already sailed. When the recruits arrived in New York, Watkins pleaded to be discharged but was denied; after three weeks, "refusing to enlist," he was discharged by the regiment and put on a warship. The ship was at sea when the discharge order arrived in New York, and although the navy would honor the discharge, the unfortunate Watkins had to wait for the ship to return to New York before he could finally be "returned to his friends" "on Board some vessel bound to England."[29]

Other men were enlisted improperly, the terms of the press act and the need for manpower apparently emboldening recruiters and crimps. David Honeyman claimed to have been "in liquor" when a party of the 52nd Regiment enlisted him in 1780, and never to have been attested, so he deserted at the first opportunity. Veteran Thomas Oltrup, discharged after seven years in the Foot Guards followed by seventeen years in the 10th Dragoons, stopped at a tavern in Leeds, Yorkshire, where there happened to be a recruiting party from the 23rd Regiment of Foot. After drinking a pint of cider he fell asleep, fatigued after walking over twenty miles that day. While he dozed, one of the recruiters slipped his pocketbook from his pocket, removed his discharge and other papers, and put them in the fire. Then they put a shilling in his hand, and when he awoke claimed he had enlisted. When he refused to stay with them, they put him into Leeds prison, and he was then sent to Savoy in London. He wrote a letter to the commander in chief of the army pleading his case, offering to "sound the horn, trumpet, and beat the drum" as he had done, or even serve as a private man, as long as he was released from prison.[30]

In the worst cases, men were outright kidnapped. In January 1781, long after the repeal of the press acts, twenty-year-old builder John Matson was looking for work in London when a man offered him a lucrative position. Matson allowed the stranger to buy some food and drink for him, then followed him to a house where it was announced that he had enlisted into the 100th Regiment of Foot. He was locked up with "three or four more, dressed in white jackets and caps, all young men, and in a sorrowful condition—some of them crying." Although "a soldier being a calling I hated more than any other," he found no opportunity to escape while confined to a barrack yard at Hilsea, and by March he was on a ship bound for India. He spent nearly six years in the 100th Regiment, finally being discharged in June 1786 after returning to England.[31]

Cases like Matson's, and the many pleas handled by the War Office of men improperly impressed, were among the factors that led to the repeal of the 1779 Press Act in May 1780. Writing in 1786, a British militia officer expounded on the bad impact the acts had not only on communities but on the army itself:

> An act for impressing soldiers took place in 1779, when all the thieves, pickpockets and vagabonds in the environs of London, too lame to run away, or too poor to bribe the parish officers, were apprehended and delivered over as soldiers to the regiments quartered in the very townes and villages where these banditti had lived and been taken; these men being thus set at large in the midst of their old companions and connections, immediately deserted, whereby the whole expence, by no means an inconsiderable one, was thrown away: nor did the soldiers of the regiments on which they were imposed, take the least pains to prevent their escape, or to retake them; as they justly considered being thus made the companions of thieves and robbers, a most grievous and cruel insult, and loudly complained of it as such, to their officers. Indeed it seems to have been a very ill judged measure, tending to destroy that professional pride, that esprit de corps which ought most assiduously to be cultivated in every regiment.[32]

The army did not press men again during the 1775–1783 conflict, relying instead solely on volunteers encouraged by substantial bounties and promises of prosperity. An extreme case was the 99th Regiment of Foot, "raised for the Defence of Jamaica only" and therefore called the Royal Jamaica Volunteers. Besides an initial bounty of five guineas, available only during the first four weeks of recruiting after which it dropped to three, soldiers were promised a supplement of five shillings per week over and above their usual wages, paid by "the Merchants and Planters of the Island," more than doubling their weekly pay. Wives and children would also be paid, and there was even a promise to provide for widows and orphans. "Lads of Spirit" were invited to "embrace this glorious Opportunity and advantageous Terms, which may never again offer," allowing them to experience "the many Advantages peculiar to that Island."[33] The advertisement did not mention the disadvantage of high mortality among Europeans not acclimated to the island's diseases.

Among the several hundred men tried by general court-martial for desertion in America between 1775 and 1783, only two testified that they had been enlisted by nefarious means. One was John Ingram, a seafaring man who was in port on the island of St. Vincents in April 1776. The 6th Regiment of Foot was there too, preparing to embark for New York. Two sergeants of the 6th claimed to have enlisted Ingram, but after arriving in New York, he signed on to the crew of a British transport ship and was not found out as a soldier for three months. On trial for desertion, he claimed that "he was in liquor, when he was enlisted, and did not know that he was so, 'till they came and carried him away." Since he had accepted pay and clothing as a soldier from April until he absconded in November, he was found guilty.[34]

In June 1777, George Hartley of the 60th told a more complex story. He had been a soldier in the 59th Regiment and was drafted into the 38th—which is confirmed by muster rolls—but claimed to have been discharged and sent back to England. He explained "That he did not voluntarily enlist in the 60th But was trepann'd by a soldier of the Foot Guards a few days after he arrived in London, and was attested when he was drunk, before Justice Goodchild; and immediately after was sent aboard the Springfield Transport." He deserted his post in New York in June and was soon after apprehended for desertion. The veracity of his story is questionable from two perspectives. First, muster rolls indicate he was still in the 38th, albeit sick, as late as April 19, 1777. For him to have been discharged, gone to England, then returned to America all in the space of two months is hardly possible. Second, the court noted that Hartley was "a Wretched, Unhappy Man, whose Conduct carries with it, Evident marks of Insanity." He was found guilty and sentenced to lashes, but the punishment was pardoned. The court did not address his story of being trepanned, the term for being enlisted while intoxicated (more specifically, for being plied with liquor by the recruiter until intoxicated). If true, it may have occurred in New York rather than London. Or it may have been a tall tale told by "a Wretched, Unhappy Man."[35]

After he deserted from the 23rd Regiment in June 1777, John Warren told an American officer that he had been "pressed in London" early that year. He arrived in New York in mid-June, went to his regiment in New Jersey, and deserted at the first opportunity.[36] A fellow 1777 recruit, Nicolas Edgar, deserted from the 23rd in South Carolina in April 1780. He made his way to Pennsylvania, where he took an oath of allegiance in August, claiming to have been "pressed in England."[37] There was no press act in effect in 1777, so these men may have been trying to gain favor by suggesting that they had not enlisted voluntarily. It is also possible they were referring to a practice that has tainted the British army in American histories ever since the war, the enlistment of criminals. The numbers were small. There were conditions to be met, in particular that the regiment receiving the man had to deem him suitable for a soldier, physically fit, and with a character that would not be abhorrent to the volunteer career soldiers alongside whom he would serve. And like all enlistments, it was voluntary—the criminal had the option to serve in the army instead of serving jail time. Nevertheless, the bad connotation has been used to characterize the generality of soldiers.[38]

Sentences of men convicted of petty larceny or misdemeanors could be reduced or remitted on the condition that those men joined the army.[39] Quarter-sessions records show numerous instances of this practice before and during the war, but the numbers amount to only a handful compared to the overall volume of wartime recruiting. Between 1775 and 1781, for example, there were fourteen such cases in Essex, three in Hertfordshire, two in Shropshire, and none in London, suggesting barely a few hundred for all counties.[40] There are also a few known instances of men opting to enlist before being sentenced. A look at the crimes involved shows that convicted enlistees were not dangerous criminals. In Leicester in March 1779, "Wm. Tomkins, for marrying Ann Dunmore (his former wife being alive); John Hill, charged with stealing a silver watch; and Wm. Brown, for stopping Dan. Hickling on the highway, were ordered to be sent for soldiers."[41] In Cornwall that October, laborer William Menadew pleaded guilty to stealing a sack worth sixpence and was sentenced to seven years in prison or enlistment.[42] A laborer in Bythorn, Cambridgeshire, guilty of housebreaking in 1780, was offered enlistment instead of jail time.[43] In 1781, Richard Barnett of Helston, Cornwall, stole "six yards of flowered cotton" worth tenpence and was sentenced to six months in jail "unless he chooses to enlist in an infantry regiment."[44] In October 1782, two Cornwall men charged with failure to pay fees to parishes for maintenance of their bastard children were offered enlistment as an alternative to prosecution, and a man convicted of stealing a silver spoon worth sixpence had a choice between a month in prison or enlistment.[45] In all cases, enlistment was a choice, and the men were under the same wartime terms as any other enlistee, discharge at the end of the conflict if they had served three years. The time in the army (or navy) might be longer than the prison sentence, but the experience was not as harsh. A royal pardon could commute the sentence of a man convicted and jailed, and allow enlistment as an alternative, but that was rare. In the five years before the American war, no such pardons were granted, and from 1775 through 1781, there were 764 granted in England and Wales, accounting for only a tiny portion of the recruits raised during that period. The majority of these men were sent to the harsh climates of Africa or the West Indies, places where rampant illness ravaged recruits and caused a steady demand for expendable manpower.[46]

In August 1776, a recruiting officer from the 46th Regiment located and enlisted "six very fine Lads now confined in Shrewsbury Gaol for petty Offences" and wrote to the secretary at war for an order to have them discharged from jail.[47] Four of them subsequently appear on the regiment's muster rolls; whether the other two were not allowed to enlist, chose not to, or failed to join the regiment for some other reason is not known. Those who did join had careers showing they were good candidates for soldiers. They arrived in America in the first half of 1777. John Herbert appears to have been killed in the Battle of Germantown that October. Edward Allen served for a year and a half, at which time the 46th was sent to the West Indies. There is a one-year gap in the muster rolls after which Allen no longer appears; we know nothing of what happened to him. William Davis served throughout the regiment's time in the American colonies and the West Indies. The regiment returned to England in 1782, and Davis was appointed corporal that November. Edward Kitson rose through the ranks more quickly. He was appointed corporal in January 1778, became a sergeant in August 1782, and was still in that capacity when the regiment returned to England.[48]

Deserters in Great Britain, many of whom fled from recruiting parties, were often held in prisons when they were caught. If they could not be returned to their regiments, such as the forty deserters from regiments in America sent to Savoy prison in December 1776,[49] they were liable to be put into other corps that needed men, especially those bound for far-flung places where they would be less likely to desert again. In February 1780, forty-three deserters and thirty-one impressed men were sent to the African Corps serving on the notoriously deadly west coast of Africa. That November, twenty-three deserters and nineteen impressed men, among the last of those still being held, were put into the 99th Regiment headed for Jamaica. In January 1781, the War Office directed that deserters "who appear to have been in two, or more Regiments" be "turned over to Regiments stationed, or serving, Abroad." In the first three months of that year, ninety-nine deserters were sent from Savoy to Portsmouth to be drafted into the 98th and 100th that later served in India; a further eleven were lucky enough to arrive too late for the embarkation, were drafted instead into the 6th Regiment of Foot, and remained in England.[50] George Townsend, recruited for the 22nd Regiment serving in America, deserted, was caught and sent to Savoy. In 1780, he was drafted into the 58th Regiment in Gibraltar along with a number of other men.[51] An officer in another corps in Gibraltar referred to these men in the 58th as "the Savoy lads."[52]

Although drafting was a long-standing practice for completing the strength of regiments going overseas and reinforcing those already deployed, it was used in a new way during the recruiting frenzy of 1778–1781, with repercussions that caused drafting in general to be mischaracterized as detrimental to military morale.[53] Drafting—transferring soldiers from one regiment to another—had been used to maintain the portion of experienced soldiers in regiments, and men could volunteer to be drafted. Meanwhile, one benefit of voluntary enlistment was that recruits could choose the regiment into which they enlisted. A man might enlist in a particular regiment "because his brother, his cousin, or several of his townsmen belong to it; or perhaps because the son of his father's landlord, or his nephew, is an officer in it; this man perhaps would not have engaged in any other corps."[54] They could choose a regiment about to go overseas, or one that had just returned if they hoped to stay in Britain for a while. The demands of global warfare changed that. Several times, in response to urgent needs for manpower, recruits rather than experienced soldiers were drafted from one regiment into another to reinforce a specific location.

In May 1778, eight hundred recruits raised for regiments in America were instead drafted into four regiments defending Gibraltar, depriving

thirty-two regiments in one war zone of badly needed men but reinforcing a critical bastion in another.[55] When a large body of recruits disembarked in America in 1780, problems arose because of "numbers of men
that were enlisted and cloath'd by one Regiment having been drafted into
another just previous to their embarkation"; not all accounts had been
settled properly, and there was "apparent hardship done both to Regiments and to the Individuals themselves."[56] A far worse problem occurred
in April 1779, when a detachment of recruits raised for the 42nd and
71st Regiments was brought to Leith, a port near Edinburgh, and informed they were drafted into the 83rd. They were highlanders, native
speakers of Erse accustomed to wearing highland garb, and they had enlisted in highland regiments. The 83rd, the Royal Glasgow Volunteers,
was an English-speaking, breeches-wearing lowland regiment. Some recruits refused to be drafted. Local troops were called to force them on
board the 83rd's transports, and in the meantime local residents brought
liquor to the recruits, fueling their belligerence. When the local troops
arrived, there was confusion over whether the recruits were being taken
prisoners, after which they could plead their case, or being forced to embark. Negotiations ensued; one recruit explained, in Erse, "That if an offer
had been made to them of a voluntary draught into the 83d," he would
have gone, but "they were going to boat them like a parcel of sheep; and,
since that was the case, he would stand out to the last." Unrest increased.
Bayonets were drawn, fighting broke out, then gunfire. "Several of His
Majesty's subjects were killed, and others wounded."

Three recruits, Charles Williamson and Archibald Maciver of the
42nd and Robert Budge of the 71st, went to trial for inciting mutiny. In
their defense, they repeated the complaints they and other recruits voiced
when refusing to be drafted—that they enlisted in highland regiments
because, having spent their lives entirely in the highlands, "they neither
could have understood the language, nor have used their arms, or perched
in the dress of any other regiment." In the 83rd, they claimed, they "could
not have performed the duties of a soldier." In addition, they included a
thoughtful legalistic argument, perhaps benefiting more from careful research after the mutiny than from great insight before it. They pointed
out that the Articles of War, with which they were familiar even as recruits and which "cannot be unknown to any soldier," stated in Section 6
Article 3 that "no non-commissioned officer or soldier shall inlist himself
in any other regiment, troop, or company, without a regular discharge
from the regiment, troop, or company, in which he last served, on the
penalty of being reputed a deserter, and suffering accordingly." Further,

any officer knowingly receiving such men could be charged. The recruits had been enlisted by the 42nd and 71st and had not been discharged, so there was no legal basis, they claimed, for them serving in the 83rd, war or no war. The court nonetheless found all three men guilty of mutiny and sentenced them to be shot. With monarchical wisdom, the king pardoned all three, two in "regard to the former commendable and distinguished behaviour of the 42d regiment" and the third because he did not "appear to have had any forward part in the mutiny." They were sent to their regiments, "in full confidence that they will endeavour, upon every future occasion, by a prompt obedience and orderly demeanour, to atone for this unpremeditated but atrocious offence."[57]

This incident has been used to characterize drafting as generally problematic, but it was a singular incident. War Office correspondence contains many complaints about men being recruited or pressed improperly, but none about drafting. Tracing careers of drafts shows no correlation between drafting and desertion or other bad behavior. Surviving records leave no way to trace the careers of men drafted as recruits, nor any way to distinguish volunteer drafts from those who did not volunteer, leaving some room for doubt. A writer in 1786 recommended "inserting the power of draughting in the attestation" rather than the current language of "a specific agreement to serve the king in one particular corps and no other," and further suggested relying only on "volunteers from the different regiments at home, a measure never known to fail, and by which a corps gets rid of those restless spirits, who are best when employed on active service."[58]

The wartime army, like the peacetime army, attracted "restless spirits." Although obliged to serve only for the duration of the war, many remained soldiers for decades, through reenlistments and drafts, at home and abroad until no longer fit for service. On the opposite end of the spectrum were occasional men like Jonathan Sawyer who "being disappointed in courtship" joined and deserted from a British militia regiment. Seventeen years old, he then enlisted in the 52nd Regiment in January 1779, only to desert three months later, stealing a horse and some money to effect his escape. He spent the next year stealing horses and robbing houses, twice escaping after capture. He was finally arrested, tried, convicted, and sentenced to death in April 1780. He "willingly resigned his life as atonement for his offences," saying on the gallows that "he hoped his end would be a warning to others."[59]

Just as before the war, training began with the recruiting party. John Robertshaw, a recruit for the 33rd Regiment, recalled going out each day "to march around with the recruiting party and exercise myself in running, jumping and learning to walk straight." When the party had enough recruits, they went to a depot—Chatham Barracks or Portsmouth in England, Cork in Ireland, Fort William in Scotland—where an officer of their regiment trained them as platoons and as a company. They received uniforms—not full regimentals, but jackets, trousers, and caps— and for the first time handled firearms. Robertshaw recalled "constantly exercising and learning the military evolutions" at Chatham Barracks in 1777, and their corporal trained the nineteen men of the 33rd so well that they, "after only six months practice, challenged the whole garrison to contend with them in military discipline."[60] How long recruits continued this training depended on when convoys sailed. Some embarked within weeks of enlisting while others trained for over two years before sailing to join their regiments abroad. Robertshaw spent "almost a year" at Chatham. Among sixty-four recruits for the 22nd Regiment for whom details are known, twenty-two spent over two years training in Britain before joining the regiment in America, and twenty-two others spent between one and two years. Of the twenty with less than a full year's training before being sent overseas, fifteen had at least five months of it.[61]

When recruits joined their regiments, they were blended in with the other soldiers in such a way that they learned their trade quickly. There were no army-wide standards for teaching recruits the basic skills of a solider: hygiene, military bearing, and other aspects of day-to-day discipline. Each regiment instead relied on knowledge passed from experienced officers and soldiers to new ones, from one regiment to another as officers advanced their careers, and through brigades and garrisons as senior officers took interest in matters beyond their own corps. An assortment of military textbooks described best practices or recommended new ones, resulting in methods that were typical if not standardized, for everything from managing a regiment's finances to tailoring each soldier's clothing.[62] *The Manual Exercise, As ordered by his Majesty, In 1764. Together with Plans and Explanations Of the Method generally Practis'd At Review and Field-Days, &c.*[63] described the basic techniques of handling the firelock and bayonet, and an assortment of formation maneuvers that varied somewhat with different editions but retained the basic elements of moving close-order formations efficiently and effectively. Wartime recruits learned these techniques in their weeks or months at depots, giving them a basis from which to learn locally adapted maneuvers from their companies, regiments, and brigades in America.

With each regiment free to manage its own internal affairs, and very few surviving regimental records, it is difficult to draw general conclusions about many things, including the extent to which recommendations in military texts were followed. There are, nonetheless, some aspects of the common soldiers' experiences that can be discerned as typical, albeit not universal. With the grenadier and light infantry companies detached, each regiment took new recruits into their eight battalion companies, becoming "battalion men."[64] Usually they were distributed equally, and other men were transferred among companies to bring them all to equal strength.[65] "The 34 Recruits including 2 Drummers that came yesterday being drawn for, are to join their companys," directed the commander of the 40th Regiment in October 1776,[66] one of several indications that recruits and drafts were usually distributed by lottery among the eight companies.

As the war progressed, some recruits arrived in America to find their regiments no longer in the region. Recruits for the 15th, 27th, 28th, and 35th Regiments, for example, arrived in New York in summer 1781 when their corps were serving in the West Indies. For expedience, in August "part of the British Recruits now here were this day drafted to the Regiments in this district."[67] The 22nd Regiment took in twenty-three from the 15th; the 38th forty-one from the 15th, six from the 27th, and fifteen from the 28th; and so forth.[68] When word of surrender at Yorktown reached New York in 1781, recruits for the then-incarcerated 17th, 23rd, 33rd, and 43rd were drafted into the 40th, which had been depleted by recent service in the harsh Caribbean climate followed by heavy casualties in an assault on Fort Griswold, Connecticut.[69]

Receipt of recruits and drafts was diligently recorded on muster rolls, but in ways that invite confusion. The rolls were prepared to reconcile the amount of money regiments distributed to pay soldiers, but recruits and drafts did not become the financial responsibility of their regiments on the same day they joined in person. Some regiments, like the 22nd, recorded the date recruits embarked in Great Britain, or in the case of the German recruits, in Germany; thus, the regiment's German recruits are shown on the rolls as joining the regiment in May 1776 when they actually arrived in New York in October. Other regiments, like the 33rd Foot, recorded the date of disembarkation in America. For drafts already in the same location as their new regiment, the date that the new corps

took over their finances was a few weeks after the transfer actually occurred. Soldiers of the 18th Regiment, for example, were drafted into
other regiments on December 5, 1775, and those of the 59th on December 11, but their accounts were "settled with to the 24th December,"[70]
and they appear on the rolls of their new regiments on December 25.[71]

"Serjt. Benson is to take out the Last Batch of Recruits every day the
weather will permit until they are perfect in marching and exercising,"[72]
the men of the 40th Regiment were told in October 1776, immediately
after their augmentation of over one hundred recruits and drafts disembarked in New York. Included were English, Irish, and Scottish recruits,
a few drafts, and German recruits, some with prior military experience,
some without. Emphasis was on "marching exercising," the organized
military movements essential for fighting effectively, which the army
under General Howe had tailored considerably for fast-moving, open-
order warfare in America. Within three weeks, Sergeant Robert Benson
discerned which men learned quickly and shifted focus to intensive drill
for those making slower progress. "As the Duty of the Battalion is become
easy the Auquard Men & undisciplin'd Recruits are to do no more duty
with Arms till they are More Perfect in the Essential part of the Exercise
& Marching &c. to effect which they are to be out three times every Day
if the Weather Permitts under the instruction of the Adjutant & Drill'd
by Serjt Benson & Parrott, who are to be struck off other duty's till further Orders." When the entire regiment paraded for training, inspections
and other activities, "the Above Recruits are to form on the Left of the
whole, and the Drill Serjts are to Attend to their Behaviour in every Respect."[73] Extra time was spent as often as possible working with the awk-
ward squad—men who found handling arms and the niceties of marching
difficult—to the point of drilling them on the decks of transports crossing
the Atlantic and sending them on shore to exercise when in easy reach
of land.[74]

Integrating recruits and drafts with their new regiments "without a
days delay after receiving them" was essential, because most arrived in
America between May and October, when regiments were actively campaigning. Having learned the fundamentals of handling arms and marching in Britain, albeit for different lengths of time between enlistment and
embarkation, in America they could focus on platoon exercise and firing
with live ammunition. To avoid false alarms, general orders announced
times of practice firing, such as in June 1777, when recruits practiced

"ball Firing between the hours of 6 & 8 in the morning," and to avoid accidents, "the Officers are to Inspect their mens Arms before they leave the field And take care that no man Returns to Camp with his Arms loaded."[75]

Training with live ammunition was not limited to recruits. As springtime approached each year, battalions, regiments, and brigades practiced maneuvers and firing in preparation for active campaigning. A brigade in New Jersey in May 1777 practiced "firing ball by platoon, sub and grand divisions and by battalion," including "on Uneven ground so as to accustom the men not to fire but when ordered and not only to level but to be taught to fire up and down hill."[76] The following March, recruits in Philadelphia fired twelve rounds, but the commanding officer did "not think it necessary for old soldiers to fire Ball."[77] In early 1781, on the other hand, old soldiers in the light infantry and grenadier battalions on Long Island honed their skills. The grenadiers fired in February at targets "by single man, by files & by Companies," in March worked on battalion firings, then in April exercised with two battalions together, for eight hours on one of the days, all with live ammunition and doing "some things over again that we did wrong yesterday, very simple when properly directed."[78]

"Superior conduct and address can only be acquired in an eminent degree by discipline of which regularity & prompt execution are the chief Ingredients," asserted the commanding officer of the 71st Regiment two years after it arrived in America.[79] The regiment raised for the American war had acquitted itself well so far but continued to train and refine skills. "The soldiers are to level constantly at the Enemy's Waist Bands and with their right Eye direct to the Barrels of their pieces on that Object the instant they pull their Triggers." Instead of firing in volleys, "When the Signal for Action is given, the firings are immediately to commence on which Occasion every man shall take the most direct aim possible at the most Favourable Object in his front and without waiting for an Officer's orders with respect to times continue to load, present, and fire with the utmost alacrity, deliberation and accuracy 'til the firings are ordered to cease." Emphasizing the fighting style so necessary in America, the orders continued, "every Soldier shall hug their coverts in the most compleat manner possible for giving annoyance to the enemy and perfect security to themselves. If the troops are ordered to move in any direction they are to spring from tree to tree, Stump, Log, & etc with the utmost Agility & continue to fire, load and spring as they advance upon or retreat from the enemy."[80] This was the way of war for British soldiers in America who had learned conventional linear warfare techniques so well, whether as long-serving soldiers or as recruits in Great Britain, that they were capable of adapting to whatever conditions American terrain and opposition offered.

CHAPTER II

Bounties, Wages, Rewards, Prizes, and Promotions

"The Method is, that every Commanding Officer regularly Accounts with the Soldiers of his Company every two Months," explained an officer when asked how soldiers of the 22nd Regiment of Foot were paid. He continued, "in general if they are Men that do not make away with their Necessaries, they pay them the Balance coming to them; if they are accustomed to Sell or loose their Necessaries, they then keep the Balance of such Men to indemnify themselves for any fresh Supply of Necessaries there may be occasion for." Each soldier signed his account in acknowledgment.[1] Simply stated, if a soldier could be trusted not to incur debts, he received the money due to him every two months; but if he was prone to lose or sell the clothing that his company commander was responsible for providing, or incur other debts, the officer held on to the money as a surety. The soldier got money in hand only when he proved himself trustworthy or left the regiment. Thomas Sullivan of the 49th recalled that payment came "mostly" in coins used for international trade—Portuguese gold Johannes and silver half-Johannes valued at thirty-six and eighteen shillings, respectively, and silver Spanish milled dollars and cob dollars. The army's exchange rate was four shillings eight pence per dollar, but inhabitants typically gave only four shillings sixpence.[2]

Records of individual soldiers' pay were kept by regiments, and with no need for the government to retain copies, few survive. Extant accounts of what soldiers actually received show that while the job was not lucrative, life as a private soldier was not as poverty stricken as some writers—even during the eighteenth century—have suggested. An account book for one company of the 71st Regiment covering September 1779 through October 1781 records in meticulous detail each soldier's expenses and credits. The balances due each man at the end of the period range from just one shilling to eleven pounds fifteen shillings, with the majority between two pounds and eight pounds.[3] Each account begins with a balance from before September 1779; muster rolls for the 71st have not survived for this period, leaving no record of how long each man had served by the time of these accounts, but the regiment was raised in 1775 and 1776, so no man had more than four years of service.

Soldiers in regiments of foot earned a nominal eight pence per day, two pence of which went toward annual regimental clothing and a few other fixed costs. The remaining sixpence—five, when posted in Ireland—was for daily expenses including food, nonannual clothing like shoes and shirts, tailoring, washing, soap, and hospitalization.[4] Some men in the 71st were paid sums of cash during the account period; these payments were recorded, such that each man's available balance was always known. The account book records only the sixpence per day, just over nine pounds per year before expenses; most men in this company of the 71st had accrued between two and eleven months' pay after expenses when their accounts were settled in 1781.

A pay receipt for one company of the 84th (Royal Highland Emigrant) Regiment records sums paid to thirty-three private men on June 24, 1782, but does not give the period over which the pay accrued. Eleven men received less than a pound, fourteen received between one and three pounds, six received between three and five pounds, one man was paid six pounds two shillings eleven pence, and one received eight pounds five shillings five and a half pence—all of this after expenses.[5]

An account book for one company of the Brigade of Guards records each man's earnings and expenses during 1778.[6] The daily subsistence in the Guards was six and six-sevenths pence, or eleven pounds three shillings nine and two-sevenths pence annually, about 16 percent more than regular infantry regiments. Of eighty-five privates, seventy had between one and four pounds remaining at the end of the year; twelve were due less than a pound, including three who died during the year, cutting short their earnings. Three were in debt at year's end. One

man had a balance of over six pounds, but that was because he was a prisoner of war for much of the year, accruing pay but bearing fewer expenses
than other men. To summarize, four-fifths of the men in this company
had expenses of only 70 to 90 percent of their income, leaving 10 to 30
percent to carry over into the next year. If this economy was typical, at
the end of a twenty-year career, a soldier might have two to six years' pay
due. But, lacking more comprehensive records, there is no way to know
if this year was typical for a soldier in the Guards, or if this information
is applicable to soldiers in other corps.

The accounts for the company of Guards in 1778 show only base pay.
Just as in peacetime, wartime soldiers had other ways to earn money. Orderly books frequently include entries for quartermasters, barrack masters,
and other officers to settle accounts with soldiers who did extra military
work,[7] but we lack quantitative information about how many days each
year an average soldier was likely to spend at this sort of labor. A receipt
for "demolishing the works left by the Rebels, & repairing redoubts now
standing, & in erecting log breast works" at Paulus Hook in October and
November 1777 shows that nine men of the 57th Regiment were paid
ten pence per day for thirty-one days of labor.[8] Working parties in Boston
scavenged firewood from every possible source while the town was under
siege, receiving five shillings per cord.[9] The garrison in Rhode Island regularly sent parties to other places for firewood for which they were paid
two shillings eleven pence per cord; during winter 1777–1778, parties of
fifty men cut for fourteen days at a time, but the quantities of wood cut
is not known, and so neither are the earnings for each man.[10] In New
York in November 1778, men employed at "fitting out quarters" for the
coming winter were paid sixpence per day for common labor, while those
with tradesman's skills—sawyers, carpenters, thatchers, masons, smiths,
and such—earned one shilling three pence per day; the work was to be
done over a two-month period, but there is no record of how many men
were employed, or for how many days.[11]

Soldier servants earned extra money caring for their officers. Tailors,
shoemakers, gunsmiths, bakers, and others with trades useful to their regiments or the army worked steadily throughout their military careers,
sometimes only when not on duty, other times being excused from duty.[12]
In December 1776, butchers in a brigade in New Jersey were allowed to
sell sheep and bull hides to local inhabitants.[13] Two unnamed soldiers of
the 63rd Regiment worked a garden in New York in 1779, earning two

pounds two shillings each for sixty-three days of work—a wage of eight pence per day.[14] Forty-four-year-old Charles Russell, a soldier with nineteen years in the army, was a shoemaker from Tipperary,[15] but in 1782 he spent eighteen days "employed in the Boat at Paulus Hook" in New Jersey. He earned four shillings per day, six times his daily pay as a private soldier in the 22nd Regiment. Eighteen days of work netted him three pounds twelve shillings, equivalent to almost four months' pay, in addition to his usual soldiers' wage. Six other men in the 22nd were on this job and earned the same substantial wage.[16]

Throughout the war, tradesmen were summoned from regiments when the army had special needs: smiths to make and repair grates for barracks fireplaces, masons and bricklayers to work for the military engineers in Boston; men with experience using fascines—bundles of saplings—to reinforce fortifications in preparation for the 1776 New York campaign, to be paid a shilling a day; caulkers and carpenters from regiments in Canada to prepare bateaux for Burgoyne's 1777 campaign, along with collar makers to fabricate harnesses for carts.[17]

In June 1777, Evan Evans of the 52nd Regiment testified at a court-martial that he "works at his trade as a Shoemaker, in a hovel, close by the Camp."[18] The following February, Edinburgh native John Murray of the 57th advertised his services in a New York newspaper, offering "that he engraves all manner of silver plate, ornaments, gold and silver watch cases, cyphers upon silver and steel seals, ladies' visiting and company cards, message cards, &c. coats of arms upon copper, for gentlemen's books, office seals, officers gorgets and sword-belt plates, neatly engraved," along with a promise "to perform his work by the greatest dispatch, and also at the Old Country price."[19] Thomas Brissbrown, a corporal in the 53rd Regiment, obtained leave of absence to work as a jeweler in Quebec in 1782.[20] Anecdotal accounts like these confirm that wartime soldiers worked outside the army as time permitted, but the numbers and their earnings are not known.

Money came from other sources. Men drafted from one regiment into another received a bounty of a guinea and a half—thirty-one shillings and sixpence—as they were effectively enlisting in a new regiment. Although drafting occurred routinely in peacetime, wartime made it more frequent; of almost 1,100 men who served in the 38th Regiment at some point during the war, at least 200 were drafts from other regiments.[21] Of just over 1,000 men who served in the 22nd during the war, at least 150

	Complaints	Where Born	Occupations
53 Foot Wm. Brumpton 50 28	Chronic Rheumatism	Ludlow C. Salop	Labourer
do. John Strange 47 28	ditto	St. Albans Glouc.	Pin Maker
do. Wm. Benbow 51 27½	ditto	New Castle C. Staff.	Buckle Maker
do. Walt. Blackburn 52 27½	ditto	Ripon C. York	Shoe Maker
do. John Strickland 48 27½	ditto	Blandford C. Dorset	Labourer
do. Wm. Sherwood 56 27	ditto	Evesham C. Worc.	Taylor
do. Dan. Downs 49 27 6	ditto	Limerick	Weaver
do. Joseph Scott 42 26	ditto and married	Salisbury Wilts	Taylor
do. John Miller 51 24	Rheumatism	Dundee Angus	Weaver
do. John Hunter 49 24	Chronic do.	Ritton C. Durham	Carpenter
do. John Mallison 56 23½	ditto	Halifax C. York	Woolcomber
do. Wm. Passmore 47 23⅝	ditto	Biddeford C. Devon	Labourer
do. Dan. McLoggish 41 16½	Fractured Thigh Bone	Inverary C. Argyll	ditto
do. John Simpson 36 16	His Feet Frostbitten	Tuxford Nottingm.	Stocking Weaver
do. John Oldham 30 11¾	Consumptive	Wisbech C. Cambridge	Taylor
do. Peter Hoyle 28 9	ditto severely	Braid Carmine C. Tyrone	Weaver
60 do. John Clarke 53 8	Wounded Legs & bones	Colchester	Labourer
do. Thos. Smith 36 8	Lost an Eye	Stow on the Wou[ld] Glouc.	Baker
62 do. Paul Daily 45 17	Wounded in the left Thigh	Kilmore C. Roscom.	Labourer
63 do. Thos. Davis Corp. 50 28½	Worn Out	Old Cliew C. Somerset	Taylor
do. Jas. Clements 40 22	ditto	Tardy C. Worcester	Needle Maker
do. John Rook 39 16	Wounded Leg	Birmingham	Brass Founder
71 do. Gilb. Paterson Serj. 32 8	Do. in head, hand Leg & Thigh	Inveresk Midlth.	Labourer
do. John Paterson Serj. 29 8	Do. in Hand & Thigh	Glasgow	ditto
do. James Wright 36 8	Hurt Breast & Side	High Church C. Renfrew	Weaver
do. Wm. McKay 34 8	Wounded leg & fits	Dornoch C. Sutherland	Labourer
do. Wm. Hamilton 26 8	Bruised Back	Munton C. Ayr	Weaver

The variety of trades among soldiers is evident in this list of men from the 53rd, 60th, 62nd, 63rd and 71st Regiments who went before the pension examination board on December 15, 1784: nine laborers, five weavers, four tailors, a pin maker, a buckle maker, a shoe maker, a carpenter, a woolcomber, a stocking weaver, a baker, a needle maker, and a brass founder. Detail from Pension Admission Books, WO 116/8. (*The National Archives*) were drafts from other regiments during those years.[22] Patrick Caufield, Jacob Ingram, William Oxford, and William Shearman all answered the call for volunteers and left their regiments in Ireland to serve in America in early 1775, taking the bounty and joining the 59th Regiment. At the end of the year, the 59th was sent home, and all four men were drafted into the 52nd, earning another bounty. When the 52nd was drafted in 1778, they were drafted yet again, for still another bounty.[23]

Prize money was another wartime benefit, albeit occasional. Men of the 1st Battalion of Grenadiers each received prize money of about one pound for the capture of an American frigate on the Delaware River near Philadelphia in 1778.[24] Privates and drummers in the Brigade of Guards and the 82nd Regiment were awarded nine shillings nine and a quarter pence in 1781 for their participation in a late-1780 expedition to Virginia that netted a number of valuable prizes; in 1784, settlement of additional prize money from this expedition yielded them three shillings eight pence more (corporals received a total of one pound two shillings five and a half pence, and sergeants one pound thirteen shillings five pence).[25] The 71st Regiment account book mentioned above includes payments of seven shillings eight pence to each of thirty-three privates involved in a capture at Wilmington, North Carolina, in 1781.[26] Privates from the Guards, 71st and 82nd, would be entitled to one pound twelve shillings in prize money awarded in 1784 for stores captured in Charleston, South Carolina, in 1780.[27]

Rewards were offered for apprehending deserters: five guineas during the expedition to South Carolina in 1776, twenty dollars on Burgoyne's 1777 campaign, as well as one hundred dollars "for the Discovery of any Person who Shall be tempering with any Soldiers, or Holding Conversation in favour of the Enemy, or Otherwise tending to Persuade Men to Disert."[28] A reward of two hundred dollars was offered for the perpetrators of a robbery near Philadelphia in September 1777, and for those who set fire to houses in New Jersey in June 1778.[29] Robert Begant of the 43rd claimed a reward in August 1774 for his "very proper and laudable instance of Fidelity and attention to his duty, in apprehending a soldier of another Corps who last night was attempting to desert in disguise," and William Burke of the 45th received a guinea from his colonel for tracking down a deserter in Ireland shortly before the war.[30] Corporals William Barker and Adam Todd of the 63rd each received two guineas in March 1778 "for their Respective Soldierlike behavior on duty." There are no details of what they did, but Barker had testified in a court-martial concerning a robbery a few months before.[31] Rewards were given for "arms taken with prisoners,"[32] and although there were many prisoners early in the war, there are no known records of how their captors were paid for them. Soldiers who encountered cattle while on campaign near Philadelphia in 1777 could sell it to the army's commissary general at the rate of a dollar per head.[33] The 1st Battalion of Light Infantry received five hundred dollars for capturing five cannons at the Battle of Brandywine in 1777, about a dollar per man.[34] Sergeant John Crookshank of the Brigade of Guards seized "a quantity of goods" being sent from New York to Long Island "without a permit" in October 1779; the goods were sold "at publick vendue" and proceeds divided between him and "the poor of the city."[35]

On rare occasions, individual soldiers were recognized for heroic deeds in battle. During the night of March 12-13, 1777, an American armed vessel named *Spitfire* ran aground in Narragansett Bay in Rhode Island, within range of British artillery. The guns forced the crew to abandon the ship but could not sink it because it was already aground. A British soldier swam out to the vessel so it could be burned. The commander of the British garrison wrote in general orders the next day that he desired "Henry Pickles, Private soldier in his Majestys 43d Regiment may be informed that he is extreamly pleased with his spirited conduct, in Swiming on Board the Galley."[36] During the Battle of Germantown, Pennsylvania, later that year, Corporal George Peacock of the 52nd Regiment carried Lieutenant Richard St. George Mansergh to safety after the officer was wounded in the head. When St. George took a promotion into another regiment a few months later, he asked a fellow officer to "take good care of Peacock" and gave the corporal the remarkable sum of fifty guineas.[37]

Private soldiers employed as servants sometimes received favors and rewards in addition to their wages. James Cairns of the 22nd Regiment, for example, was given a surtout, a type of overcoat, that the regiment's tailors made for him at the behest of the lieutenant he served.[38] When Captain William Leslie of the 17th Regiment of Foot was mortally wounded at the Battle of Princeton in January 1777, his servant Peter McDonald "put the body on a baggage cart & conducted it for a considerable time in spite of a very heavy fire from the Enemy but at last he was obliged to abandon it." Before he died, Leslie asked that McDonald be given his watch.[39] After Brigadier General James Agnew was killed at the Battle of Germantown, his effects "were equally divided among all the servants," presumably meaning the value after being sold at auction; Alexander Andrew, Agnew's servant since before the war, also received a set of silver buckles "extraordinary as a reward for good and faithful services."[40]

Some soldiers earned money by nefarious means. After hostilities began in Boston, parties were employed to cut "small wood" to make fascines, but some "cut down large branches, and even whole trees, and are selling them in a Scandalous manner about the town to the Inhabitants."[41] Three men of the 82nd Regiment were in the military prison in New York in 1780 for "coining," that is, making counterfeit coins.[42] Soldiers in Rhode Island plundered gardens and sold the vegetables to "soldiers wives, and other small retailers."[43] Four men of the 18th in Boston in 1775 were tried by regimental courts for selling or "making away with" their shirts, shoes, or stockings, as were seven men of the 44th between December 1780 and April 1784.[44] Thomas Bell of the marines sold four stolen shirts to wives of soldiers in the 4th Regiment of Foot in Boston in July 1775,[45] and John Parrott of the 54th sold "a gown, two aprons and two or three pieces of cambric" to the wife of a fellow soldier on Long Island in 1782, all stolen goods,[46] certainly only a tiny fraction of what unethical soldiers were able to fence during eight years of war.

Although accounts were regularly kept, it was up to regimental or company commanders to decide when to put cash into soldiers' hands. Men in a brigade in New Jersey in late 1776 were paid twice a week if they were not in debt.[47] At the other extreme, sometimes men went for long periods without being paid at all, sometimes for lack of specie, other times because hard money was "of little or no use to the soldiers during the active part of the campaign," as an officer told his men in New Jersey in June 1777.[48] This could cause discontent. After deserting, Richard Power of the 37th Regiment told American officers that he and his comrades were given only enough money to pay for washing, making "his Regiment very discontented for want of pay."[49] On Long Island in 1779, four soldiers of the 43rd's light infantry company claimed not to have received weekly subsistence money nor full rations for eight months, driving them to kill an ox belonging to an inhabitant; their company commander assured the court that he gave "those who had any claim what money they wanted," and "saw no use in giving men much in debt more money than was necessary to keep them clean." The men were found guilty.[50]

In August 1778, the commander of the 71st Regiment expressed dismay at how the men in this Scottish corps used their money after being paid. "It is with the utmost astonishment and passion," he wrote, to observe "the unreasonable conduct of the men since their last settlement of accounts. Instead of using their money with discretion they continue to squander it on Liquor and Debauchery by which they injure their Health, ruin their morals and Sully that valuable character, they have already acquired as soldiers." To bridle this behavior, he ordered limits on how much cash a man received each week as "pocquet money": one shilling if his balance of pay was less than nine shillings, or five shillings if his balance was more than one pound (with no explanation for balances between nine shillings and one pound). This, it was hoped, would remove "infatuation" with cash.[51]

War increased opportunities for career advancement, and consequent higher pay. The size increase authorized in 1775 added ten sergeants and ten drummers to each infantry regiment. Deserving corporals were appointed as sergeants, and deserving privates became corporals. The duties of corporals did not change during the war, but there was more turnover due to attrition. From January 1772 through April 1775, for example, sixty men in the 17th Regiment of Foot's ten companies served as corporals, whereas from May 1775 through December 1778, eighty-three individuals spent some time in that capacity.[52]

In every garrison there were a number of administrative posts for which sergeants, skilled at clerical work, were ideal. Sergeant Cornelius Killegrew of the 34th Regiment was appointed provost marshal on the campaign that besieged Fort Stanwix in 1777; for this work of managing prisoners he was paid two shillings sixpence per day.[53] Sergeant Edward Welsh of the 10th Regiment of Foot took the role of provost marshal when Rhode Island was occupied on December 8, 1776, and Sergeant Jacob Margas of the 54th, trained as an optician in London, took over from him in 1778.[54] In British-held Philadelphia, Sergeant Andrew Cunningham of the 10th and Sergeant John Jeffries of the 27th were appointed assistants to the provost marshal.[55] In 1779, there was frequent traffic between British-held New York and American-held Elizabeth, New Jersey, under flags of truce conducted by Sergeant William Lloyd of the 47th Regiment at a salary of ten shillings New York currency per day, a role that he performed from October at least through June 1780.[56] The 23rd's Sergeant Roger Lamb was appointed clerk to the commandant of the city of New York late in the war, for which he "had a good salary," and also served as adjutant of a volunteer corps in the city.[57] It was apparently positions like these that allowed Sergeant John Hutton of the 10th to save over three hundred guineas from the time he joined the army in 1746 until late 1778, when the ship carrying it was captured and it was all lost.[58]

Some appointments were sufficiently substantial that the sergeants who took them were discharged from their regiments, such as when Richard Thompson of the 37th became town adjutant of New York in 1776, and William Clarkson of the 46th became deputy barrack master of Philadelphia a year later.[59] The most significant career advancement was promotion to an officer rank. In summer 1775, the addition of six officers to each regiment for recruiting caused an immediate shortage of officers. One measure taken to compensate for this was a declaration that "for the future none but active sergeants shall be appointed to be quarter master to the regiments of infantry."[60] Sergeants were promoted to adjutant as well, relieving junior officers from doing double duty in these regimental staff positions. Through this avenue, dozens of long-serving sergeants advanced their careers thanks to wartime opportunity. Men like William Abercrombie, a veteran of the French and Indian War in the 22nd Regiment of Foot, became quartermaster in May 1776, and John Bathe, forty-four-year-old sergeant major in the 15th, became adjutant in January 1776.[61] Some changed regiments when they took new positions, like Sergeant Major Joseph Robinson of the 28th and Sergeant Major George Watson of the 27th, who became quartermaster and adjutant of the 23rd in 1777 and 1779 respectively.[62]

Not only did daily pay jump from one shilling sixpence to four shillings for adjutant or four shillings eight pence for quartermaster, the transition from most senior noncommissioned officer to most junior officer opened an entire new career path.[63] John Bathe of the 15th Regiment, for example, was commissioned as an ensign just eleven months after becoming adjutant, then promoted to lieutenant less than two years later. Opportunities also opened up for the children of these deserving former sergeants. Bathe's son, although born in 1763 when his father was still among the rank and file, obtained an ensign's commission in 1779 and eventually became the 15th's lieutenant colonel in 1799. Sergeant John Tuffie of the 44th obtained the quartermaster's post in 1776 at age thirty-two, and although he remained in that role until his death in 1794, his sons Samuel and William both became commissioned officers in the regiment.[64]

The dramatically increasing size of the wartime army opened up even more advancement opportunities. In America, regiments of Loyalists were raised, and at least sixty British sergeants accelerated their careers by taking commissions in those new corps, where their experience at training and military administration might far exceed that of their officers. Sergeant Allan Cumming of the 71st was commissioned as an ensign in the New York Volunteers; Sergeant David McFall of the 26th was promoted to lieutenant and adjutant of the Queen's Loyal Rangers; Sergeant John Hatfield of the 4th, a twenty-eight-year veteran who also directed the regiment's band of music, became a captain in the New Jersey Volunteers.[65] A senior Loyalist officer was concerned that this practice denied opportunities to qualified American-born men who were better suited for the American war, being acquainted with the "temper of its inhabitants, their manners &c." He wondered, "Should men of enlarged minds of liberal educations & extensive knowledge remain unemployed until all the serjeants of the army are provided for?"[66] The practice nonetheless continued. While most promoted sergeants served well as officers, a few found their new world difficult. Lieutenant Patrick Henry of the New Jersey Volunteers, formerly a sergeant in the 17h Regiment of Foot, was tried on several charges including "ungentlemanlike behavior," based in part on his apparent preference of the company of enlisted men over officers.[67] Lieutenant Joshua Hamilton of the Kings Orange Rangers, promoted from sergeant in the 6th Regiment of Foot, was tried and reprimanded for insulting another officer; the following year, as adjutant in the New Jersey Volunteers, he was on trial again, this time for "Mutinous, Insolent and ungentlemanlike behavior" toward his commanding officer, resulting in his discharge from the service. Quartermaster Colin Smith of the 42nd Regiment, promoted from sergeant in 1776, shot himself in December 1779, "supposed on account of some clandestine management."[68]

With twenty-three years as a drummer in the 27th Regiment, William King could be expected to keep a cadence when the regiment marched on campaign. But he had a different job: he was "employed to carry things" for an officer.[69] His lot was similar to that of many drummers at war in America. Their skills that were so vital for waking up camps and garrisons and then signaling activities throughout the day, and for training recruits and regiments to synchronize their movements, were not much needed in the fast-paced, open-order fighting that was the hallmark of British campaigning. Because "in action the noise of the Artillery and Musketry generally renders it impossible to use any Signals by the

Drum," as early as February 1776 General Howe ordered regiments in Boston "not to use the drum or fife for marching or signals when in the field."[70] When the army prepared to evacuate the city a month later, the drummers and fifers who were "not fit to carry arms" went onto ships before their regiments embarked, and in December, after the vigorous campaign through New York and New Jersey, the 17th Regiment of Foot directed that, "The Drummers who have done Duty as privates during the Campaign, are to Receive the Clothing and do Duty as Drummers."[71] In 1777, preparing for a new campaign, the 17th's brigade practiced maneuvers with "no fifing or drumming but when ordered."[72] When the army set off from Head of Elk, Maryland, toward Philadelphia in late 1777, it marched "without beat of drum."[73]

Drums did have their uses on campaign. Sixteen days after British forces marched "without beat of drum," "the signal to march was drummed everywhere" to start the final push to victory in the Battle of Brandywine, and the grenadier battalions advanced to a tune called the "Grenadiers March."[74] In the following days, the rebel army stayed just barely ahead of pursuing British columns, monitoring British progress, as an American officer recalled years later, by listening to their drums.[75] An officer in the 60th Regiment recalled drummers beating signals for advance and retreat, and playing the "Grenadiers March," during skirmishes in Georgia in 1778.[76] During the siege of Penobscot in 1779, light infantry from the 82nd Regiment twice taunted their opponents by playing "Yankee Doodle" in front of rebel artillery batteries.[77] In garrison on Long Island in August 1780, the 1st Battalion of Grenadiers practiced maneuvers that included drum signals for firing by companies, forming line from column, advancing in line (for which the signal was the "Grenadiers March"), charge, and halt.[78]

The impression that emerges, although not explicitly stated, is of one or a few drummers available to a senior officer to beat critical commands for an entire regiment, brigade, or army such as advance or halt, and occasional tunes to rouse spirits at key moments, but otherwise to remain silent, while companies and platoons relied entirely on voice commands. A 1780 military text recommended that all "except the two orderly drummers are to stay with their respective companies and assist the wounded," and one drummer of the 23rd did just that for a wounded officer on the first day of the war.[79] On a raid in Rhode Island in May 1778, when combustibles were needed to ignite and destroy enemy military stores, two drummers were sent to fetch them.[80] Preparing to move into the Carolina interior in December 1780, the Brigade of Guards ordered their drum-

Drummer of the 55th Regiment of Foot. Although bearskin caps were the warranted headwear for drummers, they were often left in storage in favor of the cocked hats worn by most infantry. Drawing by Eric H. Schnitzer.

mers to "carry a good Ax each & provide themselves with slings for the same."[81] And at the Battle of Hobkirk's Hill, South Carolina, in April 1781, drummers were armed with muskets, as was "every thing that could carry a firelock."[82]

In the early 1770s, the peacetime establishment of a British infantry regiment included one drummer in each company, ten altogether. By the end of 1775, the establishment had been increased to two per company. Regiments already in America needed more drummers. Some, like the 4th and 40th, appointed private soldiers to the newly created drummer positions.[83] These men may have started their careers as drummers before becoming private soldiers, or have been musicians in the regiment's band also doing duty as privates, because bands were not part of the wartime or peacetime establishment. Some regiments, like the 23rd, enlisted new drummers for some companies while leaving other companies with only one drummer.[84] And some, like the 22nd, left most or all of the positions open until 1780, when the bandsmen finally were appointed to drummer posts instead of being carried on the rolls as privates.[85] Throughout the war, newly appointed young drummers often had the same surnames as soldiers in the same company, suggesting the continued tradition of soldiers' children following their fathers' military careers.[86]

"I have no objection to your taking the Soldier's Son you propose for a Drummer, provided he is really of an age sufficient to learn his Duty," wrote the commander of the Royal Artillery to a company captain in January 1779. But he cautioned that the son must be listed on the muster rolls as a matross, the artillery equivalent of a private soldier, because there was no vacancy for a drummer in the company.[87] This hints at the difficulty of discerning which men on muster rolls were soldiers and which, albeit few, were children learning the drum or fife while waiting for a vacancy. Frequently men appear as "enlisted" on the rolls and were appointed as drummers soon after, like William Higgins, who "joined" the 38th Regiment as a private in January 1779 and was appointed drummer the following September. A rare tabulation of ages of soldiers in America during the war, a December 1782 return of the 31st Regiment, includes a thirteen-, a twelve- and a nine-year-old among the private soldiers, in addition to several drummers eleven and twelve. Only the nine-year-old is annotated as a soldier's son.[88] In January 1783, the 34th Regiment listed seven "privates" aged six, seven, or eight, not all with the same surnames as officers or soldiers in the regiment.[89] The captain of the 42nd's grenadier company was ordered by his colonel, in 1778, to include on his muster roll "an effective drummer that I knew nothing about,"[90] showing that even the drummers listed on muster rolls were not always drummers, at least not in the companies on whose rolls they appear.

Four months after agreeing to allow a Royal Artillery soldier's son to be a drummer, the commander mentioned the lad again, writing, "I hope you will take care to have him instructed by the Drum Major of some of the Regiments."[91] When two drummers arrived among recruits for the 40th in October 1776, they were put "under the inspection of the Drum Major." The following June, when the regiment was in New Jersey, the drum major took "the 6 boys he returned unfit to march" back to New York, presumably to continue their instruction.[92] Even though drummers were sometimes "set to Work in the Clearing & Levelling the Street in front of the Encampment," they also practiced their percussion skills for the occasions when regiments "march'd in Town with drums beating another Trumphall entry."[93]

"The line will not turn out to receive the Commander in Chief on his going into Camp unless ordered," directed General Thomas Gage in Boston in July 1774. The general was not abdicating authority but instead doing away with a bit of ceremonial ritual as tensions rose, allowing him to be present among the troops frequently and with less disruption. When General Howe took over in 1775, he gave similar orders.[94] Compliments, as saluting was called in a popular military text, were less important on campaign than vigilance, resulting in a standing order from General Clinton "that no Centry or Party upon any of the advanced posts, shall pay any compliment to officers of whatsoever rank approaching their posts." On his 1777 campaign, General Burgoyne ordered soldiers "not to stand to their Arms or pay him any Compliment" when he visited outposts.[95] All of these orders pertain to soldiers at front lines where attention to duty was more important than military formalities.

Soldiers were expected to behave toward officers "with the highest marks of honour and respect," but officers were nonetheless approachable.[96] An American officer held prisoner by a party of the 37th Regiment in a house in 1776 "was surprised at the easy familiarity which seemed to prevail between them and their officer. But," he continued, "it appeared to be perfectly understood between them, that their coteries, though so near to each other, as that every word from either might be heard by both, were yet entirely distinct."[97] When a woodcutting expedition from the Rhode Island garrison quartered themselves in an abandoned house on

Shelter Island in Long Island Sound, "The soldiers had free liberty to say what they pleased," recalled the army surgeon who accompanied them and cooked for the officers; "they joaked the Colonel, laughed with their Officers, and swore the Cook Doctor was a damned honest fellow."[98] These examples occurred when officers and soldiers were in close quarters and where duty took precedence over formality. In garrisons or encampments, it was easier to maintain polite separation between officers and soldiers. Understanding when familiarity was accepted and when not may have been ingrained from a long-standing British army custom of allowing soldiers on a long march "the liberty of talking all kind of ribaldry respecting their amours and those of their officers." Although by the 1770s this custom had "for some time been very properly abolished," it was still "the custom to allow them to talk on the long march, or after the drums have ceased beating, yet their conversation should not be suffered to rise into noise and clamour."[99]

A soldier could be charged with mutiny for disobeying an officer, as was John Brown of the 44th Regiment in Boston in December 1775. The officer saw Brown carrying boards from a house and suspected he had torn them out from inside. When called on to stop, Brown ran, and upon being caught, struggled and broke free, saying "he would not be confined by him." Brown told a court-martial that he thought the officer was a servant, "being buttoned up from head to foot, in a great coat." An officer and a sergeant gave him favorable references. He was sentenced to five hundred lashes, but pardoned "in consideration of the Prisoner's former good Character, and his orderly and Obedient behaviour in general." Sometimes duty took precedence, as when Joseph Smith of the 23rd Regiment refused an officer's request to help move an injured man because "he could not do it till he was relieved being centry" at a general officer's quarters.[100] Officers were not above asking opinions of soldiers. A young ensign in the 17th Regiment of Foot, when his post at Stony Point on the Hudson River north of New York was attacked at night, acted "as many old Officers no doubt had done before, and since, I obeyed the directions of an experienced Sergeant."[101] When Province Island in the Delaware River was under attack on October 11, 1777, the two officers in command went so far as to ask the soldiers whether or not they should surrender by raising a white handkerchief tied to a ramrod. Donald McLean, a Royal Artillery matross, begged them not to, while an artillery corporal said simply that "he was under his command, and would do as he ordered him." The two officers were charged with misbehavior before the enemy, an offense just short of cowardice. At their trial, one officer said that William Blakeney, a soldier in the 5th Regiment, "desired him to hoist" the white flag, then "got upon the gun, and hoisted it," but Blakeney testified that he was ordered to do so. The officers were found guilty and cashiered from the service.[102]

While soldiers were required to show respect to their officers, they expected to receive an appropriate degree of respect as well. Soldiers on trial could object to officers appointed to the court,[103] and occasionally appealed the verdicts of regimental courts to be considered by general courts, the latter being composed of officers from other regiments and therefore less likely to be biased.[104] Soldiers on trial frequently asked officers for character references, which usually, but not always, showed them in a favorable light. Often these were brief statements, such as a lieutenant saying that James Cairns of the 22nd Regiment "always bore a good character and he never heard his honesty called in question, except on the present occasion," and two officers of the 57th offering of drummer John Brayson that "during a Campaign he served with them, he was remarkable for being a well behaved lad."[105] A lieutenant in the 38th deposed of knowing Thomas Manning and John Clements "for some years . . . they have always distinguished themselves, not only as brave but regular soldiers, and adds, when he inlisted Manning, he had of him the best character, as a good and honest man." Arthur Cosworth of the 45th, on trial for theft, got a glowing reference from a captain who had known him "for four or five years, & he always look'd upon him to be a quiet, sober, good soldier, & in point of his honesty he had so high an opinion of it, that had he had occasion to intrust money in the hands of a soldier in the Regiment Cosworth would have been the man he would have made choice of."[106]

Of the 27th's drummer William King, a lieutenant said "during six years that he had known him, he had always behaved well except being a little addicted to liquor and that his general character in the 27th Regiment, in which he has served 23 years is a good one." Drummer Robert Mason was told directly, in front of the court, by his captain in the 23rd Regiment, "you have lately been rather inattentive, owing to an attachment to two Women of the Regiment." John Cox, a five-year veteran of the same regiment, was called by his captain "a very drunken, idle and irregular soldier," but inasmuch as Cox was on trial for theft, he informed the court that he did "not recollect his having ever been charged with theft before."[107]

Some soldiers charged with military crimes appealed to the court's sense of justice, as when Corporal John Fisher of the 28th, on trial for rape, told the officers, "I am certain my Judges would rather ten guilty persons should escape than one innocent should suffer." More often, soldiers gave pleas of youthfulness and ignorance. Patrick Sheehan of the 62nd told the court that he deserted in Ireland shortly before the regiment's embarkation because "he was but six Months in the Army & not sensible of the heinousness or consequence of his Crime, that being a married man, his friends in Ireland forced him to desert." John Wheally of the 43rd, charged with desertion, said "he was extremely sorry for his Offence," and "at the time of his Deserting, he was only 17 years of Age." James Garrity of the 46th explained that he had not intended to desert but became "rather intoxicated" and lost his way, and was "but Eighteen years of age." John Kerr of the 82nd, after telling an officer he "deserved to be run through with a Bayonet for a Bougre," offered as his only defense, "that if he had not been out of his Senses with Liquor, that he never could have made use of those Expressions, and begs that the Court will consider his Youth and throws himself upon their Mercy." Perhaps the most absurd defense came from Martin Hurley, who deserted from the 44th Regiment in Boston and joined the enemy as an officer in a New Jersey regiment. After being captured at the Battle of Germantown, "he had nothing to offer in his defence, but that he never had been guilty of such crimes before."[108]

Although soldiers knew that officers were expected to treat them fairly, some deserted rather than seek redress. Thomas Slack deserted from the 7th Regiment of Foot in New York "owing to his Officer having beat him black and blue with the Scabbard of his Sword." Patrick Fallan of the 64th deserted his post in New York after a lieutenant ordered him "to Strip off his Coat and Waistcoat and then beat him with a large Stick for being in liquor," adding that the officer "on the March threatened to beat him and told him that if he did not keep up, he might as well be with Washington; this added to other ill usage he had received two Months, being tied up and gagged with a rough Stick, which cut his Mouth, for being in liquor, induced him to go off." Another officer, however, indicated that Fallan had brought his troubles upon himself, being "apt to get in liquor and is then so impertinent and noisy that they are often obliged to gag him." A captain in the 42nd Regiment confided to his diary that he had "knock'd down" a soldier "not so much for being drunk as for swearing he was not, & tho' he deserved it I am sorry for it, for we should never punish a soldier in a passion."[109]

Remembering being cheated out of provisions by an unscrupulous sergeant when he was a young soldier, Roger Lamb wrote, "If we had boldly stated our grievances to the officer commanding, we most certainly had been redressed." Some soldiers were bold enough to take grievances directly to their officers. Thomas Edwards of the 22nd Regiment, harassed by marauding Hessian soldiers when he was a safe guard, reported the abuse directly to his company captain. Two soldiers of the 17th Regiment of Foot, convicted of robbery, wrote an impassioned plea to the commander in chief in New York, saying they had been in confinement for four months since being tried and asking the general "most mercifully to extricate them out of their present unhappy circumstances."[110]

Four companies of the 53rd Regiment were captured near Fort Ticonderoga in September 1777. When their captors separated soldiers from officers, faithful soldiers offered to carry some of the officers' personal baggage. "These things my men desir'd to carry for me," recalled one officer, "and I distributed amongst them, and I am happy to say they were all so honest, that I collected them all after two weeks march through the country."[111] While victims wrote extensively about plunder, and trial proceedings reveal all manner of crimes, honest behavior was rarely recorded even if it was prevalent. Trial transcripts contain numerous examples of soldiers with a good moral compass, or at least a healthy respect for the Articles of War. When John Sellers of the 23rd stood sentry one night, a soldier in his regiment came by and "put a bottle in his hand, and desiring him to draw the cork of it went away without saying anything further." Sellers discerned that it contained beer but imagined "that it was not honestly come by," so he put it down, "determined not to drink, and broke it with the butt of his firelock." When the man returned, Sellers "told him the consequences of taking other people's property."[112] Joseph Collins of the Brigade of Guards was offered "knives and forks and other things for sale" in Philadelphia in April 1778, but suspected them to have been stolen. John Grant of the 42nd caught two men trying to desert; one of them "took a pair of new Shoes that were wrapped up in a Handkerchief, out of his pocket, and a quarter Dollar, and told him, he would give them to him, if he would let him go home," but Grant refused the bribe.[113]

Jeremiah Nicolas, another Guardsman, assaulted an officer in a barrack room in New York in August 1778; when all of the men in the room were ordered confined, Nicolas came forward and said he "hoped he would not confine his comrades on his account." Drummer John Fisher of the 28th was found in an American uniform in New Jersey in June 1778 after being missing for over a year. On trial for desertion, he claimed he was captured and joined the rebel army to get to the front lines so he could rejoin the British. To corroborate this, he called upon John Hatter of the 17th Regiment of Foot, once a prisoner but now exchanged. Rather than support Fisher's alibi, Hatter informed the court that Fisher had never mentioned wanting to rejoin the British army, and had in fact acknowledged being a deserter.[114]

Soldiers who spoke English poorly, or not at all, could find it difficult to assimilate to the army. John Frederick Leo, his nationality unknown, enlisted in the 22nd Regiment of Foot in Great Britain in 1775 and joined the regiment in America the following year. He deserted in 1778 because he had been "beat and abused" by noncommissioned officers and said "his not complaining to any of the officers of this treatment was his ignorance of the English language."[115] At trials, bilingual soldiers interpreted, as did a sergeant of the 71st "from the Erse to the English language" for a 71st soldier in Philadelphia in December 1777, and a private of the same regiment for a witness in March 1779.[116] That July, a Scottish sergeant in the 38th interpreted for John Grant of the 42nd who had caught and questioned two deserters. The English-speaking prisoners asked, through the interpreter, "Why the Deponent cannot speak English as well now, as he could in the morning?" to which Grant responded "That he understands it enough to ask questions, but not sufficiently to tell a connected story."[117] An officer of the 76th, composed of Erse-speaking highlanders and English-speaking lowlanders, recalled that by 1780, "The Highlanders had made great progress in acquiring the English language, and began to lose that feeling of jealousy, which too often subsists between Highlanders and Lowlanders."[118]

Occasionally highlanders used their native language to benefit the service. An officer of the 42nd wrote from New Jersey in January 1777 about six men of the 71st who took only their swords with them when they went to get hay. Suddenly confronted by ten musket-armed rebels, the Scotsmen surrendered their swords and marched off as prisoners with the rebels behind them. A bilingual soldier of the 71st, "more knowing than the rest, informed them, that was not the way in which the regulars marched their prisoners; that it was unsoldier-like, and desired to march in the centre, so that there should be a prisoner between two of the guard, which was then agreed to." He then "made his design known in Erse to the rest," and they were able to suddenly seize their swords and fight their way to freedom.[119] In 1780, an official at the frontier post of Michilimackinac between Lake Huron and Lake Michigan sent a letter containing important information; "for want of a cypher," he instead sent "a private of the King's Regiment, a Highlander writing in that language."[120]

In the 9th Regiment, Sergeant John McKenzie, a Scotsman, translated English into German for a German recruit on trial. A German recruit in the 54th, Henry Kling, having prior military experience as a noncommissioned officer, was appointed sergeant and spoke English well enough to interpret for witnesses and defendants at trials of two German recruits in Rhode Island in 1778, while a German recruit in the 22nd translated for German soldiers testifying at another trial there the following year.[121]

The German recruits had a particularly difficult time, at least in some regiments. John Christian Lindorff, who joined the 40th Regiment in America in early 1777, complained that he had been promised to be put in a regiment in England and would "be among Germans," that he did not receive his full enlistment bounty, and that upon joining the 40th, the German recruits were not paid as much as other men. "Not being able to speak English, he could not make his Officers understand him." He never heard the Articles of War read, and "the other Soldiers were always calling them German Bougres."[122] That September, in Burgoyne's army making its way from Lake Champlain toward Albany, Georg Hundertmark of the 9th Regiment testified (through a translator) at his trial for desertion that "the promises which were made him when he inlisted have not been kept." He did not get all the pay due to him, nor his first year's regimental clothing, instead going on campaign wearing the recruits' clothing given to him before he embarked in 1776. When his shoes wore out, he went barefoot for two weeks before convincing an officer to give him another pair, even though shoes were among items contractually required to be replaced as often as necessary—and the officer gave an old pair of his own shoes, "throwing one of them at him which struck him on the head, so that he was Stunned for a Quarter of an hour." Soldiers' wives who did washing refused to wash his shirts, flinging them back at him and saying "they did not wash for Dutchmen." He tried to wash them himself but had no soap. And, he had never heard the Articles of War read in German.[123] In 1780, German recruits in the 16th Regiment of Foot in Mobile and Pensacola for four years had still not received all of their pay or clothing, received less food than other soldiers, and got no monetary compensation for the shortage. It had not been made clear to them that the cost of clothing was deducted from their pay. One complained that he did "not know how to behave himself as a Soldier should, as the Articles of War were never read to him."[124]

British military courts took a dim view of these complaints as justification for desertion. Hundertmark was executed, and two of the 16th's men were sentenced to death. Officers in German regiments, however, corroborated claims of German recruits in British regiments. "English regiments have frequent, severe trouble with their hired German recruits," wrote an officer in Canada. "This is not surprising, as they are treated much worse than the English, also they receive their pay quite irregularly."[125] An officer in Philadelphia in 1778 observed, "The German recruits who have been distributed among the English regiments and who are very dissatisfied (for which they have good reason indeed) are now deserting in rather large numbers."[126] And desert they did. Desertion among German recruits in the brigade composed of the 17th, 40th, 46th, and 55th was so bad that the brigadier in command ordered them "put together to sleep in one or more Rooms which rooms are to be locked at 8 at night and opened at Reveille beating in the morning, that their names may be called over every hour during the day." They were prohibited from visiting a nearby German regiment, the Articles of War were read to them, and they were told they were being treated this way because of frequent desertion.[127] The 17th Regiment lost thirteen out of thirty-five German recruits to desertion, the 22nd Regiment lost nine out of forty, and the 23rd eleven out of thirty-five; in each of these regiments, the Germans deserted at a much higher rate than British soldiers in general.[128]

Most British regiments distributed their German recruits more or less evenly among their eight battalion companies, similar to other recruits. The 22nd put five Germans into each of eight companies, resulting in about one in ten men being German before attrition reduced those numbers.[129] The intention was probably to spread inexperience or liability evenly, but this may have made it more difficult for those who could not speak English. The 17th Regiment put all the Germans into one company, perhaps because someone in that company spoke the language well; given that they experienced as much desertion as other regiments, it could also have been a measure to keep them in control.[130] This regiment ordered four of them to "carry each a spade, hatchet and saw instead of his firelock and pouch" during their first campaign.[131]

As time passed, however, some German recruits mastered military skills well enough to be moved into the active grenadier and light infantry companies. Many German recruits served out their time until the end of the war, and some continued as British soldiers for years after. Peter Federheim, from Grünstadt southeast of Frankfurt, enlisted with the German recruits at age eighteen in 1776 and joined the 17th Regiment of Foot. He served the entire war, including over a year as a prisoner of war, and remained in the regiment when the war ended. He was appointed corporal, then sergeant, suggesting he had become fluent in reading, writing, and speaking English. When he finally left the army in 1802, he signed his name as "Fetherham," an indication he had fully acclimated to British service. At the other extreme was Hinrich Peper, a nineteen-year-old Prussian who went into the 29th Regiment in Canada but deserted in September 1776 soon after joining. He found refuge with the Mohawk Indians, was adopted by them, and married into the tribe. With them he fought, "prov'd himself an useful fellow upon many occasions," and gained their "high opinion of his courage and address." In September 1782, he was confined as a deserter in Montreal. Because he had lived a "wandering life and uncontrol'd life," the senior officer in Montreal thought it unlikely he would "be brought to submit to the restraints of military discipline" and recommended returning him to his newfound people.[132]

ENDING CAREERS, ENDING THE WAR

CHAPTER 12

The Remains of Regiments

DUBLIN NATIVE JOHN DEARING was tired of being in jail, so the twenty-four-year-old soldier from the 47th Regiment and eighteen others dug their way out using "no other instrument than their knives." Dearing was part of the army that surrendered at Saratoga in 1777. He escaped in March 1778, but was captured and put into jail in Easton, Pennsylvania, for nine months before being moved to a Philadelphia jail. Over the next two and a half years, he made six more escape attempts, earning him twenty-one days in irons. Digging out in early 1782, his persistence was finally rewarded; he managed to get into British lines in New York. His regiment was still officially interned, but he did what escaped prisoners had been doing since the war began: he joined another regiment, the 57th.[1]

Life as a soldier was not easy, but it was compelling enough for Dearing to risk his life and endure great hardship to return to it. He was one of hundreds, perhaps over a thousand, to do so. Captured British soldiers escaped in droves and made their way, with the help of Loyalist citizens and their own resourcefulness, back to British lines. Some made it quickly, like Michael Tevin of the 47th who escaped with four others from a Rutland, Massachusetts, stockade in September 1778, and covered some eighty miles through rebel-held country in just twelve days to join the British garrison in Rhode Island and sign on to the 38th Regiment. Others, like George Holmes of the 53rd, spent years in the American countryside, working for a living between periods of confinement; it was three years and two months from the time he escaped Rutland to the time he got into New York and joined the 22nd Regiment of Foot. John Rhoads of the 20th attempted to cut a picket from the stockade confining him in Lancaster, Pennsylvania, only to be caught and put in a dungeon in irons for three months, after which he climbed over the stockade and, this time, got to New York. Patrick Kelly of the 31st managed to break two pickets of the stockade in Rutland, but it took him twenty months to get to New York, spending most of the time working "in the country for his livelihood" except for six weeks in a rebel militia. James Steel of the 21st, after escape and recapture, signed on to the crew of an American merchant vessel "in hopes of falling into the hands of a British Cruizer." He got his wish when the British frigate *Jason* captured his ship and brought it in to New York, where Steel joined the 22nd Regiment. John Major of the 24th signed on to a rebel privateer, and when a British warship came into view he cut away the topsail lines to slow the vessel so it could be captured.[2]

Some escaped through subterfuge. James Riley of the 31st, John Stubbs of the 62nd, and the 53rd's John Wishart, John Drury, John Duncan, and John Smith all learned that sailors in their prisons or jails were to be exchanged and managed to pass themselves off as sailors; exchanged, they rejoined the army when they reached New York. The 47th Regiment, as part of Burgoyne's captive army, was not included in exchange negotiations, but soldiers captured at Stony Point in 1779 were. William Woodside of the 47th persuaded an officer of the 17th Regiment of Foot to list him as a member of that corps so that he was exchanged with other Stony Point prisoners. Another avenue out of captivity was as a servant to an officer who was exchanged, like Samuel Millington of the 47th, who served a member of the hospital staff in order to get to New York, where he joined the 23rd Regiment.[3]

Many escapees spent months or years working at their trades while awaiting an opportunity to get through the lines: George Holmes of the 53rd as a shoemaker, James Cuffe of the 62nd as a barber, Roger Clancy of the 47th as a weaver, and Andrew Smith of the 9th as a mill carpenter to name a few. Some were allowed out of prison to work for local inhabitants, labor being in short supply because so many American men were away in the army. Edward Miller of the 20th Regiment of Foot was "bailed out" to work as a wheelwright, John Ward of the 31st was "occasionally let out in the daytime to work at his trade, as a Breeches Maker," and John Southers of the 47th was "bailed out by a farmer in order to go to work for him." All absconded and eventually found their ways into their own lines.[4]

Five men of the 17th Regiment of Foot and two of the Royal Artillery signed an affidavit on behalf of a Bucks County, Pennsylvania, resident who "secreted and supported them for a considerable time" after they escaped confinement, having been captured at Stony Point in 1779. Roger Lamb of the 23rd, after escaping from the prisoners taken at Yorktown in 1781, submitted a detailed report to the commander in chief in New York telling that he and his fellow fugitives were assisted by "friends which are numerous" in Pennsylvania but "found our friends greatly diminished in the Jerseys." They nonetheless found people to shelter and guide them. Roger Clancy of the 47th made his way from Albemarle, Virginia, to New York with the help of people who "made a practice of forwarding British prisoners," although the journey took him sixteen months. Richard Morris, a grenadier in the 34th, told of receiving "Directions from Friends to Government to call on particular Persons at different Places who would aid him" and of working for some "in order to bear his expenses."[5]

A few escapees gave depositions that, although plausible, were not entirely true. Augustine (or Augustus) Barrett, a bricklayer from Leeds who had enlisted in the 24th Regiment in 1771 at the age of just sixteen or seventeen, escaped from the prisoner of war barracks outside Boston in November 1777. When he finally reached British lines, he told of being put on a prison ship in Boston Harbor for six months before conceding to enlist in an American regiment, from which he deserted in September 1780 to get to New York. American muster rolls, however, show that he actually enlisted within days of leaving the barracks and spent almost all of the subsequent time in the Continental army, even being appointed corporal for a while and apparently marrying an American woman.[6]

These are but a handful of the escapees who gave some account of their experiences. Hundreds more left no known accounts. The number of British soldiers taken prisoner during the war cannot be determined with accuracy. Groups of several hundred were taken in Canada in 1775, at sea on the way to Boston in 1776, at Stony Point in 1779, at Cowpens, South Carolina, in 1780, and Pensacola in 1781, besides the bigger capitulations at Saratoga in 1777 and Yorktown in 1781. Countless individuals were captured throughout the war. Muster rolls record those who were "prisoner with the rebels," but rolls are not available for all regiments. Many who escaped and joined other regiments are not recorded accurately. The 33rd Regiment, for example, annotated escapees drafted into the regiment as "enlisted" rather than as soldiers from other corps.[7]

Soldiers were displaced from their regiments for reasons besides capture or desertion. When regiments marched out of garrisons on campaign, some soldiers stayed behind—convalescents recovering from wounds or illness, older men no longer fit for long marches, servants of officers with staff positions, for example. They managed the regiment's "heavy baggage," the clothing and equipment not taken on campaign, and worked in whatever roles the garrison required. A responsible noncommissioned officer managed their accounts and those of the regiment's wives and children in garrison.[8] When regiments on Staten Island marched out in August 1776, convalescents stayed behind as an ad hoc corps to do whatever duty they could.[9] "The Recovered men are regularly sent from Staten Island as soon as they are able to do their duty to their respective Corps," came orders in September.[10] A contingent of recovered men from New York arrived at Princeton, New Jersey, on January 3, 1777, "just as the action began," according to the officer escorting them, referring to the Battle of Princeton that day.[11]

Sometimes, the regiment never came back. This was the situation of George Fox and fifty-one others of the 7th Regiment of Foot, left in Quebec when their regiment went to garrison forts along the Richelieu River in 1775. They performed various duties in the region but returned to help defend Quebec from a rebel invasion that captured most of the 7th and 26th Regiments late in the year. As the only British regulars in Quebec, the little detachment of the 7th performed crucial service in the besieged city over the winter. Fox and the others joined the 47th Regiment when that corps arrived in 1776 as part of a large reinforcement. Sent on Burgoyne's expedition in 1777, Fox was among those captured and spent the rest of the war in captivity.[12] Most of Burgoyne's regiments left substantial detachments in Quebec when they marched out in 1777, and when the campaigning army moved south from Skenesboro, New York, in July 1777, it left behind detachments for the post's security "composed of the Convalesents and Men Least able to march." Included were men "in slight case of flux."[13] A year after Burgoyne's army was interned, most of the men left in Quebec were drafted into regiments still in Canada: sixty-five men of the 21st Regiment joined the 34th, eighty-five of the 62nd went into the 53rd, and so forth.[14] Six of George Fox's fellow soldiers of the 7th who had defended Quebec and then joined the 47th were still in Quebec in October 1782, and were drafted again into the 8th Regiment of Foot.[15]

Some soldiers endured years as prisoners of war, replacing worn-out clothing with garments sent by the British army or whatever else they could procure. This man from the 47th Regiment, captured in 1777 and still a prisoner in 1781, wears his old foraging cap, a linen jacket, check shirt, and canvas trousers, with his old knapsack in some disrepair. Drawing by Eric H. Schnitzer.

Trustworthy soldier servants sometimes followed their officers into new regiments, as evidenced by exchanges of individuals between regiments when officers transferred. Major Christopher French left the 22nd Regiment of Foot to join the 52nd at the end of 1777, taking with him William Goldthorp and Archibald McDonald, and the 52nd transferred James Adair and Edward Atkins to the 22nd. Goldthorp and Adair were a fair exchange, at least nominally, having been born in the early 1730s and each with twenty years in the army when they switched regiments.[16] No details have been found of the administrative aspects of trades like these, for example, whether the soldier received a bounty for joining the new regiment. Overall, it was not typical for officers to take their servants with them when they changed regiments; seventeen officers transferred into or out of the 38th from 1774 through 1783, but in only four cases is it clear from muster rolls that servants followed them.[17]

Throughout the war, regiments went back to Britain, usually because they had been overseas for years before the war broke out. Just as in peacetime, private soldiers still fit for campaigning were drafted, while the officers, noncommissioned officers, and drummers went home with the regiment. The 18th and 59th, both of which arrived in America in the 1760s, went home in December 1775, each distributing between one hundred and two hundred men to regiments in Boston. The 16th Light Dragoons and the 6th, 10th, 14th, 26th, 45th, 52nd, and 65th Regiments went home in subsequent years, similarly distributing their fit men. The 50th Regiment, after several hard years in the West Indies in the early 1770s, had officers and men who were nonetheless "desirous to serve in America."[18] When the corps arrived at Staten Island in summer 1776 from Jamaica, however, it was so under strength that it was sent home after drafting the able-bodied men. These men were seasoned soldiers and veterans of fighting in the Carib War in 1773. The 22nd Regiment received fourteen men from the 50th, including thirty-two-year-old John Coleman, who had enlisted in 1765; twenty-nine-year-old Timothy Connel, who joined the army in 1768; thirty-two-year-old William Copeland, who enlisted in 1764; forty-two-year-old John Cox, with twenty-one years in the army; forty-one-year-old John Harris, who had been a soldier since 1760; thirty-two-year-old John Reynolds, who joined in 1764; and twenty-year veteran David Williams, who was born in 1735.[19] All were veterans going into at least their second war.

While able-bodied men were drafted into other regiments, those no longer fit for active service in the infantry were discharged. Some, however, could still make active contributions to the army, even if not suited for long marches and life in far-flung encampments. Garrisons needed men, lots of men, for routine duties and defense if a threat arose. The Royal Garrison Battalion was formed in 1778 in the city of New York, composed of discharged regular and Loyalist soldiers "totally unfit for the fatigue of a Campaign" but "better calculated for the duty of a Garrison, or the defence of an Island or Fort than an equal number of Recruits sent from Europe."[20] Nominally consisting of some six hundred sergeants, drummers, and private soldiers, companies of this battalion served in the New York area, New Providence in the Bahamas, and Bermuda. Usually this was uneventful service, but sixty-two garrison battalion soldiers were captured when American troops raided the British fort at Paulus Hook, New Jersey, in August 1779. Men like Joseph Jerviss, a fifty-year-old who had served twenty-seven years in at least three regiments before joining the battalion in February 1779, and Hamilton Cross, a year older but with three fewer years in the army, were suddenly prisoners of war, though they had the good fortune to be exchanged and back in New York by January 1781.[21] As the conflict wound down and British troops were redistributed, a British officer in St. Augustine, Florida, characterized these long-serving soldiers in his suggestion that garrison battalion men replace regular troops there: "would not this be a very proper place for a company or two of old fogies, they might smoke their pipes & tell their lies in great tranquility without fear of flux or ague."[22]

No garrison battalion was authorized in Canada, but among the men left behind from regiments on Burgoyne's 1777 campaign were "a considerable number which were thought unfit for service, and the Regiments intended to discharge them, but several of these having been reported to me as capable of Garrison Duty, tho' unable to support the fatigues of a Campaign." The commander in chief in Canada ordered them to be drafted like the others, "meaning however to employ them only in the Garrisons." Unlike other drafts, the regiments receiving them were not required to pay the sending regiment; whether the individuals received a bounty like other drafts is not recorded. A year after being detained "in expectation some good might be derived to the service by their doing Garrison duty," they were embarked "as marines" on the armed ship *Brilliant* for a voyage back to Great Britain.[23]

Although regiments were the army's principal organizational component for recruiting, deployment, and management of individual soldiers, the demands of warfare often caused regiments to be fragmented in various ways. The creation of light infantry battalions and grenadier battalions—the flank battalions—in 1776 was intended as a temporary wartime measure, but the war dragged on for seven more years and sprawled across extensive territory. This caused the flank companies to be separated from their regiments for years on end, often in different regions. The 22nd and 43rd, for example, in Rhode Island from December 1776 through October 1779, consisted only of their eight battalion companies, while their grenadiers and light infantry were in flank battalions fighting in New York, New Jersey, and Pennsylvania. Each year, soldiers were transferred from the regiments to the flank companies to make up for losses, and from the flank companies back to the regiments when no longer fit for campaigning, a significant exercise when the regiments and flank companies were far apart. Soldiers who spent most of the war in flank battalions developed greater attachment to those battalions than to their own parent regiments. Richard Cotton, a light infantryman in the 38th, deserted in July 1780 when he "understood he was to be sent to the Regiment which he much lamented having serv'd so long in the light Infantry."[24]

In places with few flank companies, small battalions were created consisting of both light infantry and grenadiers. For the eighteen months of Rhode Island's occupation, only the flank companies of the 54th Regiment were in the garrison and operated together; when the 38th arrived in summer 1778, its flank companies joined those of the 54th in a little, four-company battalion. In 1783, with only five regiments remaining on Long Island, their ten flank companies were formed into a single battalion. The flank companies of the 29th, 31st, and 34th Regiments were captured at Saratoga in 1777, while their parent regiments remained in Canada. In 1781, with no prospect of recovering the captives, those regiments formed new flank companies.[25] The Brigade of Guards, originally organized into ten companies including two flank companies, reorganized several times during the war: in April 1779, they were arranged into two grenadier, two light infantry and six battalion companies; in October 1780, one of the grenadier and one of the light infantry companies were disbanded, leaving a total of eight companies; and that December, two of the battalion companies were disbanded.[26]

Fast-paced fluid warfare in America relied heavily on the active men of the flank battalions, and additional temporary composite corps were created to supplement them. For Burgoyne's 1777 campaign, two men "of Good Character, Sober, Active, Robust, and Healthy" were selected from each of six regiments and "Provided with Very Good Firelocks" so that they were "in Every Respect Proper to form A Body of Marks Men."[27] A similar corps was formed in General Howe's army in 1777 under Captain Patrick Ferguson of the 70th Regiment, composed of recruits selected and trained with breech-loading rifles of Ferguson's own design.[28] The men continued in the pay of their own regiments, and no rosters of these specialized corps survive, making it almost impossible to determine which individuals served in them.

Captain William Dansey of the 33rd Regiment commanded two composite organizations late in the war. In January 1782, he was put in charge of "the remains of the 23d, 33d & 71st Regiments" who had stayed behind or been sent back to Charleston, South Carolina, when their regiments went on the campaign that culminated in their surrender at Yorktown in October 1781. That December, he took over "Command of the Remains of the Guards and of the 33d amounting to about 100 men" at Fort Johnson near Charleston.[29] Wherever there were displaced soldiers, they were either attached to local regiments or formed into composite corps. All of these organizations, the flank battalions, the Brigade of Guards, the companies of marksmen, and other composites, were strictly temporary. When a regiment left the theater of operations, its flank companies usually went with it. Detached men were either eventually sent to their regiments or drafted into others.

Unfit to be drafted, or even to join a garrison battalion? Then it was time to go home. At least once a year, sometimes more often, when shipping was available, "invalids," men no longer fit for any service due to age or wounds or other infirmities were discharged. "Those Regiments that send Invalids to England, to give each man 8 weeks pay, deducting Six weeks provision money out of it for the time he is supposed to be on board Ship," read orders in Boston in August 1775. "A Fortnight pay is allowed each man on his landing to carry him to his place of abode."[30] Similar orders came throughout the war.[31] The commander of the 42nd Regiment's grenadier company personally visited veteran Sergeant Donald McCraw and his wife and son in July 1780, "told them to get ready to go

home in the fleet," and "gave the Boy 2 guineas," an indication of the es-
teem some officers had for long-serving, trustworthy soldiers.[32]

Even though the voyage from America to Great Britain usually took
only about a third the time as the opposite trip, it was every bit as haz-
ardous. The *Lion* transport taking home "wounded officers and soldiers"
of the 59th Regiment ran aground on the Isles of Scilly in a storm in
early 1776, and was freed after a few days only to be dashed upon rocks
again in even heavier weather. All got on shore safely, but a newspaper
reported that "several poor Wretches died there through the Want of the
common Necessaries of Life, owing to the Barrenness of the Place."[33] In
1778, the *America* transport took invalids from Philadelphia in spite of
being "for a considerable time leaky and otherwise not in a Situation to
go to sea at a time of year when Gales of wind were to be expected," and
foundered nine days after leaving the American coast. Fortunately, the
passengers were saved, and a sympathetic officer asked for an investiga-
tion to prevent future instances of "such Shameful inattention to the
safety of men who have suffered in His Majestys Service."[34] The *Henry
& Ann* transport was captured by a French privateer in February 1779 in
the English Channel, and the invalids on board were imprisoned in
France for two years.[35]

And soldiers died. Battle, illness, accidents, and even occasional suicides
claimed many soldiers during eight years of war. The 38th Regiment,
which arrived in Boston in the middle of 1774 and left New York in November 1783, saw 1,171 individuals pass through its ranks, not including
officers. Of those, 296 died during those years, including 27 in the
grenadier company and 38 in the light infantry. The 22nd Regiment, in
America from June 1775 until November 1783, lost about 200 out of just
over 1,000.[36] As discussed earlier, the majority of these deaths were due
to illness rather than battle.

Military texts described funeral procedures for every rank from private
soldier to general officer.[37] Before war broke out, deceased soldiers were
buried with some ceremony, at least in Boston, where the 18th Regiment
ordered funeral parties for private soldiers or sergeants five times from
the beginning of December 1774 to the end of January 1775. The 10th
Regiment held a funeral on March 16, 1775. In each case a sergeant, a
corporal, and twelve privates were assigned to "fire over the body" and
"all the men off duty" in the regiment attended.[38] No record has been
found of such rites after June 1775, but regimental orderly books that

sometimes include this information are themselves extremely rare, leaving it uncertain whether common soldiers were interred with any ceremony in British wartime garrisons.

Nottingham native John Budge enlisted in the 7th Regiment of Foot as a wartime recruit and was soon on his way to America. Before embarking, he had a will prepared that opened with the puzzling phrase, "As it is my misfortune to enlist in the army." He had an annual income of one hundred pounds per year bequeathed by an uncle, which he left in the management of another uncle and willed to several extended family members in the event of his death.[39] He was prescient both in preparing the will and in recognizing his misfortune, as he died in Charleston of unknown causes in 1780.[40] Only a handful of wills for soldiers who served in America are known to survive; four were registered by soldiers of the 1st Battalion of the Brigade of Guards between November 1777 and March 1779, out of some five hundred soldiers in the battalion (others may have registered wills before that).[41] Sergeant David Stuart of the 22nd Regiment's grenadier company, serving as quartermaster to the 2nd Battalion of Grenadiers, prepared a will four days before dying in New York on October 14, 1779, witnessed by a sergeant in his own regiment and two sergeants from others. He left all of his "estate, real and personal, and all arrears of pay" to his wife, Mary, who was to "pay all debts." He left "one half of what I shall die possessed of" to his nine-year-old son, James, and declared his wife the executor.[42] James Bradley, a recruit in the 7th Regiment of Foot from Broomsgrove, Worcestershire, was ill from the time he arrived in America in 1777. His will prepared in April 1779 left "all my real and personal estate, whatsoever" to New York jeweler James Bennett, also a Broomsgrove native.[43] Bradley died in May 1780. John Gilbert, private soldier and musician in the 22nd Regiment who joined the army in 1766, prepared a will two weeks before his death in England in April 1786 after serving the entire war in America. He left one hundred pounds, plus all money still owed to him including prize money, to his brother, who was to apportion it in thirds between himself and two other siblings. He also left a "silver watch & furniture" to his sister, a valuable token that he might have owned because his father and brother were both watchmakers.[44]

The 1778 account book for a company of the Brigade of Guards notes balances "due to the heirs" of deceased soldiers, amounts never exceeding five pounds.[45] The account book for a company of the 71st shows similar small balances for the eighteen men who died between September 1779 and October 1781, with a few slightly exceeding six pounds. No mention is made of where the money went, but one man's account included a charge for "a Coffin & Funeral expenses."[46] The 22nd Regiment of Foot's agent in London, the financial firm that managed the regiment's accounts, recorded payments to four widows of soldiers who died in America, including Thomas Scott, who was found "perished through the severity of the weather" on December 24, 1778, in Rhode Island.[47]

CHAPTER 13

Long and Faithful Services

WILLIAM CRAWFORD, A MAN WITH AN "ardent disposition for adventure," left the 12th Light Dragoons in Ireland to join the 20th Regiment of Foot bound for the American war. A year and a half after landing in Quebec he was a prisoner of war, among those interned at Saratoga, and spent over two years being marched first to the Boston area, then to the interior of Massachusetts, then to Virginia. This was not the adventure he had enlisted for, and with several others he effected his escape, only to be apprehended and thrown in a Virginia jail. "All my hopes of glory and promotion were likely to be at an end, unless I released myself from this place," he knew, and formed a plan. "Young, hearty, and handsome," the Irishman befriended the jailer's daughter. Her reciprocation, however, took him in a different direction than he intended. She forged a marriage certificate, spirited him out of jail, and presented him to townspeople as her husband. Rather than escape to rejoin his army, he acquiesced to the marriage and settled in America.[1]

When an end to hostilities came and British forces reduced their holdings in the newfound United States to only the area around the city of New York, there remained redcoats scattered all over the country. Prisoners of war, escapees, and deserters now had to find their way to their army or find fortunes in the new land. Some did one, some did the other. Abraham Pike, an Irishman who enlisted in 1775 at age twenty-five, was tried for plundering in 1777 (as seen in chapter 9) and deserted from the 23rd Regiment in May 1778.[2] He made his way to the Pennsylvania frontier, where he married and tried to settle. But times were unsettled in this war-torn region. His exploits in clashes with native tribesmen allied to the British government earned him the sobriquet "The Indian Killer." The town of Pike's Creek in Luzerne County, Pennsylvania, is named for him.[3] Suffolk native Henry Church came to America in 1780 as a thirty-year-old recruit for the 63rd Regiment. Taken prisoner while in the regiment's light infantry company near Petersburg, Virginia, he absconded from captivity and settled on the frontier. He lived to be one hundred nine years old, long enough to see the first railroad built past his farm, and acquired the nickname of "Old Hundred." For this reason, the town that grew up around where he settled in what is today Wetzel County, West Virginia, is named Hundred.[4]

By 1783, most British prisoners of war were held in Pennsylvania west of the Susquehanna River. The conclusion of peace negotiations left them free to return to British-held New York. An officer among them recalled that

> we remained till June, 1783, when orders were given for our march to New York, in consequence of peace. We moved off in divisions, passing through Philadelphia. . . . The soldiers received marching money daily, and the clothing not delivered out was carried in wagons. Numerous applications were made to us on the road to give away part of our stores. On our arrival at Staten Island we found transports in readiness, and all the men whose regiments were in Europe, and who embarked, were settled with for pay and clothing, and sailed for England. The others were quartered in New York and the dependencies.[5]

Prisoners who did not return were written off as deserters, causing muster rolls to show clusters of desertions on a single day in May or June. Fifteen men of the 38th's light infantry company, captured at Yorktown in October 1781, were written off on May 18, 1783. The 23rd Regiment, of which over two hundred were captured at Yorktown, wrote off thirty-five as deserters on June 24, and twenty-five more as dead, perhaps because their fates were known.

While most of the absent prisoners probably did desert and remain in America, some who were written off did not desert at all. Essex native John Overon and county Cavan native James Caffrey, both born in about 1750 and serving in the 34th Regiment's light infantry company, were

HENRY CHURCH.

Henry Church, veteran of the 63rd Regiment of Foot born in 1750, deserted and settled in what is now West Virginia. This picture of him appeared in *Harper's Magazine*, Vol. 19 (June-November 1859), page 16.

captured in an action at Fort Windecker in the Mohawk River Valley in October 1780. Written off as deserters when they failed to return to the regiment in Canada in 1783, they had actually taken a more noble path. They escaped captivity and made their way to New York, where they joined the 22nd Regiment of Foot in January 1782, remaining in that corps for several years after the war's end.[6] Countless others may have turned up in distant places, unbeknownst to the regiments that struck them off their muster rolls.

War in many parts of the world meant changing priorities, and by 1781 it was clear that there were more important places than America to send troops. That year, the established size of infantry regiments was reduced, from the seventy private soldiers per company ordered in 1778 to fifty-six per company; numbers of sergeants, corporals, and drummers remained the same. The 42nd Regiment, which was at one hundred per company, was reduced to eighty-five, and regiments captured at Saratoga in 1777 were reduced to just thirty per company, reflecting the attrition that had ravaged them during years of captivity.[7] Two years later, with peace terms settled and preparations made to finally evacuate New York, further reductions occurred. In August 1783, orders from England arrived in New York and were disseminated on the seventeenth. The army in America was to reduce its size by disbanding most of the regiments raised after the war began and decreasing the established strength of the remaining regiments. Some regiments in New York were to return to Great Britain and others were to remain in North American colonies still under British rule. For some soldiers this was just another set of marching orders, another change of station in a military career. For others, there were choices.

Seven regiments were in Canada in 1783, the 8th, 29th, 31st, 34th, 44th, 53rd, and 84th. Five regiments in New York were directed to join them, the 33rd, 37th, 42nd, 54th, and 57th. The other eleven regiments in New York—the 17th Light Dragoons, and the 7th, 22nd, 23rd, 38th, 43rd, 70th, 71st, 76th, 80th, and 82nd Regiments of Foot—prepared to return to Great Britain, where the latter four would disband. Some regiments in the West Indies stayed there, while others went home. Two of the 60th Regiment's four battalions disbanded, as did one of the 84th's two battalions. Most other infantry regiments were reduced from ten companies to eight, each with two sergeants, three corporals, two drummers, and forty-eight private soldiers, plus two fifers in the grenadier company—a reduction of one sergeant and eight private soldiers per company, plus two companies discarded altogether.[8] This meant discharging a large number of men while still in New York. Choosing whom to discharge was not difficult. Those enlisted after December 16, 1775, were entitled to be discharged at the end of the war, if they had served for at least three years. The 38th Regiment had at least 144 who met that criteria; the 3rd Regiment, in Jamaica since the end of 1782, had 232.[9] In addition, there were veterans with twenty or more years in the army who were no longer fit for service.

Soldiers discharged in America could choose one of the most valuable benefits the army had to offer: land. One hundred acres was the grant for a private soldier, more for married men and those with children. Just over eight hundred men, women, and children embarked in New York on September 26, bound for Port Roseway (now Shelburne), Nova Scotia. The men were paid through October 24, the date of discharge recorded on muster rolls, including money for undelivered regimental clothing due in 1783, and were allowed to keep their knapsacks (they also kept their clothing, having already paid for it). After landing, they were formed into militia companies under the care of officers who had also been discharged, more for the sake of managing the influx of people than for military purposes, "Until the governor of Nova Scotia shall make new arrangements in their behalf."[10] Men from regiments already in Canada received land grants in Upper Canada, present-day Ontario. The first few years of life in these rugged territories were challenging, waiting for grants to be surveyed, but for former tenant farmers accustomed to laboring on other people's land, it was the start of a new life otherwise unimaginable. James Nowland, a Catholic born in Ireland in 1743, was among the recruits who arrived sick in New York in 1779. He had the good fortune to survive, serve in the 22nd Regiment until the end of the war, and take a land grant in Nova Scotia. He married in his late fifties and then had eleven children before his wife died in 1829. On June 30, 1840, he scrawled his mark on a deposition for relief under a new act for "old soldiers" living in Canada; at the age of ninety-three, he submitted that he could no longer support himself. He was granted relief of ten pounds per year, which he was still collecting in 1843 at the age of one hundred.

Johann Philip Aulenbach came to America as a twenty-one-year-old German recruit in 1776, accompanied by his wife, Dorothea, whom he had married earlier that year. Because he had learned to play several musical instruments while working as "the attendant of a prominent and distinguished gentleman" in Hanover, he was taken into the 17th Light Dragoons as a trumpeter, soon becoming the trumpet major, the cavalry equivalent of drum major. He served for the entire war, accepted his discharge, and went with his wife to Port Roseway. In 1784, he was elected an elder in a new Lutheran congregation; five months later, when the minister left, Aulenbach conducted services. He diligently secured land in town for a church and raised funds to build it. When one of the elders absconded with the money, Aulenbach and another elder rented a house to hold services. By 1785, many veterans in Port Roseway had dispersed to other parts of Nova Scotia, and that August, Aulenbach also moved on, becoming the teacher at a parochial school in Lunenburg. Besides teaching, he officiated at services and funerals when ministers were not available. After his wife died in August 1801, he remarried that November and subsequently had six children. In a memorial written late in his life, he lamented that in 1819, "I fell and badly broke my right leg. I had already been for a long time lame in the left one, and was now a poor cripple who could earn little or nothing any more. My hearing I lost through ringing the bell, having to stand too near it. Yet I still taught the school for a few years after my unfortunate accident." He died in January 1836.[11]

William Scoles was among several hundred recruits disembarked at Halifax, Nova Scotia, in 1782 rather than continuing on to their regiments in New York. They bolstered the Halifax garrison even though they were put onto the muster rolls of regiments they never actually joined, in Scoles's case, the 33rd.[12] After about fourteen months in Halifax, with the war over and the army being downsized, Scoles and the others were discharged. Scoles "followed the business of fishing" but five years later petitioned for a vacant fifty-acre lot on Halifax Harbor "on the Western Shore, between Sleepy cove and Ferguson's Cove." His request granted, he settled there, continued to fish, married, and raised a family. The risk he took by enlisting in a wartime army rewarded him well with a new life on his own land, in return for serving three years far from any hostile action.[13]

John Drury, who was wounded three times and "always behaved himself a clean, good and obedient soldier" in the 38th Regiment, did not get a grant but instead used his own money to purchase a small plot in Port Roseway from the surveyor who allocated granted land. In spite of the disabling effects from his wounds, he quickly built a house and a slaughterhouse, and settled in with his family. Fortune soon turned against the industrious Drury. There were accusations of unfairness in the slow-moving land-allocation process. Much of the land was poor, house lots in town were in short supply, and tensions flared when white settlers complained that free blacks in town threatened jobs because they worked for lower wages. Rioting ensued, with white settlers pulling down the houses of their black counterparts. The surveyor got wind that he was soon to be targeted for his role in allocating land and fled for his own safety. Drury, trying to support his family on a subdivision of the surveyor's land, was driven off the property he had bought and developed. He lost everything.[14]

Not everyone who went to Canada did so for a land grant. For many soldiers discharged in New York, there was an immediate and familiar opportunity. The regiments bound for Canada needed new men after discharging those who were eligible, and the army was a known career. Forty-seven men discharged from the 22nd Regiment of Foot immediately enlisted in the 54th, many even though they were eligible for land grants or return to Britain—including three German recruits who had joined in 1776. The 57th took on 147 new men in this way, mostly from British regiments and a few from disbanded Loyalist corps. The 42nd added nearly 100, and the two companies of the 37th for which rolls survive took on 42, suggesting a total of about 160 in all eight companies. In each regiment, a few of their own discharged men reenlisted.[15] None wrote down their reasons, but the army offered all the incentives that had compelled them to enlist in the first place—including an enlistment bounty of five pounds.[16] For those who had been drafted already, like thirty-three-year-old Bryan Sweeny, who had joined the 50th Regiment in 1768 and been drafted into the 22nd in 1776, it was the third enlistment bounty of this career and the biggest so far, and he saw yet another when he joined the 20th Regiment in 1788.[17]

Some discharged soldiers were fond enough of North America to remain even without a land grant. County Wexford native Garrett Barron spent much of the war along the Richelieu River between Lake Champlain and Montreal, and settled there after being discharged from the 29th Regiment in June 1784.[18] He established a farm at Caldwell Manor, Quebec, just over the border from the United States. He married a local woman (apparently his second marriage, although no details are known of the first), and they took in travelers. One of their guests in November 1787 was an army officer with whom Barron had served, who wrote, "we Rowed as far as Barrons farm where we stopped to breakfast and were entertained with very excellent Tea and sausages. The owner of the house was an old acquaintance of mine having been a Sergeant in the 29th Regt many Years. His house is extremely neat and clean and is by far the best Public house on the whole Communication between Albany and Montreal."[19]

In spite of his comfortable situation, Barron sold his property and moved forty miles into the wilderness, where he and his father-in-law settled on adjacent properties in Hinchinbrook. He was a captain in the local militia, had some minor involvement when war came to his area in 1813, and lived until 1835, having spent twenty-three years in the army followed by fifty-one years farming in Canada. A local history wrote of him:

> Mrs Barron felt very lonesome in her new home, when her husband remarked that with 5 gallons of rum she had all the company needed. Like all old soldiers of that time, he was fond of his dram, but never got intoxicated. He was tall, over 6 feet, and in his prime must have been a powerful man. He was rough-spoken, and fond of contradiction, and especially prone to controversy with Presbyterians (he was an Episcopalian) and Catholics.[20]

When a man was discharged from the army, he received a paper called a discharge stating clearly that he was released from his service obligation. It was a crucial document, affording proof that he was not a deserter. Usually a printed form with individual details written into blanks, the discharge recorded the man's name, age, place of birth, length of service, trade, the regiment from which he was discharged, and sometimes some details of his service history. Usually the reason for discharge was given, whether it was a malady that rendered him unfit for service, a reduction in forces, or simply in consideration of long and faithful service. Some included descriptive information such as height, hair and eye colors, complexion, and "visage"—the shape of the face, such as oval, round, square, or what have you. It included a statement that the man had received all pay and clothing due to him, and was signed by the soldier and at least one officer or noncommissioned officer.

Men eligible for discharge from regiments returning to Great Britain could stay in their regiments for the journey home, leaving the ranks after

The one-page discharge form was usually printed with personal information filled in by hand. The format varied, but always included the soldier's name, age, place of birth, trade, and length of service. Some, like this one for Alexander Andrew of the 44th Regiment discharged in 1793, include more details about service. Andrew was recommended for a pension "for his long and Faithfull Service, also having been Wounded in the right side at the Battle of Germantown near Philadelphia on the 4th Day of October 1777." WO 119/1/4. (*The National Archives*)

The reverse side of the discharge gave a signed statement that the man had received all arrears of pay and clothing due to him. It was countersigned by an officer or sergeant. Some, like this one, also included a statement from an army surgeon concerning any infirmities the man incurred in the service. WO 119/1/4. (*The National Archives*) disembarking. Those discharged in America also could return to the British Isles at the army's expense, one more ocean voyage in a transport ship. Once in Britain, discharged soldiers born in England were paid for an extra fourteen days "to carry them to the places of their former residence"; those who enlisted in Scotland or Ireland received twenty-eight days' worth "in consideration of their homes being more distant."[21] And each man had the option of going to Chelsea Hospital on the outskirts of London, where the army's pension examining board sat, in the hope that the board would grant a pension of five pence per day, five-eighths of his base pay as a soldier.

Each man went before the pension board in person to make his case. He presented his discharge, which often included an explicit recommendation from an officer in his former regiment. The board kept a record of every man it examined, listing his name, age, years of service, place of birth, trade, reason for discharge, and the regiment from which he was discharged. No examination proceedings are known to survive, however, leaving us ignorant of the interactions between the applicant and the examiners. Most men were granted pensions if they had incurred an infirmity rendering them unable to earn a living, or if they had served for at least twenty years. The examination board's admission books record all sorts of health issues, mostly in just one or a few words. Some had explicit injuries, from the general term "wounded" to specifics like "hurt leg," "lost the use of his left arm," "lost a leg," or "wounded thro' the body." Far more common were ailments contracted from long service, like "asthma," "rheumatick," "dropsy," "paralytic," "bad sight," "ruptured," "delirious," "lame," or most common of all, "worn out."

The system had room for abuse. The all-important discharge was the applicant's proof of his length of service. These forms were usually filled out by noncommissioned officers like Roger Lamb of the 23rd Regiment, a good writer who later became a school teacher. Soon after his regiment returned to England in early 1784, he "was employed to fill up the soldiers discharges." He wrote, in a manuscript passage that he opted to omit from the two books he published:

> In filling up the soldiers discharges which were signed by the Colonel before they were sent to me, the soldiers were asked "How long have you served" their answer would be seven or eight years more than they really were in the service, this they said in order that they might the more readily pass the Board by having a longer servitude. I then wrote the number of years they mentioned. But

in filling up my own discharge I wrote Twelve just the number I really did serve. It is a false notion to think soldiers are served by putting down in their papers more years than they actually were in the service. No it is bringing a curse on them by lying and perjury! They are obliged to swear in a most solemn manner before a Magistrate every quarter of a year, that they have served the number of years specified in their discharge. And I do not wonder at the misery some of these poor old men undergo after leaving the Army seeing that the curse of lying and perjury are upon them.[22]

Lamb's claims are difficult, if not impossible, to prove. Lamb himself went before the pension board on March 8, 1784, along with sixty-one other veterans of the 23rd.[23] Some of their entries in the pension board examination book record more years of service than reflected on the regiment's muster rolls, but among them are drafts, escaped prisoners of war from other regiments, and wartime enlistees who may have had prior service.[24] For the most part, when the years of service can be verified, the information recorded on discharges is accurate to within a year or two.

The pension board filed away its copy of each man's discharge, and a substantial number survive—perhaps as many as ten thousand for men who served in the American war,[25] albeit only for men who appeared before the board after 1785; many are discharges from corps men served in later in their careers, rather than those they were in while in America. These documents are useful for demographic studies, such as determining the proportion that signed their own names versus using "his mark," but many also carry rich, albeit brief, details about service and ailments. Some have general statements like "worn out in the service in North America," or "twice wounded & unfit for service,"[26] but others are very specific.

John Hawkins, a writing clerk from Shankill in county Armagh who served in the 37th Regiment, was "wounded in the head in the action at Brandywine the 11 of September 1777 and Melancholy." Edinburgh native James Forest of the 57th, a blacksmith, was "worn out and wounded in his thigh 26th May 1782 in an Engagement with the Enemy at Sandy Hook." Thomas Witherill, a clothier from Bidell, Yorkshire, "lost part of one finger of his left hand at German Town North America and wounded in the left arm at York Town Virginia" while in the 63rd Regiment. Leicester stocking weaver Anthony Townshend of the 29th was discharged "by reason of being worn out and having received a cut in the

Leg with an Ax when on Duty in America, which renders him unfit for His Majesty's service." Allen Cameron of the 74th, an Argyllshire native, was "severely wounded in the head, and his shoulder dislocated in the siege of Penobscot in America, by which his brain is so affected as to be frequently out of his senses, and brought on other complaints." Samuel Newby, a musician in the 10th Regiment of Foot and a Limerick native, after thirty years of service was "worn out on account of his long service and Constant Practice on Musical Wind Instruments." Londonderry blacksmith William McCreally of the 3rd Regiment was disabled by "having both his arms broke in a Hurricane in Jamaica and having received a Ball in his leg, at the Eutaws in America."[27] These are but a few of hundreds upon hundreds.

Some soldiers served in more than one part of the world during the years of the American war, such as Westmoreland native James Rennison, a weaver who served twenty-nine years in the 59th Regiment and "was present at the engagements at Bunkers Hill & Lexington in North America in the year 1775, at the latter of which he was wounded in the thigh by a musket ball; and has served at the Siege of Gibraltar, but having contracted a Rupture, and being Old & worn out in the Service" was recommended for a pension.[28] Others fought and were wounded in more than one war. The 6th Regiment of Foot was in the Carib War, where Samuel Stratton was "wounded in the neck & head the 25th January 1773, in the Island of St. Vincents in the West Indies." Drafted into the 37th in 1776, he was wounded again, "thro' the right Arm & right leg at Brandywine in North America the 11th September 1777," but nonetheless soldiered on until 1790, when twenty-two years in the army left him "worn out in the service."[29] Benjamin Noble left his native Bedfordshire and enlisted in the 14th Regiment of Foot in 1765, was wounded on St. Vincent during the Carib War and again at the Battle of Great Bridge, Virginia, in 1775. He was drafted into the grenadier company of the 44th Regiment just in time to participate in the Battle of Princeton in January 1777, where he was wounded a third time, but he remained an active soldier until 1786, "worn out with long service."[30] Heinrich Lücke of Hildesheim in Lower Saxony served for over eighteen years in the Hanoverian army, including at the Battle of Minden in 1759, where he was wounded in the wrist. This did not stop him from serving with the 4th Regiment of Foot, a German recruit enlisted in 1776, until he was fifty-four years old in March 1791.[31] Also in the 4th was John Smith, who was wounded for the second time at Concord on April 19, 1775, through the thigh; his first wound was in the leg at one of the invasions of Martinique during the Seven Years' War, in either 1759 or 1762 (the discharge does not say which one), but the dyer from Norfolk stayed at his military profession for thirty-four years, finishing in 1788.[32]

Some discharges included statements of the man's meritorious service, either on the forms themselves or in attached affidavits. Of a Dumbarton shoemaker in the 7th Regiment of Foot, an officer wrote, "The within named Alexander Brice during twenty two years service having never been brought to a Court Martial it is with great Pleasure & satisfaction I give this testimony of his merit."[33] Wickham, Kent, native John Evident, a chair maker, spent twenty-four and a half years in the 7th Regiment before taking his discharge in 1788. At forty-four, he was swarthy, just over six feet tall, with hazel eyes and dark hair, and "having been wounded in the right thigh & the hip at the storming of Fort Montgomery, suffered much by long confinement when Prisoner of War in America, & worn out with long servitude, has obtained the honor of the first Class of the Badge of Distinction for his Fidelity and Virtue."[34] Besides being wounded in America while in the 55th Regiment, Perthshire native James Shaw "served most faithfully, with remarkable diligence, sobriety, & good character," and was "hereby recommended as a proper & deserving object of His Majesty's Royal Bounty of Chelsea Hospital."[35] An officer glowingly wrote of the 17th Regiment's Mark Green, who was "taken prisoner twice in America at the famous Battle of Princeton in the Jersies & at Stony Point in confinement in Jail for more than 34 months," saying that he served "with the greatest Credit never having been tried by a Court Martial or confined for any Misdemeanor. His Behaviour has been ever praiseworthy for all the Rigors he suffered in unwholesome Jails during his long Confinements, or the purswasion and Endeavors of the Americans to make him desert his King and Country could never have the least affect on him to make him swerve from his duty, for he even broke out of Jail & made his Escape."[36]

Roger Lamb was denied a pension because he had served only twelve years and had no disability; he was still capable of earning his own living. Some men probably knew this would be the decision and did not even go before the pension board. For the 22nd Regiment, for example, about 40 percent of the men discharged during or after the war never went before the board.[37] Some soldiers were intent on getting home rather than making the journey to Chelsea, such as Archibald MacIndow, "disabled at the siege of York Town in Virginia by the kick of a horse in the forehead and afterwards taken prisoner." When released and discharged from the 71st Regiment in Perth, the native of Ardnamurchan, Argyllshire, "returned to his family in the highlands where he has lived since," but the effects of his wound caught up with him. In 1792 he finally made his way to the pension board and handed over a discharge newly prepared by one of his former officers explaining that he was "subject to convulsion fits, which and real poverty, prevented his coming to solicit the pension sooner."[38] A fellow soldier in the 71st, Allen Roy Cameron, from the same Argyllshire town, went before the pension board on the same day. He was wounded in the right leg in a redoubt at Yorktown in 1781, but after discharge "returned to Scotland without being properly recommended where he remained with his family till lately in a lingering state of health." His discharge explained "that his not being recommended was owing entirely to the hurry peculiar to embarkation of the sick & wounded at that time."[39]

In spite of spending six years in the British army, language remained a barrier to some highlanders who did not understand that they could seek benefits. Inverness native Alexander McKinnon, wounded at the 1781 Battle of Green Spring in Virginia, "was glad to go and see his friends and return to his native place: forgetting his misfortunes" when his regiment, the 76th, was disbanded in Stirling, Scotland, after the war. His discharge money, however, ran out and "he found himself incapable of supporting himself on account of his wound which rendered him very lame, and grew dayly worse." One of his former officers wrote a letter to the examining board on his behalf in 1790, explaining of the tenacious disabled veteran, "at length he determined to collect what little money he could from his friends, to bear his expenses to London (part of which he came by water, and paid fifteen shillings for) and throw himself on the mercy of the honorable board of Chelsea College to admit him into the house, not speaking a word of English, and being unable to support himself."[40] The same officer also endorsed 76th Regiment veteran John McDonald, who had "received a wound in his back by the Bursting of a shell at Yorktown, Virginia," and, in 1790, at age fifty-seven, was old and infirm. The officer had seen McDonald's scars and wrote to the pension board that the wound was not mentioned at the time of his discharge because no sufficiently senior officer was present. The endorsement continued, "These poor ignorant Highlanders not speaking a word of English are not able to state their own case when called upon."[41]

Chelsea Hospital had accommodations for a few hundred residents, called in-pensioners. The thousands of other applicants were granted out-pensions, allowing them to live at their own places of residence. The pension office sent a list of pensioners to each region's excise office, and twice each year the pensioner visited the office to collect his stipend of five pence per day for a private soldier, proportionally more for drummers, corporals, or sergeants. Failure to collect the pension resulted in being struck off the pension list, ensuring that the deceased were not maintained on the rolls even if their deaths were not directly reported.[42] Other circumstances could cause removal from the rolls, including further military service, after which the man could appear again before the examining board or make his case in another way. Samuel Debnam served in the 22nd Regiment of Foot from 1766 until 1784, when he was granted a pension. He remained a pensioner for a few years, perhaps also working at his trade as a wheelwright in his native Warminster, Wiltshire, before joining the army again. He spent five years in three different corps and was finally discharged again in 1795, but could not appear in person in Chelsea. He instead wrote an eloquent, page-long petition to the pension board outlining his service and situation, including being "very lame by having an ulcered leg," and asked "that your Lordships will through your great Goodness, be pleased to order him to be reanstablished on the Books, he being an object of Charity."[43]

The pension did carry an obligation: in times of military crisis, pensioners could be called to serve in British garrisons where the inability to march long distances and perform heavy labor was not a liability. Corps with names like "Veteran Battalion," "Invalid Company," and "Garrison Battalion" guarding coastal locations in Great Britain increased and decreased in number and size as circumstances demanded. Some men went directly into these corps after discharge from infantry regiments, such as John Corbett of the 22nd Regiment, discharged because of a wound in 1779 after only two and a half years of service, who spent the next thirty-three years and five months in various veteran battalions.[44] Others were summoned when needed. In early 1776, when large numbers of men were being drafted in Ireland to serve in America, the weakened regiments were temporarily bolstered by pensioners. Newspaper notices directed pensioners to appear before local examining boards on certain dates to assess whether they were fit for service.[45] Thirty pensioners served with the 32nd Regiment for most of 1776, as did similar numbers in the 36th and 67th; they were released at the end of the year.[46]

Failure to respond to a call to duty resulted in being struck from the pension rolls, as it did for Donald Wright, discharged from the 22nd Regiment of Foot in 1784. He found work as a cook on the herring-fishing sloop *Janet*, which was at sea from May through November 1790. During that time, pensioners in the Glasgow area were summoned; since Wright did not appear, he was struck from the rolls. He petitioned the pension board to be reinstated, providing several sworn statements attesting to his whereabouts and asserting that he "payed his rent and sofar as I know is an honest man."[47] Also in 1790, John Mayell, a pensioned musician from the 22nd who had been wounded in the shoulder, was summoned to Bristol but was unable to report there because of poor health. He was instead examined at Devizes and found unfit for service, but he was struck off the rolls because he failed to appear at Bristol. He, too, petitioned to be reinstated as a pensioner.[48]

John Lawson joined the 22nd Regiment of Foot in 1750, when he was twenty years old, and served in America from the siege of Louisbourg in 1758 until his regiment returned to England in 1764. After a decade of respite in Great Britain, he stepped onto a wharf in America again, this time in Boston, in June 1775, greeted by a fresh new war against the same colonists he'd fought alongside a dozen years earlier.

This time his stay was short. As one of his regiment's longest-serving soldiers, Lawson was chosen for recruiting service in Britain. He and his counterparts sailed back to the British Isles in December 1775. Lawson spent the next sixteen months working hard to raise men for the war in America. In April 1777, he was discharged, "worn out" after spending more than half his life in the army, and was among the limited number of recipients of a twelve-pence-per-day pension rather than the usual five pence, "in consideration of his long and faithful services in the Army, & to keep him from Want." He returned to his place of birth, the Glasgow suburb of Cathcart, where he stood to live a reasonably comfortable retirement.

Within a few years, though, he took up a cause on behalf of his fellow pensioners. Army pensions were distributed through local excise offices, and the law allowed those offices to retain 5 percent of the pension payments as compensation for their services. For pensioners in western Scotland, however, there was a difference: they collected their pensions in Glasgow, but the designated place was in Edinburgh on the other side of the country. The Glasgow excise collector withheld an additional service fee of two shillings a year from each pension, besides the 5 percent with-held in Edinburgh. In 1785, John Lawson made a stand against this decades-old practice by filing a lawsuit on behalf of himself and other pensioners asserting that the extra charge was unfair. The court agreed and ordered Lawson and others to be paid the sums withheld since they went onto the pension rolls. Eight years after he left active service, Lawson had won a victory for his fellow former soldiers.[49]

Archibald Maclaren of Inveraray, Scotland, arrived in America in 1777 as a twenty-one-year-old recruit in the 26th Regiment of Foot. He returned with his regiment to Great Britain just two years later, after being wounded three times, once in the head. He left no record of where he received those wounds, but they did not prevent him from being appointed sergeant in 1780. He used his free time to write and publish plays, the first of which, the farce *The conjurer, or the Scotsman in London*, was published in Dundee in 1781. It opened in Edinburgh in 1783, the same year his second play, a "musical entertainment" called *Coup de Main, or the American Adventurers*, also opened. Maclaren took advantage of the military drawdown to obtain his discharge and recognized that his wounds were good grounds for seeking a pension. He set off for Chelsea,

> But the very day on which I had purposed to commence my journey to London, I was seized with a fever, which confined me six weeks, and to augment my disaster, I found my landlady had lighted her pipe with my discharge, at which she seemed so little concerned, that she gravely told me—she always lighted her pipe with Jock's copy-books when they were all written upon: this was a heavy stroke, for the Regt. had by that time returned to America, and my discharge was no phoenix—from the ashes of which I could expect to see another rise: so what was to be done?

His regiment had actually gone to Ireland, leaving Maclaren without the essential documentation to show the pension board. He toured with a theater company for a while, taking advantage of his highland accent to play Scottish, Irish, and French characters, but the company went out of business. Needing a source of income, in November 1784 he enlisted again, returning to his former rank in a Scottish corps, the Dunbartonshire Fencible Infantry. It fought in the 1798 Irish rebellion, after which he was discharged and once again set out for Chelsea, this time from Ireland, "but still my unfriendly stars continued to twinkle upon me—for in the course of my passage to Bristol (as if fire and water had combined to ruin me) my knapsack, which contained my discharge, by the carelessness of an officious passenger, fell overboard."

Now with a family to support, he moved to London in 1799 and threw himself into his literary pursuits and an ongoing campaign to win a pension. He had published eleven more plays since 1789. In 1803, he began including introductions in some, first telling readers that "the little Productions of my Pen are my only source of support for myself and Family," and in 1805 waxing philosophical about his modest following:

"And as for the few who have—but why should I complain? If every body was to buy, I would grow too rich; and if nobody was to buy, I should starve; so, between those that do, and those that do not, thank Providence I make a shift to move on towards the end of my long journey."

In response to questions frequently asked by prospective buyers, in 1811 he wrote an essay in the April issue of the London magazine *The Satirist: Or, Monthly Meteor*. Titled "To the Public," it began:

"'If you are an old soldier, why don't you live upon your pension?' said a gentleman to me 'tother day. Now, my good reader, as in all probability you may be inclined to propose the same question, I shall endeavour to tell you, in as few words as possible, how I happen to have no pension, and yet I am an old soldier."

He explained that he had obtained a written recommendation from one of his former officers, but the pension board would not accept his application without a printed discharge.

The introduction to his 1813 "dramatic piece with songs" *The Prisoner of War, or a most excellent Story*, brought readers the latest news on his tribulations with the pension board. He had finally obtained a printed discharge and was summoned to Chelsea, but a young officer on the examining board deemed it unacceptable, saying, "This man's discharge will not do, being agreeable to neither the new nor the old form." Maclaren lamented,

Now my good readers, though my services were not doubted, and my wounds were too conspicuous to be disputed, you see that owing to a small deficiency in point of form, I am cut off from all hopes of obtaining the veteran's reward. But no reflections—perhaps they did well, and perhaps they did ill, in rejecting my claim; but in spite of all the perhaps that ever can be perhapsed, I cannot help thinking that I was as much entitled to the pension as many of my more fortunate brother soldiers who have it. Disappointment is the fate of man, and I have had my share of it, yet why should I repine, as long as I can say that several of the Royal Family, Nobility, Gentry, and others, encourage my little attempts.

Sometime between 1814 and 1816, Maclaren's fortunes with the military administration changed. He obtained an acceptable discharge, on which his trade was recorded as "comedian." He was granted a pension of nine pence per day since he had been a sergeant for much of his career, but this new income did not stop him from writing. By the time he died in 1826, Archibald Maclaren had published at least eighty-three plays, some revisions of a few of those plays, two prose works dealing with the history of the Irish rebellion, and three collections of poetry, making him one of the most prolific Scottish authors of the age. Quite an accomplishment for an old soldier and self-described comedian.[50]

Samuel Lee, the grenadier of the 18th Regiment described in this book's introduction, was captured on the April 19, 1775, expedition to Concord, Massachusetts, one of the war's first prisoners. In spite of having a wife and family with his regiment in Boston, he chose to remain in Concord, remarry, and work as a tailor until he died in August 1790, at age forty-five.[51] John Young, the soldier in the 5th Regiment who saw a bullet splash into the water near his post in Boston in July 1774, discussed in chapter 1, was killed at the Battle of Germantown on October 4, 1777.[52] Roger Lamb, mentioned frequently throughout this book, served in the 9th and 23rd Regiments, was twice taken prisoner and twice escaped; he took his discharge in 1784 and, denied a pension because he was in good health after less than twelve years in the army, opened a religious school in his native Dublin where he taught into the early nineteenth century, and wrote more about his service than any other British soldier of the era, including two published books.[53] Thomas Walker, the drummer in the 29th called a "black rascal" by Bostonians in 1770 (chapter 3) was captured at Saratoga in 1777 and died four years later as a prisoner of war in Lancaster, Pennsylvania.[54] William Nicholson, whose claim of being kidnapped is related in chapter 4, was found on the crew of a captured privateer; he was convicted of desertion (it was his third infraction) and executed in New York on December 28, 1776.[55] Thomas McMahon, who with his wife, Isabella, was convicted of receiving stolen goods in Boston (chapter 7), took his discharge from the 43rd Regiment in Rhode Island in March 1779, then joined the Royal Garrison Battalion, which took him to Bermuda. Discharged in 1784 at age fifty after twenty-seven years in the army, the butcher from Clare was granted a pension, but there is no information on the fate of his wife.[56]

Chapter 8 saw Richard Hallum of the 22nd Regiment go fishing in Rhode Island. In 1780, he was taken prisoner at the Battle of Connecticut Farms in New Jersey, and he died as a prisoner of war in a Philadelphia jail in early 1781.[57] Sergeant Mathew Hayes, mentioned in chapter 9 as another of the war's first prisoners taken on April 19, 1775, fared much better: he escaped and made his way to the city of New York in early 1776, where he took command of a small band of soldiers that successfully defended Sandy Hook lighthouse from rebel attacks before British forces came to the area that summer. He rejoined the 52nd Regiment, returned to Great Britain with his regiment in 1778, obtained a commission in the new-raised 90th Regiment of Foot, and was able to retire as an officer when that corps was disbanded in 1783.[58] George Peacock, the corporal who was rewarded with fifty guineas for saving an officer's life (chapter 11), remained in the army for two more decades and became a sergeant, finally taking his discharge and receiving a pension in 1799 at age fifty-two after thirty-six years in the army.[59] Michael Tevin of the 47th Regiment, who we saw in chapter 12 escape from captivity and join the 38th Regiment, was discharged in 1784, and then served in an Irish invalid corps from 1793 until 1802, when he received a pension at age fifty-eight, having spent thirty-one years as a soldier.[60]

Ten soldiers with ten very different lives, and throughout this book are dozens more, too many to relate the rest of their stories. For the hundreds about whom this much is known, there are thousands more with stories waiting to be discovered. Laborers, weavers, tailors, shoemakers, carpenters, coopers, miners, musicians, blacksmiths, bakers, bricklayers, bookbinders, butchers, barbers, even the occasional comedian—these were British soldiers who fought the American Revolution. English, Scottish, Irish, Welsh, German, sometimes American, Nova Scotian, Swedish, Swiss, Polish, Austrian, Dutch, Danish—all were among the ranks of redcoats in America. In any company of fifty or so men might be a few teens and quinquagenarians, but mostly men in their late twenties to early forties. They were veterans of decades of campaigns and previous wars, and recruits setting foot for the first time on foreign shores. Young romantics far from home, married men with wives in tow, some with schooling, some with none, some reprieved from bad deeds done. A smattering of criminals and ne'er-do-wells, malcontents as dissatisfied with the army as they were with society, wanderers who wandered into the army and wandered out again, men who succumbed to the temptations of itinerant military life, but most who did their duty faithfully and well. Uniforms, drill, and discipline molded masses of men into regiments that travelled, worked, and fought together, integrating them so completely that the historical record is largely focused on the exploits of the organizations rather than the people who composed them. Studying battles, campaigns, and wars, it is easy to forget that each gallant regiment and heroic corps was composed of individuals.

Inside each uniform, inside each soldier, was a person whose formative years had led him to the army. They enlisted for reasons as individual as themselves: to seek adventure, to escape boredom, to earn income, to flee relationships, for reasons mostly unrecorded. Some joined against the advice of peers, others at the urging of peers. Once in the army, each man moved with hundreds of others, and yet each man followed a distinctive path, changing companies and comrades, switching regiments and regions, serving a few years or a few decades, until the chances of any two careers being alike were slim. Only a few left accounts of those careers, narratives and memoirs that provide tantalizing details but leave much unsaid. More can be discerned by piecing together fragments from a plethora of sources, yielding patchwork biographies that, when taken together, begin to give a sense of how varied were the lives of soldiers. Studying their distinctive careers reveals the true texture of the army, bringing into focus the souls who were the soldiers, every one with a story to tell.

"I faithfully served my king all the best of my days," related an aged pensioner, "and like a good master, he now supports me." He then told of his own encounters, as a sheep-herding English youth, with a disabled pensioner who mused on his martial exploits with great pleasure, diagramming trenches and breastworks with a stick in the soil as he spoke of sallies and sieges. The old veteran's stories convinced the boy that "there is a glitter in the life of a soldier unknown to every other profession": at eighteen, the young man left home and became a soldier himself, serving thirty-five years before drawing a pension of his own.[61] While probably an allegorical story, it nonetheless captures the influence that old soldiers, after long careers, had in creating the next generation of soldiers. The British citizens who chose careers in the army, fought to quell rebellion in America, and either died there, settled there, went on to other exploits, or returned to their native land, are too often overlooked as individuals because the fortunes of war overshadowed their personal endurance and triumphs. They were soldiers, lured to their colors, in the words of one, by "the glory of victory, the comforts of a pension in old age, and the pleasure of recounting my adventures to others."

Of adventures in America, there were as many as there were soldiers, and far too few recollections survive. "It is impossible to conceive with what eagerness and satisfaction every soldier step't into the boat which was to carry him to the scene of action. Good humour, self complacency, and determined resolution were painted upon every countenance," wrote an officer from the South Carolina coast in 1776.[62] This spirit endured even as the war went badly for British soldiers. At the final humiliation of surrender at Yorktown in 1781, a Scottish officer vividly recalled the emotions of a man who had done his duty only to have it go for naught: "A corporal next to me shed tears, and, embracing his firelock, threw it down, saying, 'May you never get so good a master.'"[63]

NOTES

ABBREVIATIONS

ACC   Adirondack Community College, Queensbury, New York
ADM   Admiralty records, The National Archives, Kew, UK
AO   Audit Office records, The National Archives, Kew, UK
CO   Colonial Office records, The National Archives, Kew, UK
ECP   Eyre Coote Papers, William L. Clements Library,
            University of Michigan, Ann Arbor
FL   Firestone Library, Princeton University, Princeton, New Jersey
FMP   Frederick Mackenzie Papers, William L. Clements Library,
            University of Michigan, Ann Arbor
HCP   Henry Clinton Papers, William L. Clements Library,
            University of Michigan, Ann Arbor
HL   Huntington Library, San Marino, CA
HSD   Historical Society of Delaware, Wilmington
HSP   Historical Society of Pennsylvania, Philadelphia
LOC   Library of Congress, Washington, DC
MAHS   Massachusetts Historical Society, Boston
NAM   National Army Museum, London
NARA   National Archives and Records Administration,
            Washington, DC
NAS   National Archive of Scotland, Edinburgh
NLI   National Library of Ireland, Dublin
NMS   National Museums of Scotland, Edinburgh
NYHS   New York Historical Society, New York
PA   Parliamentary Archives, Houses of Parliament, London
PAC   Public Archives of Canada, Ottawa
PRO   Domestic Records of the Public Record Office,
            The National Archives, Kew, UK
PROB   Prerogative Court of Canterbury and related Probate
            Jurisdictions, The National Archives, Kew, UK

RFM	Royal Fusiliers Museum, Warwick, UK
RL	Rubenstein Library, Duke University, Durham, North Carolina
T	Treasury records, The National Archives, Kew, UK
TGP	Thomas Gage Papers, American Series, William L. Clements Library, University of Michigan, Ann Arbor
WO	War Office records, The National Archives, Kew, UK
WYA	West Yorkshire Archives, Calderdale, West Yorkshire, UK

INTRODUCTION

1. Muster rolls, 18th Regiment of Foot, WO 12/3501; *Concord, Massachusetts Births, Marriages and Deaths, 1635–1850* (Boston: Thomas Todd, 1895), 420; trial of John Green, WO 71/79 pp. 234-257; for having a family in Boston, see Prisoners in Concord Jail, December 6, 1775, Revolutionary War Records SC1 Series 57, vol. 8, Massachusetts State Archives.

CHAPTER 1. SEDUCED, KIDNAPPED, AND CRUELLY USED

1. Report by Lt. Alexander Robertson, 43rd Regiment of Foot, July 19, 1774, Thomas Gage Papers, American Series (hereafter TGP), vol. 121, William L. Clements Library, University of Michigan, Ann Arbor (hereafter WLC).

2. The full strength of each regiment included 35 officers and 442 other ranks at this time. It was increased twice during the course of the war, first to 662 other ranks, then to 792; the number of officers remained the same. Establishments, WO 379/1. Actual strength was often somewhat less depending on attrition and the arrival of recruits.

3. A 1765 census recorded 2,941 white males older than sixteen in Boston. J. H. Benton Jr., *Early Census Making in Massachusetts, 1643–1765* (Boston: Charles E. Goodspeed, 1905), 74.

4. For details on the events leading up to March 5, 1770, see Serena Zabin, *The Boston Massacre: A Family History* (Boston: Houghton Mifflin Harcourt, 2020), and Hiller B. Zobel, *The Boston Massacre* (New York: W. W. Norton, 1970).

5. TGP, vol. 120. The letter is handwritten and found its way into General Thomas Gage's papers; it is possible that many copies of it were distributed.

6. Trial of Robert Gaul, WO 71/83 pp. 336-339.

7. Trial of John Man, WO 71/79 pp. 407-413.

8. Trial of John Winters, WO 71/82 pp. 426-428.

9. Trial of Robert Hall, WO 71/79 pp. 387-395. Hall's term "11th Instant," abbreviated in the trial transcript, referred to the 11th of the same month as the trial.

10. Trial of Thomas Watson, WO 71/83 pp. 30-41.

11. Trial of Thomas Sewell, WO 71/83 pp. 48-52.

12. Trial of John Jermon, WO 71/79 pp. 413-419.

13. Summaries of trials in general orders, WO 36/1.

14. Muster rolls of the several regiments in Boston during this period, WO 12. If a man deserted and returned within the same six-month muster period, it is often not recorded on the muster rolls, as demonstrated by court-martial proceedings for men whose desertions are not recorded, WO 71.

15. "Extracts of a Letter from Captain Balfour," undated, TGP, vol. 126.

16. *Belfast Newsletter*, October 25, 1774.

17. *Freeman's Journal* (Dublin), January 31, 1775. The man who houghed Thompson, a butcher named John Murphy, was caught, tried, and executed for the crime. Ibid., February 3 and March 7, 1775.

18. *Freeman's Journal*, February 4, 1775.

19. *Hibernian Chronicle*, February 13, 1775.

20. Based on reports in the *Freeman's Journal*.

21. Disabled soldiers to be placed on the Military Establishment in Ireland, September 11, 1776, Treasury records (hereafter T) 14/15.

22. *Freeman's Journal*, February 2, 1775.

23. The names of the two soldiers are given in "Copy of a letter from Captain Maginis of the 38th regiment in Boston to his brother in Drogheda, dated Dec. 14, 1774," *Hibernian Chronicle*, January 23, 1775. Another account of the event is in *Rivington's New-York Gazetteer*, December 29, 1774. Phineas Baker died July 17, 1775, of wounds received at the Battle of Bunker Hill a month before; Henry Drennan remained in the regiment until he was discharged in 1784, having attained the rank of sergeant. Muster rolls, 38th Regiment of Foot, WO 12/5171 and WO 12/5172.

24. Depositions of Thomas Ditson and John Clancy, TGP, vol. 126.

25. See for example Zabin, *Boston Massacre*, 69, 146-49, and soldier testimonies, CO 5/88.

26. General orders, June 12, 1774, WO 36/1.

27. *Boston Gazette*, August 29, 1774.

28. *Massachusetts Spy*, September 28, 1774.

29. "At an Examination . . . with Regards to ill Usage, alleged to have been received by some Servants of the Town of Roxbury," TGP, vol. 127.

CHAPTER 2. ROVING DISPOSITIONS AND SOARING SPIRITS

1. Don N. Hagist, *British Soldiers, American War: Voices of the American Revolution* (Yardley, PA: Westholme, 2012), 106.

2. Muster rolls, 23rd Regiment of Foot, WO 12/3959.

3. Trial of Thomas Watson, WO 71/83 pp. 30-41.

4. For an analytical approach to determining why men enlisted, based on economic data, see Sylvia R. Frey, *The British Soldier in North America* (Austin: University of Texas Press, 1983), 3-21.

5. Hagist, *British Soldiers*, 84.

6. Ibid., 229; muster rolls, 44th Regiment of Foot, WO 12/5637.

7. Edmund Bott, *A Collection of Decisions of the Court of King's Bench upon the Poor's Laws, down to the Present Time*, 2nd ed. (London: W. Strachan and M. Woodfall, 1773), 394.

8. Roger Lamb, *A British Soldier's Story: Roger Lamb's Narrative of the American Revolution*, ed. Don N. Hagist (Baraboo, WI: Ballindalloch Press, 2005), 7.

9. Brian Gee, *Francis Watkins and the Dollond Telescope Patent Controversy* (Farnham, Surrey, UK: Ashgate, 2014), 38-39; discharge of Jacob Margas, WO 121/159/97.

10. *Appleton's Cyclopedia of American Biography*, vol. 5 (New York: D. Appleton, 1888), 122, s.v. "Thomas Machin"; muster rolls, 23rd Regiment of Foot, WO 12/3959 and WO 12/3960; Carrie Rebora Barratt and Lori Zabar, *American Portrait Miniatures in the Metropolitan Museum of Art* (New Haven, CT: Yale University Press, 2010), 168; muster rolls, 38th Regiment of Foot, WO 12/5171; *Appleton's Cyclopedia of American Biography*, vol. 1 (New York: D. Appleton, 1887), 394, s.v. "Andrew Brown"; muster rolls, 47th Regiment of Foot, WO 12/5871; Thomas Heitmann, *Historical*

Register of Officers of the Continental Army (Washington, DC: W. H. Lowdermilk, 1893), 123, 207, 371. Machin's work with Brindley has not been confirmed by primary sources, and many other aspects of his published background conflict with primary sources. Brown's attendance at Trinity College has not been confirmed by primary sources.

11. *British Chronicle or Pugh's Hereford Journal*, August 31, 1775.

12. Leah Leneman, *Living in Atholl: A Social History of the Estates, 1685–1785* (Edinburgh: Edinburgh University Press, 1986), 130.

13. Hagist, *British Soldiers*, 61.

14. Trial of Edward Hall, WO 71/79 pp. 387-395; muster rolls, 43rd Regiment of Foot, WO 12/5561.

15. Thomas Sullivan, *From Redcoat to Rebel: The Thomas Sullivan Journal*, ed. Joseph Lee Boyle (Bowie, MD: Heritage Books, 1997), 3.

16. Robert Huish, *Memoirs of William Cobbett, Esq.* (London: John Saunders, 1836), 10, 20.

17. Thomas Simes, *The Military Medley*, 2nd ed. (London, 1768), 34; Colonel Sir Bruce Seton, "Infantry Recruiting Instructions in England in 1767," *Journal of Army Historical Research* 4, no. 16 (April–June 1925): 86.

18. Simes, *Military Medley*, 33; Bennet Cuthbertson, *A System for the Compleat Interior Management and Œconomy of a Battalion of Infantry* (Dublin, 1768), 56.

19. Seton, "Infantry Recruiting Instructions," 86; *British Chronicle or Pugh's Hereford Journal*, August 31, 1775; Recruiting Instructions for the Royal Fusiliers, November 27, 1775, Royal Fusiliers Museum, Warwick, UK (hereafter RFM).

20. Cuthbertson, *System*, 59.

21. Recruiting Instructions for the Royal Fusiliers, RFM.

22. Simes, *Military Medley*, 33.

23. Cuthbertson, *System*, 55-56.

24. Recruiting Instructions for the Royal Fusiliers, RFM; Simes, *Military Medley*, 33; Cuthbertson, *System*, 56.

25. Cuthbertson, *System*, 59, 62.

26. Walter Home Memorandum Book, George Chalmers collection, Peter Force Manuscripts, Library of Congress (hereafter LOC).

27. Data from discharges for 133 men of the 22nd Regiment and 252 men from other regiments, from soldiers' discharges, WO 97, WO 119, and WO 121. Only men whose service could be traced to their initial enlistment, and who served in the 1775–1783 American war, were considered for this study. Discharge forms give age on the date of discharge and the number of years of service; the age at enlistment is deduced from these figures and could be off by as much as a year for each man, but this inaccuracy does not significantly change the overall distribution.

28. Cuthbertson, *System*, 12.

29. Muster rolls, 35th Regiment of Foot, WO 12/4949.

30. Pension Admission Books, WO 116/7 and WO 116/8.

31. "Examinations of Invalid Soldiers," April 2, 1792, Pension Admission Book, WO 116/9; discharge of Alexander Major, WO 121/13/311.

32. Regimental orders, January 24, 1766, Henry Clinton Papers (hereafter HCP), vol. 265:15, WLC.

33. Alexander Graydon, *Memoirs of His own Time* (Harrisburgh: John Wyeth, 1811), 19, 70-71.

34. Trial of Luke Murphy, WO 71/79 pp. 367-374.

35. Trial of John Man, WO 71/79 pp. 407-413.

36. Trial of Charles Toomey, WO 71/86 pp. 396-399. Toomey was brought to trial in New York in August 1778 after deserting from a British regiment, enlisting in a Loyalist regiment, then deserting from it and attempting to enlist in yet another.

37. Based on court-martial testimony, primarily WO 71/79 through /94.

38. Reasons for desertion are given in court-martial testimony, WO 71/79 through /94.

39. *Edinburgh Advertiser*, July 24, 1772.

40. Ibid., July 28, 1772.

41. *London Packet*, September 1, 1773.

42. Cuthbertson, *System*, 130.

43. Inspection Returns, 17th, 49th, and 55th Regiments of Foot, WO 27/32. Welsh are not enumerated separately from the English on these returns.

44. Soldiers' discharges, WO 97, WO 119, WO 121. This sample includes only men who began their careers in the 22nd Regiment.

45. For a study of nationalities in several regiments, see Frey, *British Soldier*, 23-26.

46. Cuthbertson, *System*, 66-67.

47. Standing orders, 37th Regiment, Eyre Coote Papers, William L. Clements Library, University of Michigan, Ann Arbor (hereafter ECP); Cuthbertson, *System*, 17.

48. William Dansey, *Captured Rebel Flag: The Letters of Captain William Dansey, 33rd Regiment of Foot, 1776–1777*, ed. Paul Dansey (Godmanchester, Huntington, UK: Ken Trotman Press, 2010), 12, 25.

49. *Pennsylvania Gazette*, November 7, 1771.

50. As determined from Pension Admission Books, WO 116, which includes only those men who eventually applied for pensions. No comprehensive demographic data exists for these regiments when they were in Boston.

51. Birthplace information in soldiers' discharges, WO 97, WO 119, and WO 121; and Pension Admission Books, WO 116.

52. *Pennsylvania Gazette*, December 6, 1770.

53. Ibid., November 7, 1771.

54. Hagist, *British Soldiers*, 252.

55. M. M. Gilchrist, "Captain Hon. William Leslie (1751–76): His Life, Letters and Commemoration," *Military Miscellany II* (Stroud, Gloucestershire: Sutton Publishing, for the Army Records Society, 2005), 142.

56. WO 1/610 pp. 299-304.

CHAPTER 3. CLOSENESS AND SMARTNESS IN EVERYTHING HE DOES

1. "Examinations of Invalid Soldiers," June 10, 1774, Pension Admission Book, WO 116/6; Discharge of Robert Andrews, WO 121/140/297.

2. Anon., *Observations on the Prevailing Abuses in the British Army* (London, 1775).

3. John Williamson, *A Treatise on Military Finance* (London, 1782), 10-13, 19.

4. See Don N. Hagist, "Maintaining Military Roads: Orders for Sergeant McGregor's Party, 1772," *Journal of the Society for Army Historical Research* 93, no. 375 (Autumn 2015): 210-213.

5. General orders, August 18, 1774, WO 36/1.

6. General orders, September 2, 1774, ibid.

7. General orders, October 2, 1774, ibid.

8. General orders, October 3, 1774, ibid.

9. An Account of Working Parties employed . . . in cutting through the Gate Way, in "Proceedings of a Garrison Court of Enquiry regarding the Destruction of His Majesty's Fort of Crown Point," CO 5/91.

10. Muster rolls, 22nd Regiment of Foot, WO 12/ 3871 and WO 12/3872.

11. John Montresor, "The Montresor Journals," *Collections of the New York Historical Society for the year 1881* (New York: New York Historical Society, 1882): 401-402.

12. The percentage is based on several data sets that yield similar results: a sample of 322 men of the 22nd Regiment of Foot between 1775 and 1783 for whom trades are known, based primarily on soldiers' discharges, WO 121; a sample of soldiers' discharges of 442 men who served in various regiments in America, WO 121; trades listed in pension admission books for infantry men between 1774 and 1782, Pension Admission Book, WO 116/7.

13. Cuthbertson, *System*, 76. The few surviving returns indicating which men were employed suggest that one man per company was typical. See, for example, state of the 37th Regiment light company, April 6, 1780, orderly books, 1st Battalion of Light Infantry, ECP. For notes on tailors and their work, see John Peebles, *John Peebles American War: the Diary of a Scottish Grenadier, 1776–1782*, ed. Ira D. Gruber (Mechanicsburg, PA: Stackpole Books, for the Army Records Society, 1998), 252, 256, 258, 308-309, 313, 315, 404, 405.

14. See for example testimony in the trial of John Green, WO 71/79 pp. 234-257.

15. See for example regimental orders, October 21, 1776, orderly book, 40th Regiment of Foot, MAHS; regimental orders, October 2, 1777, orderly books, 37th Regiment, ECP.

16. See for example State of the 37th Regiment light company, April 6, 1780, orderly books, 1st battalion of light infantry, ECP; Morning Report of the 17th Regiment of Dragoons, September 21, 1780, HCP, vol. 124: 12.

17. Regimental orders, January 25 and February 27, 1775, orderly book, 18th Regiment of Foot, National Army Museum, London (hereafter) NAM.

18. Morning Report of the 17th Regiment of Dragoons, September 21, 1780, HCP, vol. 124:12.

19. See for example "Scheme of an Ensign's Constant Expence," Thomas Simes, *A Military Guide for Young Officers* (London, 1776), 314.

20. Testimony of John Irish in the trial of Benjamin Charnock Payne, WO 71/81 pp. 2-165.

21. "Of working Men, with the Restrictions necessary to be laid on them," Cuthbertson, *System*, 152-154.

22. Trial of William King, WO 71/53 pp. 1-16. Most of the 14th Regiment was in America at this time.

23. Hagist, *British Soldiers*, 253.

24. General orders, August 2, 1774, WO 36/1.

25. Robert Donkin, *Military Collections and Remarks* (New York: H. Gaine, 1777), 130-132. See also Cuthbertson, *System*, 128-129, and *Northampton Mercury*, June 25, 1770. The seven-year medal is described as gilded or brass.

26. *The Diaries of a Duchess: Extracts from the Diaries of the First Duchess of Northumberland*, ed. J. Grieg (New York: Hodder and Stoughton, 1926), 84-85.

27. Two medals of the 37th Regiment of Foot are illustrated in H. C. Wylly, *A Life of Lieutenant General Sir Eyre Coote, K. B.* (Oxford: Clarendon Press, 1922), and are mentioned in regimental orders for September 15, 1775, orderly books, 37th Regiment, ECP. The 22nd Regiment of Foot adopted a medal in 1785. Bernard Rigby, *Ever Glorious: The Story of the 22nd (Cheshire) Regiment* (Cheshire, UK: W. H. Evans and Sons, 1982), 92.

28. Cuthbertson, *System*, 153.

29. Muster rolls, 22nd Regiment of Foot, WO 12/3871.

30. Lamb, *British Soldier's Story*, 8.
31. Ibid., 9.
32. Cuthbertson, *System*, 5.
33. Discharge of Alexander Andrew, WO 119/1/4; "Examinations of Invalid Soldiers," March 8, 1784, WO 116/8.
34. Cuthbertson, *System*, 8.
35. Based on a survey of soldiers' discharges in WO 121. See chapter 8 for more details on this proportion.
36. Hagist, *British Soldiers*, 107.
37. Thomas Simes, *The Regulator* (London, 1780), 2, and Simes, *Military Guide*, 164.
38. Standing orders, 37th Regiment, ECP. The orders are undated, but the owner of the book, Eyre Coote, obtained his first commission in the regiment in April 1774, and the book appears to have been his own record of orders already in effect at that time.
39. Regimental orders for March 21, May 13, and May 14, 1776, orderly book, 32nd Regiment of Foot, National Library of Ireland, Dublin (hereafter NLI); general orders for July 7 and August 5, 1776, orderly books kept in Halifax, New York Public Library; standing orders, orderly book, 2nd Battalion 71st Regiment, Huntington Library, San Marino, CA (hereafter HL).
40. Standing orders, 37th Regiment, ECP.
41. Recruiting accounts of Joab Aked, West Yorkshire Archives, Calderdale, West Yorkshire, UK (hereafter WYA).
42. George Smith, *An Universal Military Dictionary* (London, 1779), 193.
43. Lamb, *British Soldier's Story*, 7.
44. Cuthbertson, *System*, 161-162.
45. Standing orders, 37th Regiment, ECP.
46. Lamb, *British Soldier's Story*, 7.
47. *The Manual Exercise, As ordered by his Majesty, In 1764. Together with Plans and Explanations Of the Method generally Practis'd At Review and Field-Days, &c.* (London, 1764).
48. See for example Timothy Pickering, *An Easy Plan of Discipline for a Militia* (Boston: S. Hall, 1776), 8.
49. Standing orders, 37th Regiment, ECP.
50. See for example regimental orders for April 26, 1776, orderly book, 32nd Regiment, NLI.
51. Standing orders, 37th Regiment, ECP.
52. Cuthbertson, *System*, 163.
53. Standing orders, 35th Regiment of Foot, MAHS.
54. Lamb, *British Soldier's Story*, 8.
55. Cuthbertson, *System*, 163.
56. J. A. Houlding, *Fit for Service: The Training of the British Army 1715–1795* (Oxford, UK: Clarendon Press, 1981), 144-145.
57. Standing orders, 37th Regiment, ECP.
58. A survey of twenty-one regiments inspected in Ireland in 1774 showed a minimum of twenty-three recruits and a maximum of ninety-six, with most regiments having between forty and sixty. Inspection returns, WO 27/32.
59. Smith, *Universal Military Dictionary*, 175.
60. Bennett Cuthbertson and George Smith each wrote that messes consisted of five to eight men; the wife of a soldier in the 26th Regiment mentioned that the mess she and her husband belonged to consisted of nine men when garrisoned at Crown

Point, New York, in April 1773. Cuthbertson, *System*, 25; Smith, *Universal Military Dictionary*, 171; testimony of Jane Ross, "Proceedings of a Garrison Court of Enquiry regarding the Destruction of His Majesty's Fort of Crown Point," CO 5/91.
61. Returns of camp equipage, WO 4/274 p. 56-59, 91, 183-184, 281-282.
62. Cuthbertson, *System*, 25.
63. General orders, June 1, 1774, WO 36/1.
64. Smith, *Universal Military Dictionary*, 238; Simes, *Military Guide*, 168. Orders for the 35th Regiment were for "Each company to be divided into as many squads as there are Serjeants, with the Corporals to assist them." Standing orders, 35th Regiment, MAHS.
65. Cuthbertson, *System*, 14; orderly book, 28th Regiment of Foot, special collections, Alexander Library, Rutgers University.
66. Cuthbertson, *System*, 107-108.
67. Simes, *Regulator*, 15.
68. Standing orders, 35th Regiment, MAHS.
69. Williamson, *Treatise on Military Finance*, 19.
70. Based on a survey of muster rolls for several regiments, WO 12.
71. Standing orders, 37th Regiment, ECP; muster rolls, 22nd Regiment of Foot, WO 12/3871 and WO 12/3872.
72. Simes, *Regulator*, 16.
73. Trial of Andrew Conway, WO 71/77 pp. 193-196.
74. Standing orders, 37th Regiment, ECP.
75. All trial data is from regimental punishment books, HL/PO/JO/10/7/544, Parliamentary Archives, Houses of Parliament, London, UK (hereafter PA). The estimated number of corporals is based on the muster rolls for the four regiments; gaps in the surviving rolls make it impossible to know the exact number. Muster rolls, 3rd Regiment of Foot, WO 12/2105; muster rolls, 36th Regiment of Foot, WO 12/5025; muster rolls, 67th Regiment of Foot, WO 12/7536 and WO 12/7537; muster rolls, 68th Regiment of Foot, WO 12/7622 and WO 12/7623.
76. Muster rolls, 22nd Regiment of Foot, WO 12/3872. Muster rolls give the date of death but not the cause; illness is inferred because the regiment was not involved in any combat at the time of Graves's reduction or death.
77. John Barker, *British in Boston: The Diary of Lt. John Barker*, ed. Elizabeth Ellery Dana (Cambridge, MA: Harvard University Press, 1924), 6-7. Earlier in the century the symbol of rank for corporals was a knot of cord on the shoulder; regulations in 1768 replaced the knot with an epaulet, but the term "knot" remained a metaphor for the rank.
78. Battalion orders, July 24, 1780, orderly books, 1st battalion of light infantry, ECP; muster rolls, 37th Regiment of Foot, WO 12/5101.
79. "Examinations of Invalid Soldiers," April 14, 1784, Pension Admission Book, WO 116/8; muster rolls, 22nd Regiment of Foot, WO 12/3871 and WO 12/3872.
80. "Examinations of Invalid Soldiers," June 12, 1786, Pension Admission Book, WO 116/9; muster rolls, 22nd Regiment of Foot, WO 12/3871 and WO 12/3872.
81. As seen from muster rolls of various regiments, WO 12.
82. Williamson, *Treatise on Military Finance*, 19. Pay was slightly higher in the Foot Guards, cavalry, and artillery.
83. Simes, *Regulator*, 19.
84. The term "pay sergeant" appears in the testimony of Sergeant Paul Hadfield of the 23rd Regiment of Foot, Boston, August 1774, WO 71/79 pp. 375-378; "paymaster sergeant" is used in Simes, *Regulator*, 21.

85. Many desertion trials feature testimony of sergeants discussing the circumstances of the man's disappearance, the state of his belongings, and his general character. WO 71/80 through /98.

86. "The humble Petition of the Non Commissioned Officers and Private Men of the four Companies now stationed on this Island," signed by four sergeants, April 1, 1776, CO 5/168 f316.

87. Regimental punishment books, HL/PO/JO/10/7/544, PA.

88. Lamb, *British Soldier's Story*, 8.

89. Regimental orders, June 14, 1776, orderly books, 37th Regiment, ECP.

90. Regimental punishment books, HL/PO/JO/10/7/544, PA.

91. Standing orders, 35th Regiment, MAHS.

92. Regimental punishment books, HL/PO/JO/10/7/544, PA.

93. Ibid.

94. Muster rolls, 22nd Regiment of Foot, WO 12/3871 and WO 12/3872; Return of Invalids of the 22nd, 43rd, & 54th Regiments of Foot, discharged by order of Major General Pigot, as unfit for Service, Newport, January 1778, HCP, vol. 30:40; regimental returns of pensioners, WO 120.

95. Simes, *Regulator*, 37–46. The Quartering Act of 1765, and that of 1774, directed that American colonies provide quarters in barracks, public houses, inns, ale houses, livery stables, uninhabited homes, or outbuildings.

96. Ibid., 37.

97. Ibid., 28-29.

98. Examples appear in regimental punishment books, HL/PO/JO/10/7/544, PA, and in several general courts-martial, WO 71/80 through /98.

99. Regimental orders, November 14, 1774, orderly book, 18th Regiment of Foot, NAM. Five more companies of the 18th were in New Jersey, and the remaining two in Illinois; the orders pertaining to the sergeant major and the quartermaster sergeant were recorded in an orderly book for the detachment of three companies, but it is not clear whether they applied only to that detachment or to the regiment as a whole.

100. Discharge of James Anderson, WO 121/11/337.

101. Discharge of Hiram Murphy, WO 97/382/59.

102. Kilmainham Pensioners living in 1807, WO 118/35.

103. Discharge of Donald Forbes, WO 119/1/22.

104. Petition of Ranald McDonell, Malcolm Fraser Papers, vol. 32, PAC. His name appears on the muster rolls as "Randal McDonald." Muster rolls, 52nd Regiment of Foot, WO 12/6240.

105. Standing orders, 37th Regiment, ECP.

106. Muster rolls, 22nd Regiment of Foot, WO 12/3871 and WO 12/3872.

107. Discharge of Thomas Huggans, WO 121/13/310.

108. Simes, *Military Guide*, 207.

109. Muster rolls, 22nd Regiment of Foot, WO 12/3871 and WO 12/3872.

110. Cuthbertson, *System*, 13-14.

111. Discharge of John Hardman from the 22nd Regiment, WO 121/1/135; discharge of John Hardman from the 2nd Royal Veteran Battalion, WO 121/164/301.

112. Discharge of John Hogg, WO 121/10/39. Hogg served in the 19th Regiment of Foot during the American war. Muster rolls, 19th Regiment of Foot, WO 12/3593.

113. Muster rolls, 29th Regiment of Foot, WO 12/4493; "Examinations of Invalid Soldiers," July 17, 1783, Pension Admission Book, WO 116/8.

114. Discharges of Thomas Smith, WO 121/35/127 and WO 97/1140B/191.

115. *Boston Evening Post*, October 6, 1768.

116. Ellen Chase, *The Beginnings of the American Revolution based on Contemporary Letters, Diaries and Other Documents* (New York: Baker and Taylor, 1910), 1:173.

117. Standing orders, 37th Regiment, ECP.

118. Discharges of Michael Clarke, WO 121/158/244 and WO 121/185/552; muster rolls, 22nd Regiment of Foot, WO 12/3871 and WO 12/3872.

119. Discharge of William McLeod, WO 119/2/16; muster rolls, 22nd Regiment of Foot, WO 12/3872. Early muster rolls give his name as Hugh, until 1774, when it changes to William.

120. Williamson, *Treatise on Military Finance*, 19.

121. Cuthbertson, *System*, 9.

122. Ibid., 13; regimental orders, July 29, 1776, orderly book, 32nd Regiment, NLI.

123. Regimental Ledger Books, 22nd Regiment of Foot, Lloyds Bank Archives, London.

124. Cuthbertson, *System*, 9-10; Standing orders, 37th Regiment, ECP. Cuthbertson recommended payment of half a guinea per student, while the 32nd Regiment ordered a full guinea "when completed in their Duty." Orderly book, 32nd Regiment, NLI.

125. Regimental orders, December 15, 1774, orderly book, 18th Regiment of Foot, NAM.

126. Cuthbertson, *System*, 11.

127. Ibid., 9.

128. Muster book, *Robust*, October 1781, ADM 36/8499. A portion of the regiment was put on board this warship, and six men are denoted as "musick." The remainder of the regiment was on another ship, but no list of them has been found.

129. Muster rolls, 22nd Regiment of Foot, WO 12/3871 and WO 12/3872.

130. Discharge of John Mayell, WO 121/140/158; discharge of Richard Street, WO 121/3/21; discharge of James Harvey, WO 119/4/175; entry for William Tarrant, WO 25/1126.

131. Standing orders, 37th Regiment, ECP.

132. *Edinburgh Advertiser*, October 9, 1772; *St. James's Chronicle* (London), August 28, 1777; *Edinburgh Advertiser*, February 9, 1776; *Boston Chronicle*, February 9, 1769; *New York Gazette or Weekly Post Boy*, September 10, 1770.

133. *Public Advertiser* (London), September 4, 1770.

134. *Hibernian Chronicle* (Cork), October 9, 1773.

135. Regimental orders, July 27, 1775, orderly books, 37th Regiment, ECP of Foot.

136. Frederick A. Pottle and Charles H. Bennett, *Boswell's Journal of a Tour to the Hebrides with Samuel Johnson, 1773* (New York: McGraw-Hill, 1936), 94.

137. *Pennsylvania Gazette*, July 11, 1771.

138. Ibid., November 28, 1771. Philip Roth was listed a private soldier in the regiment in 1775 and 1776, and as a sergeant in 1781. Muster rolls, 21st Regiment of Foot, WO 12/3378/2.

139. *Pennsylvania Gazette*, July 28, 1773.

140. *Boston Gazette*, April 11, 1774.

141. See for example Barker, *British in Boston*, 15 (snow); brigade orders, June 11, 1777, orderly book, Major Acland's Grenadier Battalion, New York Historical Society, New York (hereafter NYHS) (clearing); general orders, January 5, 1778, orderly books, 37th Regiment, ECP (latrines).

142. Trial of William Ferguson, WO 71/80 pp. 176-184.

143. *Rules and articles for the better government of His Majesty's horse and foot guards, and all other forces in Great Britain and Ireland, dominions beyond the seas, and foreign parts, from the 24th of March, 1777* (London, 1777). Other annual editions from this era are substantially similar.

144. Regimental punishment books, HL/PO/JO/10/7/544, PA.

145. Barker, *British in Boston*, 14.

146. See for example trial of Elija Reeves, WO 71/79 p. 157-177.

147. Robert Hamilton, *Duties of a Regimental Surgeon Considered* (London, 1787), 2:28.

148. Ibid., 2:25-87.

149. Francis Grose, *Military Antiquities Respecting a History of the English Army from the Conquest to the Present Time* (London: S. Hooper, 1786), 2:200; John Shipp, *Flogging and its Substitute: A voice from the ranks* (London: Whittaker, Treacher, 1831), 21.

150. Lord Chief Baron Macdonald at the trial of Governor Wall for the flogging death of Sergeant Armstrong at Goree, 1789, in Henry Marshall, *Military Miscellany; comprehending a history of the recruiting of the army, military punishments, etc.* (London: John Murray, 1846), 257. The trial was in 1802, making it unclear whether the description pertained to that time or to the time of the punishment in question.

151. John Blatchford, *The narrative of John Blatchford, detailing his sufferings in the revolutionary war, while a prisoner with the British* (New York: privately printed, 1865), 31.

152. Hamilton, *Duties*, 2:62.

153. Regimental punishment books, HL/PO/JO/10/7/544, PA.

154. Hamilton, *Duties*, 2:75.

CHAPTER 4. WORKING HARD AT THE FIRELOCK

1. General orders, August 4, 1774, WO 36/1.

2. Hugh Earl Percy, *Letters of Hugh Earl Percy from Boston and New York 1774–1776*, ed. Charles Knowles Bolton (Boston: Charles E. Goodspeed, 1902), 34.

3. In the 43rd Regiment of Foot at the beginning of January 1775, for example, were 328 private soldiers, of whom 69 had enlisted since June 25, 1771—leaving over three quarters of the men with more than three and a half years in the army. Muster rolls, 43rd Regiment of Foot, WO 12/5561. Inspection returns from 1774 for nine regiments that arrived in Boston in 1775 show a range of 13 percent to 32 percent of their men had ten or more years in the army, with the average about 24 percent. These numbers may have decreased a bit when the regiments prepared for overseas service, discharging some long-serving men and recruiting new ones.

4. Houlding, *Fit for Service*, 24-57.

5. The typical camp layout is described in Lewis Lochée, *Essay on Castremetation* (London: 1778), 17-31; the camp kitchen is described in Grose, *Military Antiquities*, 2:240-242.

6. General orders, June 12, 1774, WO 36/1.

7. Cuthbertson, *System*, 108.

8. General orders, July 14, 1774, WO 36/1. Orders given in other places also allowed bathing only in the morning and evening; some suggest it was unhealthful to bathe in the middle of the day but do not indicate what the perceived dangers were.

9. General orders, July 15, 1774, WO 36/1.

10. General orders, July 13, 1774, WO 36/1.

11. General orders, July 15, 1774, WO 36/1.

12. Barker, *British in Boston*, 3.

13. General orders, undated entry (late November or early December 1774), WO 36/1 mss. p. 57.

14. Frederick Mackenzie, *The Diary of Frederick Mackenzie* (Cambridge, MA: Harvard University Press, 1930), 554.

15. Regimental orders, December 11, 1774, orderly book, 18th Regiment of Foot, NAM.

16. Barker, *British in Boston*, 11.

17. Regimental orders, December 26, 1774, orderly book, 18th Regiment of Foot, NAM.

18. An officer noted on December 15, "Two men of the 43d died of the disorder above mention'd," and these two died on that date; three other men of the regiment died earlier in the month. Muster rolls, 43rd Regiment of Foot, WO 12/5561; Barker, *British in Boston*, 12.

19. Barker, *British in Boston*, 12, referring specifically to the 43rd Regiment.

20. Expenses incurred on his Majesty's Service in the Engineers Department from the 25th Decr 1774 to the 24th March inclusive 1775, TGP vol. 127.

21. Barker, *British in Boston*, 18.

22. Smith, *Universal Military Dictionary*, 240.

23. General orders, July 6, 11, and 21, 1774, WO 36/1.

24. Trial of Luke Murphy, WO 71/79 pp. 367-374; trial of Robert Hall, WO 71/79 pp. 387-395; trial of William Nicholson, WO 71/83 pp. 69-70.

25. Trial of William Ferguson, WO 71/80 pp. 176-184.

26. Barker, *British in Boston*, 9. The King's Own was the 4th Regiment of Foot.

27. *Quebec Gazette*, May 12, 1774.

28. Regimental punishment books, HL/PO/JO/10/7/544, PA.

29. Steven M. Baule and Don N. Hagist, "The Regimental Punishment Book of the Boston Detachments of the Royal Irish Regiment and 65th Regiment, 1774–75," *Journal of Army Historical Research* 88 (2010): 5-18.

30. *Massachusetts Spy*, September 29, 1774. The newspaper spelled the prisoner's name "Fanthrop," but it appears as Fanthorp on the muster rolls. Muster rolls, 5th Regiment of Foot, WO 12/2289.

31. Trial of Robert Vaughan, WO 71/80 pp. 199-206.

32. General orders, June 26, 1774, WO 36/1.

33. Baule and Hagist, "Regimental Punishment Book," 14-18.

34. John Pitcairn to John Mackenzie, December 10, 1774, MacKenzie Papers, Add. Mss. 39190, British Library, London.

35. Muster rolls, 23rd Regiment of Foot, WO 12/3960.

36. Muster rolls, 43rd Regiment of Foot, WO 12/5561.

37. General orders, July 18, 1774, WO 36/1.

38. Standing orders, 37th Regiment, ECP.

39. General orders, August 14, 1774, WO 36/1.

40. Charles James, *A New and Enlarged Military Dictionary* (London: T. Egerton, 1802), entry for "Fugel-Man."

41. W. Glanville Evelyn, *Memoir and Letters of Captain W. Glanville Evelyn, of the 4th Regiment, ("King's Own,") from North America, 1774–1776*, ed. G. D. Scull (Oxford: Parker, 1879), 30.

42. General orders, November 21, 1774, WO 36/1.

43. *The Manual Exercise, As Ordered by His Majesty, in 1764*. Although this document was widely reprinted, the text of the manual exercise portion does not vary with the exception of typographical changes.

44. Simes, *Military Guide*, 196.

45. William Windham, *A Plan of Discipline composed for the use of the Militia of County of Norfolk* (London: J. Shuckburgh, 1759), plate 1.

46. Houlding, *Fit for Service*, 144-145.

47. General orders, June 26, 1774, WO 36/1.

48. General orders, November 18, 1774, WO 36/1.

49. Barker, *British in Boston*, 7, 9.

50. Regimental orders for December 1, 1774 (10 rounds); and January 16 (8), February 7 (8), and 21 (8), March 14 (10), 23 (10), and 31 (15), and April 15 (15), 1775, orderly book, 18th Regiment of Foot, NAM.

51. Mackenzie, *Diary*, 4.

52. Robert Honyman, *Colonial Panorama, 1775: Dr. Robert Honyman's Journal for March and April*, ed. Philip Radford (San Marino, CA: Huntington Library, 1939), 44, 50.

53. Barker, *British in Boston*, 11, 18, 23, 25.

54. Mackenzie, *Diary*, 6.

55. Ibid., 7.

56. Regimental orders for December 14 and 19, 1774, and January 21 and 31, and February 8, 11, and 27, 1775, orderly book, 18th Regiment of Foot, NAM.

57. Mackenzie, *Diary*, 13.

58. Barker, *British in Boston*, 27-28.

59. Mackenzie, *Diary*, 15.

CHAPTER 5. EVIDENT SUPERIORITY EVEN IN WOODS

1. Francis Rawdon, *Report on the Manuscripts of the late Reginald Rawdon Hastings, Esq.*, ed. Francis Bickley (London: Historical Manuscripts Commission, 1934), 167.

2. Barker, *British in Boston*, 31.

3. Each company had at least one of its three officers present, but working alongside other companies for the first time, the whole overseen by a pro-tem commander, and having many supernumerary officers on the expedition may have caused considerable confusion about the source and meaning of spoken orders.

4. Barker, *British in Boston*, 39.

5. Undated entry, mss. p. 79, WO 36/1.

6. General orders, undated entry, mss. p. 83, ibid.

7. General orders, undated entry, mss. p. 90, ibid.

8. General orders, undated entry, mss. p. 83, ibid.

9. General orders, May 31, 1775, ibid.

10. General orders, undated entry, mss. p. 79, ibid.

11. Muster rolls, 23rd Regiment of Foot, WO 12/3960, and 38th Regiment of Foot.

12. For example, the 38th Regiment received Joseph Blackwell, who had fifteen years in the army before being drafted from the 36th Regiment; Adam Forbes, with twelve years from the 42nd Regiment; William Marsh, with fourteen years from the 20th Regiment of Foot; and Henry Thomas, with thirty years from the 40th Regiment. "Examinations of Invalid Soldiers," June 6, 1776 (Marsh), December 5, 1780 (Thomas), March 4, 1783 (Blackwell), and September 12, 1783 (Forbes), Pension Admission Books, WO 116/7 and /8.

13. General orders, June 11, 1775, WO 36/1.

14. General orders, June 14, 1775, WO 36/1.

15. General orders, June 3 and 4, 1775, WO 36/1.

16. General orders, June 12, 1775, WO 36/1.

17. Muster rolls for various regiments in Boston, WO 12.

18. General orders, June 17, 1775, WO 36/1. The amount of provisions is not stated in the orders; for later campaigns, three days' worth, consisting usually of a pound and a half each of precooked meat and bread, was typical.

19. James Abercrombie to Sir Jeffrey Amherst, June 20, 1775, Amherst mss., U1350 080/3, Center for Kentish Studies, Maidstone, Kent, UK.

20. *The Lost War: Letters from British Officers during the American Revolution*, ed. Marion Balderston and David Syrett (New York: Horizon Press, 1975), 33; Rawdon, *Manuscripts*, 157.

21. Richard Williams, *Discord and Civil Wars* (Buffalo, NY: Easy Hill Press, 1954), 21-22.

22. William Carter, *A genuine detail of the several engagements, positions, and movements of the Royal and American armies, during the years 1775 and 1776* (London, 1784), 5-6.

23. General orders, August 10, 1775, WO 36/1.

24. William Howe, *General Sir William Howe's Orderly Book*, ed. B. F. Stevens (Port Washington, NY: Kennikat Press, 1980), 251-252.

25. "Discipline established by Major General Howe for Light Infantry in Battalion," NAM; Houlding, *Fit for Service*, 336-337.

26. Howe, *Orderly Book*, 269. The order reads "39," apparently including corporals in the number.

27. Ibid., 272-273. The marines contributed two companies of grenadiers but no light infantry.

28. Ibid., 251-252.

29. General orders, June 3, 1775, WO 36/1.

30. Howe, *Orderly Book*, 294.

31. Ibid., 243, 251, 274, 292.

32. General orders, May 29 and 30, 1776, "British Army Orders," *Collections of the New York Historical Society for the year 1883* (New York: New York Historical Society, 1884), 374, 375.

33. Don N. Hagist and Erik Goldstein, "Short Land Muskets for the British Light Infantry in America," *Man at Arms* (December 2009): 18-25.

34. Howe, *Orderly Book*, 284-285.

35. Ibid., 255, 264, 275, 291.

36. General orders, August 12, 1776, WO 36/5.

37. General orders, August 1, 1776, WO 36/5.

38. Percy, *Letters*, 68.

39. James Murray, *Letters from America, 1773 to 1780*, ed. Eric Robson (New York: Barnes & Noble, 1950), 33-34.

40. The preeminent study of British tactical discipline during the American Revolution is Matthew H. Spring, *With Zeal and Bayonets Only: The British Army on Campaign in North America, 1775–1783* (Norman: University of Oklahoma Press, 2008).

41. General orders, September 13, 1776, WO 36/5.

42. Loftus Cliffe to "Jack," September 21, 1776, Loftus Cliffe Papers, WLC. Matthew Johnson commanded the light infantry company of the 46th Regiment;

this company joined the army on Staten Island during the summer, and as part of the 3rd Battalion of Light Infantry may not have been taught, or had time to thoroughly train with, the exercise that the other battalions learned in Halifax.

43. Dansey, *Captured Rebel Flag*, 20.

44. Murray, *Letters*, 40.

45. Dansey, *Captured Rebel Flag*, 27.

46. Peebles, *Diary*, 111.

47. Ray W. Pettengill, trans., *Letters from America 1776–1779, Being Letters of Brunswick, Hessian, and Waldeck Officers with the British Armies during the Revolution* (Boston: Houghton Mifflin, 1924), 70.

48. General orders, June 20, 1777, orderly book, Major Acland's Grenadier Battalion, NYHS.

49. Francis-Carr Clarke, "Letters to Lord Polwarth from Sir Francis-Carr Clerke, Aide-de-Camp to General John Burgoyne," ed. Ronald F. Kingsley, *New York History* 79, no. 4 (October 1998): 429.

50. Thomas Hughes, *A Journal by Thos: Hughes* (Cambridge, MA: Harvard University Press, 1947), 10.

51. "Diary of Joshua Pell, junior," *Magazine of American History* 2, no. 2 (February 1878): 109.

52. "Narrative of William Grant," *Documents Relative to the Colonial History of the State of New York, Procured in Holland, England and France*, ed. E. B. O'Callaghan (Albany, NY: Weed, Parsons, 1857), 733-734.

53. F. von Münchausen, *At General Howe's Side, 1776–1778: The Diary of General William Howe's Aide de Camp, Captain Friedrich von Muenchausen*, ed. S. Smith (Monmouth Beach, NJ: Philip Freneau, 1974), 31A.

54. Francis Downman, *The Services of Lieut. Colonel Francis Downman, R. A. in France, North America and the West Indies, between the years 1758 and 1784*, ed. F. A. Whinyates (Woolwich, UK: Royal Artillery Institution, 1896), 35.

55. Peebles, *Diary*, 194.

56. Thomas George Barretté to Henry Clinton, August 26, 1780, HCP, vol. 118:41.

57. General orders, April 5, 1781, orderly books, 1st battalion of light infantry, ECP.

58. Ebenezer Denny, *Military Journal of Major Ebenezer Denny* (Philadelphia: J. B. Lippincott, 1859), 37.

59. Gaillard Hunt, *Fragments of Revolutionary History. Being hitherto unpublished writings of the men of the American Revolution* (Brooklyn: Historical Printing Club, 1892), 50.

60. Carter, *Genuine Detail*, 48.

61. Anonymous British Journal, 1776–78, ms. no. 409, November 18, 1776, Sol Feinstone Manuscripts Collection, American Philosphical Society Library, Philadelphia; Thomas Glyn Journal, November 20, 1776, Firestone Library, Princeton University, Princeton, New Jersey (hereafter FL).

62. Henry Stirke, "A British Officer's Revolutionary War Journal, 1776–1778," *Maryland Historical Magazine* 56 (June 1961): 169.

63. Anonymous British Journal, 1776–78, ms. no. 409, September 11, 1777.

64. Stinson Jarvis, ed., "Reminiscences of a Loyalist," *Canadian Magazine* 26, no. 3 (January 1906): 232.

65. Lamb, *British Soldier's Story*, 81.

66. "Letters of Charles O'Hara to the Duke of Grafton," ed. G. C. Rogers, *South Carolina Historical Magazine* 65 (1964): 175.

67. Charles Cornwallis to Lord George Germain, March 17, 1781, *The Cornwallis Papers: The Campaigns of 1780 and 1781 in the Southern Theatre of the American Revolutionary War*, 6 vols., ed. Ian Saberton (Uckfield: Naval & Military Press, 2010), 4:17-18.

68. Patrick Ferguson to Clinton, August 1778, Howard H. Peckham, *Sources of American Independence: Selected Manuscripts from the Collections of the William L. Clements Library* (Chicago: University of Chicago Press, 1978), 2:307.

69. General orders, June 23, 1776, orderly books, 37th Regiment, ECP.

70. General orders, October 15, 1776, "British Army Orders," 389.

71. William Haslewood, "Journal of a British Officer during the American Revolution," *Mississippi Valley Historical Review* 7, no. 1 (June 1920), 55.

72. General orders for September 17, 1776, WO 36/5.

73. Peckham, *Sources*, 2:304.

74. *et qui pis étuit* (and what is worse), Murray, *Letters*, 40-41.

75. Peebles, *Diary*, 216, 223.

76. Ibid., 133.

77. Lt. George Duke, letter dated German Town Camp, October 13, 1777, sold at auction 2008, Heritage Auctions, https://historical.ha.com/itm/military-and-patriotic/revolutionary-war/battle-of-brandywine-manuscript-copy-letter/a/683-56040.s.

78. Robert Francis Seybolt, "A Contemporary British Account of General Sir William Howe's Military Operations in 1777," *Proceedings of the American Antiquarian Society* 40 (April 1930): 78, 79.

79. John André, *Journal, Major André's Journal*, ed. C. Willcox (Tarrytown, NY: William Abbatt, 1930), 46.

80. Cornwallis to Germain, March 17, 1781, *Cornwallis Papers*, 4:19.

81. "Letters of Charles O'Hara to the Duke of Grafton," 177.

82. Trial of Duncan Robertson, WO 71/84 pp. 205-208.

83. Anonymous British Journal, ms. no. 409, June 26, 1777.

84. Montresor, "Journals," 425.

85. Loftus Cliffe to "Jack," October 24, 1777, Loftus Cliffe Papers, WLC.

86. Anonymous British Journal, ms. no. 409, September 11, 1777.

87. Montresor, "Journals," 511-512.

88. Stephen Kemble, "Journals of Lieut.-Col. Stephen Kemble," *Collections of the New York Historical Society for the year 1883* (New York, 1884), 154.

89. Anonymous British Journal, ms. no. 409, June 28, 1778.

90. Peebles, *Diary*, 194.

91. *Lost War*, 126.

92. General orders, May 25, 1775, WO 36/1.

93. General orders, August 20, 1775, ibid.

94. Ibid.

95. Kemble, "Journals," 59.

96. Mackenzie, *Diary*, 163.

97. Discharge of Donald MacDonald, WO 121/1/195; discharge of John McIntosh, WO 121/2/91.

98. Peter Traille to John André, HCP, vol. 91:31.

99. TGP, vol. 126.

100. Martin Hunter, *The Journal of Gen. Sir Martin Hunter* (Edinburgh: Edinburgh Press, 1894), 43.

101. Battalion orders, November 5, 1778, orderly books, 1st battalion of light infantry, ECP.

102. Muster rolls, 16th Light Dragoons, WO 12/1246, and muster rolls,17th Regiment of Foot, WO 12/3406.

103. Present State of the 15 Companys of Light Infantry Commanded by Lieut Colonel Robert Abercromby, April 25, 1779, Southampton, New York, George Washington Papers, ser. 4. F, LOC.

104. Trial of John Cochrall, 44th Regiment, WO 71/90 pp. 82-84; trial of Robert Mason and James Watson, 23rd Regiment, WO 71/90 pp. 129-131.

105. Trial of William Hudson, WO 71/94 pp. 310-31.

106. Mackenzie, *Diary*, 458.

107. Cornwallis to Clinton, December 3, 1780, *Cornwallis Papers*, 3:25.

108. Cornwallis to Money, November 13, 1780, ibid., 3:309; Cornwallis to McArthur, November 30, 1780, ibid., 3:321.

109. Clinton to Phillips, April 25, 1781, ibid., 5:50; Banastre Tarleton, *A History of the Campaigns of 1780 and 1781 in the Southern Provinces of North America* (London: T. Cadell, 1787), 295-296; Cornwallis to Leslie, July 14, 1781, *Cornwallis Papers*, 5:186.

110. David Syrett, *Shipping and the American War, 1775–83: A Study of British Transport Organization* (Oxford: Oxford University Press, 1970), 77-105.

111. *Edinburgh Advertiser*, July 30, 1776.

112. Archibald Campbell to William Howe, June 19, 1776, *Naval Documents of the American Revolution,* 13 vols., ed. William James Morgan et al. (Washington, DC: Government Printing Office, 1964-2019), 5:620.

113. Peebles, *Diary*, 50; Mackenzie, *Diary*, 114.

114. Lewis Butler, *The Annals of the King's Royal Rifle Corps.* Vol. 1 (London: John Murray, 1813), 299.

115. John Enys, *The American Journals of Lt. John Enys*, ed. Elizabeth Cometti (Blue Mountain Lake, NY: Adirondack Museum, 1976), 18.

116. Ibid., 20; muster rolls, 29th Regiment of Foot, WO 12/4493. Enys wrote that "5 or 6 men and a Drummer" of the 29th were killed, but the muster rolls show only three died that day. A few other men died within the next few days, possibly of wounds.

117. William Dansey to his mother, July 28, 1778, William Dansey Letters, Historical Society of Delaware, Wilmington (hereafter HSD).

118. André, *Journal*, 82.

119. Ibid.

120. Christian M. McBurney, *The Rhode Island Campaign: The First French and American Operation in the Revolutionary War* (Yardley, PA: Westholme, 2011), 129-131.

121. Muster rolls, 23rd Regiment of Foot, WO 12/3960.

122. Peebles, *Diary*, 483.

123. General orders, February 28, 1779, orderly book, Captain Clayton's company, 17th Regiment of Foot, HL.

CHAPTER 6. GONE VOLUNTEER TO AMERICA

1. Land Grant Petition by William Morgan Esquire, Upper Canada Land Grant Petitions "M" Bundle 10, 1809–1816, PAC; muster rolls, 5th Dragoons, WO 12/682, and muster rolls for other cavalry regiments, WO 12.

2. Muster rolls, 12th Dragoons, WO 12/1037; muster rolls, 15th Dragoons, WO12/1192; muster rolls, 17th Light Dragoons, WO 12/1306.

3. Two hundred drafts were taken from regiments in Ireland by having each regiment contribute ten men; sixty more drafts were drawn from regiments in England. WO

1/680 pp. 291-292. The specific distribution of drafts into the 35th, 49th, and 63rd Regiments that embarked in April are not recorded on their muster rolls but are mentioned in the journal of Thomas Sullivan, a soldier in the 49th. Sullivan, *From Redcoat to Rebel*, 8-9. The drafts joining regiments in Boston are recorded on the rolls for those regiments; the 10th Regiment, for example, received twenty-two drafts from sixteen different regiments. Muster rolls, 10th Regiment of Foot, WO 12/2750.

4. Muster rolls, 23rd Regiment of Foot, WO 12/3960; muster rolls, 59th Regiment of Foot, WO 12/6786.

5. Muster rolls, 17th Regiment of Foot, WO 12/3406; muster rolls, 27th Regiment of Foot, WO 12/4328; muster rolls, 55th Regiment of Foot, WO 12/6471. The rolls of the 17th and 27th denote only a few of the drafts, and those of the 55th denote the drafts but not the regiments from which they came; the cavalry drafts were discerned by comparing names of drafts on cavalry muster rolls to those on the infantry rolls, based on several explicitly identified on the 17th's rolls.

6. The embarking regiments were the 15th, 28th, 33rd, 37th, 46th, 54th, and 57th. None of their rolls enumerate the drafts completely. The rolls of the 11th, 32nd, and 36th Regiments, which remained in Ireland, indicate 160 drafts to the embarking regiments. There may have been others from other infantry regiments, and a few cavalry drafts are enumerated. Muster rolls for these regiments, WO 12.

7. Muster rolls for these eight regiments, WO 12.

8. Muster rolls, 1st Regiment of Foot 1st Battalion, WO 12/1882 and 2nd Battalion, WO 12/1948. Six of these men went into the 17th Regiment and another six into the 22nd Regiment. Orderly Book, 17th Regiment of Foot, NYHS; muster rolls, 22nd Regiment of Foot, WO 12/3872.

9. Regimental orders, August 25, 1775, orderly books, 37th Regiment, ECP.

10. Regimental orders, February 20, 1776, orderly book, 32nd Regiment, NLI.

11. Secretary at War to the commanding officer of the 2nd Battalion, 1st Regiment of Foot, April 19, 1776, WO 4/97 pp. 57-58.

12. Hagist, *British Soldiers*, 141.

13. See for example muster rolls, 5th Dragoons, WO 12/682, and muster rolls, 13th Dragoons, WO 12/1084.

14. Land Grant Petition by William Morgan Esquire. No copy of the order has been found.

15. Trial of John Reilly and James Barry, WO 71/82 p. 388-402; trial of David Taylor, Patrick Shanley, William McGill, John Hughes, and Thomas Burnell, WO 71/87 p. 29-51.

16. The off-reckonings, the portion of pay allocated for everything besides subsistence (food), was three pence per day for private soldiers in the cavalry, two pence per day in the infantry. The difference in subsistence pay was much greater. Edward R. Curtis, *The Organization of the British Army in the American Revolution* (Gansvoort, NY: Corner House Historical Publications, 1998), 158.

17. Edward Harvey to Lt. Col. Smith, September 7, 1775, WO 3/5 p. 71.

18. See for example Curtis, *Organization*, 77-80.

19. Based on a study of all of the men who served in the 22nd Regiment of Foot in America from 1775 through 1783, and soldiers' discharges for soldiers who served in America in various regiments. WO 12, WO 97, WO 119 and WO 121.

20. Muster rolls, 3rd Regiment of Foot, WO 12/2105; muster rolls, 10th Regiment of Foot, WO 12/2750; muster rolls, 45th Regiment of Foot, WO 12/5718.

21. Muster rolls, 3rd Regiment of Foot, WO 12/2105; muster rolls, 59th Regiment of Foot, WO 12/6786; muster rolls, 38th Regiment of Foot, WO 12/5171.

22. Muster rolls, 7th Regiment of Foot, WO 12/2474; muster rolls, 24th Regiment of Foot, WO 12/4059; muster rolls, 67th Regiment of Foot, WO 12/7537.
23. Muster rolls, 1st Regiment of Foot 2nd Battalion, WO 12/1948; muster rolls, 19th Regiment of Foot, WO 12/3593; muster rolls, 22nd Regiment of Foot, WO 12/3872; muster rolls, 30th Regiment of Foot, WO 12/4561; "Examinations of Invalid Soldiers," March 26, 1782, Pension Admission Book, WO 116/7; "Examinations of Invalid Soldiers," April 14, 1784, WO 116/8; discharge of Jacob Holts, WO 121/37/113.
24. Muster rolls, 36th Regiment of Foot, WO 12/5025.
25. Gavin Cochrane to William, Viscout Barrington, April 30, 1776, WO 991/1 p. 33.
26. Barrington to Cochrane, April 27, 1776, WO 4/97 p. 100.
27. Harvey to Cochrane, May 9, 1776, WO 3/6 p. 34.
28. Punishment book, 3rd Regiment of Foot, HL/PO/JO/10/7/544, PA; muster rolls, 22nd Regiment of Foot, WO 12/3872.
29. John Nairne to Richard Lernoult, September 3, 1782, John and Thomas Nairne fonds, MG 23, GIII23, vol. 3 pp. 234-235, PAC.
30. Muster rolls, 38th Regiment of Foot, WO 12/5171 and WO 12/5172; the fate of three of the drafts is unknown because of gaps in the muster rolls.
31. Muster rolls, 23rd Regiment of Foot, WO 12/3960; the fate of two drafts is unknown.
32. Howe, *Orderly Book*, 132, 302.
33. Thomas Cranfield, *The Useful Christian; a Memoir of Thomas Cranfield, for about Fifty Years a Devoted Sunday-School Teacher* (Philadelphia: American Sunday-School Union, Philadelphia, no date), 11.
34. S. P. Julliott to Clinton, HCP, vol. 228:41; the letter is undated but is filed with papers from 1779.
35. Andrew Scott, *Poems, Chiefly in the Scottish Dialect* (Kelso, Scotland: Andrew Leadbetter, 1811), x.
36. John MacDonald, *Autobiographical Journal of John MacDonald: Schoolmaster and Soldier* (Edinburgh: Norman MacLeod, 1906), 33, 36.
37. A Narrative of the Life of Serjeant William Pell, E06-003, Grenadier Guards Archives, London.
38. Jeremiah Clinton to Sir Henry Clinton, April 26, 1780, HCP, vol. 95:12.
39. "The last Speech, Confession and dying words of James Andrew, who was executed in the Grassmarket of Edinburgh, upon Wednesday the 4th day of February 1784 for the horrid crime of Highway Robbery," in R. C. and J. M. Anderson, *Quicksilver: A Hundred Years of Coaching 1750–1850* (Newton Abbot, UK: David & Charles, 1973), 174-177.
40. Hagist, *British Soldiers*, 15.
41. W. Griffith, "Memoirs and Spiritual Experience of the late Mr. W. Griffith, Senior (Written by himself)," *Spiritual Magazine, and Zion's Casket* (1848): 152.
42. General orders, November 17, 1775, WO 36/1.
43. General orders, November 26, 1775, WO 36/1.
44. WO 4/133-134, 196-198.
45. Harvey to Cornwallis, July 6, 1775, WO 3/5.
46. *Belfast Newsletter*, September 8, 1775.
47. *Freeman's Journal* (Dublin), August 15, 1775.
48. *Hibernian Chronicle* (Cork), September 21, 1775.
49. Philip Tisdall Attorney General, June 27, 1775, WO 40/1.

50. Commander in chief in Munster to Barrington, in J. E. Norton, ed., *Letters of Edward Gibbon* (London: Cassell, 1956), 2:89.

51. Richard Temple to Barrington, December 26, 1775, WO 1/994.

52. Muster rolls, 17th Regiment of Foot, WO 12/3406.

53. Muster rolls 55th Regiment of Foot.

54. Muster rolls, 9th Regiment of Foot, WO 12/2653, and 24th Regiment of Foot.

55. *London Gazette*, December 16, 1775.

56. Report of the Number of Men Entertain'd in the Additional Companys by Wm. Cowley Capt. 22d Regt. Foot to 5 Jany 1776, WO 991/1 p. 106.

57. List of Recruits Raised for the 46th Regiment of Foot, WO 1/992. The 46th Regiment had sailed in late 1775, but its ships were driven back to Great Britain by storms. This allowed these recruits to join the regiment before it set off once again in 1776.

58. Ibid.

59. *Norfolk Chronicle*, March 30, 1776.

60. *Edinburgh Advertiser*, April 21, 1775.

61. Ibid., June 14, 1776.

62. Gilchrist, "Captain Hon. William Leslie," 146.

63. John Murray to Barrington, October 10, 1775, Lord John Murray Papers, Bagshawe Muniments, John Rylands University Library of Manchester.

64. *Edinburgh Advertiser*, October 27, 1775.

65. At this writing, three descriptive lists of von Scheither recruits have been found that give place of birth, age, prior military service, and other data for 996 men; of those, 329 had prior military service. List of Lt. Colonel v. Scheither's Recruits Embarked at Stade for England on 18 December 1775, WO 43/405 p. 266-274; Liste Des Recrués Anglois embarqués á Stade pour Spithead en Irlande ce 14me de Mai 1776, WO 43/405, pp. 369-375; 7th-25th Scheither Recruit Transports Halting at Münden, Hannover, Hann.41.V.Nr.4, f.191-223 (April-Sept 1776), Sta-Hannover.

66. Edward Harvey to "Maj. Gen. C.," April 1, 1776, WO 3/6 fol. 2.

67. Harvey to "Major Roberts," May 3, 1776, WO 3/6 p. 32; WO 4/98 pp. 439-440.

68. H. Lewis to William Knox, May 24, 1776, CO 5/168 p. 169.

69. Georg Pausch, *Georg Pausch's Journal and Reports of the Campaign in America*, trans. Bruce E. Burgoyne (Bowie, MD: Heritage Books, 1996), 16.

70. Barrington to Amherst, April 16, 1776, CO 5/168.

71. Barrington to Germain, May 10, 1776, CO 5/168 p. 157; H. Lewis to William Knox, May 24, 1776, CO 5/168 p. 169.

72. Recruiting leaflet, 71st Regiment, M.1982.97, National Museums of Scotland, Edinburgh (hereafter NMS).

73. Discharge of Allan Roy Cameron, WO 121/14/364; discharge of Donald McPhee, WO 121/10/149; discharge of Archibald McMillan, WO 121/12/204; discharge of Hugh Duncan, WO 121/2/90; discharge of John Bogg, WO 121/7/185; discharge of Hugh Cameron, WO 121/10/10; recruiting leaflet, 71st Regiment, NMS.

74. Recruiting instructions for Sergeant Miller of the Northumberland Militia, Bayard-Campbell-Pearsall Collection, Campbell Accounts and Papers, 1773-1781, Box 17, folder 2, New York Public Library.

75. Peebles, *Diary*, 24-25.

CHAPTER 7. BARRACKS AND BARNS, TRANSPORTS AND TENTS, WIGWAMS AND BLANKETS

1. Hagist, *British Soldiers,* 153.

2. David Syrett, "Living Conditions on the Navy Board's Transports during the American War, 1775–1783," *Mariner's Mirror* 55 (1969): 88.

3. Syrett, *Shipping,* 110-14.

4. See for example Germain to the Admiralty, February 21, 1776, and George Jackson to Molyneux Shuldham, March 16, 1776, *Naval Documents,* 4:925, 977-978; Zabin, *Boston Massacre,* 11-16.

5. See for example Return of three Detachments that embarked for America . . . at Charles Fort 12th April 1776, and Return of three Detachments ordered for embarkation from the Additional Companies at Charles Fort 7th May 1776, WO 1/992.

6. See for example CO 5/168 pp. 17, 24, and letters of April 12 and May 20, 1776, WO 1/992.

7. Orders and Instructions for His Majesty's 33d Regiment of Foot, November 29, 1775, WO 26/29 pp. 156-157.

8. Orders to be observed by Officers Commanding Detachments on Board Transport Vessels, May 15, 1780, Frederick Mackenzie Papers (hereafter FMP), box 1, folder 2, William L. Clements Library, University of Michigan, Ann Arbor.

9. Ibid. The exception was when the recruits were completing size increases of regiments in 1776 and 1779; the regiments needed additional arms, and they were brought by the recruits.

10. Peebles, *Diary,* 27.

11. Orders for the 2d Battn. of the 71st Regt. on its Embarkation for North America, April 25, 1776, Abbott and Lane Papers, box 1, folder 36, Concord Antiquarian Society Collection, Concord Free Public Library.

12. *Reading Mercury,* March 18, 1776.

13. Orders to be observed by Officers Commanding Detachments on Board Transport Vessels, May 15, 1780, FMP, box 1, folder 2.

14. John Row to Jane Innes, March 9, 1776, GD113/5/74, National Archive of Scotland, Edinburgh (hereafter) NAS.

15. Lamb, *British Soldier's Story,* 21.

16. Journal of Ensign William Johnson, 29th Regiment of Foot, Collections of Fort Ticonderoga Museum.

17. Ibid.

18. Peebles, *Diary,* 27-28.

19. Sullivan, *From Redcoat to Rebel,* 12.

20. Lamb, *British Soldier's Story,* 31-32. Lamb identified Brooks by name. A gap in the muster rolls of the 9th Regiment prevents identification of the two unnamed men.

21. Stirke, "British Officer's Revolutionary War Journal," 167; muster rolls, 22nd Regiment of Foot, WO 12/3872.

22. Journal of Ensign William Johnson, 29th Regiment of Foot, Collections of Fort Ticonderoga Museum; Peebles, *Diary,* 31-33; Ambrose Serle, *The American Journal of Ambrose Serle* (San Marino, CA: Huntington Library, 1940), 241; discharge of Robert Reeves, WO 121/3/293; discharge of James McKilligan, WO 121/7/194; discharge of James McPherson, WO 121/2/183; discharge of Henry Brown, WO 121/8/258.

23. George Inman, "George Inman's Narrative of the American Revolution," *Pennsylvania Magazine of History and Biography* 7, no. 3 (1883): 238; see also, for example, Thomas Glyn Journal, August 14, 1776, FL, and Peebles, *Diary*, 35.

24. Hagist, *British Soldiers*, 253-254.

25. Mungo Campbell to the Secretary at War, Boston, January 16, 1776, WO 991/1 p. 98.

26. Hagist, *British Soldiers*, 22-24.

27. Mackenzie, *Diary*, 84.

28. Peebles, *Diary*, 325.

29. George, Mathew, "Mathew's Narrative," *Historical Magazine* 1 (1857), 103.

30. CO 5/98, p. 493.

31. Mackenzie, *Diary*, 243.

32. Peebles, *Diary*, 155.

33. Memorial of Mary Clarke, Headquarters Papers of the British Army in America, PRO 30/55/8549.

34. General orders, November 11, 1777, *General Orders, Rhode Island*, ed. Don N. Hagist (Bowie, MD: Heritage Books, 2001), 74.

35. "Instructions for the Barrack Masters of Montreal & Quebec," in *The Correspondence of General Thomas Gage with the Secretaries of State and with the War Office and the Treasury, 1763–1775*, ed. Edwin Clarence Carter (New Haven, CT: Yale University Press, 1931); general orders, November 12, 1774, WO 36/1.

36. General orders, November 21, 1774, WO 36/1.

37. Regimental orders, March 14, 1778, orderly books, 37th Regiment, ECP.

38. Cuthbertson, *System*, 37-38.

39. General orders, December 23, 1774, WO 36/1; general orders, December 12, 1777, *General Orders, Rhode Island*, 79.

40. Cuthbertson, *System*, 38; regimental orders, December 14, 1776, orderly book, 15th Regiment of Foot, Historical Society of Pennsylvania, Philadelphia (hereafter HSP).

41. Cuthbertson, *System*, 34; regimental orders, January 4, 1777, orderly book, 15th Regiment of Foot, HSP.

42. Brigade orders, December 20, 1776, orderly book, 17th Regiment of Foot, NYHS.

43. General orders, undated entry, mss. p. 69, WO 36/1.

44. General orders, February 11, 1777, *General Orders, Rhode Island*, 31.

45. Stephen Payne Adye to Colebrooke Nesbitt, November 12, 1779, "Official Letters of Major General James Pattison," *Collections of the New York Historical Society for the year 1875* (New York: New York Historical Society, 1876), 298.

46. Cuthbertson, *System*, 28-29.

47. Trial of Thomas Owen and Henry Johnston, WO 71/82 pp. 203-206; trial of Thomas and Isabella McMahon, WO 71/82 pp. 207-210.

48. Orders for January 15 and 22, orderly book, 15th Regiment of Foot, HSP.

49. William Maxwell to the Secretary at War, September 20, 1773, CO 5/176 fol. 80.

50. Peebles, *Diary*, 230-233.

51. Ibid., 233-234, 237.

52. Ibid., 303, 309.

53. "Mathew's Narrative," 103.

54. Peebles, *Diary*, 413, 416.

55. Ibid., 422; Battalion orders, November 20, 1779, orderly books, 1st battalion of light infantry, ECP; Peebles, *Diary*, 415; muster rolls, 43rd Regiment of Foot, WO 12/5561.

56. Peebles, *Diary*, 448.

57. Clerke, "Letters to Lord Polwarth," 417.

58. As mentioned elsewhere, a few regiments were larger than the typical size, therefore requiring more tents per company.

59. Until 1781, camp equipage included "tin water flasks," but in 1781, wooden canteens were sent instead. Returns of camp equipage, WO 4/98 p. 146, WO 4/101 p. 397, WO 26/29 p. 468 (tin); WO 4/275 pp. 89-93 (wood).

60. See for example CO 5/169 fols., 109-110.

61. Troops in Rhode Island initially received thirty-five pounds per tent in May 1777, and five, ten, fifteen, or twenty pounds per tent every few weeks through November. *General Orders, Rhode Island*, 48, 57, 59, 64, 66, 73. The 40th Regiment procured thirty-five pounds of straw to fill fifteen bolsters per company in New Jersey in December 1776. Regimental orders, December 27, 1776, orderly book, 40th Regiment of Foot, MAHS.

62. Carter, *Genuine Detail*, 15.

63. This was written on November 20, and the regiment went into barracks on December 11. *Lost War*, 53.

64. Rawdon, *Manuscripts*, 161.

65. For example, in April 1782, the 29th Regiment in Canada faced the prospect of using the same tents for a third year in a row, the previous year's having been mistakenly put into stores. Christopher Carleton to Richard Lernoult, April 26, 1781, WO 28/2 p. 3.

66. Serle, *American Journal*, 56.

67. William Digby, *The British Invasion From the North: The Campaigns of Generals Carleton and Burgoyne from Canada, 1776–1777, with the Journal of Lieut. William Digby* (Albany, NY: Joel Munsell's Sons, 1887), 121-22.

68. Mackenzie, *Diary*, 190 (October 10, 1777), 351 (August 12, 1778) and 397 (September 23, 1778).

69. Peebles, *Diary*, 285.

70. Cuthbertson, *System*, 40; regimental orders, October 17, 1776, orderly book, 17th Regiment of Foot, NYHS.

71. Mackenzie, *Diary*, 212.

72. Peebles, *Diary*, 453.

73. See for example Mackenzie, *Diary*, 198-199.

74. General orders, June 8, 1777, orderly book, Major Acland's Grenadier Battalion, NYHS. The orders specified eighteen yards between the bell tents, which leaves about twelve yards from the front of one tent to the front of the tent opposite it on the next street.

75. General orders, June 9, 1777, orderly book, Major Acland's Grenadier Battalion, NYHS.

76. General orders, June 20, 1777, orderly book, Major Acland's Grenadier Battalion, NYHS.

77. Regimental orders, August 30, 1776, orderly books, 37th Regiment, ECP.

78. See for example general orders, August 29, 1777, orderly book, 47th Regiment of Foot, Adirondack Community College, Queensbury, New York (hereafter ACC).

79. See for example general orders, November 13, 1776, orderly book, 17th Regiment of Foot, NYHS; Loftus Cliffe to "Bat," February 17, 1778, Loftus Cliffe Papers,

WLC (concerning preparations for the Philadelphia campaign the previous year).

80. Loftus Cliffe to [unknown], July 9, 1776, Loftus Cliffe Papers, WLC.

81. General orders, August 24, 1776, orderly book, 4th Battalion of Grenadiers, NAS.

82. Mackenzie, *Diary*, 50, 68.

83. Thomas Glyn Journal, November 28, 1776, FL.

84. Regimental orders, December 4 and 8, and brigade orders, December 20, 1776, orderly book, 17th Regiment of Foot, NYHS.

85. Peebles, *Diary*, 70, 72

86. *Georg Pausch's Journal*, 31.

87. For example, in September 1780, when the grenadier battalions moved into barns on Long Island while building huts. Peebles, *Diary*, 410.

88. Hunter, *Journal*, 27.

89. Charles Cochrane to Archibald, ninth Earl of Dundonald, March 8, 1777, in James Paterson, *History of the County of Ayr: with a Genealogical Account of the Families of Ayrshire*, vol. 2 (Edinburgh: Thomas George Stevenson, 1852), 28.

90. Linnea M. Bass, "Bloody Footprints in the Snow? January 1777 at Brunswick, New Jersey," *Military Collector & Historian* 45 (Spring 1993): 9-10.

91. William Murray to Mungo Murray, June 5, 1777, GD68/2/117, NAS.

92. Cochrane to Archibald, Paterson, *History of the County of Ayr*, 28.

93. Münchausen, *At General Howe's Side,* 46.

94. William Bamford, *A Redcoat in America: The Diaries of Lieutenant William Bamford, 1757–1765 and 1776* (Warwick, UK: Helion, 2019), 214.

95. Mackenzie, *Diary*, 52.

96. Battalion orders, September 27, 1777, orderly book, 2nd Battalion of Light Infantry, LOC.

97. Haslewood, "Journal," 58.

98. Phillips to Clinton, March 30, 1781, *Cornwallis Papers*, 5:13.

99. James, *New and Enlarged*, entry for "Wigwam."

100. Samuel Graham, *Memoir of General Graham*, ed. Colonel James J. Graham (Edinburgh: R. & R. Clark, 1862), 269.

101. Hunter, *Journal*, 33.

102. Peebles, *Diary*, 268.

103. Enys, *American Journals*, 26; muster rolls, 29th Regiment of Foot, WO 12/4493.

104. Samuel Adams Drake, *Bunker Hill: The Story Told in Letters from the Battle Field by British Officers Engaged* (Boston: Nichols and Hall, 1875), 38.

105. Carter, *Genuine Detail*, 5.

106. *Pennsylvania Gazette*, September 4, 1776.

107. Gilchrist, "Captain Hon. William Leslie," 153-154.

108. Ibid., 160. Some words abbreviated in the original have been spelled out for clarity.

109. Mackenzie, *Diary*, 24.

110. Haslewood, "Journal," 55.

111. Downman, *Services*, 30.

112. Münchausen, *At General Howe's Side,* 26.

113. Peebles, *Diary*, 338.

114. Mackenzie, *Diary*, 389; Todd W. Braisted, *Grand Forage 1778: The Battleground around New York City* (Yardley, PA: Westholme, 2016), 57-60.

115. Orders given to the 37th Regiment, typical of those for all of the regiments ordered on the expedition, Frederick Mackenzie to James Cousseau, June 6, 1780,

HCP, vol. 104:23.

116. George Washington Papers, ser. 4, General Correspondence, June 7, 1780, LOC; muster rolls, 43rd Regiment of Foot, WO 12/5561.

117. Mackenzie, *Diary*, 284.

118. John Burgoyne, *A State of the Expedition from Canada, as Laid before the House of Commons* ... (London: J. Almon, 1780), 148. As early as 1794, authors began dramatically overstating this load, giving weights as much as 125 pounds. Charles Stedman, *History of the Origin, Progress, and Termination of the American War* (London, 1794), 1:128.

119. James Stuart, "Letters from America, 1780 and 1781," ed. K. C. Corsar, *Journal of the Society for Army Historical Research* 20, no. 79 (Autumn 1941): 135.

120. Don N. Hagist, "Unpublished Military Writings of Roger Lamb, Soldier in the 1775–1783 American War, Part 1," *Journal of the Society for Army Historical Research* 89, no. 360 (Winter 2011): 283-284.

CHAPTER 8. BEEF AND BREAD, FEVER AND FLUX, SWIMMING AND SACK RACES

1. Discharge of John Hopwood, WO 121/14/459.

2. General Orders, June 1, 1774, WO 36/1.

3. Trial of Benjamin Williams, WO 71/86 pp. 124-129.

4. General orders, June 1, 1774, WO 36/1.

5. Mackenzie, *Diary*, 435.

6. Daniel Chamier to Clinton, July 12, 1777, HCP, vol. 21:41.

7. General orders, November 14, 1776, orderly book, 17th Regiment of Foot, NYHS; general orders, June 24, 1777, orderly book, Major Acland's Grenadier Battalion, NYHS.

8. Edward Harvey to "Mr. Johnson," April 26, 1776, WO 3/6.

9. General orders, November 14 and 27, 1776, orderly book, 17th Regiment of Foot, NYHS.

10. Regimental orders, December 4, 1776, orderly book, 17th Regiment of Foot, NYHS; regimental orders for June 20, 1777, orderly book, 40th Regiment of Foot, LOC.

11. General orders, September 20, 1775, WO 36/1

12. General orders, January 5, 1776, WO 36/1.

13. Carter, *Genuine Detail*, 21.

14. Mackenzie, *Diary*, 395, 404.

15. Ibid., 432.

16. Regimental orders, June 20, 1777, orderly book, 40th Regiment of Foot, LOC.

17. Trial of Thomas Cook, WO 71/84 pp. 154-158.

18. André, *Journal*, 40.

19. Trial of Benjamin Reynard, WO 71/88 pp. 536-537.

20. Trial of Robert Mason and James Watson, WO 71/90 pp. 129-131.

21. Trial of Benjamin Allen, Thomas Jones and George McCulloch, WO 71/84 pp. 326-331; trial of John Walker, WO 71/85 pp. 302-305.

22. Regimental orders, October 19 and November 17, 1776, orderly book, 17th Regiment of Foot, NYHS.

23. Trial of William Fenton, William Hodgets, James Croker and John Betsworth, WO 71/85 pp. 196-202.

24. S. Sydney Bradford, ed., "Lord Francis Napier's Journal of the Burgoyne Campaign," *Maryland Historical Magaine* 57, no. 4 (December 1962): 315.

25. Mackenzie, *Diary*, 45.
26. Regimental orders, April 19, 1775, orderly book, 18th Regiment of Foot, NAM.
27. Trial of Thomas Parker, WO 71/82 pp. 80-89.
28. General orders, June 24, 1776, orderly books, 37th Regiment, ECP.
29. Inman, "George Inman's Narrative," 241.
30. Colin Lindsay, *Extracts from Colonel Tempelhoffe's History of the Seven Years War . . . to which is added a Narrative of Events at St. Lucie and Gibraltar* (London: T. Cadell, 1793), 339.
31. General orders, April 14, 1776, Howe, *Orderly Book*, 252.
32. Inman, "George Inman's Narrative," 238.
33. Thomas Glyn Journal, August 17, 1776, FL; Mackenzie, *Diary*, 227.
34. Trial of Thomas Sewell, WO 71/83 pp. 48-52.
35. Serle, *American Journal*, 71.
36. Loftus Cliffe to "Jack," September 21, 1776, Loftus Cliffe Papers, WLC.
37. Trial of Henry White, WO 71/92 pp. 213-217.
38. Peebles, *Diary*, 401.
39. Bamford, *Redcoat*, 198.
40. Thomas Glyn Journal, January 9, 1777, FL.
41. *Lost War*, 39; Thomas Stanley to "My Dear Friend," October 10, 1775, Thomas Stanley Letters, Boston Public Library.
42. General orders, September 17, 1775, WO 36/1; Mackenzie, *Diary*, 185-186.
43. Howe, *Orderly Book*, 193.
44. Rawdon, *Manuscripts*, 160.
45. *Lost War*, 57.
46. Peter Force, *American Archives*, 5th ser. (Washington, DC: M. St. Clair Clarke and Peter Force, 1848), 1:200.
47. See for example "Return of the Sick and Wounded in his Majesty's Hospital at New York," weekly returns for various weeks in 1777 and 1780, FMP, box 1, folders 6, 23, 24, and 25; and HCP, vols. 104:47, 118:47, 124:33a, 125:21.
48. For example, the 22nd, 43rd, and 54th Regiments, all serving in Rhode Island, prepared two years' worth of semiannual rolls in October 1778, covering periods from June through December 1776, January through June 1777, June through December 1777, and January through June 1778 (specifically, muster rolls cover December 25 through June 24, or June 25 through December 24 of each year). On these rolls, all prepared at the same time, the same men are listed as "sick" throughout the entire two-year period unless some other event caused their service to be discontinuous. Also, men unfit for service for any reason are recorded as "sick," including those wounded in battle. Because of this, the rolls prepared in October 1778 list men wounded in the Battle of Rhode Island, on August 29, 1778, as "sick" for the entire period from June 1776 through October 1778. Muster rolls, 22nd Regiment of Foot, WO 12/3872; muster rolls, 43rd Regiment of Foot; muster rolls, 54th Regiment of Foot, WO 12/6399; Return of the Killed, Wounded and Missing at Rhode Island, August 29, 1778, HCP, vol. 40:22.
49. Thomas Dickson Reide, *A View of the Diseases of the Army* (London: J. Johnson, 1793), 99-168.
50. Ibid., 40.
51. Robert Knox to Barrington, September 20, 1777, WO 1/11 pp. 179-180.
52. Hughes, *Journal*, 12.
53. "State of the Troops which arrived in the fleet from England under the Com-

mand of Vice admiral Arbuthnot, New York 1st. Septr. 1779," CO 5/98, p. 493.

54. Mariot Arbuthnot to George Germain, May 2, 1779, *Report on the Manuscripts of Mrs. Stopford-Sackville* (Hereford: Hereford Times Co., 1910), 2:127.

55. "State of the Troops," CO 5/98, p. 493.

56. Peebles, *Diary*, 289-290.

57. Ibid., 291. At that time there were fifteen grenadier companies organized into a single battalion; a week later they were split into two battalions. Ibid., 292.

58. Ibid., 296.

59. Henry Clinton, *The American Rebellion; Sir Henry Clinton's Narrative of His Campaigns, 1775–1782*, ed. William B. Willcox (New Haven, CT: Yale University Press, 1954), 141.

60. Peebles, *Diary*, 313.

61. Muster rolls, 42nd Regiment of Foot, WO 12/5553.

62. Muster rolls, 37th Regiment of Foot, WO 12/5101.

63. Muster rolls, 54th Regiment of Foot, WO 12/6399.

64. Minutes of an Hospital Board held at the College Hospital at New York 27th Sepr. 1779, HCP, vol. 69:27.

65. L. H. Butterfield, ed., *Letters of Benjamin Rush* (Princeton, NJ: Princeton University Press, 1951), 1:154-155.

66. Peebles, *Diary*, 296.

67. Robert Jackson, *Treatise on the Fevers of Jamaica* (London: J. Murray, 1791), 86-87.

68. Cornwallis to Clinton, August 10, 1780, *Cornwallis Papers*, 1:180. Each battalion of the 71st Regiment, when the grenadiers and light infantry were detached, consisted of eight companies with a full strength of one hundred private soldiers.

69. Jackson, *Treatise*, 299-300.

70. Rawdon to Cornwallis, August 2, 1780, *Cornwallis Papers*, 1:228.

71. Cornwallis to Clinton, September 23, 1780, ibid., 2:44; Cornwallis to Balfour, September 12, 1780, ibid., 2:80; Cornwallis to Balfour, September 13, 1780, ibid., 2:82.

72. Reide, *View of the Diseases*, 50.

73. Ibid., 161, 165.

74. Muster rolls, 29th Regiment of Foot, WO 12/4493; Reide, *View of the Diseases*, 155; Enys, *American Journals*, 26.

75. Return of the Killed, Wounded and Missing at Rhode Island, August 29, 1778, HCP, vol. 40:22; muster rolls, 22nd Regiment of Foot; Mackenzie, *Diary*, 435. Four officers were also wounded, of whom two died within three weeks and two recovered.

76. Return of the Killed Wounded & Missing of the Troops under the Command of Lt. Genl. Sr. Henry Clinton in the Storm of Forts Clinton & Montgomery on the 6th Octr 1777, CO 5/94 p. 699; muster rolls, 52nd Regiment of Foot, WO 12/6240; muster rolls, 57th Regiment of Foot, WO 12/6633; muster rolls 63rd Regiment of Foot, WO 12/7241.

77. Battalion orders, September 19, 1776, orderly book, 4th Battalion of Grenadiers, NAS.

78. Brigade orders for June 2, 1777, orderly book, 40th Regiment of Foot, LOC.

79. Battalion orders, June 5, 1777, orderly book, Major Acland's Grenadier Battalion, NYHS; general orders, June 8, 1777, *General Orders, Rhode Island*, 54.

80. Trial of Benjamin Allen, Thomas Jones and George Mculloch, WO 71/84 pp.

326-331.

81. Trial of John Walton and John Connell, WO 71/84 pp. 317-325.

82. Trial of John Connolly, WO 71/87 pp. 14-16.

83. Trial of Thomas Clarke and Joseph Taylor, WO 71/87 pp. 1-9.

84. Edward Harvey to Lord Lennox, July 27, 1776, WO 3/6.

85. Benjamin Rush to Anthony Wayne, September 29, 1776, in *Letters of the Delegates to Congress 1774–1789*, ed. Paul H. Smith (Washington, DC: Library of Congress, 1976), 5:262-263.

86. In May 1758, during the French and Indian War, Brigadier General George Howe, brother of the officer who would command in America in 1776, had "induced the army to cut their hair short leaving it not more than two finger's breadth long." François Pouchot, *Memoir upon the Late War in North America, between the French and English, 1755–60*, ed. Frederick Benjamin Hough (Roxbury, MA: W. E. Woodward, 1866), 1:110.

87. *Connecticut Courant*, May 19, 1777; muster rolls, 40th Regiment of Foot, WO 12/5318.

88. *Pennsylvania Gazette*, July 23, 1777.

89. Battalion orders, August 24, 1776, orderly book, 4th Battalion of Grenadiers, NAS.

90. Regimental orders, June 25 and August 15, 1776, orderly book, Royal Regiment of Artillery, May 8, 1776–June 29, 1777, Lloyd W. Smith Collection, Morristown National Historical Park.

91. Regimental orders, January 10, 1778, orderly book, Royal Artillery, September 28, 1777–February 21, 1778, James Pattison Papers, Royal Artillery Institution Library, Woolwich, UK.

92. Trial of John Love, Thomas Manning and John Clements, WO 71/87 pp. 245-250; muster rolls, 38th Regiment of Foot, WO 12/5171.

93. Murray, *Letters*, 27.

94. Rawdon, *Manuscripts*, 177.

95. Bamford, *Redcoat*, 183; *Lost War*, 75.

96. Peebles, *Diary*, 74, 75.

97. Regimental orders for June 8, 1777, orderly book, 40th Regiment of Foot, LOC.

98. Peebles, *Diary*, 172.

99. Ibid., 248, 255, 256.

100. *New York Gazette*, May 22, 1780.

101. *Lost War*, 126.

102. Peebles, *Diary*, 303; Enys, *American Journals*, 148; Joseph Strutt, *The Sports and Pastimes of the People of England* (London, 1801), 272.

103. Enys, *American Journals*, 148.

104. *Essex Gazette*, June 27, 1774; muster rolls, 64th Regiment of Foot, WO 12/7313.

105. Trial of Patrick Henry, WO 71/85 pp. 399-422.

106. John C. Dann, ed., *The Revolution Remembered* (Chicago: University of Chicago Press, 1980), 47.

107. Orders for July 22, 1775, orderly books, 37th Regiment, ECP.

108. Orders for April 6, 1780, recruiting accounts of Joab Aked, WYA.

109. Trial of Luke Murphy, WO 71/79 pp. 367-374; trial of William Norrington, WO 71/82 pp. 377-388; trial of John Dunn and John Lusty, WO 71/82 pp. 412-424; trial of Duncan Robinson, WO 71/86 pp. 393-396; trial of Jeremiah Nicolas, WO 71/86 pp. 239-250; trial of Thomas McChesnie, WO 71/90 pp. 95-102; trial of Bartholomew Gilmore, WO 71/90 pp. 26-34; trial of John and Sophie Sinclair,

WO 71/91 pp. 22-27.

110. Sullivan, *From Redcoat to Rebel*, 3.

111. Thomas Pasley, *Private Sea Journals, 1778–1782, Kept by Admiral Sir Thomas Pasley, bart.: when in command of H. M. ships Glasgow (20), Sybil (28) and Jupiter (50)*, ed. Robert M. S. Pasley (London: J. M. Dent and Sons, 1931), 204.

112. Memoir of William Hunter, private collection. At this writing, the memoir is being incorporated into a biography of William Hunter expected to be published in the next few years.

113. Scott, *Poems*, x-xi.

114. Butler, *Annals*, 317.

115. Trial of James Edwards and William Moran, WO 71/80 pp. 351-355.

116. Alexander Grant to "Ever Honoured father," August 19, 1775, private collection, sold by Swann Auction Galleries, Sale 2391–Lot 29, September 2015.

117. Thomas Plumb to Alexander Johns, February 22, 1777, HCA 30.272, The National Archives, Kew, UK.

118. Muster rolls, 22nd Regiment of Foot, WO 12/3872.

119. Duncan Grant to Lachlan Grant, September 12, 1777, GD248/509/3, NAS.

120. Richard Williams to Rosanna Williams, November 23, 1780, Bradford Family Papers, Box 23, HSP.

121. Trial of Owen Smith, WO 71/82 pp. 429-434.

122. Charles Hay, August 28, 1776, and John Elborn, August 28, 1776, WO 1/993.

123. Peleg W. Chandler, *Notes from American Criminal Trials* (Boston: Charles C. Little and James Brown, 1844), 2:43; Lamb, *British Soldier's Story*, 59.

124. Trial of William Naylor, WO 71/89 pp. 77-193.

125. Soldiers' discharges, WO 121/1 through /15. The sample includes only those discharge forms that explicitly mention service in America. The collection includes discharges for many more men who served in America but whose service there has not been confirmed by correlating their discharges to muster rolls.

126. Trial of Benjamin Charnock Payne, WO 71/81 pp. 2-165.

127. See for example regimental orders, Royal Artillery, January 6, 1776, WO 55/677.

128. Peebles, *Diary*, 204.

129. Simes, *Military Medley*, 33.

130. Gregory J. W. Urwin, "Irish Catholics in the British Army of the American Revolution: The Article behind the Uniform," *Brigade Dispatch* 14, no. 1 (Summer 1978): 20-21.

131. Liste Des Recrués Anglois embarqués á Stade pour Spithead en Irlande ce 14me de Mai 1776, WO 43/405.

132. Trial of Benjamin Charnock Payne, WO 71/81 pp. 2-165.

133. "Letter of a Dying Soldier," *Evangelical Magazine* 5 (1797): 414. The letter was reprinted, with variations, in a number of publications, including Roger Lamb, *An Original and Authentic Journal of Occurrences during the Late American War* (Dublin: Wilkinson & Courtney, 1809), 35. The letter was either signed by, or submitted to the magazine by, "John Randon," and names Corporal Samuel Pierce.

134. Jonas Hanway, *The Seaman's Christian Friend* (London, 1779), iii; John Wesley, *The Journal of the Reverend John Wesley* (New York: J. Collord, 1832), 2:518.

135. Sullivan, *From Redcoat to Rebel*, 222.

136. Rawdon, *Manuscripts*, 183-184.

137. Hagist, *British Soldiers*, 120.

138. Don N. Hagist, "Unpublished Military Writings of Roger Lamb, Part 2," *Jour-*

nal of the Society for Army Historical Research 90, no. 362 (Summer 2012): 81.

139. Hagist, *British Soldiers,* 67.

140. John Shuttleworth to John Spencer, Quebec, January 2, 1774; A. M. W. Stirling, *Annals of a Yorkshire House, from the papers of a Macaroni & his Kindred* (London: John Lane, 1911), 2:340.

141. R. Arthur Bowler, *Logistics and the Failure of the British Army in America* (Princeton, NJ: Princeton University Press, 1975), 8; Norman Baker, *Government and Contractors: The British Treasury and War Supplies, 1775–1783* (London: Athlone Press, 1971), 162; Loftus Cliffe to "Jack," September 21, 1776, Loftus Cliffe Papers, WLC.

142. Peebles, *Diary,* 432.

143. Trial of Bartholomew Gilmore, WO 71/90 pp. 26-34; trial of Thomas McCowan, WO 71/97 pp. 243-246; trial of John Betsworth, Robert Wilkins and George Hewston, WO 71/90 pp. 408-410; trial of Hamilton Henry, WO 71/92 pp. 53-55.

144. Trial of Evan Evans, WO 71/84 p. 48-51; trial of John Sullivan, WO 71/84 pp. 147-149.

145. Violet Biddulph, "Letters of Robert Biddulph, 1779–1783," *American Historical Review* 29, no. 1 (October 1923): 90.

146. Peebles, *Diary,* 368.

147. Jackson, *Treatise,* 303-304.

148. "Extract of a letter from an Officer of the 15th regiment, to his friend here, dated at the Camp near Cape Fear, North Carolina, May 17th," *Caledonian Mercury* (Edinburgh), August 2, 1776.

CHAPTER 9. THE PLUNDER PROBLEM

1. James Abercrombie to Cadwallader Colden, May 2, 1775, *Proceedings of the Massachusetts Historical Society,* 2nd ser., vol. 11 (Boston: printed by the Society, 1897), 306. He arrived in America from Great Britain on April 23.

2. Williams, *Discord,* 14.

3. General orders, undated entry (shortly after April 19, 1775), mss. p. 79, WO 36/1.

4. General orders, December 5, 1775, WO 36/1.

5. General orders, December 31, 1776, January 8, April 8, May 22, and August 29, 1777, and proclamation of March 31, 1777, *General Orders, Rhode Island,* 40-41. Some of these orders pertained to the effect of damaging fencing on agriculture rather than explicitly referring to theft of rails for firewood.

6. General orders, December 24, 1776, and May 22, 1777, *General Orders, Rhode Island,* 15, 48.

7. For an example of the losses incurred by one inhabitant, see Susan Stanton Brayton, "Silas Cooke—A Victim of the Revolution," *Rhode Island Historical Society Collections* 31 (1938): 110-116.

8. General orders, August 23, 1776, WO 36/5; general orders, August 26, 1776, WO 36/5.

9. General orders, September 6, 1776, WO 36/5; Mackenzie, *Diary,* 40.

10. Trial of John Kelly, John Scofield, Henry Swaffield and Thomas Ingram, WO 71/82 pp. 405-425. John Kelly, the only man convicted, deserted two years later. Muster rolls, 27th Regiment of Foot, WO 12/4328.

11. Mackenzie, *Diary,* 56.

12. Trial of Bryan Sweeny and James Gardner, WO 71/83 pp. 41-48; muster rolls, 22nd Regiment of Foot, WO 12/3872; discharge of Bryan Sweeny, WO 121/12/371.

Sweeny's name is also written as McSweeny and Swyneyard.

13. Kemble, "Journals," 91, 96, 98.

14. For more on attitudes of British officers toward their German allies, see Stephen R. Conway, "The British Army, 'Military Europe,' and the American War of Independence," *William and Mary Quarterly* 67, no. 1 (January 2010): 98-99.

15. Brigade orders, December 15, 1776, orderly book, 17th Regiment of Foot, NYHS.

16. Peebles, *Diary*, 7; Hunter, *Journal*, 27.

17. André, *Journal*, 29, 33. No records from these trials have been found.

18. Deposition of William Tay Jr., December 13, 1775, in Richard Frothingham, *History of the Siege of Boston* (Boston: Little, Brown, 1851), 369.

19. *Proceedings of the Lexington Historical Society*, vol. 1 (Lexington, MA: Lexington Historical Society, 1890), 52-53.

20. Kemble, "Journals," 97-98.

21. *Military Instructions by the King of Prussia*, trans. T. Forster (London, 1762), 31-33.

22. Force, *American Archives*, 1:814; muster rolls, 40th Regiment of Foot, WO 12/5318.

23. Force, *American Archives*, 1:814.

24. General orders, September 18, 1777, orderly book, 47th Regiment of Foot, ACC.

25. André, *Journal*, 37.

26. General orders, August 26, 1777, "British Army Orders," 477-478.

27. Downman, *Services*, 30.

28. General orders, August 29, 1777, "British Army Orders," 480.

29. André, *Journal*, 42; Peebles, *Diary*, 129.

30. Proceedings of trials between August 29, 1777, and January 31, 1778, WO 71. These figures include only charges of plundering and robbery. There were trials for a number of other crimes, particularly desertion, during this period. One trial, that of Edward Riley of the 15th Regiment, is mentioned in general orders but not recorded in WO 71. General orders, September 24, 1777, "British Army Orders," 504.

31. Trial of William Johnstone, WO 71/84 pp. 197-200.

32. Trial of Abraham Pike, William Houston and John Smith, WO 71/84 pp. 200-202; trial of William King, WO 71/84 pp. 202-204.

33. General orders, September 2, 1777, in "British Army Orders," 483.

34. Downman, *Services*, 31.

35. Peebles, *Diary*, 129.

36. Richard Fitzpatrick to Lady Ossory, September 1, 1777, in Horace Walpole, *Characteristic Sketches of Society, Politics, and Literature; comprised in a series of letters addressed to The Countess of Ossory* (London: Richard Bentley, 1848), 1:311n.

37. General orders, September 10, 1777, "British Army Orders," 491; muster rolls, 1st Regiment of Foot 1st Battalion, WO 12/1882; muster rolls, 10th Regiment of Foot, WO 12/2750.

38. Muster rolls, 49th Regiment of Foot, WO 12/6032.

39. Trial of Robert Hicks and Thomas Burrows, WO 71/84 pp. 262-266; trial of Thomas Burford, John Jackson and Richard Jones, WO 71/84 pp. 266-270; general orders, September 20 and 24, 1777, "British Army Orders," pp. 499-500, 504.

40. "Diary of Robert Morton," *Pennsylvania Magazine of History and Biography* 1, no. 1 (1877): 9-10.

41. Trial of John Walton and John Connell, WO 71/84 pp. 317-325; general orders,

October 5, 1777, "British Army Orders," 510-511.

42. Trial of Benjamin Allen, Thomas Jones and George McCulloch, WO 71/84 pp. 317-325; general orders, October 5, 1777, "British Army Orders," 511; "Men that are Dead of the Coldstream Regt. in the Detachment of Foot Guards in America," Orders, Returns, Morning Reports and Accounts of the Brigade of Foot Guards, National Archives and Records Administration (hereafter NARA), Washington, DC; muster rolls, 49th Regiment of Foot, WO 12/6032.

43. Ferguson to Clinton, October 9, 1779, Peckham, *Sources*, 2:336-337, 339.

44. Robert Pigot to William Howe, September 30, 1777, HCP, vol. 24:28.

45. Trial of Murtoch Laughlan, Charles Neal and Robert Pearce, WO 71/85 pp. 159-166.

46. Brayton, "Silas Cooke," 110-116.

47. Muster rolls, 38th Regiment of Foot; "Examinations of Invalid Soldiers," March 8, 1783, Pension Admission Book, WO 116/8.

48. Trial of John Love, Thomas Manning and John Clements, WO 71/85 pp. 209-216.

49. General orders, December 7, 1776, *General Orders, Rhode Island*, 3.

50. Trial of Thomas Edwards, WO 71/83 pp. 102-108.

51. See for example general orders, November 30, 1776, orderly book, 17th Regiment of Foot, NYHS; Ferguson to Clinton, October 9, 1779, Peckham, *Sources*, 2:336-337, 339.

52. Trial of Thomas Clark and Joseph Taylor, WO 71/87 pp. 1-9.

53. Trial of John Sutherland, WO71/87 pp. 335-337.

54. Muster rolls, 44th Regiment of Foot, WO 12/5637.

55. Trial of John Sutherland, WO71/90 pp. 9-11; Peebles, *Diary*, 276, 279.

56. Trial of Alexander Cumming, Hugh Mulloy, Allan Boyd, Archibald Campbell, Donald McDonald and Simon Frazer, WO 71/88 pp. 346-350.

57. Recruiting leaflet, 71st Regiment, NMS.

58. Trial of Thomas Reedman, WO 71/88 pp. 324-330; trial of William Steedman, Donald Monroe and Thomas Martin, WO 71/88 pp. 330-334; trial of Michael Farrell, WO 71/88 pp. 336-338.

59. Trial of Patrick Welsh, Thomas Adams, George Boyce, Walter George, Charles Toyee and Henry Rigby, WO 71/88 pp. 362-372.

60. Peebles, *Diary*, 255, 260.

61. Ibid., 303, 310. There are no general court-martial records associated with these punishments; they were apparently tried by battalion courts instead of general courts.

62. Trial of William Deane, WO 71/90 pp. 410-416; trial of John Gaurnsey, William McGlaughlin and William Belshar, WO 71/92 pp. 37-44.

63. Trial of John Harris, James Carey and John Williams, WO 71/88 pp. 393-398; trial of William Green and Thomas Salim, WO 71/90 pp. 376-383; trial of Robert Hughes, WO 71/90 pp. 405-408.

64. Data from WO 71/88 through 71/96.

65. "Examinations of Invalid Soldiers," November 10, 1780, Pension Admission Book, WO 116/7.

66. Peebles, *Diary*, 316.

67. Trial of nine soldiers of the Kings American Regiment, WO 71/92 pp. 227-238.

68. Peebles, *Diary*, 421-422; trial of Alexander McDonald, WO 71/92 pp. 411-419.

69. Peebles, *Diary*, 456-457; trial of Alexander McDonald, WO 71/94 pp. 297-302.

70. Muster rolls, 42nd Regiment of Foot, WO 12/5553.

71. That many British army officers understood the detrimental effects of plundering,

but also advocated harsh treatment of rebellious Americans, is discussed in Stephen Conway, "To Subdue America: British Army Officers and the Conduct of the Revolutionary War," *William and Mary Quarterly*, 3rd ser., vol. 43, no. 3 (July 1986): 381-407, and Stephen Conway, "'The Great Mischief Complain'd of': Reflections on the Misconduct of British Soldiers in the Revolutionary War," *William and Mary Quarterly*, 3rd ser., vol. 47, no. 3 (July 1990): 370-390.

CHAPTER 10. BRINGERS HANDSOMELY REWARDED

1. John Hawthorn, "The Journey and Observations of a Countryman," *Poems* (Printed for the author and sold by E. Easton [Salisbury, UK], J. Dodsley, and J. Wilkie [London], 1779), 31-32.
2. Establishments, 1777–1779, WO 379.
3. Recruiting poster for the 22nd Regiment circa 1778, Cheshire Military Museum, Chester, UK; 52nd Regiment recruiting poster circa 1779, courtesy Eric H. Schnitzer; 45th Regiment recruiting poster circa 1779, print 2006-18,1, Colonial Williamsburg Foundation, Williamsburg, VA.
4. 22nd Light Dragoons (Sussex Light Dragoons) recruiting poster circa 1779, NAM; 88th Regiment recruiting poster circa 1780, NAM.
5. *Public Advertiser* (London), February 17, 1778; *Aris's Gazette* (Birmingham), January 21, January 26, February 2, February 5, March 16, April 27, 1778.
6. Inspection return, 74th Regiment, April 13, 1778, WO 34/195.
7. Inspection return, 76th Regiment, May 11, 1778, WO 34/195.
8. Inspection return, 80th Regiment, May 11, 1778, WO 34/195.
9. Inspection return, 82nd Regiment, April 16, 1778, WO 34/195.
10. Graham, *Memoir*, 9-11.
11. 45th Regiment recruiting poster circa 1779, Colonial Williamsburg; 52nd Regiment recruiting poster circa 1779, courtesy Eric H. Schnitzer; 88th Regiment recruiting poster circa 1780, NAM; 22nd Regiment recruiting poster circa 1778, Cheshire Military Museum.
12. Francis Grose, *A Classical Dictionary of the Vulgar Tongue*, ed. Eric Partridge (New York: Dorset Press, 1992), 105.
13. James Miller, "Memoirs of an Invalid," Amherst Papers, U1350 Z9A, Centre for Kentish Studies, Maidstone, UK, quoted in Peter Way, "Locating the Lower Orders: Recovering the Lives of 18th Century Soldiers," presented at Canada on Display: Celebrating the Teaching of History at Trent, Trent University, Peterborough, Ontario, April 13, 2007, scholar.uwindsor.ca/historypres/5.
14. Stephen Brumwell, *Redcoats: The British Soldier and War in the Americas, 1755–1763* (Cambridge: Cambridge University Press, 2002), 63-64.
15. Curtis, *Organization*, 59-60.
16. William Jackson to Leonard Morse, November 22, 1778, WO 34/225 pp. 3-4.
17. WO 4/966 pp. 402-407.
18. Curtis, *Organization*, 66; Stephen R. Conway, "The Recruitment of Criminals into the British Army, 1775–81," *Historical Research* 58 (May 1985): 48.
19. Additional companies alone recruited almost 3,500 men between March 1 and October 31, 1779; added to the 7,700 in the eleven new-raised regiments, over 11,000 men were recruited, of whom fewer than 1,000 were pressed. Returns of recruits raised by additional companies, CO 5/171 pp. 152-218.
20. Embarkation Return of the Additional Companies Embarked from Chatham Barracks to compleat the Regiments in North America, March 26, 1779, HCP, vol. 55:5.
21. "Extract of a letter from Chatham, June 2," *Post and Daily Advertiser* (London),

June 3, 1779.

22. Embarkation Return of the Additional Companies Embarked from Chatham Barracks to compleat the Regiments in North America, March 26, 1779, HCP, vol. 55:5.

23. WO 34/150 fol. 129.

24. WO 4/966 pp. 402-407.

25. *Leicester Journal*, March 13, 1779.

26. Barrington to sheriffs in various shires, June 25, 1778, WO 4/965 pp. 8-10.

27. Letters dated March 20 and March 23, 1779, WO 4/966.

28. WO 4/966 pp. 402-407.

29. Charles Jenkinson to commanding officer of the 37th Foot at New York, June 30, 1779, PRO 30/55/17/64; William Watkins to Jenkinson, July 17, 1780, PRO 30/55/24/100; Clinton to Jenkinson, October 28, 1780, PRO 30/55/26/48; muster rolls, 37th Regiment of Foot, WO 12/5101.

30. Memorandum concerning David Honeyman, WO 34/225 p. 386; Thomas Oltrup to Amherst, September 9, 1781, WO 34/225 p. 414.

31. John Matson, *Indian Warfare: or, the Extraordinary Adventures of John Matson the Kidnapped Youth, late of Kingsland Road, London; formerly of Bridlington Quay, in the County of York; Architect and Builder* (London: Effingham Wilson, 1842), 16-18.

32. Grose, *Military Antiquities*, 1:100.

33. *Belfast Newsletter*, March 3, 1780.

34. Trial of John Ingram, WO 71/83 pp. 171-172.

35. Trial of George Hartley, WO 71/83 pp. 420-426; muster rolls, 59th Regiment of Foot, WO 12/6786; muster rolls, 38th Regiment of Foot, WO 12/5171; general orders, July 10, 1777, "British Army Orders," 468.

36. Samuel Hazard, ed., *Pennsylvania Archives* (Philadelphia: Joseph Severns, 1853), 5:410; muster rolls, 23rd Regiment of Foot, WO 12/3960.

37. Muster rolls, 23rd Regiment of Foot, WO 12/3960; Thompson Westcott, *Names of Persons who took the Oath of Allegiance to the State of Pennsylvania between the years 1777 and 1780* (Philadelphia: John Campbell, 1865), 68.

38. See for example Curtis, *Organization*, 56.

39. Among the acts of Parliament providing the option of military service are the 1744 Salt Duties Act, 17 Geo. II, c. 5; the 1776 Insolvent Debtors Relief Act, 16 Geo. III c. 38; and the 1776 Natural-born Children of Aliens Act, 18 Geo. III c. 52.

40. Conway, "Recruitment," 46-58.

41. *Leicester Journal*, March 20, 1779.

42. Sessions held at Bodmin, October 1779, QS/1/4/247, Cornwall Record Office.

43. Huntingdonshire Quarter Sessions, 1780, HCP/1/1 - HCP/1/9, Cambridgeshire County Record Office.

44. Sessions held at Truro, April 26, 1781, QS/1/4/299-306, Cornwall Record Office.

45. Sessions held at Truro, October 10, 1782, QS/1/4/367 and QS/1/4/370, Cornwall Record Office.

46. Conway, "Recruitment." Records for Scotland and Ireland are not available.

47. John Ridout to Barrington, August 10, 1776, WO 1/993.

48. Muster rolls, 46th Regiment of Foot, WO 12/5797. Herbert's given name is John on the August 1776 letter but William on the muster rolls. Inconsistencies of first names are not uncommon on muster rolls, but it is also possible they are not the same man; William Herbert joined the regiment on the same date as two of the

other men from Shrewsbury jail.

49. *Edinburgh Advertiser*, December 6, 1776.

50. WO 34/225 pp. 159, 267, 294, 336.

51. WO 34/203 pp. 226.

52. John Spilsbury, *A Journal of the Siege of Gibraltar 1779–1783 by Captain Spilsbury, 12th Regiment*, ed. B. H. J. Frere (Gibraltar: Gibraltar Garrison Library, 1908), 65.

53. For examples of emphasizing the negative aspects of drafting, see Curtis, *Organization*, 78-80, and Houlding, *Fit for Service*, 120-125.

54. Grose, *Military Antiquities*, 1:185n.

55. Return of the Eight Hundred Privates Draughted from the Additional Companies of the American Regiments to the Regiments at Gibraltar, May 2, 1778, WO 34/225 p. 414.

56. Report dated October 25, 1780, CO 5/100, quoted in Curtis, *Organization*, 80n91.

57. "A Trial for Mutiny," *Scots Magazine* 41 (1779): 271-272, 305-308.

58. Grose, *Military Antiquities*, 1:186n.

59. *Leeds Intelligencer*, March 23, 1779; *Whitehall Evening Post* (London), April 1, 1780; *Norfolk Chronicle*, April 15, 1780; *Gazetteer and New Daily Advertiser* (London), April 18, 1780.

60. Hagist, *British Soldiers*, 17-18.

61. Recruiting accounts of Joab Aked, WYA; Service Returns, WO 25/1126; muster rolls, 22nd Regiment of Foot, WO 12/3872.

62. For example, Cuthbertson, *System*, and Simes, *Military Medley*.

63. This manual was widely reprinted throughout Great Britain and in the American colonies in the 1760s and 1770s.

64. For examples of this terminology see the trial of Robert Hicks and Thomas Burrows, WO 71/84 pp. 262-266, and the trial of William Grinsell, Edward Webb and Eleanor Webb, WO 71/91 pp. 40-47.

65. This can be seen in the muster rolls of any regiment, with few exceptions.

66. Regimental orders, October 21, 1776; orderly book, 40th Regiment of Foot, MAHS.

67. Mackenzie, *Diary*, 580.

68. Muster rolls, 22nd Regiment of Foot, WO 12/3872; muster rolls, 38th Regiment of Foot, WO 12/5172.

69. Mackenzie, *Diary*, 696. Mackenzie wrote on November 18, 1781, "138 Recruits lately drafted to the 17th, 23rd & 33rd Regiments, were drafted this day to the 40th, 54th, & 57th at Brooklyn," but only the muster rolls of the 40th Regiment show receipt of drafts from those regiments. The 40th received at least 114, and some recruits for the 43rd Regiment, also taken at Yorktown, were put into the 54th and 57th Regiments.

70. General orders, December 3 and 10, 1775; Howe, *Orderly Book*, 159, 163.

71. See for example muster rolls, 38th Regiment of Foot, WO 12/5171.

72. Regimental orders, October 22, 1776, orderly book, 40th Regiment of Foot, MAHS.

73. Regimental orders, November 13, 1776, orderly book, 40th Regiment of Foot, MAHS.

74. See for example Peebles, *Diary*, 35, 40.

75. General orders, June 3, 1777, orderly book, 40th Regiment of Foot, LOC.

76. Brigade orders, May 13, 1777, orderly book, 40th Regiment of Foot, LOC.

77. General orders, March 30, 1778, orderly books, 37th Regiment, ECP.

78. Peebles, *Diary*, 429, 434, 436.
79. Regimental orders, June 1, 1778, orderly book, 2nd Battalion 71st Regiment, HL.
80. Standing orders, June 30, 1778, ibid.

CHAPTER II. BOUNTIES, WAGES, REWARDS, PRIZES, AND PROMOTIONS

1. Trial of Isaac Neuman, WO 71/96 pp. 106-112.
2. Sullivan, *From Redcoat to Rebel*, 27.
3. Robert Campbell Account Book, Rubenstein Library, Duke University, Durham, North Carolina (hereafter RL).The book contains accounts for seventy private soldiers, of which the final balance due is clearly stated for forty-seven. Of those, four were due less than one pound, seven between one and two pounds, seven between two and three pounds, three between three and four pounds, eight between four and five pounds, seven between five and six pounds, four between six and seven pounds, five between seven and eight pounds, one was due nine pounds ten shillings, and one was due eleven pounds fifteen shillings.
4. Williamson, *Treatise on Military Finance*, 10-13, 19.
5. "Acquittance Roll of Brigadier General Macleans Co.," Malcolm Fraser Papers, vol. 32, PAC.
6. Orders, Returns, Morning Reports and Accounts of the Brigade of Foot Guards, NARA.
7. For example, "All money due by the different departments to the troops for work, to be paid weekly into the hands of the Quarter Masters of the several Corps, and the Commanding Officers will order it to be accounted for to the men at proper periods." General orders, October 14, 1775, WO 36/1.
8. "An Account of Work done by the 57th Regiment at Paulus Hook," private collection; the work was done from October 11 to November 20, 1776. An additional ten men were paid ten pence per day for ten days of work in January 1777.
9. Sullivan, *From Redcoat to Rebel*, 26.
10. Mackenzie, *Diary*, 245. In April, the 43rd Regiment was paid four dollars per cord for 150 cords they had cut during the course of a month. Ibid., 264.
11. General orders, November 31, 1778, orderly books, 1st Battalion of Light Infantry, ECP.
12. For example, "The Shoemakers of the Regt are exqused attending parade in order that the mens shoe as may require it." Regimental orders, February 28, 1779, orderly book, Captain Clayton's company, 17th Regiment of Foot, HL.
13. Brigade orders, December 24 and 26, orderly book, 17th Regiment of Foot, NYHS.
14. Account of Cash paid by J: Smith for His Excellency Sir H. Clinton K.B. HCP, vol. 68:14.
15. "Examinations of Invalid Soldiers," April 14, 1784, Pension Admission Book, WO 116/8,.
16. "Abstract of Pay due for Men employed in the Boat at Paulus Hook, from 27th May to 30th June 1782, being 35 days," PRO 30/55/4964.
17. General orders, November 3, 7 and 9, 1775, WO 36/1; general orders, August 12, 1776, WO 36/5; general orders, June 7, 1777, orderly book, Major Acland's Grenadier Battalion, NYHS; general orders, July 28, 1777, orderly book, 47th Regiment of Foot, ACC.
18. Trial of Evan Evans, WO 71/84 pp. 48-51.
19. *Royal Gazette* (New York), February 28, 1778. The first line of the ad incorrectly

gives his regiment as the 52nd, but the final line, and the 57th's muster rolls, confirm it as the 57th. Muster rolls, 57th Regiment of Foot, WO 12/6633.

20. Forbes MacBean to John Nairne, April 4, 1782, John and Thomas Nairne fonds, MG 23, GIII23, vol. 3, Entrybook of Correspondence, p. 221, PAC.

21. A total of 1,072 men, excluding officers, served in the regiment between the middle of 1774 and the end of 1783; 197 are explicitly annotated as drafts during those years, and a few more are known from other sources to be drafts. Muster rolls, 38th Regiment of Foot, WO 12/5171 and WO 12/5172.

22. Muster rolls, 22nd Regiment of Foot, WO 12/3872.

23. Muster rolls, 52nd Regiment of Foot, WO 12/6240; muster rolls, 59th Regiment of Foot, WO 12/6786.

24. Each company received forty-five pounds thirteen shillings, before a deduction of 4 percent, divided equally among the men. Soldiers in the 42nd Regiment's grenadier company received eighteen shillings nine pence each, a lower amount than most because that company was bigger than most. Peebles, *Diary*, 244.

25. Payments to sergeants, corporals, private men and drummers on Major General Leslie's expedition to Virginia, 1780, Parker Family Papers, City of Liverpool Public Libraries.

26. Robert Campbell Account Book, RL.

27. Based on "List of Non Commissioned Officers Drums & private men of the Light Compy of the 22d Regt intitled to prise Money Canterbury Feby 19 1784," D/DB 1059, Essex Record Office, Chelmsford, UK.

28. General orders, July 6, 1776, orderly books, 37th Regiment, ECP; general orders, August 21, 1777, orderly book, 47th Regiment of Foot, ACC.

29. General orders, September 27, 1777, orderly book, 2nd Battalion of Light Infantry, LOC; general orders, June 23, 1778; orderly book, 2nd Battalion of Grenadiers, LOC.

30. General orders, August 2, 1774, WO 36/1; Hagist, *British Soldiers*, 253.

31. Brigade orders, March 25, 1778, orderly books, 37th Regiment, ECP; trial of Charles Fraser, Dudley Wells, Henry Hart and Cornelius Drewry, WO 71/85 pp. 155-158.

32. General orders, August 28, 1776, WO 36/5.

33. General orders, August 29, 1777, "British Army Orders," 480.

34. Stirke, "British Officer's Revolutionary War Journal," 170.

35. Stephen Payne Adye to Andrew Elliot, December 29, 1779, "Official Letters of Major General James Pattison," 328.

36. *General Orders, Rhode Island*, 37.

37. Hunter, *Journal*, 21-22.

38. Trial of James Cairns, WO 71/82 pp. 241-250.

39. Gilchrist, "Captain Hon. William Leslie," 171.

40. Hagist, *British Soldiers*, 231.

41. General orders, August 31, 1775, WO 36/1.

42. Weekly State of the Provost New York, August 28, 1780, HCP, vol. 119:14.

43. *Newport Gazette*, August 26, 1779.

44. Baule and Hagist, "Regimental Punishment Book," 13-18; Punishment Book of the 44th Regiment of Foot, MG23, K6(2), PAC.

45. Trial of Thomas Bell, WO 71/80 pp. 356-360.

46. Trial of John Porter, William Webb and James Wollaner, WO 71/96 pp. 27-34.

47. Brigade orders, December 23, 1776, orderly book, 17th Regiment of Foot,

NYHS.
48. Regimental orders, October 10, 1776, orderly book, 17th Regiment of Foot, NYHS; regimental orders, June 24, 1777, orderly book, 40th Regiment of Foot, LOC.
49. Miscellaneous Numbered Records, No. 31,726, NARA.
50. Trial of Thomas Reedman, William Steedman, Donald Monroe and Thomas Martin, WO 71/88 pp. 324-334.
51. Regimental orders, August 15, 1778, orderly book, 2nd Battalion 71st Regiment, HL.
52. Muster rolls, 17th Regiment of Foot, WO 12/3406.
53. William L. Stone, *Orderly book of Sir John Johnson during his campaign against Fort Stanwix* (New York: A. S. Barnes, 1881), 74.
54. General orders, December 8, 1776, *General Orders, Rhode Island*, 4; discharge of Jacob Margas, WO 121/11/337.
55. General orders, October 2, 1777, orderly book, 2nd Battalion of Light Infantry, LOC.
56. Stephen Payne Adye to Henry Bruen, June 30, 1780, "Official Letters of Major General James Pattison," 405.
57. Lamb, *British Soldier's Story*, 113.
58. Memorial of John Hutton, PRO 30/55/54/82.
59. General orders, September 30, 1776, WO 36/5; general orders, October 2, 1777, orderly book, 2nd Battalion of Light Infantry, LOC.
60. General orders, July 31 1775, orderly books, 37th Regiment, ECP.
61. Muster rolls, 22nd Regiment of Foot, WO 12/3871 and WO 12/3872; muster rolls, 15th Regiment of Foot, WO 12/3229; 1783 inspection return, 15th Regiment of Foot, WO 27/51.
62. Muster rolls, 23rd Regiment of Foot, WO 12/3960; muster rolls, 27th Regiment of Foot, WO 12/4328.
63. Williamson, *Treatise on Military Finance*, 19. Pay rates were slightly higher in the Foot Guards, cavalry, and artillery. Ibid., 14-20.
64. Muster rolls, 44th Regiment of Foot, WO 12/5637; *Gentleman's Magazine* 76 (November 1794): 1062; Thomas Carter, *Historical record of the Forty-Fourth: or the East Essex regiment* (Chatham, UK: Gale & Polden, 1887), 33.
65. Loyalist Regiment Muster Rolls: New York Volunteers, RG 8, "C" ser., vol. 1874, p. 51, PAC; CO 42/46/246-253; CO 5/111/446-462.
66. Draft letter of Edward Winslow, c-1781, Winslow Papers, vol. 2, no. 41, University of New Brunswick.
67. Trial of Patrick Henry, WO 71/85 pp. 399-422.
68. Peebles, *Diary*, 317.
69. Trial of William King, WO 71/84 pp. 202-204.
70. Cuthbertson, *System*, 169; General orders, February 6, 1776, Howe, *Orderly Book*, 209.
71. General orders, March 13, 1776, "British Army Orders," 236; regimental orders, December 19, 1776, orderly book, 17th Regiment of Foot, NYHS.
72. Brigade orders, May 10, 1777, orderly book, 40th Regiment of Foot, LOC.
73. Peebles, *Diary*, 128.
74. Münchausen, *At General Howe's Side*, 31; Hunter, *Journal*, 29; W. H. Wilkin, ed., *Some British Soldiers in America* (London: H. Rees, 1914), 231. Today, the "Grenadiers March" is called "The British Grenadiers."
75. Enoch Anderson, *Personal recollections of Captain Enoch Anderson, an officer of the Delaware regiments in the revolutionary war* (Wilmington: Historical Society of

Delaware, 1896), 39-40.

76. Butler, *Annals*, 305, 315.

77. George A. Wheeler, "Sergeant Lawrence's Journal," *History of Castine, Penobscot and Brooksville, Maine* (Bangor: Burr & Robinson, 1875), 317.

78. Papers of Lt., later Capt., John Peebles of the 42nd. Foot ("The Black Watch"), 1776–1782, Cunninghame of Thorntoun Papers (GD 21/492), book 11, pp. 16-21, NAS.

79. Simes, *Regulator*, 204; Jeremy Lister, *Concord Fight: Being so much of the Narrative of Ensign Jeremy Lister of the 10th Regiment of Foot as pertains to his services on the 19th of April, 1775, and to his experiences in Boston during the early months of the siege* (Cambridge, MA: Harvard University Press, 1931), 33.

80. Mackenzie, *Diary*, 286.

81. General Orders, December 15, 1780; A. R. Newsome, ed., "A British Orderly Book, 1780–1781," *North Carolina Historical Review* 9 (1932): 179.

82. Rawdon to Cornwallis, April 26, 1781, *Cornwallis Papers*, 4:181.

83. Muster rolls, 4th Regiment of Foot, WO 12/2194; muster rolls, 40th Regiment of Foot, WO 12/5318.

84. Muster rolls, 23rd Regiment of Foot, WO 12/3960.

85. Muster rolls, 22nd Regiment of Foot, WO 12/3872. The band members are identified on the muster book of the *Robust*, which carried part of the regiment briefly in 1781. Muster book, HMS *Robust*, ADM 36/8499.

86. See for example drummer George Burch Jr. and George Burch Sr. in the 10th Regiment, and drummer Edward Royce and Sergeant Edward Royce of the 59th Regiment, Muster rolls, 10th Regiment of Foot, WO 12/2750; muster rolls, 59th Regiment of Foot, WO 12/6786.

87. James Pattison to Anthony Farrington, January 19, 1779, "Official Letters of Major General James Pattison," 7.

88. Return of the 31st Regiment of Foot, WO 28/10 pp. 158-174.

89. Return of the 34th Regiment of Foot, WO 28/10 pp. 194-201.

90. Peebles, *Diary*, 204.

91. James Pattison to Anthony Farrington, April 12, 1779, "Official Letters of Major General James Pattison," 36.

92. Regimental orders, October 22, 1776, orderly book, 40th Regiment of Foot, MAHS; regimental orders, June 10, 1777, orderly book, 40th Regiment of Foot, LOC.

93. Regimental orders, May 23, 1777, orderly book, 40th Regiment of Foot, LOC; Peebles, *Diary*, 105.

94. General orders, July 8, 1774, WO 36/1; general orders, October 13, 1775, WO 36/1.

95. Cuthbertson, *System*, 148; general orders, May 21, 1776, orderly books, 37th Regiment, ECP; general orders, June 20, 1777, orderly book, Major Acland's Grenadier Battalion, NYHS.

96. Cuthbertson, *System*, 148.

97. Graydon, *Memoirs*, 192.

98. Diary of Thompson Forster, Staff Surgeon to His Majesty's Detached Hospital in North America, private collection, 129.

99. Grose, *Military Antiquities*, 2:253-54; John Williamson, *The Elements of Military Arrangements, Comprehending the Tactick, Exercise, Manoevres, and Discipline of the British Infantry* (London, 1781), 160-61.

100. Trial of John Brown, WO 71/82 pp. 232-235; trial of Richard Symes, WO

71/80 pp. 336-350.
101. Journal of Frederick Philipse Robinson, FC3071.1.R58 1814, Massay Library, Royal Military College of Canada.
102. Trial of John Vatass, WO 71/84 pp. 355-380; trial of Richard Blackmore, WO 71/84 pp. 381-397.
103. See for example trial of John Man, WO 71/79 pp. 407-413, and trial of Benjamin Cotton, WO 71/92 pp. 239-242.
104. See for example trial of Elija Reeves, WO 71/79 pp. 157-177, and trial of Bartholomew Gilmore, WO 71/90 pp. 26-34.
105. Trial of James Cairnes, WO 71/82 pp. 241-250; trial of John Brayson, WO 71/88 pp. 428-430.
106. Trial of John Love, Thomas Manning and John Clements, WO 71/87 pp. 245-250; trial of Arthur Cosworth and William Pinches, WO 71/83 pp. 57-68.
107. Trial of William King, WO 71/84 pp. 202-204; trial of Robert Mason and James Watson, WO 71/90 pp. 129-131; trial of Benjamin Doran, William Lamb, John Cox and John Woods, WO 71/81 pp. 405-430.
108. Trial of John Fisher, WO 71/85 pp. 290-307; trial of Patrick Sheehan, WO 71/84 pp. 224-228; trial of John Wheally, WO 71/86 pp. 129-131; trial of James Garraty, WO 71/85 pp. 281-283; trial of John Kerr, WO 71/92 pp. 371-375; trial of Martin Hurley, WO 71/84 pp. 342-345.
109. Trial of Thomas Slack, WO 71/90 pp. 408-410; trial of Patrick Fallan, WO71/86 pp. 413-417; Peebles, *Diary*, 368.
110. Lamb, *British Soldier's Story*, 8; trial of Thomas Edwards, WO 71/83 pp. 102-108; petition of John Gaurnsey and William McGlaughlin, August 4, 1780, HCP, vol. 115:30.
111. Hughes, *Journal*, 13-14.
112. Trial of Benjamin Doran, William Lamb, John Cox and John Woods, WO 71/81 pp. 405-430.
113. Trial of Richard Collins, Thomas Lamb and Mary Collins, WO 71/86 pp. 70-76; trial of George Watkins and Richard Sharpe, WO 71/88 pp. 528-532.
114. Trial of Jeremiah Nicolas, WO 71/86 pp. 239-250; trial of John Fisher, WO 71/87 pp. 202-208.
115. Trial of John Frederick Leo, WO 71/86 pp. 97-98.
116. Trial of Murdock McLeod, WO 71/85 pp. 151-154; trial of Alexander Cumming, Hugh Mulloy, Allan Boyd, Archibald Campbell, Donald McDonald and Simon Frazer, WO71/88 pp. 346-350.
117. Trial of George Watkins and Richard Sharpe, WO 71/88 pp. 528-532.
118. Graham, *Memoir*, 244.
119. *Leeds Intelligencer*, April 1, 1777.
120. The "King's Regiment" was the 8th Regiment of Foot. Patrick Sinclair to Frederick Haldimand, February 17, 1780, "Papers from Canadian Archives," *Collections of the State Historical Society of Wisconsin*, vol. 11 (Madison: Democrat Printing, 1888), 147-148.
121. Trial of Georg Hundertmark, WO 71/84 pp. 181-186; trial of Leonard Carl, WO 71/87 pp. 241-243, and trial of Hubertus Römer, WO 71/87 pp. 234-235; trial of Bartholomew Gilmore, WO 71/90 pp. 26-34.
122. Trial of John Christian Lindorff, WO 71/85 pp. 128, 145-146.
123. Trial of Georg Hundertmark, WO 71/84, pp. 181-186.
124. Trial of Godfrey Bushman, Francis Uss, Lewis Mason, and Henry Urban, WO

71/92 pp. 163-179.

125. Journal of Johann Ernst Schueler von Senden, Musketeer Regiment Specht, Morristown National Historical Park, Morristown, NJ.

126. Münchausen, *At General Howe's Side,* 48.

127. Brigade orders, May 6, 1777, orderly book, 40th Regiment of Foot, LOC.

128. Don N. Hagist, "Von Scheither Recruits in the 17th Regiment of Foot," *The Hessians: Journal of the Johannes Schwalm Historical Association* 17 (2014): 23; Don N. Hagist, "Forty German Recruits: The Service of the von Scheither Recruits in the 22nd Regiment of Foot, 1776–1783," *Journal of the Johannes Schwalm Historical Association* 6, no. 1 (1997): 63–66; Don N. Hagist, "Von Scheither Recruits in the 23rd Regiment of Foot," *The Hessians: Journal of the Johannes Schwalm Historical Association* 18 (2015): 30.

129. Muster rolls, 22nd Regiment of Foot, WO 12/3872.

130. Regimental orders, October 23, November 18, and December 27, 1776, orderly book, 17th Regiment of Foot, NYHS.

131. Regimental orders, November 23, 1776, orderly book, 17th Regiment of Foot, NYHS.

132. Barry St. Leger to Richard Lernoult, December 2, 1782, WO 28/2 p. 34.

CHAPTER 12. THE REMAINS OF REGIMENTS

1. Deposition of John Dearing, Board of Inquiry, PRO 30/55/6884.

2. Discharge of Michael Tevin, WO 119/6/278; depositions of Michael Tevin, George Holmes, John Rhoads, Patrick Kelly, James Steel, and John Major, Board of Inquiry, PRO 30/55/6884.

3. Depositions of James Riley, John Stubbs, John Wishart, John Drury, John Duncan, John Smith, William Woodside, and Samuel Millington, Board of Inquiry, PRO 30/55/6884.

4. Depositions of George Homes, James Cuffe, Roger Clancy, Andrew Smith, Edward Miller, John Ward, and John Southers, Board of Inquiry, PRO 30/55/6884.

5. Memorial of Joseph Tomlinson, AO 13/21 f. 423 and 435; "Journal of three serjeants of the 23rd Regiment, who made their escape from York, in Pennsylvania, the 1st March, and arrived at New York the 23rd March 1782," HCP, vol. 191:47; depositions of Roger Clancy and Richard Morris, Board of Inquiry, PRO 30/55/6884.

6. Deposition of Augustine Barrett, Board of Inquiry, PRO 30/55/6884; muster rolls, 24th Regiment of Foot, WO 12/4059; "Roll of the Officers of Col. David Henley's Regt & all of the men which has been Inlisted in said Regt," April 18, 1778, Revolutionary War Rolls, NARA; "Descriptive list of the Non-Commission'd Officers and Privates, Deserters, from the late 16th Masstts. Regt., Revolutionary War Rolls; Muster roll of the 5th Company in the Battalion of Massachusetts Forces, in the Service of the United States, Commanded by Col. Hy. Jackson," Revolutionary War Rolls; "Return of the Non Commiss'd Officers & Soldiers Inlisted for the War in the Cols Compy," Muster rolls, 16th Massachusetts Regiment, Henry Jackson Papers, LOC; *Massachusetts Soldiers and Sailors of the Revolutionary War* (Boston: Wright and Potter Printing, 1896), 1:677.

7. Muster rolls, 33rd Regiment of Foot, WO 12/4803.

8. Brigade Orders, October 27, 1777, orderly book, Royal Artillery, September 28, 1777–February 21, 1778, James Pattison Papers, Royal Artillery Institution Library, Woolwich, UK.

9. General orders, August 19, 1776, WO 36/5.

10. General orders, September 14, 1776, WO 36/5.

11. Hunter, *Journal*, 25.

12. For George Fox's full story, see Hagist, *British Soldiers,* 200-214.

13. General orders, July 27, 1777, orderly book, 47th Regiment of Foot, ACC.

14. Muster rolls, 34th Regiment of Foot, WO 12/4866; muster rolls, 53rd Regiment of Foot, WO 12/6317.

15. Muster rolls, 47th Regiment of Foot, WO 12/5871.

16. Muster rolls, 22nd Regiment of Foot, WO 12/3872; muster rolls, 52nd Regiment of Foot, WO 12/6240; "Examinations of Invalid Soldiers," December 18, 1778, Pension Admission Book, WO 116/7; discharge of James Adair, WO 97/418/1.

17. Muster rolls, 38th Regiment of Foot, WO 12/5171 and WO 12/5172.

18. Henry Ogilvy to Barrington, July 2, 1776, WO 1/993.

19. Muster rolls, 22nd Regiment of Foot, WO 12/3872; "Examinations of Invalid Soldiers," April 14, 1778 (Cox), February 13, 1782 (Copeland and Williams), and March 26, 1782 (Harris), Pension Admission Book, WO 116/7; "Examinations of Invalid Soldiers," March 31, 1783 (Coleman) and April 14, 1784 (Reynolds), Pension Admission Book, WO 116/8, "Examinations of Invalid Soldiers," November 8, 1785, Pension Admission Book, WO 116/9 (Connel).

20. "A Sketch of an Establishment for a Garrison Battalion to be form'd from the Invalid'd Men of this Army," FMP.

21. List of Prisoners in Jail taken at Paulus Hook, Bradford Family Papers; muster rolls, 22nd Regiment of Foot, WO 12/3872; "Examinations of Invalid Soldiers," June 22 and 30, 1784, Pension Admission Book, WO 116/8; muster rolls, Royal Garrison Battalion, RG 8 C Series, vol. 1873, PAC.

22. Archibald McArthur to Alexander Leslie, October 30, 1782, PRO 30/55/53/34.

23. Carleton to Barrington, July 29, 1778, WO 1/11 p. 72; general orders, July 28, 1778, WO 1/11 p. 74; Haldimand to Jenkinson, September 18, 1779, WO 1/11 pp. 126-128.

24. Trial of Benjamin Cotton, WO 71/92 pp. 239-242. His name appears in the muster rolls as Richard.

25. Enys, *American Journals,* 53.

26. Brigade orders, April 3, 1779, orderly book, Brigade of Guards, 1779, NYHS; Newsome, "British Orderly Book," 165, 179.

27. This corps was embodied in September 1776, and was rebuilt a year later after losses at the Battle of Bennington. General orders, September 2, 1777, orderly book, 47th Regiment of Foot, ACC.

28. General orders, May 30, 1777, Thomas Glyn Journal, FL; M. M. Gilchrist, *Patrick Ferguson A Man of Some Genius* (Edinburgh: NMS Publishing, 2003), 20-45.

29. Colebrooke Nesbitt to Dansey, January 25, 1782, Dansey Letters, HSD; Dansey to his mother, December 4, 1782, Dansey Letters, HSD.

30. General orders, August 10, 1775, WO 36/1.

31. See for example general orders, March 23, 1777, Thomas Glyn Journal, FL, and general orders, February 27, 1779, orderly book, Captain Clayton's company, 17th Regiment of Foot, HL.

32. Peebles, *Diary,* 392.

33. *Daily Advertiser* (London), March 13, 1776. For a more detailed account of the shipwreck of the *Lion,* see *Derby Mercury,* February 23, 1776.

34. Richard St. George to Clinton, London, July 1, 1778, HCP, vol. 36:24.

35. *New Lloyd's List* (London), February 16, 1779; Memoir of William Hunter, pri-

vate collection.

36. Muster rolls, 38th Regiment of Foot, WO 12/5171 and WO 12/5172; muster rolls, 22nd Regiment of Foot, WO 12/3872.

37. See for example Simes, *Military Guide*, 301-304.

38. Regimental orders, December 1, 11, and 24, 1774, and January 1 and 22, 1775, orderly book, 18th Regiment of Foot, NAM; regimental orders, March 16, 1775, orderly book, 10th Regiment of Foot, WLC.

39. Will of John Budge, PROB 11/1094/344.

40. Muster rolls, 17th Regiment of Foot, WO 12/3406.

41. "Register of Wills of the Men of the First Battalion of Guards," Orders, Returns, Morning Reports and Accounts of the Brigade of Foot Guards, NARA.

42. Will of David Stuart, "Abstracts of Wills on File in the Surrogate's Office, City of New York," *Collections of the New York Historical Society*, 1901 (New York: Printed for the Society, 1902), 3.

43. Will of James Bradley, ibid., 110.

44. Will of John Gilbert, PROB 11/1142/318.

45. Orders, Returns, Morning Reports and Accounts of the Brigade of Foot Guards, NARA.

46. Robert Campbell Account Book, RL.

47. Regimental Ledger Books, 22nd Regiment of Foot, Lloyds Bank Archives; Mackenzie, *Diary*, 435.

CHAPTER 13. LONG AND FAITHFUL SERVICES

1. Hagist, *British Soldiers*, 68-71.

2. Muster rolls, 23rd Regiment of Foot, WO 12/3960.

3. *Wyoming Republican* (Kingston, PA) September 4, 1833; Hendrick Bradley Wright, *Historical Sketches of Plymouth, Luzerne Co., Penna* (Plymouth, PA: T. B. Peterson, 1873), 208-217.

4. "B. & O. R. R. Engineering before and after the War," *Engineers' Society of Western Pennsylvania Proceedings* 6 (Pittsburg: Engineer's Society of Western Pennsylvania, 1890), 91-92; James D. Dilts, *The Great Road: The Building of the Baltimore and Ohio, the Nation's First Railroad, 1828–1858* (Palo Alto, CA: Stanford University Press, 1996); "Artists' Excursion Over the Baltimore & Ohio Railroad," *Harper's New Monthly Magazine* 109, no. 19 (June 1859): 16-18.

5. Graham, *Memoir*, 333.

6. Gavin K. Watt, *The Burning of the Valleys: Daring Raids from Canada against the New York Frontier in the Fall of 1780* (Toronto: Dundurn Press, 1997), 342; muster rolls, 22nd Regiment of Foot, WO 12/3872, and 34th Regiment of Foot.

7. Peebles, *Diary*, 431.

8. General orders, August 17, 1783, Sir Guy Carleton orderly book, FMP.

9. Muster rolls, 38th Regiment of Foot, WO 12/5172; muster rolls, 3rd Regiment of Foot, WO 12/2106.

10. General orders, September 14, 17, 21, and 26, 1783, New York orderly book, British Library.

11. Don N. Hagist, "John Philipp Aulenbach: von Scheither Recruit in the 17th Light Dragoons," *The Hessians: Journal of the Johannes Schwalm Historical Association* 16 (2013): 54-56.

12. Scoles's name appears as "Seals" on the muster rolls, perhaps because he never joined the regiment in person. Muster rolls, 33rd Regiment of Foot, WO 12/4803.

13. Petition of William Scoles, 1788, Nova Scotia Land Papers, Nova Scotia

Archives, Halifax, NS. The date of Scoles's enlistment is not recorded, but he had served the requisite three years when he was discharged, including his time in Great Britain and in Nova Scotia.

14. Petition of John Drury (Drurey), 1786, Nova Scotia Land Papers, Nova Scotia Archives.
15. Muster rolls, 37th Regiment of Foot, WO 12/5101; muster rolls, 42nd Regiment of Foot, WO 12/5553; muster rolls, 54th Regiment of Foot, WO 12/6398.
16. General orders, August 17, 1783, Sir Guy Carleton orderly book, FMP.
17. Discharge of Bryan Sweeny, WO 121/12/371.
18. Muster rolls, 29th Regiment of Foot, WO 12/4493.
19. Enys, *American Journals,* 173.
20. Robert Sellar, *The History of the County of Huntingdon* (Huntington, QC: Canadian Gleaner, 1888), 55.
21. General orders, August 17, 1783, Sir Guy Carleton orderly book, FMP.
22. Hagist, "Unpublished Military Writings of Roger Lamb, Part 2," 79.
23. "Examinations of Invalid Soldiers," March 8, 1784, Pension Admission Book, WO 116/8.
24. Muster rolls, 23rd Regiment of Foot, WO 12/3960.
25. This estimate is based on study of discharges of men in the 22nd Regiment of Foot; about two hundred discharges survive, out of about one thousand men who served in the regiment in America between 1775 and 1783. Many went before the pension board years after their American service. Soldiers' discharges, WO 97, WO 119, WO 121.
26. Discharges of William Chester, WO 121/1/332, and William Begg, WO 121/1/333, among others; discharge of Michael Donnelly, WO 121/3/308.
27. Discharge of John Hawkins, WO 121/1/6; discharge of James Forest, WO 121/1/85; discharge of Thomas Witherill, WO 121/1/166; discharge of Anthony Townshend, WO 121/13/171; discharge of Allen Cameron, WO 121/3/337; discharge of Samuel Newby, WO 121/5/34; discharge of William McCreally, WO 121/5/117.
28. Discharge of James Rennison, WO 121/3/157.
29. Discharge of Samuel Stratton, WO 121/10/51.
30. Discharge of Benjamin Noble, WO 121/10/94.
31. Muster rolls, 4th Regiment of Foot, WO 12/2194 and WO 12/2195; Liste Des Recrués Anglois embarqués á Stade pour Spithead en Irlande ce 14me de Mai 1776, WO 43/405; discharge of "Henry Lytch," WO 121/11/18.
32. Discharge of John Smith, WO 121/5/226.
33. Discharge of Alexander Brice, WO 121/2/145.
34. Discharge of John Evident, WO 121/6/36.
35. Discharge of James Shaw, WO 121/9/104.
36. Discharge of Mark Green, WO 121/12/178.
37. More accurately, there is no evidence that they did so. It is possible that some reenlisted and received pensions after being discharged from other regiments. Some discharges include explicit enumerations of the man's career, others do not.
38. Discharge of Archibald MacIndow, WO 121/14/368.
39. Discharge of Allan Roy Cameron, WO 121/14/364.
40. Discharge of Alexander McKinnon, WO 121/8/120.
41. Discharge of John McDonald, WO 121/8/119.
42. *Report of the Commissioners Appointed to Inquire into and to State the Mode of Keep-*

ing the Official Accounts in the Principal Departments Connected with the Receipts and Expenditure for the Public Service (London: Printed for His Majesty's Treasury, 1829), 266-267.

43. Petition of Samuel Debnam, WO 121/150/50.

44. Discharge of John Corbett, WO 121/178/96.

45. See for example the notice directed "To the Out-Pensioners of Chelsea-College," *Edinburgh Advertiser*, March 17, 1775.

46. General orders, March 14, 1776, orderly book, 32nd Regiment, NLI; muster rolls, 36th Regiment of Foot, WO 12/5025; muster rolls, 67th Regiment of Foot, WO 12/7537.

47. Petition of Donald Wright, WO 121/140/157.

48. Petition of John Mayell, WO 121/140/158.

49. *Information for John Lawson late serjeant in the 22d regiment of foot, pursuer; against Duncan Campbell, Esq; collector of excise as Glasgow, defender* (Edinburgh, 1788); *Information for Duncan Campbell, Esq; collector of excise in Glasgow, defender; against John Lawson late serjeant in the 22d regiment of foot, one of the out-pensioners of Chelsea Hospital, pursuer* (Edinburgh, 1788). The excise office appealed, and Lawson escalated the matter, charging the excise officer directly with being in violation of a statute concerning fair distribution of funds. If he was right, Lawson stood to collect a 100 pound reward as the informant against a corrupt official. The case continued into 1788, and the outcome, at this writing, has not been determined.

50. Discharge of Archibald Maclaren, WO 97/1173/429; muster rolls, 26th Regiment of Foot, WO 12/4250; "Archibald Maclaren," *Dictionary of National Biography*, vol. 35, ed. Sidney Lee (New York: Macmillan, 1893), 192-194; Archibald Maclaren, "To the Public," *The Satirist: Or, Monthly Meteor* 8, no. 4 (April, 1811): 295-297; introductions in Maclaren's plays *The Lottery Chance; Or, the Drunkard Reclaim'd* (London, 1803), *A Touch at the Times; or, an Attempt to Please* (London, 1805), *The Ways of London: Or Honesty the Best Policy* (London, 1812), *The Prisoner of War* (London, 1813), *The Last Shift; Or the Prisoners Released* (London, 1814), *The Debating Club* (London, 1816), *Live and Hope; or the Emigrant Prevented* (London, 1817), *Filial Duty: or, the Maid of Oban* (London, 1819), and *The Royal Visit* (London, 1822).

51. *Concord Births*, 258, 420.

52. Muster rolls, 5th Regiment of Foot, WO 12/2289.

53. After extensive correspondence and interviews that he duly recorded, Roger Lamb was finally granted a pension in 1809. He published two books, *An Original and Authentic Journal of Occurrences during the Late American War* (Dublin, 1809) and *Memoir of His Own Life* (Dublin, 1811), and maintained an extensive book of notes and drawings, his Commonplace Book, in the Methodist Historical Society of Ireland Archives, Belfast. Some of Lamb's letters survive in other archives.

54. "List of British Prisoners Brought to Lancaster by Major Baily the 16th June 1781," July 18, 1781, Peter Force Papers ser. 9, reel 106, pp. 675-685, LOC.

55. Trial of William Nicholson, WO 71/83 pp. 69-70; "British Army Orders," 428, 431.

56. Muster rolls, 43rd Regiment of Foot, WO 12/5561; muster rolls, Royal Garrison Battalion, RG 8 "C" Series, vol. 1873 p. 35, PAC; "Examinations of Invalid Soldiers," June 30, 1784, Pension Admission Book, WO 116/8 .

57. List of Prisoners sent from Morris Town to Philadelphia, June 17, 1780, Bradford Family Papers V1:46; muster rolls, 22nd Regiment of Foot, WO 12/3872.

58. Lindsay, *Extracts*, 484-485.

59. Discharge of George Peacock, WO 121/42/174.

60. Discharge of Michael Tevin, WO 119/6/278.
61. Anon., *The Veteran Soldier; an interesting Narrative of the Life, and Religious Experience, of the Late Serjeant Greenleigh* (London: William Whittemore, 1822), 19, 25-27.
62. Murray, *Letters*, 28.
63. Graham, *Memoir*, 278.

SELECTED BIBLIOGRAPHY

PRIMARY SOURCES

Manuscripts

Adirondack Community College, Queensbury, New York
    Orderly book, 47th Regiment of Foot
American Philosophical Society Library, Philadelphia
    Anonymous British Journal, 1776–78, Feinstone no. 409
Archibald S. Alexander Library, Rutgers, State University of New Jersey,
New Brunswick, New Jersey
    Orderly book, General Charles Grey's company, 28th Regiment of Foot
British Library, London
    Additional Manuscripts
Center for Kentish Studies, Maidstone, Kent, UK
    Amherst manuscripts, U1350
Colonial Williamsburg Foundation, Williamsburg, VA
    Recruiting poster, 45th Regiment of Foot, 2006-18, 1
Firestone Library, Princeton University, Princeton, New Jersey
    Thomas Glyn Journal
Historical Society of Delaware, Wilmington
    William Dansey Letters
Historical Society of Pennsylvania, Philadelphia
    Bradford Family Papers, Thomas Bradford Series
    Orderly book, 15th Regiment of Foot, Hamilton Collection no. 1612
Huntington Library, San Marino, CA
    Orderly book, Captain Clayton's company, 17th Regiment of Foot
    Orderly book, 2nd Battalion 71st Regiment
Library of Congress, Washington, DC
    George Washington Papers, Orderly book, 2nd Battalion of Grenadiers
    (64th Regiment's company)

George Washington Papers, Orderly book, 2nd Battalion of Light Infantry (64th Regiment's company)

George Washington Papers, Orderly book, 40th Regiment of Foot

Walter Home Memorandum Book, George Chalmers Collection, Peter Force Manuscripts

Lloyds Bank Archives, London

Regimental Ledger Books, 22nd Regiment of Foot, A56e/102, Cox & Company

Massachusetts Historical Society, Boston

Standing Orders, 35th Regiment of Foot

Orderly book, 40th Regiment of Foot

Massachusetts State Archives, Boston

Revolutionary War Records

Morristown National Historical Park, Morristown, New Jersey

Journal of Johann Ernst Schueler von Senden, Musketeer Regiment Specht, Lloyd W. Smith Collection

National Archives and Records Administration, Washington, DC

Orders, Returns, Morning Reports and Accounts of the Brigade of Foot Guards

Papers of the Continental Congress

National Archives, Kew, UK

AO 13: American Loyalist Claims

CO 5: Board of Trade and Secretaries of State: America and West Indies, Original Correspondence

CO 42: Canada, formerly British North America, Original Correspondence

PRO 30/55: Guy Carleton Papers

PROB 11: Will Registers

T 14/15: Out Letters concerning Ireland

WO 1: Secretary-at-War and Commander-in-Chief, In-letters

WO 3: Office of the Commander-in-Chief, Out-letters

WO 4: Secretary-at-War and Commander-in-Chief, Out-letters

WO 12: General muster books and pay lists

WO 25: Service Returns

WO 26: Entry Books of Warrants, Regulations and Precedents

WO 27: Inspection Returns

WO 34: Jeffrey Amherst Papers

WO 36: Entry Books, American Revolution

WO 40: Secretary-at-War, in-Letters and Reports

WO 43: Secretary-at-War Correspondence, Very Old Series

WO 71: Judge Advocate General's Office: Courts Martial Proceedings

WO 97: Royal Hospital Chelsea: Soldiers Service Documents

WO 116: Disability and Royal Artillery Out-Pensions, Admission Books

WO 118: Kilmainham Pensioners living in 1807

WO 119: Royal Hospital, Kilmainham: Pensioners' Discharge Documents

WO 120: Royal Hospital, Chelsea: Regimental Registers of Pensioners

WO 121: Royal Hospital, Chelsea: Discharge Documents of Pensioners
WO 379: Establishments
National Archives of Scotland, Edinburgh
 Orderly book, 4th Battalion of Grenadiers, in Papers of John Peebles, 42nd
 Regiment, Cunninghame of Thorntoun Papers (GD 21/492)
National Army Museum, London
 Ms. 1976-09-3: Orderly book, 18th Regiment of Foot
 Ms. 6807-157-6: Discipline established by Major General Howe for Light
 Infantry in Battalion, Sarum, September 1774
National Library of Ireland, Dublin
 MS 3750: Orderly book, 32nd Regiment of Foot
New-York Historical Society, New York
 Orderly book, 17th Regiment of Foot
 Orderly book, Brigade of Guards, 1779
 Orderly book, Major Acland's Grenadier Battalion
New York Public Library, New York
 Bayard-Campbell-Pearsall Collection, Campbell Accounts and Papers
Nova Scotia Archives, Halifax
 Nova Scotia Land Papers
 Orderly books kept in Halifax, Nova Scotia
Parliamentary Archives, Houses of Parliament, London
 HL/PO/JO/10/7/544: Return of Courts Martial held in Ireland
Public Archives of Canada, Ottawa
 CO transcripts, Q series
 John and Thomas Nairne fonds
 Malcolm Fraser Papers
 MG23, K6(2): Punishment Book of the 44th Regiment of Foot
Royal Artillery Institution Library, Woolwich, UK
 James Pattison Papers
Royal Fusiliers Museum, Warwick, UK
 Recruiting Instructions for the Royal Fusiliers, November 27, 1775
Rubenstein Library, Duke University, Durham, North Carolina
 Robert Campbell Account Book, 1779–1781
West Yorkshire Archives, Calderdale, West Yorkshire, UK
 SH17/A: Recruiting Accounts and Ledger of Lt. Joab Aked
William L. Clements Library, University of Michigan, Ann Arbor
 Eyre Coote Papers:
  Orderly books, 1st Battalion of Light Infantry, 37th Regiment Company
  Orderly books, 37th Regiment of Foot
  Standing orders, 37th Regiment of Foot
 Frederick Mackenzie Papers
 Henry Clinton Papers
 Loftus Cliffe Papers
 Orderly book, 10th Regiment of Foot
 Thomas Gage Papers, American Series

Newspapers

BRITISH

Aris's Gazette (Birmingham), 1778
Belfast Newsletter, 1774–1780
British Chronicle or Pugh's Hereford Journal, 1775
Caledonian Mercury, 1776
Daily Advertiser (London), 1776
Derby Mercury, 1776
Edinburgh Advertiser, 1772–1776
Freeman's Journal (Dublin), 1775
Gazetteer and New Daily Advertiser (London), 1780
Hibernian Chronicle (Cork), 1773–1775
Leeds Intelligencer, 1777–1779
Leicester Journal, 1779
London Gazette, 1775
London Packet, 1773
New Lloyd's List (London), 1779
Norfolk Chronicle, 1776–1780
Northampton Mercury, 1770
Post and Daily Advertiser (London), 1779
Public Advertiser (London), 1770–1778
Reading Mercury, 1776
St. James's Chronicle (London), 1777
Whitehall Evening Post (London), 1780

NORTH AMERICAN

Boston Chronicle, 1769
Boston Gazette, 1774
Connecticut Courant (Hartford), 1777
Essex (MA) Gazette, 1774
Massachusetts Spy (Boston), 1774
Newport Gazette, 1779
New York Gazette, 1770–1780
Pennsylvania Gazette (Philadelphia), 1770–1777
Quebec Gazette (Quebec City), 1774
Rivington's New-York Gazetteer, 1774
Royal Gazette (New York), 1778–1781
Thomas's Massachusetts Spy Or, American Oracle of Liberty (Worcester), 1779
Wyoming Republican (Kingston, PA), 1833

PUBLISHED PRIMARY SOURCES

Anderson, Enoch. *Personal recollections of Captain Enoch Anderson, an officer of the Delaware regiments in the revolutionary war.* Wilmington: Historical Society of Delaware, 1896.
André, John. *Major André's Journal.* Edited by C. Willcox. Tarrytown, NY: William Abbatt, 1930.

Anon. *Observations on the Prevailing Abuses in the British Army.* London, 1775.

Anon. *The Veteran Soldier; an interesting Narrative of the Life, and Religious Experience, of the Late Serjeant Greenleigh.* London: William Whittemore, 1822.

Balderston, Marion and David Syrett., eds. *The Lost War: Letters from British Officers during the American Revolution.* New York: Horizon Press, 1975.

Bamford, William. *A Redcoat in America: The Diaries of Lieutenant William Bamford, 1757–1765 and 1776.* Warwick, UK: Helion, 2019.

Barker, John. *The British in Boston: The Diary of Lt. John Barker.* Edited by Elizabeth Ellery Dana. Cambridge, MA: Harvard University Press, 1924.

Biddulph, Violet. "Letters of Robert Biddulph, 1779–1783." *American Historical Review* 29, no. 1 (October 1923): 87-109.

Blatchford, John. *The narrative of John Blatchford, detailing his sufferings in the revolutionary war, while a prisoner with the British.* New York: privately printed, 1865.

Boston under Military Rule (1768-1769): As Revealed in a Journal of the Times. Edited by Oliver Morton Dickerson. Boston: Chapman and Grimes, 1936.

Bradford, Sydney S., ed. "Lord Francis Napier's Journal of the Burgoyne Campaign." *Maryland Historical Magaine* 57, no. 4 (December 1962): 285-333.

"British Army Orders." *Collections of the New York Historical Society for the year 1883.* New York, 1884.

Burgoyne. John. *A State of the Expedition from Canada as Laid Before the House of Commons, by Lieutenant-General Burgoyne, and Verified by Evidence, with a Collection of Authentic Documents, and an Addition of Many Circumstances Which were Prevented from Appearing Before the House by the Prorogation of Parliament.* London: J. Almon, 1780.

Carter, William. *A genuine detail of the several engagements, positions, and movements of the Royal and American armies, during the years 1775 and 1776.* London, 1784.

Clerke, Francis-Carr. "Letters to Lord Polwarth from Sir Francis-Carr Clerke, Aide-de-Camp to General John Burgoyne." Edited by Ronald F. Kingsley. *New York History* 79, no. 4 (October 1998): 393-424.

Clinton, Henry. *The American Rebellion; Sir Henry Clinton's Narrative of His Campaigns, 1775–1782.* Edited by William B. Willcox. New Haven, CT: Yale University Press, 1954.

Cranfield, Thomas. *The Useful Christian; a Memoir of Thomas Cranfield, for about Fifty Years a Devoted Sunday-School Teacher.* Philadelphia: American Sunday-School Union, n.d.

Cuthbertson, Bennett. *A System for the Compleat Interior Management and Œconomy of a Battalion of Infantry.* Dublin, 1768.

Dann, John C., ed. *The Revolution Remembered.* Chicago: University of Chicago Press, 1980.

Dansey, William. *Captured Rebel Flag: The Letters of Captain William Dansey, 33rd Regiment of Foot, 1776–1777.* Edited by Paul Dansey. Godmanchester, Huntington, UK: Ken Trotman Press, 2010.

Denny, Ebenezer. *Military Journal of Major Ebenezer Denny.* Philadelphia: J. B. Lippincott, 1859.

"Diary of Joshua Pell, junior." *Magazine of American History* 2, no. 2 (February 1878): 107-112.

Digby, William. *The British Invasion From the North: The Campaigns of Generals Carleton and Burgoyne from Canada, 1776–1777, with the Journal of Lieut. William Digby.* Albany, NY: Joel Munsell's Sons, 1887.

Donkin, Robert. *Military Collections and Remarks.* New York: H. Gaine, 1777.

Downman, Francis. *The Services of Lieut. Colonel Francis Downman, R. A. in France, North America and the West Indies, between the years 1758 and 1784.* Edited by F. A. Whinyates. Woolwich, UK: Royal Artillery Institution, 1896.

Drake, Samuel Adams. *Bunker Hill: The Story Told in Letters from the Battle Field by British Officers Engaged.* Boston: Nichols and Hall, 1875.

Enys, John. *The American Journals of Lt. John Enys.* Edited by Elizabeth Cometti. Blue Mountain Lake, NY: Adirondack Museum, 1976.

Evelyn, W. Glanville. *Memoir and Letters of Captain W. Glanville Evelyn, of the 4th Regiment, ("King's Own,") from North America, 1774–1776.* Edited by G. D. Scull. Oxford: Parker, 1879.

Force, Peter. *American Archives,* 5th ser. Washington, DC: M. St. Clair Clarke and Peter Force, 1848.

Gage, Thomas. *The Correspondence of General Thomas Gage with the Secretaries of State and with the War Office and the Treasury, 1763–1775.* Edited by Edwin Clarence Carter. New Haven, CT: Yale University Press, 1931.

General Orders, Rhode Island. Edited by Don N. Hagist. Bowie, MD: Heritage Books, 2001.

Gilchrist, Marianne. "Captain Hon. William Leslie (1751–76): His Life, Letters and Commemoration." In *Military Miscellany 2,* edited by David Chandler, 134-196. Stroud, UK: Sutton Publishing, for the Army Records Society, 2005.

Graham, Samuel. *Memoir of General Graham.* Edited by Colonel James J. Graham. Edinburgh: R. & R. Clark, 1862.

Graydon, Alexander. *Memoirs of His own Time.* Harrisburg: John Wyeth, 1811.

Grieg, J., ed. *The Diaries of a Duchess: Extracts from the Diaries of the First Duchess of Northumberland.* New York: Hodder and Stoughton, 1926.

Griffith, W. "Memoirs and Spiritual Experience of the late Mr. W. Griffith, Senior (Written by himself)." *Spiritual Magazine, and Zion's Casket* (1849): 151-156.

Grose, Francis. *A Classical Dictionary of the Vulgar Tongue.* Edited by Eric Partridge. New York: Dorset Press, 1992.

————. *Military Antiquities Respecting a History of the English Army from the Conquest to the Present Time.* London: S. Hooper, 1786.

Hamilton, Robert. *Duties of a Regimental Surgeon Considered.* Vol. 2. London, 1787.

Hanway, Jonas. *The Seaman's Christian Friend.* London, 1779.

Hawthorn, John. *Poems.* Printed for the author and sold by E. Easton [Salisbury, UK], J. Dodsley, and J. Wilkie [London], 1779.

Haslewood, William. "Journal of a British Officer during the American Revolution." *Mississippi Valley Historical Review* 7, no. 1 (June 1920): 51-58.

Honyman, Robert. *Colonial Panorama, 1775: Dr. Robert Honyman's Journal for March and April.* Edited by Philip Radford. San Marino, CA: Huntington Library, 1939.

Howe, William. *General Sir William Howe's Orderly Book.* Edited by B. F. Stevens. Port Washington, NY: Kennikat Press, 1980.

Hughes, Thomas. *A Journal by Thos. Hughes.* Cambridge, MA: Harvard University Press, 1947.

Hunter, Martin. *The Journal of Gen. Sir Martin Hunter.* Edinburgh: Edinburgh Press, 1894.

Information for Duncan Campbell, Esq; collector of excise in Glasgow, defender; against John Lawson late serjeant in the 22d regiment of foot, one of the outpensioners of Chelsea Hospital, pursuer. Edinburgh: n.p., 1788.

Information for John Lawson late serjeant in the 22d regiment of foot, pursuer; against Duncan Campbell, Esq; collector of excise as Glasgow, defender. Edinburgh: n.p., 1788.

Inman, George. "George Inman's Narrative of the American Revolution." *Pennsylvania Magazine of History and Biography* 7, no. 3 (1883): 237-248.

Jackson, Robert. *Treatise on the Fevers of Jamaica.* London: J. Murray, 1791.

James, Charles. *A New and Enlarged Military Dictionary.* London: T. Egerton, 1802.

Jarvis, Stinson, ed. "Reminiscences of a Loyalist." *Canadian Magazine* 26, no. 3 (January 1906): 227-233.

Kemble, Stephen. "Journals of Lieut.-Col. Stephen Kemble." *Collections of the New York Historical Society for the year 1883.* New York, 1884.

Lamb, Roger. *A British Soldier's Story: Roger Lamb's Narrative of the American Revolution.* Edited by Don N. Hagist. Baraboo, WI: Ballindalloch Press, 2005.

————. *An Original and Authentic Journal of Occurrences during the Late American War.* Dublin: Wilkinson & Courtney, 1809.

Letters from America 1776–1779, Being Letters of Brunswick, Hessian, and Waldeck Officers with the British Armies during the Revolution. Translated by Ray W. Pettengill. Boston: Houghton Mifflin, 1924.

"Letters of Charles O'Hara to the Duke of Grafton." Edited by G. C. Rogers. *South Carolina Historical Magazine* 65 (1964): 156-180.

Letters of the Delegates to Congress 1774–1789. Edited by Paul H. Smith. Washington, DC: Library of Congress, 1976.

Lindsay, Colin. *Extracts from Colonel Tempelhoffe's History of the Seven Years War . . . to which is added a Narrative of Events at St. Lucie and Gibraltar* (London: T. Cadell, 1793).

Lister, Jeremy. *Concord Fight: Being so much of the Narrative of Ensign Jeremy Lister of the 10th Regiment of Foot as pertains to his services on the 19th of April, 1775, and to his experiences in Boston during the early months of the siege.* Cambridge, MA: Harvard University Press, 1931.

Lochée, Lewis. *Essay on Castremetation.* London, 1778.

MacDonald, John. *Autobiographical Journal of John MacDonald: Schoolmaster and Soldier.* Edinburgh: Norman MacLeod, 1906.

Mackenzie, Frederick. *The Diary of Frederick Mackenzie.* Cambridge, MA: Harvard University Press, 1930.

MacLaren, Archibald. *The Debating Club.* London, 1816.

———. *Filial Duty: or, the Maid of Oban.* London, 1819.

———. *The Last Shift; Or the Prisoners Released.* London, 1814.

———. *Live and Hope; or the Emigrant Prevented.* London, 1817.

———. *The Lottery Chance; Or, the Drunkard Reclaim'd.* London, 1803.

———. *The Prisoner of War, or a most excellent Story.* London, 1813.

———. *The Royal Visit.* London, 1822.

———. "To the Public." *The Satirist: Or, Monthly Meteor* 8, no. 4 (April 1811): 295-297.

———. *A Touch at the Times; or, an Attempt to Please.* London, 1805.

———. *The Ways of London: Or Honesty the Best Policy.* London, 1812.

The Manual Exercise, As ordered by his Majesty, In 1764. Together with Plans and Explanations Of the Method generally Practis'd At Review and Field-Days, &c. London: 1764.

Mathew, George. "Mathew's Narrative." *Historical Magazine* 1 (1857): 102–106.

Matson, John. *Indian Warfare: or, the Extraordinary Adventures of John Matson the Kidnapped Youth, late of Kingsland Road, London; formerly of Bridlington Quay, in the County of York; Architect and Builder. Written by Himself.* London: Effingham Wilson, 1842.

Military Instructions by the King of Prussia. Translated by T. Forster. London, 1762.

Montresor, John. "The Montresor Journals." *Collections of the New York Historical Society for the year 1881.* New York, 1882.

Morton, Robert. "Diary of Robert Morton." *Pennsylvania Magazine of History and Biography* 1, no. 1 (1877): 1-39.

Münchausen, F. von. *At General Howe's Side, 1776–1778: The Diary of General William Howe's Aide de Camp, Captain Friedrich von Muenchausen.* Edited by S. Smith. Monmouth Beach, NJ: Philip Freneau, 1974.

Murray, James. *Letters from America, 1773 to 1780.* Edited by Eric Robson. New York: Barnes & Noble, 1950.

"Narrative of William Grant." *Documents Relative to the Colonial History of the State of New York, Procured in Holland, England and France.* Edited by E. B. O'Callaghan. Albany, NY: Weed, Parsons, 1857.

Naval Documents of the American Revolution. 13 volumes. Edited by William James Morgan et al. Washington, DC: Government Printing Office, 1964–2019.

Newsome, A. R., ed. "A British Orderly Book, 1780–1781." *North Carolina Historical Review* 9 (1932): 57-78.

Norton, J. E., ed. *Letters of Edward Gibbon.* London: Cassell, 1956.

"Official Letters of Major General James Pattison." *Collections of the New York Historical Society for the year 1875.* New York, 1876.

Pasley, Thomas. *Private sea journals, 1778–1782, kept by Admiral Sir Thomas Pasley, bart.: when in command of H. M. ships Glasgow (20), Sybil (28) and Jupiter (50).* Edited by Robert M. S. Pasley. London: J. M. Dent and Sons, 1931.

Pausch, Georg. *Georg Pausch's Journal and Reports of the Campaign in America.* Translated by Bruce E. Burgoyne. Bowie, MD: Heritage Books, 1996.

Peckham, Howard H., ed. *Sources of American Independence: Selected Manuscripts from the Collections of the William L. Clements Library.* Chicago: University of Chicago Press, 1978.

Peebles, John. *John Peebles American War: The Diary of a Scottish Grenadier, 1776–1782.* Edited by Irea D. Gruber. Mechanicsburg, PA: Stackpole Books, for the Army Records Society, 1998.

Percy, Hugh. *Letters of Hugh Earl Percy from Boston and New York 1774–1776.* Edited by Charles Knowles Bolton. Boston: Charles E. Goodspeed, 1902.

Pickering, Timothy. *An Easy Plan of Discipline for a Militia.* Boston: S. Hall, 1776.

Pouchot, François. *Memoir upon the Late War in North America, between the French and English, 1755–60.* Edited by Frederick Benjamin Hough. Roxbury, MA: W. E. Woodward, 1866.

Rawdon, Francis. *Report on the Manuscripts of the late Reginald Rawdon Hastings, Esq.* Edited by Francis Bickley. London: Historical Manuscripts Commission, 1934.

Reide, Thomas Dickson. *A View of the Diseases of the Army.* London: J. Johnson, 1793.

Report of the Commissioners Appointed to Inquire into and to State the Mode of Keeping the Official Accounts in the Principal Departments Connected with the Receipts and Expenditure for the Public Service. London: Printed for His Majesty's Treasury, 1829.

Report on the Manuscripts of Mrs. Stopford-Sackville. Hereford: Hereford Times Co., 1910.

Rules and articles for the better government of His Majesty's horse and foot guards, and all other forces in Great Britain and Ireland, dominions beyond the seas, and foreign parts, from the 24th of March, 1777. London, 1777.

Saberton, Ian, ed. *The Cornwallis Papers: The Campaigns of 1780 and 1781 in the Southern Theatre of the American Revolutionary War.* 6 vols. Uckfield, UK: Naval & Military Press, 2010.

Scott, Andrew. *Poems, Chiefly in the Scottish Dialect.* Kelso, Scotland: Andrew Leadbetter, 1811.

Serle, Ambrose. *The American Journal of Ambrose Serle*. San Marino, CA: Huntington Library, 1940.

Seybolt, Robert Francis. "A Contemporary British Account of General Sir William Howe's Military Operations in 1777." *Proceedings of the American Antiquarian Society* 40 (April 1930): 69-92.

Shipp, John. *Flogging and its Substitute: A voice from the ranks*. London: Whittaker, Treacher, 1831.

Simes, Thomas. *A Military Guide for Young Officers*. London, 1776.

———. *The Military Medley*. 2nd ed. London, 1768.

———. *The Regulator*. London: n.p., 1780.

Smith, George. *An Universal Military Dictionary*. London, 1779.

Spilsbury, John. *A Journal of the Siege of Gibraltar 1779–1783 by Captain Spilsbury, 12th Regiment*. Edited by B. H. J. Frere. Gibraltar: Gibraltar Garrison Library, 1908.

Stedman, Charles. *History of the Origin, Progress, and Termination of the American War*. London: printed for the author, 1794.

Stirke, Henry. "A British Officer's Revolutionary War Journal, 1776–1778." *Maryland Historical Magazine* 56 (June 1961): 150-73.

Stirling, A. M. W. *Annals of a Yorkshire House, from the papers of a Macaroni & his Kindred*. London: John Lane, 1911.

Stone, William L. *Orderly book of Sir John Johnson during his campaign against Fort Stanwix*. New York: A. S. Barnes, 1881.

Stuart, James. "Letters from America, 1780 and 1781." Edited by K. C. Corsar. *Journal of the Society for Army Historical Research* 20, no. 79 (Autumn 1941): 130-135.

Sullivan, Thomas. *From Redcoat to Rebel: The Thomas Sullivan Journal*. Edited by Joseph Lee Boyle. Bowie, MD: Heritage Books, 1997.

Tarleton, Banastre. *A History of the Campaigns of 1780 and 1781 in the Southern Provinces of North America*. London: T. Cadell, 1787.

Walpole, Horace. *Characteristic Sketches of Society, Politics, and Literature; comprised in a series of letters addressed to The Countess of Ossory*. London: Richard Bentley, 1848.

Wesley, John. *The Journal of the Reverend John Wesley*. New York: J. Collord, 1832.

Wheeler, George A. "Sergeant Lawrence's Journal." *History of Castine, Penobscot and Brooksville, Maine*. Bangor: Burr & Robinson, 1875.

Wilkin, W. H., ed. *Some British Soldiers in America*. London: H. Rees, 1914.

Williams, Richard. *Discord and Civil Wars*. Buffalo, NY: Easy Hill Press, 1954.

Windham, William. *A Plan of Discipline composed for the use of the Militia of the County of Norfolk*. London: J. Shuckburgh, 1759.

SECONDARY SOURCES

Books

"Abstracts of Wills on File in the Surrogate's Office, City of New York." *Collections of the New York Historical Society*, 1901. New York: Printed for the Society, 1902.

Anderson, R. C., and J. M. *Quicksilver: A Hundred Years of Coaching 1750–1850*. Newton Abbot, UK: David & Charles, 1973.

Appleton's Cyclopedia of American Biography. Vols. 1-5. New York: D. Appleton, 1887–1888.

Baker, Norman. *Government and Contractors: The British Treasury and War Supplies, 1775–1783*. London: Athlone Press, 1971.

Barratt, Carrie Rebora, and Lori Zabar. *American Portrait Miniatures in the Metropolitan Museum of Art*. New Haven, CT: Yale University Press, 2010.

Benton, J. H., Jr. *Early Census Making in Massachusetts, 1643–1765*. Boston: Charles E. Goodspeed, 1905.

Bott, Edmund. *A Collection of Decisions of the Court of King's Bench upon the Poor's Laws, down to the Present Time*. 2nd ed. London: W. Strachan and M. Woodfall, 1773.

Bowler, R. Arthur. *Logistics and the Failure of the British Army in America*. Princeton, NJ: Princeton University Press, 1975.

Braisted, Todd W. *Grand Forage 1778: The Battleground around New York City*. Yardley, PA: Westholme, 2016.

Brumwell, Stephen. *Redcoats: The British Soldier and War in the Americas, 1755–1763*. Cambridge: Cambridge University Press, 2002.

Butler, Lewis. *The Annals of the King's Royal Rifle Corps*. Vol. 1. London: John Murray, 1813.

Butterfield, L. H., ed. *Letters of Benjamin Rush*. Princeton, NJ: Princeton University Press, 1951.

Carter, Thomas. *Historical record of the Forty-Fourth: or the East Essex regiment*. Chatham, UK: Gale & Polden, 1887.

Chandler, Peleg W. *Notes from American Criminal Trials*. Boston: Charles C. Little and James Brown, 1844.

Chase, Ellen. *The Beginnings of the American Revolution based on Contemporary Letters, Diaries and Other Documents*. New York: Baker and Taylor, 1910.

Concord, Massachusetts Births, Marriages and Deaths, 1635-1850. Boston: Thomas Todd, 1895.

Curtis, Edward R. *The Organization of the British Army in the American Revolution*. Gansevoort, NY: Corner House Historical Publications, 1998.

Dictionary of National Biography, vol. 35. Edited by Sidney Lee. New York: Macmillan, 1893.

Dilts, James D. *The Great Road: The Building of the Baltimore and Ohio, the Nation's First Railroad, 1828–1858*. Palo Alto, CA: Stanford University Press, 1996.

Frey, Sylvia R. *The British Soldier in North America*. Austin: University of Texas Press, 1983.

Frothingham, Richard. *History of the Siege of Boston*. Boston: Little, Brown, 1851.

Gee, Brian. *Francis Watkins and the Dollond Telescope Patent Controversy*. Farnham, UK: Ashgate, 2014.

Gilchrist, M. M. *Patrick Ferguson, A Man of Some Genius*. Edinburgh: NMS Publishing, 2003.

Hagist, Don N. *British Soldiers, American War: Voices of the American Revolution*. Yardley, PA: Westholme, 2012.

Hazard, Samuel, ed. *Pennsylvania Archives*. 1st ser., vol. 5. Philadelphia: Joseph Severns, 1853.

Heitmann, Thomas. *Historical Register of Officers of the Continental Army*. Washington, DC: W. H. Lowdermilk, 1893.

Houlding, J. A. *Fit for Service: The Training of the British Army 1715–1795*. Oxford, UK: Clarendon Press, 1981.

Huish, Robert. *Memoirs of William Cobbett, Esq.* London: John Saunders, 1836.

Hunt, Galliard. *Fragments of Revolutionary History. Being hitherto unpublished writings of the men of the American Revolution*. Brooklyn: Historical Printing Club, 1892.

Leneman, Leah. *Living in Atholl: A Social History of the Estates, 1685–1785*. Edinburgh: Edinburgh University Press, 1986.

Marshall, Henry. *Military Miscellany; comprehending a history of the recruiting of the army, military punishments, etc.* London: John Murray, 1846.

Massachusetts Soldiers and Sailors of the Revolutionary War. 17 vols. Boston: Wright and Potter Printing, 1896-1908.

McBurney, Christian M. *The Rhode Island Campaign: The First French and American Operation in the Revolutionary War*. Yardley, PA: Westholme, 2011.

Paterson, James. *History of the County of Ayr: with a Genealogical Account of the Families of Ayrshire*. Vol. 2. Edinburgh: Thomas George Stevenson, 1852.

Pottle, Frederick A., and Charles H. Bennett. *Boswell's Journal of a Tour to the Hebrides with Samuel Johnson, 1773*. New York: McGraw-Hill, 1936.

Proceedings of the Lexington Historical Society. Vol. 1. Lexington, MA: Lexington Historical Socity, 1890.

Proceedings of the Massachusetts Historical Society. 2nd ser., vol. 11. Boston: printed by the Society, 1897.

Rigby, Bernard. *Ever Glorious: The Story of the 22nd (Cheshire) Regiment*. Cheshire, UK: W. H. Evans and Sons, 1982.

Sellar, Robert. *The History of the County of Huntingdon*. Huntingdon, QC: Canadian Gleaner, 1888.

Spring, Matthew H. *With Zeal and Bayonets Only: The British Army on Campaign in North America, 1775–1783*. Norman: University of Oklahoma Press, 2008.

Strutt, Joseph. *The Sports and Pastimes of the People of England*. London, 1801.

Syrett, David. *Shipping and the American War, 1775–83: A Study of British Transport Organization*. Oxford: Oxford University Press, 1970.

Watt, Gavin K. *The Burning of the Valleys: Daring Raids from Canada against the New York Frontier in the Fall of 1780.* Toronto: Dundurn Press, 1997.

Westcott, Thompson. *Names of Persons who took the Oath of Allegiance to the State of Pennsylvania between the years 1777 and 1780.* Philadelphia: John Campbell, 1865.

Wright, Hendrick Bradley. *Historical Sketches of Plymouth, Luzerne Co., Penna.* Plymouth, PA: T. B. Peterson, 1873.

Wylly, H. C. *A Life of Lieutenant General Sir Eyre Coote, K. B.* Oxford: Clarendon Press, 1922.

Zabin, Serena. *The Boston Massacre: A Family History.* Boston: Houghton Mifflin Harcourt, 2020.

Zobel, Hiller B. *The Boston Massacre.* New York: W. W. Norton, 1970.

Articles and Theses

"Artists' Excursion Over the Baltimore & Ohio Railroad." *Harper's New Monthly Magazine* 109, no. 19 (June 1859): 16-18.

"B. & O. R. R. Engineering before and after the War." *Engineers' Society of Western Pennsylvania Proceedings* 6 (1890): 89-107.

Baule, Steven M., and Don N. Hagist. "The Regimental Punishment Book of the Boston Detachments of the Royal Irish Regiment and 65th Regiment, 1774-1775." *Journal of Army Historical Research* 88, no. 353 (2010): 5-18.

Brayton, Susan Stanton. "Silas Cooke—A Victim of the Revolution." *Rhode Island Historical Society Collections* 31 (October 1938): 108-121.

Conway, Stephen R. "The British Army, 'Military Europe,' and the American War of Independence." *William and Mary Quarterly* 67, no. 1 (January 2010): 69-100.

———. "'The Great Mischief Complain'd of': Reflections on the Misconduct of British Soldiers in the Revolutionary War." *William and Mary Quarterly*, 3rd ser., vol. 47, no. 3 (July 1990): 370-390.

———. "The Recruitment of Criminals into the British Army, 1775–81." *Historical Research* 58 (May 1985): 46-58.

———. "To Subdue America: British Army Officers and the Conduct of the Revolutionary War." *William and Mary Quarterly*, 3rd ser., vol. 43, no. 3 (July 1986): 381-407.

Hagist, Don N. "Forty German Recruits: The Service of the Von Scheither Recruits in the 22nd Regiment of Foot, 1776–1783." *Journal of the Johannes Schwalm Historical Association* 6, no. 1 (1997): 63-66.

———. "John Philipp Aulenbach: von Scheither Recruit in the 17th Light Dragoons." *The Hessians: Journal of the Johannes Schwalm Historical Association* 16 (2013): 54-56.

———. "Maintaining Military Roads: Orders for Sergeant McGregor's party, 1772." *Journal of the Society for Army Historical Research* 93, no. 375 (Autumn 2015): 210-213.

———. "Unpublished Military Writings of Roger Lamb, Soldier in the 1775–1783 American War, Part 1." *Journal of the Society for Army Historical Research* 89, no. 360 (Winter 2011): 280-290.

———. "Unpublished Military Writings of Roger Lamb, Soldier in the 1775–1783 American War, Part 2." *Journal of the Society for Army Historical Research* 90, no. 362 (Summer 2012): 77-89.

———. "Von Scheither Recruits in the 17th Regiment of Foot." *The Hessians: Journal of the Johannes Schwalm Historical Association* 17 (2014): 23-28.

———. "Von Scheither Recruits in the 23rd Regiment of Foot." *The Hessians: Journal of the Johannes Schwalm Historical Association* 18 (2015): 30-33.

Seton, Colonel Sir Bruce. "Infantry Recruiting Instructions in England in 1767." *Journal of Army Historical Research* 4, no. 16 (April–June 1925): 84-90.

Syrett, David. "Living Conditions on the Navy Board's Transports during the American War, 1775–1783." *Mariner's Mirror* 55 (1969): 87-94.

Urwin, Gregory J. W. "Irish Catholics in the British Army of the American Revolution: The Article behind the Uniform." *Brigade Dispatch* 14, no. 1 (Summer 1978): 20-21.

ACKNOWLEDGMENTS

THIS BOOK DRAWS ON MATERIAL ACCUMULATED over several decades, during which time so many people have generously offered assistance of all sorts that it is impossible for me to remember them all. I regret any omissions from this list of those whose contributions great and small made this book possible.

Thanks to the staffs of the archives and research institutions preserving the documents that keep history alive, especially The National Archives of Great Britain and the William L. Clements Library at the University of Michigan. Special thanks to Katherine Ludwig, librarian at the now-defunct David Library of the American Revolution, who was always welcoming and helpful.

Todd W. Braisted has broadened the scope of my research from the beginning, uncovering new sources and sharing his own findings. Michael Barrett provided invaluable assistance obtaining materials from The National Archives. Eric H. Schnitzer graciously contributed his artistic talents for illustrations in this and my other books, as well as his subject-matter expertise in reviewing the manuscript. Rick Atkinson ensured there would be some excellent writing among these pages by contributing the foreword. Patrick K. O'Donnell provided expert guidance on the overall narrative style. Gregory J. W. Urwin, Steven M. Baule, and Robbie McNiven provided excellent and insightful feedback on the draft.

Bruce H. Franklin of Westholme Publishing asked me to write this book; it is the book that I've long planned to write but might never have started had it not been for his request.

Among the many individuals who pointed me to information or freely shared their own findings are Linnea Bass, Drew Keanu Bell, J. L. Bell,

Joel Bohy, Ed Brumby, Stephen Brumwell, John Coghlan, Andrew Cormack, Stephen Gilbert, Erik Goldstein, Alex Good, John Houlding, Vincent J-R Kehoe, Don Londahl-Smidt, Brendan Morrissey, Paul Pace, Gene Procknow, Steve Rayner, John U. Rees, Gilbert V. Riddle, John K. Robertson, William P. Tatum, Gavin K. Watt, and Matthew Zembo.

Most of all, Jennifer P. Klein provided endless support, writing guidance, editorial suggestions, encouragement, optimism, and patience throughout the process of turning piles of cluttered research materials into a coherent manuscript. No one could ask for a better partner.

INDEX

102nd Regiment of Foot, 178
100th Regiment of Foot, 187, 191
103rd Regiment of Foot, 178
Ormond Market, 7
Orr, Alexander, 95
Overon, John, 238
Owen, John, 159
Oxford, 94
Oxford, William, 204

Parker, Thomas, 138
Parliament, 3-4, 154, 268n75, 294n39
Parrott, John, 206
Paulus Hook, 139, 201-202, 231
Peacock, George, 205, 257
Pearce, John, 102
Peebles, John, 122-124, 142, 161
Pell's Point, 82
Pell, William, 104
Penobscot, 210
pensions, xiii, 16, 20, 25, 100, 153, 203,
    245, 247-259
Peper, Hinrich, 221
Petty, Arthur, 102
Phillips, William, 87, 130
Pickles, Henry, 205
Pike, Abraham, 164
Pike, Abraham, 237-238
Piscadore, Henry, 51
Plan of Discipline (Windham), 67
Platt, Phillip, 173
plunder, 157-167, 169, 171, 173, 175-
    176, 217
Port Roseway, 241-242
Post, Henry, 173
Power, Richard, 206
Press Act, 182-189
Princeton, 147, 149, 161, 205, 228, 249-
    250
Printzell, Leonard, 26
The Prisoner of War, 255-256
Pudner, William, 48

Quakers, 154
Quarter Guard, 62-63
Quartering Act, 45, 57, 119, 269n95
Quebec, 4, 47, 49, 63, 83, 97, 102, 115,
    118, 126, 136, 155, 202, 228, 237,
    243

Queen's Loyal Rangers, 209
Queen's Rangers, 174

Ralph, Thomas, 184
Raritan River, 146
rations, 135-139, 155, 169, 206
Rawley, Samuel, 100
recruiting, xvii-xviii, 12-18, 22-28, 37,
    41, 44-45, 97-98, 103-109, 112,
    173, 177-191, 194, 208, 232, 253
Reeves, Robert, 116
Reide, Thomas, 141, 144
The Relief (Bunbury), 9
religious affiliations, 152-155, 256
Rennison, James, 249
Reynard, Benjamin, 138
Reynolds, John, 230
rheumatism, 45, 144
Rhoads, John, 226
Richelieu River, 228, 243
Riley, Edward, 167
Riley, James, 226
Robertshaw, John, 104, 118, 194
Robertson, Duncan, 91
Robinson, Archibald, 117
Robinson, Duncan, 150
Robinson, Joseph, 208
Roth, Philip, 51
Rowland, William, 93
Royal Artillery, 92, 147, 152, 212-214,
    227
Royal Garrison Battalion, 231, 256
Royal Glasgow Volunteers, 179, 192
Royal Highland Emigrants, 178, 200
Royal Irish Regiment, 51
Royal Jamaica Volunteers, 187
Royal Manchester Volunteers, 179
Royal Navy, 95, 113, 117
Royal North British Fusiliers, 51, 108
Royal Regiment of Artillery, 4, 75
Royal Welch Fusileers, 65
Russell, Charles, 202

Sag Harbor, 173
The Satirist, 255
Savoy prison, 184, 186, 190-191
Sawyer, Jonathan, 193
Schnitzer, Eric H., 101, 165, 183, 211,
    229
Scoles, William, 242